Radical Uncertainty

Also by John Kay and Mervyn King

The British Tax System

John Kay
Mervyn King

·

Radical Uncertainty

Decision-Making Beyond the Numbers

W. W. NORTON & COMPANY
Independent Publishers Since 1923

Photo of Florentine church circa 1950, designed by the Renaissance
architect Filippo Brunelleschi, found on the bottom of page 143,
© Hulton Archive/Getty Images.

For information about permission to reproduce selections from this book,
write to Permissions, W. W. Norton & Company, Inc.,
500 Fifth Avenue, New York, NY 10110

For information about special discounts for bulk purchases, please contact
W. W. Norton Special Sales at specialsales@wwnorton.com or 800-233-4830

Manufacturing by LSC Harrisonburg
Production manager: Julia Druskin

ISBN 978-1-324-00477-6

W. W. Norton & Company, Inc., 500 Fifth Avenue, New York, N.Y. 10110
www.wwnorton.com

W. W. Norton & Company Ltd., 15 Carlisle Street, London W1D 3BS

1 2 3 4 5 6 7 8 9 0

For Mika and Barbara

CONTENTS

Part IV
Economics and Uncertainty

Part V
Living with Uncertainty

I prefer true but imperfect knowledge, even if it leaves much indetermined and unpredictable, to a pretence of exact knowledge that is likely to be false.

—FRIEDRICH VON HAYEK,
Nobel Prize lecture, 1974

ACKNOWLEDGEMENTS

As the final words of this book were written in the summer of 2019 its two authors celebrated, if that is the word, fifty years of life as professional economists. Much has happened to economies and the study of economics over that period. The first Nobel Prize in Economic Sciences was awarded in 1969, and the announcement of the latest winner has become a regular part of the economist's calendar. In public, private and academic sectors, the number of economists has expanded greatly. We have had the good fortune to work with colleagues in all three domains. As we describe in this book, progress is made collectively and through communication with others. Our biggest debt of gratitude must, therefore, be to our professional colleagues, too numerous to mention, from around the world with whom we have interacted for half a century. Their influence on us, both conscious and unconscious, is immense.

Our immediate thanks are to those with whom we have discussed the ideas in this book during its writing: Rachel Barkow, Tim Besley, Amar Bhidé, David Bodanis, Alan Budd, Paul Collier, Samuel Issacharoff, Peter Kellner, Richard Pildes, Stuart Proffitt, Adam Ridley, Paul Seabright, Robert Skidelsky, Ed Smith, David Tuckett, and colleagues at NYU Stern School of Business and NYU Law School, as well as at the London School of Economics and the Bank of England. Some of the ideas were presented over several years to seminar participants at a number of places including All Souls College, Oxford, the Norwegian School of Economics in Bergen, NYU Law School and Yale Law School.

Others have made this venture feasible. Our personal assistants, Rachel Lawrence in England and Gail Thomas in New York, organised our lives to make it possible to work on the book. Andrew Wylie proved once again what an energetic and supportive literary agent he is. And our publishers – Tim Whiting and Zoe Gullen at The Bridge Street Press, and Drake McFeely at W.W. Norton – provided encouragement and advice at every stage.

Doris Nikolic and Matthew Ford not only provided excellent research assistance but persisted in asking difficult questions to which we felt impelled to try to provide answers. Their insights have greatly enriched the book.

Finally, our thanks must go to our long-suffering spouses, Mika Oldham and Barbara Melander-King, who not only gave us excellent comments and editorial suggestions but patiently allowed us the time to complete the manuscript.

PREFACE

Forty years ago, we wrote a well-received book, *The British Tax System*, describing the failures — intellectual and practical — of the tax system. We were neither academic scribblers inventing a tax system from scratch nor tax accountants engrossed in excruciating detail. Instead, as young academics we set out to look carefully at how the tax system actually worked in practice and then to design improvements based on a small number of carefully thought through principles. Forty years later, we discovered that we had independently come to the view that economics as a whole faced a similar challenge and was in need of a fresh look. So we decided to collaborate again. This book is the result.

The British Tax System sold well and went into several editions. But our careers then went in different directions. John became the Director of the Institute for Fiscal Studies, started a successful consulting company focusing on business economics, and was the first director of the Saïd Business School at Oxford University and for twenty years a columnist for the *Financial Times*. Mervyn became an academic in various universities in the UK and US before joining the Bank of England as Chief Economist and later Governor from 2003 to 2013.

During those forty years we saw at first hand both the power of economics as a way of approaching practical problems, and also its limitations. As students and academics we pursued the traditional approach of trying to understand economic behaviour through the assumption that households, businesses, and indeed governments take actions in order to optimise outcomes. We learnt to approach economic problems by asking what rational individuals were maximising. Businesses were maximising shareholder value, policy-makers were trying to maximise social welfare, and households were maximising their happiness or 'utility'. And if businesses were not maximising shareholder value, we inferred that they must be maximising something else – their growth, or the remuneration of their senior executives.

The limits on their ability to optimise were represented by constraints: the relationship between inputs and outputs in the case of businesses, the feasibility of different policies in the case of governments, and budget constraints in the case of households. This 'optimising' description of behaviour was well suited to the growing use of mathematical techniques in the social sciences. If the problems facing businesses, governments and families could be expressed in terms of well-defined models, then behaviour could be predicted by evaluating the 'optimal' solution to those problems.

Although much can be learnt by thinking in this way, our own practical experience was that none of these economic actors were trying to maximise anything at all. This was not because they were stupid, although sometimes they were, nor because they were irrational, although sometimes they were. It was because an injunction to maximise shareholder value, or social welfare, or household utility, is not a coherent guide to action. Business people, policy-makers and families could not even imagine having the information needed to determine the actions that would maximise shareholder value, social welfare or household utility. Or to know whether they had succeeded in doing so after the event. Honest and capable executives and politicians, of which there are many, try instead to make incremental decisions which they think will improve their business, or make the world a better place. And happy households are places where family members work together to ensure that tomorrow is at least as good as today.

Most economists would readily acknowledge that no one actually engages in the kinds of calculation which are described in economic models. But since the work of Paul Samuelson, economists have relied on the claim that if people observed certain axioms which constituted 'rationality' they would – unconsciously – be optimising, rather as Molière's M. Jourdain had been talking prose for forty years without knowing it. And when this axiomatic approach is applied to consumer behaviour, as it was by Samuelson, the method is more fruitful than the sceptical observer might expect.

But we show in this book that the axiomatic approach to the definition of rationality comprehensively fails when applied to decisions made by businesses, governments or households about an uncertain future. And this failure is not because these economic actors are irrational, but because they *are* rational, and – mostly – do not pretend to knowledge they do not and could not have. Frequently they do not know what is going to happen and cannot successfully describe the range of things that *might* happen, far less know the relative likelihood of a variety of different possible events.

The financial crisis of 2007–08 brought home the intellectual failures of optimising models to capture the disruptive behaviour that results from confronting an unknowable future. But this is not another book about that financial crisis, or even another book about economics, although we believe that the implications for the study of economics are considerable. It is a book about how real people make choices in a radically uncertain world, in which probabilities cannot meaningfully be attached to alternative futures.

As we wrote this book, and discussed our ideas with friends and colleagues, we encountered very different reactions from general readers, on the one hand, and specialists, on the other. Most people find the concept of radical uncertainty natural and indeed obvious. For them, the challenge is not to accept the existence of radical uncertainty but to find ways of coping with it. We hope they will find answers to that challenge in the chapters that follow. Many people who have been trained in economics, statistics or decision theory, however, find it difficult to accept the centrality of radical uncertainty. And to these we need to add some who work in computer science and artificial intelligence – or who have simply read enough about these things to be caught up in the wave of popular enthusiasm for the style of reasoning at which computers excel.

In trying to persuade those two different audiences of the importance of radical uncertainty, the risk is that one thinks we are flogging a dead horse; the other that we are flogging the winner of the Kentucky Derby by decrying a set of techniques which has transformed our thinking in economics, statistics, decision-making and artificial intelligence. We hope that general readers will nevertheless enjoy the spectacle of the flogging and that specialists will feel at least some of the sting of the lash.

Part I

Introduction:
The Nature of Uncertainty

1

THE UNKNOWABLE FUTURE

All we can know is that we know nothing. And that is
the sum total of human wisdom.

—LEO TOLSTOY, *War and Peace*, 1867[1]

Unknowable unknowns

In September 1812, Napoleon's troops defeated the Russian
forces at Borodino, and cleared the way for the capture of
Moscow. The French entered the now-deserted capital and
razed its wooden structures to the ground. But the fruitless
occupation marked the end of the Emperor's campaign of con-
quests. The freezing, starving, disease-ridden Grande Armée
began its long retreat to Paris. Most of its soldiers never made it
home.[2] Napoleon abdicated in April 1814.

Napoleon was the greatest political and military leader of
the age, at the height of his power and achievement, and commander of the largest army the world had seen.[3] But he had
little understanding of what was going on at Borodino. Nor,
even today, do we truly understand why he was there. And

the complex, many-faceted relationship between Russia and Western Europe remains unresolved two centuries later.

On 3 August 1492, Christopher Columbus sailed from Spain with the hope of finding a new route to the Indies. Most experienced sailors at the time believed that a westerly route to Asia was impracticable, given the distance involved and the problem of carrying sufficient food and water. And they were right. Against all reasonable advice, the Spanish Crown agreed to sponsor his expedition. Columbus did not know what his journey would entail, or how long it would take him, and after re-stocking in the Canary Islands, he landed in the Bahamas. He did not know that the New World, as it came to be called, even existed, and he did not know what he had found even after he had found it. He maintained that he had indeed landed in Asia, which is why America is named after his contemporary, Amerigo Vespucci, who had a better idea of where his own explorations had led. Whatever counted as cost-benefit analysis in the Spanish court took no account of the possibility of a New World; nor could it.

In February 1972, Richard Nixon met the Chinese leader Mao Tse-tung in Beijing. The meeting had long been planned, secretly, by the US President and his national security adviser, Henry Kissinger. Its purpose was by no means clear, although Nixon was struggling to extricate his country from Vietnam and both American and Chinese leaders wished to put distance between the two leaders of global communism, China and the Soviet Union. The much-feted meeting ended with a bland communiqué characteristic of global summits. Later that year, five men were arrested during a break-in at the Watergate complex in Washington and the subsequent cover-up led to Nixon's resignation in 1974. Two years after that, the ailing Mao died.

No one knew what the consequences of the Nixon/Mao meeting would be – it was not even certain when Nixon's plane arrived that Mao himself would meet the President. And, almost half a century later, no one really knows what the consequences were. Was its significance merely symbolic, a media event involving two leaders in failing political or physical health? Or was it a key milestone in the integration of China into the global economy, probably the most important economic development of the subsequent half century?

Emperors, explorers and presidents made decisions without fully understanding either the situation they faced or the effects of their actions. And so must we.

The global financial crisis

On 9 August 2007, the French bank BNP Paribas announced that it was suspending transactions in three of its funds. The holdings of investors, which had been placed in securities linked to the US housing market, were effectively frozen. The failure of a small group of hedge funds was in itself a minor event. But within days the global financial crisis of 2007–08 was under-way. That crisis peaked in September 2008 with the failure of Lehman Brothers, and only extraordinary efforts by central banks around the world prevented the collapse of the Western financial system. Nevertheless, the failures in financial markets which followed led to the most severe recession in the industri-alised world since the Great Depression of the 1930s.

As the days passed and the position of the banks deteriorated, we were seeing events that had not been observed for several generations, if at all. Why was the banking system experienc-ing a crisis of confidence of the kind that we thought had been relegated to history? As the crisis passed and there was time for reflection, both authors sought to explain the background to the events that took us all by surprise. Mervyn King wrote *The End of Alchemy* and John Kay *Other People's Money*. From differing perspectives, the authors had arrived at a common view. The narrative of the pre-crisis period was falling apart. Markets in new, complex financial instruments were supposed to ensure that risks were placed with people who were best able to bear them. Or so the story had gone. As the crisis evolved, a new narrative was required; one which recognised that humans do not necessarily comprehend the consequences of their innovations. The risks had not been placed with those who had most capacity to handle them, but with those who did not understand them. And the institutions that sold those instruments understood little more and lacked the financial capacity to hold them when the market dried up.

The 25 standard deviation event

On 13 August 2007, four days after BNP Paribas had suspended redemptions from three of its funds, the chief financial officer of Goldman Sachs, David Viniar, told the *Financial Times* 'we were seeing things that were 25-standard deviation moves several days in a row'.[4] Taken literally, Viniar's statement was not credible. A 25 standard deviation event is one whose probability is less than .000000000000000000000000000000000000 00000000000000000000000000000000000000000000000000 00000000000000000000000000000000000000000000000000 0003.[5] Our universe has not existed long enough for there to have been several days on which 25 standard deviation events could occur. Mr Viniar has a degree in economics from Union College and an MBA from Harvard Business School, so he would have known this, unless he had forgotten the content of his elementary courses. But what he really meant, although his claim was wrapped up in statistical jargon, was that moves in the prices of financial assets were much larger than anything his risk managers had previously experienced or thought possible.

The risk models used by Goldman Sachs and other financial firms were incapable of coping with the stress in markets seen in 2007 and more starkly in 2008. The models used by economists in central banks and elsewhere to make forecasts of the economy also failed to predict or explain these events. The inability of experts to anticipate the crisis was not simply the result of incompetence, or wilful blindness, but reflected much deeper problems in understanding risk and uncertainty. Today we can send rockets to land a man on the moon, and probes to the planet Mercury. Why are more immediate and superficially simpler problems on Earth – such as whether it will rain next week in New York, or what will be the result of today's election, or the demand for oil next year – harder to manage? Why does planning for future contingencies cause so much difficulty for those charged with making decisions – whether they are employed in private institutions, such as banks, or in charge of public bodies, such as governments and armies?

The war on terror

Osama bin Laden masterminded the attack on Manhattan's World Trade Center on 11 September 2001, and US military preparations for a possible invasion of Iraq began almost immediately thereafter. In February of the following year, Donald Rumsfeld, the United States Secretary of Defense, gave a press briefing. Rumsfeld was asked to comment on reports that no evidence linked Baghdad to terrorist activity. His famous response was widely derided: 'There are known knowns; there are things we know we know. We also know there are known unknowns; that is to say we know there are some things we do not know. But there are also unknown unknowns – the ones we don't know we don't know.'[6]

Yet Rumsfeld was saying something important.[7] The follow-up question to Rumsfeld's musings is less well remembered than the observation that provoked it. The Defense Secretary was asked in which category – known knowns, known unknowns or unknown unknowns – did intelligence about terrorism and weapons of mass destruction fall? Rumsfeld's response was 'I am not going to say which it is'.[8] But no link between Iraq and the 9/11 attack has been established, and no weapons of mass destruction were found. The Iraq invasion was a military success: US forces rapidly reached Baghdad and toppled Saddam Hussein. But with hindsight the operation was a comprehensive failure of intelligence, judgement and contingency planning; a failure as politically damaging as the similar failures of intelligence, judgement and contingency planning in the financial sector were economically damaging. In the light of these failures, US government agencies were required to implement a more structured process for providing advice to the President.[9] Analysts were expected to quantify their confidence levels and express them as probabilities.

And so almost a decade later, in spring 2011, President Barack Obama met with his senior security advisers in the White House situation room to consider what he knew would be one of the defining decisions of his presidency. Should he approve the proposed raid by US Navy SEALs on the Abbottabad compound in Pakistan where Osama bin Laden was believed to be hiding? Obama was well aware that a similarly daring plan in 1979 to rescue hostages from the Tehran embassy had ended in fiasco and may have cost Jimmy Carter a second term as President. 'John', the CIA team leader, was 95% certain that bin Laden was in the compound. But others were less sure. Most placed their probability estimate at about 80%. Some were as low as 40% or even 30%.

The President summed up the discussion. 'This is 50–50. Look guys, this is a flip of the coin. I can't base this decision on the notion that we have any greater certainty than that.'[10] Obama did not mean that the probability that the man in the compound was bin Laden was 0.5; still less that he planned to decide by tossing a coin.[11] His summary recognised that he had to make his decision without knowing whether the terrorist leader was in the compound or not. Obama would reflect on that discussion in a subsequent interview: 'In this situation, what you started getting was probabilities that disguised uncertainty as opposed to actually providing you with more useful information.'[12]

Either bin Laden was there, or he wasn't – though the plan involved many other risks and uncertainties, military, technological and political. Obama might have said to his colleagues something like 'if you guys can tell me there is a greater than 60% chance that the man in the compound is bin Laden, I will give the order to go ahead'. But he did not; to have done so would have been to pass responsibility for the decision from the Oval Office, where it belonged, to the intelligence agencies. But such passing on of responsibility did occur in the financial sector, where senior bank executives, such as Mr Viniar, had effectively delegated the management of uncertainty to the risk professionals and their models. Obama understood this issue; Viniar and his colleagues did not.

In the run-up to the global financial crisis, as in the preparations for the Abbottabad raid, policy advisers not only chose to express uncertainties as probabilities but were required to do so. Regulators prescribed the risk models used by financial institutions; Congress insisted on the quantification of judgements based on intelligence reports. In both finance and politics, this expression of uncertainty was at best unhelpful and at worst actively misleading. The precision of the numbers presented to Viniar and Obama was spurious. Obama understood that he had to arrive at a decision on the basis of limited information, and made what, with hindsight, proved a good call. He did so not by probabilistic reasoning but by asking 'What is going on here?'

In writing this book, we found inspiration in an anecdote from Richard Rumelt's *Good Strategy/Bad Strategy*, by some distance the best book on business strategy written in the last decade. Rumelt describes a conversation with a colleague at UCLA who had observed some of his case-based MBA classes:

> We were chatting about pedagogy ... John gave me a side-long look and said 'it looks to me as if there is really only one question you're asking in each case'. That question is 'what's going on here?' John's comment was something I've never heard said explicitly but it was instantly and obviously correct. A great deal of strategy work is trying to figure out what is going on. Not just deciding what to do, but the more fundamental problem of comprehending the situation.[13]

The question 'What is going on here?' sounds banal, but it is not. In our careers we have seen repeatedly how people immersed in technicalities, engaged in day-to-day preoccupations, have failed to stand back and ask, 'What is going on here?' We have often made that mistake ourselves.

Retirement planning

Most readers will never be called upon to make decisions as momentous as those which Obama and Viniar faced – although they may be asked to judge the performance of those who make these critical decisions. But all of us make choices which require thinking about the future. House purchase and preparing for retirement are the most important financial decisions for most households. But few plan in any organised way. They decide, often rather quickly, which house to buy based on a reaction rather than a checklist. Given choices – to opt in or out of pension schemes, to select one investment fund over another – they often prefer to avoid choices. The default option – which requires no action – is usually most popular.[14]

A few households approach the issue of retirement more systematically. There are software programs to help; some asset managers[15] offer free assistance and some economists have written commercial programs.[16] These calculate how much an individual or household should save and whether they are on track for a comfortable retirement. To start using these programs you must have a lot of information at your side: current facts, such as age and marital status, and information about your future self, such as the age at which you plan to retire, and how much you will then need to spend each year. You will need to disclose not just your current salary but what you expect it to be many years from now. You may even be asked to predict how long you will live. The principal uncertainty President Obama faced was binary – either bin Laden was there in Abbottabad, or he was not. Judging how long you will live is more difficult. You know that you are most unlikely to reach 125 years old and you can consult the carefully constructed life tables used by the actuaries of insurance companies. But the program may also ask you to express views on the economy and financial markets in the future. A historic series on inflation and investment returns will give you some sense of possible answers. You might sketch a range of possibilities even if you would struggle – and be unwise – to come up with an answer.

One answer to such questions the programs generally do not allow is 'I don't know'. But that is the answer which the authors, professional economists all our lives, would give to many of these questions. And frankly we think that is the answer you should give as well. There are many questions – such as 'Who is the man in the compound in Pakistan?' – to which the only sensible answer is 'I don't know'; and if this may be true of the present, it is even more true of the future. We all have to make decisions about retirement plans even though we do not know what our income or the inflation rate will be twenty years from now. If we knew the answers to all the questions the programs pose, we could determine exactly how much we need to save to enjoy our retirement. But we do not make good decisions by professing knowledge we do not and cannot have. After we have consulted the programs, we at least know what we don't know, and we may be able to do a little to reduce our ignorance.

An intellectual failure

The crisis of 2007–08 represented – obviously – a failure of economic analysis and economic policy. But while recognising the seriousness and cost of the financial crisis, economists have generally been reluctant to accept that their intellectual framework is in need of revision. Economists (used to) distinguish risk, by which they meant unknowns which could be described with probabilities, from uncertainty, which could not. They had already adopted mathematical techniques which gave the term 'risk' a different meaning from that of everyday usage. In this book we will describe the considerable confusion and economic damage which has arisen as a result of the failure to recognise that the terms 'risk', 'uncertainty' and 'rationality' have acquired technical meanings in economics which do not correspond to the everyday use of these words. And over the last century economists have attempted to elide that historic distinction between risk and uncertainty, and to apply probabilities to every instance of our imperfect knowledge of the future.

The difference between risk and uncertainty was the subject of lively debate in the inter-war period. Two great economists – Frank Knight in Chicago and John Maynard Keynes in

Cambridge, England – argued forcefully for the continued importance of the distinction. Knight observed that 'a measurable uncertainty, or "risk" proper, as we shall use the term, is so far different from an unmeasurable one that it is not in effect an uncertainty at all'.[17]

Keynes made a similar distinction. In an article summarising his magnum opus, *The General Theory of Employment, Interest and Money*, he wrote:

> By 'uncertain' knowledge, let me explain, I do not mean merely to distinguish what is known for certain from what is only probable. The game of roulette is not subject, in this sense, to uncertainty; nor is the prospect of a Victory bond being drawn. Or, again, the expectation of life is only slightly uncertain. Even the weather is only moderately uncertain. The sense in which I am using the term is that in which the prospect of a European war is uncertain, or the price of copper and the rate of interest twenty years hence, or the obsolescence of a new invention, or the position of private wealth-owners in the social system in 1970. About these matters there is no scientific basis on which to form any calculable probability whatever. We simply do not know.[18]

The title of this book, and its central concept, is *radical uncertainty*. Uncertainty is the result of our incomplete knowledge of the world, or about the connection between our present actions and their future outcomes. Depending on the nature of the uncertainty, such incomplete knowledge may be distressing or pleasurable. I am fearful of the sentence the judge will impose, but look forward to new experiences on my forthcoming holiday. We might sometimes wish we had perfect foresight, so that nothing the future might hold could surprise us, but a little reflection will tell us that such a world would be a dull place.

We have chosen to replace the distinction between risk and uncertainty deployed by Knight and Keynes with a distinction between *resolvable* and *radical* uncertainty. Resolvable uncertainty is uncertainty which can be removed by looking something up (I am uncertain which city is the capital of Pennsylvania) or which can be represented by a known probability distribution of outcomes (the spin of a roulette wheel). With radical uncertainty, however, there is no similar means of resolving the uncertainty – we simply do not know. Radical uncertainty has many dimensions: obscurity; ignorance; vagueness; ambiguity; ill-defined problems; and a lack of information that in some cases but not all we might hope to rectify at a future date. These aspects of uncertainty are the stuff of everyday experience.

Radical uncertainty cannot be described in the probabilistic terms applicable to a game of chance. It is not just that we do not know what will happen. We often do not even know the kinds of things that might happen. When we describe radical uncertainty we are not talking about 'long tails' – imaginable and well-defined events whose low probability can be estimated, such as a long losing streak at roulette. And we are not only talking about the 'black swans' identified by Nassim Nicholas Taleb – surprising events which no one could have anticipated until they happen, although these 'black swans' *are* examples of radical uncertainty.[19] We are emphasising the vast range of possibilities that lie in between the world of unlikely events which can nevertheless be described with the aid of probability distributions, and the world of the unimaginable. This is a world of uncertain futures and unpredictable consequences, about which there is necessary speculation and inevitable disagreement – disagreement which often will never be resolved. And it is that world which we mostly encounter. So the ramifications of radical uncertainty go well beyond financial markets; they extend to individual and collective decisions, as well as economic and political ones; and from decisions of global significance taken by statesmen to everyday decisions taken by the readers of this book.

For both Knight and Keynes, recognition of the pervasive nature of radical uncertainty was essential to an understanding of how a capitalist economy worked. Knight believed that it was radical uncertainty that created profit opportunities for entrepreneurs and that it was their skill and luck in navigating radical uncertainty which drove technical and economic progress. Fifteen years before the *General Theory*, Keynes had published *A Treatise on Probability*, and an appreciation of his evolving views on risk and uncertainty is necessary in interpreting his later work. But in the *General Theory* he re-expressed Knight's thinking with characteristic literary flourish: 'If the animal spirits are dimmed and the spontaneous optimism falters, leaving us to depend on nothing but the mathematical expectation, enterprise will fade and die.'[20] Keynes' concern was less with the microeconomic drivers of innovation than with the macroeconomic factors behind the Great Depression. In his view it was (non-mathematical) expectations – 'the state of confidence' – which made it difficult to achieve or restore the equilibrium which the classical economists had described.

But Keynes and Knight lost the battle to put radical uncertainty at the heart of economic analysis (in chapter 5 we explain why). Most economists today pay – at best – lip service to the difference between risk and uncertainty. The problem of radical uncertainty has supposedly been tamed by probabilistic reasoning. That belief has infected other areas of social science, including statistics, sociology and psychology, and even the law.

And so instead of recognising radical uncertainty, and adopting policies and strategies that will be robust to many alternative futures, banks and businesses are run with reliance on models which claim knowledge of the future that we do not have and

never could have. Those models attempt to manage uncertainty
by assuming that the analysis of commercial and financial risk
is analogous to the analysis of roulette. We do not know how a
particular spin will fall, but we do know the possible outcomes
and the frequency of each of those outcomes if we played the
game over and over. But uncertainty takes many forms, few of
which can be represented in this way.

Three main propositions run through this book. First, the
world of economics, business and finance is 'non-stationary' – it
is not governed by unchanging scientific laws. Most important
challenges in these worlds are unique events, so intelligent
responses are inevitably judgements which reflect an interpretation of a particular situation. Different individuals and groups
will make different assessments and arrive at different decisions,
and often there will be no objectively right answer, either before
or after the event. And because what we observe is not the outcome of a stationary process, conventional statistical inference
rarely applies and forecasts are often based on shifting sands.

Second, individuals cannot and do not optimise; nor are
they irrational, victims of 'biases' which describe the ways they
deviate from 'rational' behaviour. The meaning of rational
behaviour depends critically on the context of the situation
and there are generally many different ways of being rational.
We distinguish axiomatic rationality, as used by economists,
from evolutionary rationality, as practised by people. Many
so-called 'biases' are responses to the complex world of radical
uncertainty. Evolution in this uncertain world has led characteristics which are primarily adaptive to become embodied
in human reasoning. Humans are successful at adapting to
the environment in which they find themselves, and have not
evolved to perform rapid calculations of well-defined problems
at which computers excel. This is because the problems which
humans face, whether sparkling at dinner party conversations

or conducting international trade negotiations, are not well-defined problems amenable to rapid calculation.

Third, humans are social animals and communication plays an important role in decision-making. We frame our thinking in terms of narratives. And able leaders – whether in business, in politics, or in everyday life – make decisions, both personal and collective, by talking with others and being open to challenge from them. Humans, uniquely, produce artefacts of extraordinary complexity and are able to do so only by the successful development of networks of trust, cooperation and coordination. Market economies function only by virtue of being embedded in a social context.

Sensible – adaptive – public policy and business strategy cannot be determined by quantitative assessments of policies and projects, made by an industry of professional modellers using probabilistic reasoning. In this book we explain how it is that so many clever people came to believe otherwise – and why they are wrong. We reassert the distinction between risk and uncertainty, and suggest that if we control risk we can not only manage but positively enjoy uncertainty. If that seems paradoxical, read on.

2

———— · ————

PUZZLES AND MYSTERIES

The worst historian has a clearer view of the period he
studies than the best of us can hope to form of that in
which we live. The obscurest epoch is to-day.

—ROBERT LOUIS STEVENSON[1]

In August 2004, NASA launched the probe MESSENGER
from Cape Canaveral. Although Mercury is on average 'only'
60 million miles from Earth,[2] the rocket travelled 4.9 billion
miles at a speed of 84,500 mph before it finally entered its investigative orbit of the planet, according to plan, in March 2011.[3]

This remarkable feat of computation was possible because:

- the equations of planetary motion have been comprehensively understood since the seventeenth century, thanks to
  Johannes Kepler and his successors;
- the equations of planetary motion are stationary, in the
  sense that those equations governed their motion for

millions of years before Kepler's discoveries and have continued to govern them since ('stationary' is a technical term in mathematics and statistics and does not relate to the movements of the planets themselves but to the underlying determinants of planetary motion, which do not change over time: we will make frequent use of the word 'stationary' in this sense);[4]

- the motion of the planets is not significantly affected by human actions[5] or at all by human beliefs about their motion.

Accurate calculations, such as those undertaken by NASA scientists, can be made when the underlying process is more or less completely understood, when that process remains constant over time, and when the process is independent of our actions and beliefs. And extremely detailed forward planning – in this case, mapping the trajectory of a probe moving at rocket speed for years ahead – is then possible. MESSENGER entered its orbit of Mercury at the exact location NASA had anticipated six and a half years earlier.

Puzzles and mysteries

NASA is a product of its time. We live in an age of enlightenment in which scientific reasoning has displaced argument from authority, whether religious or secular. Scientific evidence is the new authority. But is it possible to extend to other disciplines the methods of analysis which have led to so much progress in natural science? Can there be laws of human behaviour analogous to laws of physics?

Is anything, in either the physical or the political world, really random? 'God does not play dice,' said Einstein, expressing a belief that the world is, fundamentally, deterministic.[6] And, at some deep and unimaginable level of understanding, this may be true. But whatever the playwright of the universe intended, we actors are faced with uncertainty, either because of our ignorance or because of the changing nature of the underlying processes.

The risk managers at Goldman Sachs and the policy advisers at intelligence agencies whom we met in chapter 1 expressed their assessments in probabilistic language. In both cases these assessments were unhelpful, though for different reasons (at Goldman because the probabilistic estimates were taken seriously; in the White House because they were not). In neither case did the probabilities which were expressed provide the information the decision-makers required. Where there is no adequate basis for formulating probabilities – and there was none at 200 West Street[7] or 1600 Pennsylvania Avenue – we face radical uncertainty.

The probabilists of financial institutions and intelligence agencies believed such conditions of radical uncertainty were rare and that they could estimate probabilities for most of the relevant contingencies. Since the seventeenth century it has been increasingly common to express uncertainty in probabilistic terms. The 'probabilistic turn' gathered pace in the twentieth century, and in the last two decades probabilistic reasoning has almost completely dominated the description and analysis of decision-making under uncertainty.

Other writers have made similar distinctions to the 'known' and 'unknown' unknowns described by Donald Rumsfeld. Greg Treverton, chairman of President Obama's National Intelligence Council and for many years a senior figure in the US intelligence community, stressed the difference between 'puzzles and mysteries'.[8] A puzzle has well-defined rules and a single solution, and we know when we have reached that solution. Puzzles deliver the satisfaction of a clear-cut task and a correct answer.

Even when you can't find the right answer, you know it exists. Puzzles can be solved; they have answers. But the solutions may be difficult to find. Economists have thrived on the difficulty of solving complex models of the economy precisely because they have been trained to tackle well-defined problems which have an answer. And (Nobel) prizes are awarded to those who solve the most difficult puzzles.

Mysteries offer no such clarity of definition, and no objectively correct solution:[9] they are imbued with vagueness and indeterminacy. We approach mysteries by asking 'What is going on here?', and recognise that even afterwards our understanding is likely to be only partial. They provide none of the comfort and pleasure of reaching the 'right' answer. Columbus thought he had landed in Asia. And even today, 'What was going on here?' in the global financial crisis, or during bin Laden's sojourn in Pakistan, is hotly contested. What will be the future of the Middle East? Or the development of mobile computing, or the automobile industry? Will banks as we know them survive? What is the future of capitalism, or democracy? A mystery cannot be solved as a crossword puzzle can; it can only be framed, by identifying the critical factors and applying some sense of how these factors have interacted in the past and might interact in the present or future. Puzzles may be more fun, but in our real lives the world increasingly offers us mysteries – either because the outcome is unknowable or because the issue itself is ill defined.

The political scientist Philip Tetlock has for three decades studied the performance of 'expert' forecasters, with mostly dispiriting results.[10] To find objective measures of the quality of expert judgement – and identify the determinants of good and bad judgement – Tetlock needs to specify problems with verifiable outcomes. In 2010 and 2011, the questions he set were of the kind, 'Will Serbia be officially granted European Union candidacy by 31 December 2011?' and 'Will Italy restructure or default on its debts by 31 December 2011?'[11]

But these well-defined short-term questions are not really the questions to which policy-makers seek answers. More important is to know whether the United States and China will find a peaceful solution to the growing trade and military tensions between them. Or whether the European Union will continue its expansion, and what will be the shape of monetary union in five years' time. Replacing complex mysteries with puzzles that have unambiguously right and wrong answers limits the interest and relevance of both problems and answers. While there are some problems for which the quantification of probabilities is an indispensable guide to solutions, most decisions in business, finance, politics and personal development, and their outcomes, are too complex and imprecisely defined to be approached in this way. They are subject to radical uncertainty.

Radical uncertainty and practical knowledge

Treverton's striking distinction between puzzles and mysteries is reproduced wherever practical decision-making is required. The urban planners Horst Rittel and Melvin Webber observed in 1973 that although the well-defined needs of communities for roads, sanitation, etc. had been met, their clients remained dissatisfied. More was needed; but the planners did not know what it was and the population was not able to articulate clearly its needs. Rittel and Webber distinguished the 'tame' problems which had been solved from the 'wicked' problems which might never be solved, and these terms are now often used in social policy and medicine.[12] A broken leg is a tame problem; but many patients present with symptoms whose cause is difficult to diagnose and which require treatment whose outcomes are uncertain. Their doctors must tackle wicked problems.

Engineers also distinguish between puzzles and mysteries, and give them technical names – 'aleatory' and 'epistemic' uncertainty, respectively. Meteorological records will describe the regular tides and winds to which a bridge is likely to be exposed (aleatory uncertainty), but since every bridge and every bridge location is different the effect of these conditions on the structure is never completely known (epistemic uncertainty). The tides and winds are the subject of known frequency distributions (tables showing how frequent are particular values of tide and wind speed); uncertainty remains because every complex structure is necessarily idiosyncratic. This distinction between the uncertainty which can be described probabilistically and the uncertainty which surrounds every unique project or event is important in all applications of practical knowledge and central to the argument of this book.

Donald Rumsfeld was not the first person to describe 'unknown unknowns'. British scientists invented the jet engine before the Second World War and by 1944 both Britain and Germany were able to produce jet fighters; the first commercial jets were Comets manufactured just outside London by the de Havilland company. The greater speed of jet propulsion promised – and in due course delivered – a transformation in international passenger travel. *American Aviation* magazine commented: 'Whether we like it or not, the British are giving the US a drubbing in jet transport.'[13] But a BOAC (now British Airways) Comet disintegrated in mid-air in 1954 soon after taking off from Rome airport. The planes were grounded for almost three months during which modifications were made 'to cover every possibility that imagination has suggested as a likely cause of the disaster'.[14] Two weeks after flights resumed, a South African Airways Comet suffered the same fate, coincidentally also shortly after leaving Rome. The remains of the crashed aircraft were recovered from the Mediterranean and subjected to exhaustive testing at the Royal Aircraft Establishment in Farnborough. The two accidents were the result of metal fatigue originating from the corners of the square windows. No one had imagined this could happen until it did. The lessons from the lengthy investigation which established the embarrassingly trivial source of the problem enabled de Havilland's American rival Boeing to design a plane whose windows, as with all modern aircraft, are oval rather than square. The Boeing 707 became the workhorse of jet travel and almost one thousand were built. The Boeing engineers who created the 707 described the problem that had grounded the Comets as an 'unknown unknown', anticipating Rumsfeld's use of the term by almost fifty years.[15]

Concern for 'unk-unks', as they were described at Boeing, has been integral to the company's thinking ever since. Ironically, over sixty years later, in 2019, it was Boeing that suffered the loss of two of its newest planes, in crashes that had similarities to the fate of the Comets. Engineers can solve the puzzles of aerodynamic flows and the stresses of high-speed flight at altitude. But the only way to resolve the mystery of what happens to a metal tube flying at 500 mph at 35,000 feet is to try it.

What Churchill knew

The conduct of war is, in every sense, a wicked problem. The months that followed the outbreak of the Second World War in September 1939 became known as the 'phoney war'. There were no major land operations. In April 1940, the British Prime Minister, Neville Chamberlain, told a Conservative Party meeting that 'Hitler missed the bus'.[16] Four days after Chamberlain's ill-judged speech, German troops crossed into Denmark and were trans-shipped to Norway. A British expedition at Narvik in northern Norway ended in embarrassing withdrawal. The fiasco led to Chamberlain's resignation and Winston Churchill became Prime Minister. Just as Churchill was being invited by the King to form a government, the Nazi blitzkrieg began. German troops raced through the Netherlands and Belgium and engaged the British and French armies. Within a week, the battle to defend France was lost.

In June 1941, Nazi Germany attacked Russia. The German army approached Moscow but failed to reach it, perhaps due to a mistaken focus on securing oil fields in the south rather than the seat of government in the north. On 7 December 1941, Japanese aircraft sank an American fleet at Pearl Harbor. On the following day, Congress declared war on the Empire of Japan, and three days later Hitler issued a declaration of war on the United States.

Historians still debate the crucial uncertainties of 1940. What would have happened if the British had sought a negotiated peace, as Lord Halifax, Churchill's rival for the premiership, had proposed? Some argue that, with Britain disarmed, Germany could have achieved comprehensive victory in Europe. Others contend that the crucial events of Hitler's invasion of Russia and the Japanese attack on Pearl Harbor would have occurred in any event, and the final outcome would have been the same. We do not know for sure why Hitler abandoned the invasion of Britain and focused on Russia instead; by opening a second front he greatly reduced his prospects of success in either.

The German and Japanese attacks took Stalin and Roosevelt, respectively, by surprise. Although both leaders had been given ample warning, they were unprepared. They did not believe these attacks would happen because they seemed foolish acts. And they *were* foolish acts – the likely results of engaging the Soviet Union and the United States in war were the crushing defeats that followed for the aggressors.

Churchill was impetuous, stubborn, and often mistaken in his judgements. His early political career foundered on the failure of the Dardanelles expedition in 1915, and, as Chancellor of the

Exchequer from 1924 to 1929, he was responsible for one of the worst decisions in British economic history – the return in 1925 to the gold standard at the pre-war parity. But Churchill is justly pre-eminent among statesmen because from the beginnings of Hitler's rise to power he understood 'what is going on here', and because, when the war which he saw as inevitable came, he not only provided inspirational leadership but displayed a sure grasp of the central strategic issues.

Churchill recognised that British survival depended on securing American engagement in the war against Hitler, but he also appreciated the difficulty of bringing about that engagement. Like Roosevelt, he did not anticipate a Japanese attack on the United States, nor Hitler's response to it. Though the most impatient of men, he waited on events, and was vindicated by history. Like President Obama, though in a much more complex situation, Churchill did not think that the uncertainties involved in big decisions could be represented by probabilities and (unlike Obama) no one suggested to him that they could. The environment was radically uncertain; the problems he faced were 'wicked', not 'tame'.

Military campaigns are complex and evolve in unpredictable ways. The contrast between the five-and-a-half-year history of the Second World War, with innumerable unexpected twists and turns, and the six-and-a-half-year progress of MESSENGER to Mercury along a complex but completely anticipated trajectory, could hardly be more stark. Still, even war operations are responses towards defined objectives and generally proceed to a resolution, bloody though that may be. The Second World War was prompted by Nazi aggression, the issue was how that aggression was to be contained, and in 1945 there was a definitive outcome. Many issues in business, finance and politics are ill defined and never concluded. If anything, they are even more 'wicked' than those of military strategy.

What Steve Jobs knew

Thomas Watson Jr followed his father, Tom Sr, as CEO of IBM and over half a century they built a company which came to dominate the global computer market from its beginnings in the 1950s until the personal computer revolution of the 1980s. The observation – widely attributed to Watson Jr – that there would be a world market for only five computers is apocryphal. But these IBM machines were enormous. In the 1970s, a university or a large corporation would have a single computer. The authors remember carrying boxes of punched cards to the Oxford University computer, housed in a vast air-conditioned basement in Banbury Road, or to the Cambridge University computer at the appropriately named New Museums Site.

Ken Olsen was then chief executive of America's second largest computer company, Digital Equipment Corporation (DEC). In 1977, Olsen declared, 'There is no reason anyone would want a computer in their home.'[17] Olsen anticipated extensive use of computers. But, like many others, he assumed that millions of people would obtain computing capacity by plugging into a few very large central facilities, rather as they draw power from an electricity grid linking large power stations to their home appliances.

A different vision of the digital future imagined a range of smaller purpose-specific machines. By the early 1980s, most professional offices used word processors. Such machines made it easy to correct documents and cut and paste material, and could be linked to a high-quality printer. They transformed the job of the copy typist and almost eliminated the electric typewriter. Wang Laboratories was market leader in word processors. Small programmable calculators displaced the engineer's slide rule. Specialist machines from Hewlett-Packard and Casio which could calculate redemption yields or option values were substitutes for the instinct, or seat of the pants, of market traders.

These problem-specific machines were, however, super-seded when the industry developed in a different way. In 1971, Intel developed a general-purpose chip, or microprocessor. As a result, a single small device could serve many functions. Intel's innovation paved the way for the construction of a mini-computer. At Xerox Parc in 1972, Butler Lampson built the Alto, a machine which differs little in appearance from a modern desktop computer. Lampson's team added many of the features we take for granted today. But it was years before the Xerox Corporation attempted to market a commercial version, and the company never succeeded in establishing a foothold in the computer business.

While Xerox was perfecting the Alto, personal computers were developed by hobbyists. The Altair desktop, a self-assembly kit with a price of $400, was first advertised in *Popular Electronics* magazine in December 1974. Two young high-school friends in Seattle, Paul Allen and Bill Gates, adapted a simple program-ming language, BASIC, for the Altair. Some large companies outside the conventional computer industry recognised the potential of small computers. Home computers used tape cas-settes for storage and television sets as monitors. AT&T and Sony sold desktop machines. All these initiatives failed.

Then in 1981, IBM launched a 'personal computer', immedi-ately abbreviated to PC. IBM's reputation and market presence were such that whatever the company supported commanded wide acceptance. It didn't matter that many users thought the performance of the PC was inferior to that of machines already on the market. When software developers decided which format to use, IBM's system was the obvious choice. Within months, 'PC' had become the generic term for a small computer.

In order to avoid its own slow-moving decision processes, and bypass managers who – rightly – feared that the innovation threatened their position, IBM had outsourced much of the development of the PC. For the operating system, the corporation turned to a small company, Microsoft, run by Gates and Allen. The pair in turn developed an off-the-shelf system they had bought for $50,000. The computer giant had no real sense of the revolution it had launched and the rights to MS-DOS remained with Microsoft. When IBM attempted to regain control with a new and more sophisticated operating system, OS/2, it was too late. MS-DOS (powering Windows 3.1) was everywhere.

Meanwhile, Steve Jobs and Steve Wozniak began assembling Apple machines in 1976 in Jobs's garage, now designated a historic site.[18] Although Gates and Microsoft had understood that ease of use was as important as technical sophistication to commercial success, Jobs extended this vision further and conceived a computer that you could use without understanding anything about computers. To achieve this goal, Jobs drew on another invention from Xerox Parc – the graphical user interface. Apple machines had screens with icons which created the appearance of a desktop, and friendly aids such as a mouse and trash bin – innovations that seemed like gimmicks to the nerds who then predominated among computer users, but which opened computing to a much wider audience. Apple machines were more fun.

But you could access these capabilities only by buying Apple's integrated software and hardware. Apple's determination to maintain its proprietary system failed in the face of widespread adoption of the more open standard of the IBM PC: Windows, a combination of Apple's graphical user interface with Microsoft's ubiquitous MS-DOS, swept the world, and almost swept Apple from that world. By the mid-1990s, Apple was on the edge of bankruptcy, its market share falling, its innovations failing.

But 1997 was the year of the Second Coming of Steve Jobs (he had been forced out of the company a decade earlier by

the board). The return of Jobs to the company he had founded
twenty years earlier enthused the dwindling band of Apple
devotees, but few in the business world had high expectations.
In 1998, Dick Rumelt, the UCLA strategy professor we met in
chapter 1, interviewed Jobs about his plans. The Apple CEO
responded, 'I'm going to wait for the next big thing.'[19] The
'next big thing' proved to be music. Music publishers resisted
digital downloads, proclaiming them piracy. They sought
to protect their established business of selling compact discs
through record stores. Napster and other illegal file-sharing
services flourished. Apple secured the rights to sell millions of
downloadable tracks at 99 cents each through the iTunes Store,
and launched the iPod in 2002. 'One thousand songs in your
pocket', Jobs proclaimed.

The iPod prepared the ground for something much bigger
still – the handheld computer. High-end portable devices for
business people had been available since the turn of the century;
the Palm Pilot was succeeded by the BlackBerry. But Apple
aimed its products at consumers and then opened its systems to
enable developers to provide 'apps'. Combine the music player
with the increasingly ubiquitous mobile phone, add a screen,
and you could devise almost unlimited applications for a gadget
that would fit in your pocket. Steve Ballmer, CEO of Microsoft,
laughed derisively when the iPhone appeared – who, he asked
rhetorically, would pay $500 for a phone?[20]

A lot of people would; ten years on, more than 1.5 billion
smartphones had been sold. The smartphone changed the nature
not just of entertainment, but of business communication. And
by the time Jobs died in 2011, Apple had outstripped Microsoft
to become the most valuable company in the world. Gates and
his successor Ballmer were wrongfooted by the popularity of
Apple's mobile devices, as was Nokia, the Finnish company
which had become the world's largest supplier of mobile phones.

In 2014, these two companies huddled together against the storm, as Microsoft acquired the remains of Nokia's handset division. Palm became part of Hewlett-Packard; BlackBerry is today a shadow of its former self.

But perhaps Olsen, who doubted that there would be a need for a home computer, was right after all. We no longer need or want computers in our home because we carry a computer wherever we go and plug into the limitless memory and processing power of the great servers in the cloud. But Olsen's company will not benefit from his belated vindication. The struggling Digital Equipment Corporation was absorbed into Compaq, which in turn was absorbed into Hewlett-Packard, which in turn was split in two in 2015 and is now known primarily as a manufacturer of printers. Wang, which had popularised the word processor, went bankrupt in 1992.

The history of personal computing combines extraordinary success in meeting the evolving needs of consumers with comprehensive failure by the corporations involved to anticipate how the market would develop. DEC failed to benefit from the company's leading position in a market for small computers which was about to experience exponential growth. Wang, Casio, Palm, BlackBerry and Nokia soared towards the sun and fell as quickly to earth. IBM pioneered a development which destroyed its established business. Apple's insistence on proprietary systems failed in the 1980s, but proved a success twenty years later. Microsoft failed to anticipate the importance of mobile computing. And the Xerox Corporation, which had contributed more than any other company to the innovations that made mobile computing possible, never derived commercial benefit from the inventiveness of its scientists. The pioneers of computing had built puzzle-solving machines of extraordinary power. But they had failed to understand the mysteries of business strategy as applied to their industry.

From unknown unknowns to known unknowns

Mysteries can sometimes be resolved by advances in knowledge. Dinosaurs dominated Earth for 130 million years (humans have done so for perhaps 100,000 years). But around 65 million years ago, an extraordinary event in our planet's history led to the disappearance of most species, including the dinosaurs – the Cretaceous–Paleogene extinction. At school, we were told that the problem was that dinosaur brains were too small relative to their bodies. That was nonsense, but the claim may have encouraged us to do our homework. The extinction of the dinosaurs was for long an unresolved mystery. But the accumulation of scientific knowledge has turned the mystery into a puzzle whose solution is gradually being pieced together. In the past thirty years, scientists have formulated a plausible explanation of that extinction. An asteroid at least six miles in diameter hit Earth near the Yucatán peninsula in Mexico, filling the atmosphere with debris which covered the sky for years and fundamentally altered climate conditions.[21] The resulting extinctions changed the course of evolution, and that is why we, and other mammals, are here today, and dinosaurs are not.

The largest object to have hit our planet and been the subject of contemporaneous record landed in a fortunately uninhabited area at Tunguska in Siberia in 1908. The energy from the impact was a thousand times that released at Hiroshima, and if the object had hit Manhattan, the city of New York would have been destroyed. The Yucatán asteroid was probably more than ten thousand times larger.

Many historic catastrophes, such as the Black Death or the San Francisco earthquake, can now be avoided or minimised. The mystery of what killed almost half the population of Europe became a puzzle as medical knowledge advanced, and has now been resolved. We understand seismology better, and can construct buildings that are more robust to tremors and fire, but when the next quake will occur remains a mystery. 'On the last Sabbath day of 1879, which will be remembered for a very long time', the Tay Bridge, a recently completed structure in Scotland which carried the North British Railway from Fife to Dundee, collapsed in strong winds.[22] A train was on the bridge at the moment of destruction and ninety people died in the disaster.[23] Many bridges were built in the nineteenth century as railways and railroads expanded and, with little understanding of the relevant physics, there were many failures. Just three years earlier, the US had experienced the collapse of the Ashtabula rail bridge in Ohio, which the president of the Lake Shore and Michigan Southern Railroad had himself designed.

More prudent rail executives sought the aid of engineers. The chastened North British Railway reviewed an even more ambitious project to span the River Forth between Edinburgh and Fife. Many experiments to ascertain the effects of wind on metal took place before the Forth Bridge – a spectacular and over-engineered structure – was completed in 1890. Even so, the similar Quebec Bridge collapsed during construction in 1907. The most vividly documented of all bridge collapses, through a dramatic contemporaneous film, is that of the Tacoma Narrows Bridge across the Puget Sound near Seattle. Even though storm stresses were relatively well understood in 1940, aerodynamic effects were not. Today, similar bridges are tested in wind tunnels in the design phase. Over the course of a century, the scope of mysteries has been diminished, and the effects of weather on bridges and other structures can today largely be treated as a soluble puzzle.

Some mysteries will remain just that because the solution will never be found. On 5 December 1872, the *Mary Celeste* was found abandoned in the Atlantic Ocean off the Azores. The vessel was undamaged and well provisioned, and its log book remained on board. But the lifeboat and the ship's papers were missing. As were the captain, his wife and daughter, and the crew of seven. Nothing was seen or heard of them again.

No sea mystery has ever received more attention. Seemingly plausible hypotheses, such as piracy or mutiny, appear inconsistent with the evidence, prompting speculation about outlandish ones, such as sea monsters. The incident is famous in part because Arthur Conan Doyle, the creator of Sherlock Holmes, wrote a fictional (and wholly implausible) account of what took place.[24] But his theory was to be the first of many.[25] What happened to the *Mary Celeste* will almost certainly remain a mystery, despite the efforts of successive generations of crime novelists to treat the question as a puzzle. Even though there is an answer, we will never know what it is. The claim of the modern science of decision theory is that most mysteries can be reduced to puzzles by the application of probabilistic reasoning. Such reasoning can provide solutions to puzzles, but not to mysteries. How to think about and cope with mysteries is the essence of managing life in the real world and is what this book is all about.

3

———— • ————

RADICAL UNCERTAINTY
IS EVERYWHERE

Time and chance happeneth to them all.

—Ecclesiastes 9:11

Forecasting is difficult. But as we have seen, the physicists and engineers of NASA were able, with uncanny accuracy, to predict the position of MESSENGER. NASA was dealing with a problem that was completely specified, comprehensively understood, and stationary. And that system was unchanged by human interaction with it. Its behaviour was not affected by what people understood of it or by what people did. If economic problems were like those faced by NASA, economists could have the same predictive capability as NASA.

But economic relationships change over time – the property of non-stationarity. And movements in the economy reflect our expectations. The sociologist Robert K. Merton[1] identified *reflexivity* as a distinctive property of social systems – the system itself is influenced by our beliefs about it. The idea of reflexivity was developed by the Austrian émigré philosopher Karl Popper and became central to the thinking of Popper's student, the highly successful hedge fund manager George Soros.[2] And it would form part of the approach to macroeconomics of the Chicago economist Robert Lucas and his followers, which we describe in chapter 19, although their perspective on the problem and its solution would be very different.

Reflexivity undermines stationarity. This was the essence of 'Goodhart's Law' – any business or government policy which assumed stationarity of social and economic relationships was likely to fail because its implementation would alter the behaviour of those affected and therefore destroy that stationarity.[3] In an early illustration of reflexivity, Jonah prophesied the destruction of Nineveh, having received inside information concerning God's plans to punish the city (his journey to Nineveh was interrupted by a bizarre encounter with a whale). But after his arrival the citizens repented on hearing his forewarning and the city was spared. This outcome 'displeased Jonah exceedingly, and he was very angry', feeling (unlike many modern forecasters) despondent at the very public refutation of his prediction. But God persuaded Jonah that the happy outcome was more important than the failure of his forecast.

The King of Nineveh wore sackcloth and sat in ashes; the titans of Wall Street had no similar opportunity or inclination. The collapse of Lehman Brothers on 15 September 2008 could not have been widely predicted because if it had been it would not have happened on that date. Either the bank would have collapsed earlier, or the regulators or Lehman itself would have taken steps to avoid, or at least minimise, the event. And because beliefs influence behaviour the economic system is forever changing.

The scope of probabilistic reasoning

The Oxford Dictionary defines uncertainty as 'the state of being uncertain', and the meaning of uncertain as 'not able to be relied on, not known or definite'.[4] Such uncertainty is a product of our incomplete knowledge of the state of the world – past, present or future. Or our incomplete knowledge of the connection between actions and outcomes. We talk about uncertainty only if incomplete knowledge leads to a state of doubt – we are only too familiar (some politicians come to mind) with people who are ignorant but not in doubt, and therefore experience no uncertainty.

A person may be uncertain which city is the capital of Pennsylvania, or mistakenly believe that it is Philadelphia, but unless he is intending to meet the Governor it probably does not matter much. Sometimes, as in that case, we can resolve uncertainty by consulting a reference book or the internet, or by approaching someone who knows. These resolvable uncertainties represent one pole of uncertainty, at which we can remove our doubt by further investigation. Other resolvable uncertainties are the product of stationary probability distributions – tossing a fair coin, or Brownian motion (the random movement of small particles in a liquid or gas). Everything which can be known about these uncertainties is known and quantified. Probabilistic reasoning was devised for games of chance which are based on randomness – card games, roulette wheels, lotteries. But these problems are artificial. The rules of the game, the composition of the pack of cards, are completely specified and what remains unknown – where the spin of the wheel will take the ball, whether the next card will be an ace – is not capable of being known.

Or that is what is intended. In the world of randomness, strategies which attempt to give one player an advantage through the acquisition of superior knowledge are regarded as 'cheating', and if detected incur social disapproval and exclusion from the gaming room. In 2004, a group won over £1 million at the Ritz casino in London by using laser measuring equipment to compute the trajectory of the ball – bets can be placed until the ball completes its third spin. They were arrested, and only after a nine-month investigation did police conclude that no offence had been committed: Section 17 of the Gaming Act 1845 forbade 'unlawful devices', but the suspects had not interfered with the outcome of the game.[5] They had, however, prevented the achievement of a 'level playing field' on which the objective frequency distribution was known and was the same for all players.

Many gamblers believe they have a system. What distinguished the Ritz players was that they really did. So did Edward Thorp, a mathematics professor at MIT, who in the 1960s used statistical analysis to devise a winning strategy for blackjack. Blacklisted by operators, he wore false beards and other disguises to gain access to Las Vegas casinos. Ultimately, he found easier and more profitable applications of his skills on Wall Street.[6] Regulators of securities markets restrict the activities of traders with superior information for superficially different but substantively similar reasons.

Unknown unknowns

At the opposite pole of uncertainty from true randomness are the genuinely unknown unknowns. Taleb's metaphor of the 'black swan' describes the unknown unknowns of business and finance, which are no less important than those of aviation. The origin of the metaphor is that Europeans believed all swans to be white – as all European swans are – until the colonists of Australia observed black swans. A century ago, a telephone that would fit in your pocket, take photographs, calculate the square root of a number, navigate to an unknown destination, and on which you could read any of a million novels, was not improbable; it was just not within the scope of imagination or bounds of possibility. Before the wheel was invented (by the Sumerians, ancient Iraqis, around 3500 BC) no one could talk about the probability of the invention of the wheel, and afterwards there was no uncertainty to discuss; the unknown unknown had become a known known. To identify a probability of inventing the wheel is to invent the wheel. To ask, either before or after the event, 'What was the probability of such an event?' is not an intelligible question.[7]

True 'black swans' are states of the world to which we cannot attach probabilities because we cannot conceive of these states. The dinosaurs fell victim to an unknown unknown – even as they died they did not know what had happened to them. Human extinction will more likely come about in another way. Martin Rees, a Cambridge scientist and the Astronomer Royal, has founded a Centre for the Study of Existential Risk, to identify such potential threats and suggest measures to mitigate them. He warns of the possibility of runaway climate change, pandemics, artificial intelligence and robots which run out of control. These are threats we can at least perceive. But the observation of a black swan was not a low-probability event; it was an unimaginable event, given European knowledge of swans. As the convict colonists boarded the First Fleet, no one would plausibly have offered, or accepted, a wager of the kind 'I bet you one thousand to one all the swans in Australia are white'. Natural phenomena are more likely than social ones to be the result of stationary processes – the structure of the physical world changes less than do global business, finance and politics. But the impact of a pandemic is determined as much or more by the state of medical knowledge as by the pathogens of disease. The Black Death will not recur – plague is easily cured by antibiotics (although the effectiveness of antibiotics is under threat) – and a significant outbreak of cholera in a developed country is highly unlikely. But we must expect to be hit by an epidemic of an infectious disease resulting from a virus which does not yet exist. To describe catastrophic pandemics, or environmental disasters, or nuclear annihilation, or our subjection to robots, in terms of probabilities is to mislead ourselves and others. We can talk only in terms of stories. And when our world ends, it will likely be the result not of some 'long tail' event arising from a low-probability outcome from a known frequency distribution, nor even of one of the contingencies hypothesised by Martin Rees and colleagues, but as a result of some contingency we have failed even to imagine.

In 1896, Lord Kelvin, one of the greatest physicists of his age, wrote that 'I have not the smallest molecule of faith in aerial navigation other than ballooning or of expectation of good results from any of the trials we hear of. So you will understand that I would not care to be a member of the aëronautical Society.'[8] His observation was followed in an embarrassingly short time by the first controlled flight, covering 300 yards and just under a minute long. And today, two centuries after the First Fleet reached Botany Bay with no expectation of observing black swans, an Airbus A380 weighing 360 tonnes can carry 550 passengers over 9000 miles from England to Australia. Something that would have been incomprehensible even a hundred years ago. The next hundred years will be no less radically uncertain.

Through a glass, darkly

For more than half a century a single approach to rational choice under uncertainty has dominated economics and provided the basis for what is taught in universities and business schools as 'decision science'. Agents optimise, subject to defined constraints. They list possible courses of action, define the consequences of the various alternatives, and evaluate these consequences. Then they select the best available option, if necessary anticipating how others will react to their choices. People make plans for consumption across their lifetime, from education, through child rearing, through retirement. Corporations select strategies to maximise shareholder value. Governments choose policies to maximise social welfare.

A moment's introspection is enough to tell us that they don't. They could not conceivably have the information required to do so. They do not know all the available options, and they are uncertain what the consequences of them will be. They do not even know whether what they wish for today will be what they still want if they achieve it tomorrow. Young people do not know what their career progression will be, or what they will earn over the next forty years, or whether and when they will marry or divorce, or what they will need in retirement, or whether they will live that long. No chief executive knows what will maximise shareholder value, or after the event whether it has indeed been maximised. And the notion that a government could calculate what maximises social welfare is simply ridiculous. The consequences of policies and actions are far too uncertain.

Real households, real businesses and real governments do not optimise; they cope. They make decisions incrementally. They do not attain the highest point on the landscape, they seek only a higher place than the one they occupy now. They try to find outcomes that are better and avoid outcomes that are worse. The major part of this book will describe how people manage and adapt to a radically uncertain world.

Why has this seemingly obvious critique been so widely ignored? The hegemony of optimisation as the goal of decision-making is made possible by ignoring radical uncertainty. Building on the success of probabilistic reasoning in illuminating games of chance, the approach of decision theory bifurcates uncertainty into the unknown and unknowable, and the unknown but capable of being characterised by a known probability distribution. The practitioners of this approach wash their hands of the former, describing the unknown and unknowable as 'shifts' and 'shocks', as unpredictable and inexplicable as the Yucatán asteroid. Other uncertainties are treated as resolvable. There is no room for radical uncertainty.

But people routinely need to make decisions with imperfect information. Most of real life lies in between the opposing poles of randomness and black swans; we know something, but not enough, and the knowledge which is held collectively is widely and unequally distributed. Regulators and counterparties (firms which traded with the now defunct bank) might have known Lehman was poorly managed and inadequately capitalised, although even the latter was the subject of contention. They might have known that the bank was likely to fail, but not how or when. We see, but through a glass, darkly.

It is easy to understand why economists and statisticians, in search of clear and comprehensive solutions, have sought wide extension of the scope of probabilistic reasoning. The underlying mathematics has a certain simplicity and beauty, and in practice can be applied by those who have acquired the requisite modest technical skill. Arguably the two most brilliant economists of the post-war period, Paul Samuelson and Robert Solow, occupied adjoining offices at MIT for over half a century. As Samuelson relates, 'When young he [Solow] would say, if you don't regard probability theory as the most interesting subject in the world, then I feel sorry for you. I always agreed with that.'[9]

The appeal of probability theory is understandable. But we suspect the reason that such mathematics was, as we shall see, not developed until the seventeenth century is that few real-world problems can properly be represented in this way. The most compelling extension of probabilistic reasoning is to situations where the possible outcomes are well defined, the underlying processes which give rise to them change little over time, and there is a wealth of historic information. The length of your daily commute is an example; and so are those risks, such as motor accident and mortality, which can be handled in insurance markets. For thousands of years, farmers anticipated the weather and knew that it followed an annual cycle although they had no idea why. But with careful records and computer modelling, forecasts have become more accurate and weather forecasting has become a successful business.

Meteorologists and their prognostications, however, have no influence over whether or not it will rain tomorrow. Probabilities become less useful when human behaviour is relevant to outcomes. We can consult statistics on the number of pedestrians killed crossing the road, or the life expectancy of a man aged sixty-five, but that does not help us much in deciding whether to cross the road, or how much to save for retirement. The probability of an accident or becoming a centenarian depends not just on aggregate statistics but on factors personal to us, and not necessarily known by us. And these statistics are themselves influenced by our beliefs: many fewer pedestrians are killed by cars today than in the 1920s despite the increase in traffic because we have learnt that roads are dangerous.[10]

Aggregate data help to reduce the significance of those individual factors. But the advisability of crossing the road depends on the nature of the road and our agility, eyesight and hearing. We can be reasonably confident we will not die tomorrow, or live to be 120, but this does not tell us much − or perhaps anything − about the probability that we will live to exhaust our savings. All these 'wicked' problems are in the territory of radical uncertainty. Knowledge of the underlying processes is imperfect, the processes themselves are constantly changing, and the ways in which they operate depend not just on what people do, but on what people think. Probabilistic reasoning may appear beautiful and appealing, but sadly its applicability to real-world problems is limited.

Sometimes the relevant state of the world, although a present fact, is not known to the decision-makers even after their best endeavours – is the man in the compound bin Laden? And sometimes the actual state of the world is a present or past fact, but one which is not known to anyone – what happened to the *Mary Celeste*? Or, in an issue of rather greater moment to the modern world, how many votes did Bush and Gore actually receive in Florida in the 2000 US presidential election?

Where the question is known, but the range of answers is unbounded, application of the mathematics of probability is questionable and the results ambiguous. When the question is known – 'What will happen in the Middle East in the next five years?' or 'What will be the position of private property twenty years from now?' – but the nature of the question means that the answers are ill defined, then there are no states to which we can sensibly attach probabilities.

Explaining uncertainty

The results of most medical treatments are uncertain. Doctors learn frequency distributions from their own experience and that of the medical profession as a whole. But even if extensive data are available the circumstances of every patient are unique. The modern requirement for informed consent obliges doctors to communicate this uncertainty to their patients. But their patients typically crave certainties. They place great trust in the judgement of doctors, and want to believe that doctors understand more than they do. One London doctor obtained feedback from a patient group on the wording of an information leaflet for patients in intensive care who might wish to partic- ipate in a trial involving different antibiotic therapies. The lay patient group did not like the wording 'doctors wish to carry out this trial as they do not know which antibiotic therapy is best' and preferred the wording 'doctors wish to carry out this trial to help decide which antibiotic is best'. One patient's com- ment was that 'everything is uncertain in intensive care and the last thing I want is the doctors not to know what to do'. The doctor's reaction was that 'expressing uncertainty sometimes is not helpful, but context is all'.[11]

We have found no evidence that Harry Truman ever said 'give me a one-handed economist' and think it unlikely that the shrewd former President, who was alive to the importance of radical uncertainty, said anything of the kind. But politicians also look for certainties even when none are available. One of the authors was, as Deputy Governor of the Bank of England, asked to give evidence before the House of Commons Select Committee on Education and Employment on the subject of whether Britain should join the European Monetary Union. How, the MPs asked, could we know when the UK business cycle had converged with that on the Continent? The answer was that since business cycles are of the order of ten years in duration, and at least twenty or thirty observations would be needed to assess the issue, it would be two hundred years or more before we would know. Underlying the question was the assumption that the process driving business cycles was stationary, and that over time we could learn enough about that process to provide an answer. But it would be absurd to claim that economic cycles had been unchanging since the beginning of the Industrial Revolution. There was no basis for pretending that we could simply wait and learn more about a fixed process. 'You will never be at a point where you can be confident that the cycles have genuinely converged, it is always going to be a matter of judgement.'[12] Such radical uncertainties are irresolvable.

Economic processes generating growth or fluctuations do not remain stable for long enough to allow useful estimates of probabilities of economic variables. For most interesting macro-economic questions, such as what will be the economic impact of Brexit, or the nature and timing of the next financial crisis, there is no basis on which we can easily attach probabilities to all the various possible outcomes or even define other than in vague terms what these outcomes are. The sensible answer to the question 'Will there be another global financial crisis in the next ten years?' is 'I don't know'. Both professional economists and economic agents, whether businesses or households, grapple with the question of 'What is going on here?' When experts claim knowledge they do not and could not have, they invite the response that people have 'had enough of experts'.

Practical decision-making

The different dimensions of uncertainty mean that the strategies we adopt to cope with risk and uncertainty will depend upon the particular problem with which we are faced. Most hypothetical questions – what is the capital of Pennsylvania? – are of no concern to most of the population of the world, and mostly the ignorance that results does not matter. The authors of this book have not the slightest interest in the question 'Which horse will win the 2020 Kentucky Derby?' They do not know who the runners and riders are, far less their form, or when the race will take place. Nor do they intend to bet on the outcome, or to find out the name of the winner when the finishing list is posted.

When decisions do matter, rational people delegate them to those who have, or are willing to invest in acquiring, relevant information and the capacity to interpret that information. For all that has recently been said about 'the wisdom of crowds', the authors prefer to fly with airlines which rely on the services of skilled and experienced pilots, rather than those who entrust the controls to the average opinion of the passengers.[13]

There is no general theory of how best to make decisions. Much of the academic literature on decision-making under uncertainty tries to frame the challenge as a puzzle. All decisions, it is assumed, can be expressed as mathematical problems. And potentially capable of being solved by computers. Your smartphone will tell you what restaurants are nearby, how to get there, and perhaps what you ate last night; but not where and what you want to eat now. The probably apocryphal but nevertheless illuminating story about a decision theorist contemplating whether or not to accept a job offer from a rival university illustrates this well: upon being urged by his colleague to apply tenets of rational decision-making under uncertainty and maximise his expected utility, as his academic papers suggested, he responded with exasperation, 'Come on, this is serious.'[14]

Humans have evolved to cope with problems which are not amenable to probabilistic reasoning – an issue to which we return in chapter 9. Our brains are not built like computers but as adaptive mechanisms for making connections and recognising patterns. Good decisions often result from leaps of the imagination. Creativity was the quality exhibited by that unknown Sumerian who invented the wheel, by Einstein, and by Steve Jobs. And, as Knight and Keynes emphasised, creativity is inseparable from uncertainty. By its nature, creativity cannot be formalised, only described after the event, with or without the help of equations.

The founding of California

Johann Suter, a wannabe businessman, abandoned his creditors and his family in Baden (now part of Germany) in 1834. After much travel he reappeared in 1839 on the west coast of America as John Sutter. Ambitious to establish an agricultural empire, he settled in what we call today the Bay Area. At the time, San Francisco was a modest trading post with a harbour, and home to around a thousand people.

In 1848, the Treaty of Guadalupe Hidalgo ended the Mexican War and led to the annexation of California by the United States. And in the same year, one of Sutter's employees discovered gold on the property. Sutter tried to conceal the find, partly so that he could enjoy the full benefit himself, and partly because he sensed the negative implications for his farming interests. But concealment proved impossible. The *San Francisco Examiner* published a rumour of gold and in 1849 as many as a hundred thousand people are thought to have arrived in California. Some struck it rich, most did not. Others realised that a different, if less adventurous, route to success was to provide services to the '49ers. One of them was Leland Stanford. Stanford built a successful trading business, and served a single two-year term as Governor of the fledgling state. But he was most famous for his contemporaneous role in creating the Central Pacific Railroad in 1861. The Central Pacific then built a stretch of line from Sacramento to Promontory Point in Utah, where in 1869 it joined the Union Pacific, and thus completed the first rail link between the east and west coasts of the United States. Stanford drove in a golden spike where the track surmounted the Rockies to celebrate the achievement.

And John Sutter? His fear that his land would be overrun by prospectors was well founded. He sold his interests to repay the debts incurred in his now struggling agricultural ventures. To add insult to injury, the courts revoked the land grant he had received under Spanish administration. He retired to the East Coast to nurse his losses and petition Congress for redress, and was still arguing the case at his death.

But the name Stanford is today associated less with the robber baron of the Gilded Age than with the university which bears his name. Stanford endowed what he envisaged would be an agricultural college, with a donation which might be the equivalent of $1 billion today. And a century later, the teaching and research of Stanford University, in fields far divorced from agriculture, would be central to the development of 'Silicon Valley'.

Neither Sutter nor Stanford could have imagined the consequences of their decisions, and that is the essence of radical uncertainty. They followed a long line of explorers and entrepreneurs who had to make decisions in a fog of uncertainty. In the wake of the gold discoveries in America and the investment boom in railways *The Economist* wrote in 1853, 'Astonishingly rapid now is the progress of society . . . but whither the progress is to lead, and where it is to end – except in the bosom of the Almighty, where it began – human imagination cannot conceive.'[15] Is it possible that probabilistic reasoning could take the place of such imagination?

In the next chapter, we describe 'the probabilistic turn' in human thought and how the scope of these ideas was progressively extended. At the beginning of the twenty-first century, bank executives would not be alone in discovering that the estimates of probabilities in their models bore no relationship to outcomes in the world. Matters which they and their regulators thought were soluble – and solved – puzzles turned out to be mysteries after all. And everyday experience, for ordinary citizens as well as statesmen and for consumers as well as executives, is that life comprises many more mysteries than puzzles.

Part II

The Lure of Probabilities

4

·

THINKING WITH PROBABILITIES

SOCRATES: 'I dare say that you are familiar with Tisias.
Does he not define probability to be that which the
many think?'

PHAEDRUS: 'Certainly, he does.'

—PLATO, *Phaedrus*[1]

The 'probabilistic turn' in human reasoning reportedly
began when the Chevalier de Méré, an inveterate gambler,
sought the advice of the mathematician and philosopher Blaise
Pascal. Pascal in turn consulted an even more distinguished
French polymath, Pierre de Fermat. The resulting exchange
of letters between Pascal and Fermat in the winter of 1653–4
represents the first formal analysis of probability.[2]

Historians of mathematics have speculated on why the discoveries of Pascal and Fermat came so late in the history of human
thought. Some of the finest and most original mathematicians

ever known lived in classical Athens. And Athenians gambled. Why did they not succeed in relating their mathematical skill to their common pastime? After all, as mathematics goes, the theory of probability is not very difficult.

Plato sought and found truth in logic; for him there was a sharp distinction between truth, which was axiomatic, and probability, which was merely the opinion of man. In pre-modern thought there was no such thing as randomness, since the course of events reflected the will of the gods, which was determinate if not fully known. The means of resolving uncertainty was not to be found in mathematics, but in a better appreciation of the will of the gods. Hence actions which seem to us absurd, such as inspecting the entrails of sacrificial animals or consulting an oracle, were employed for millennia. And traces of this approach linger on today, among those who follow astrology, read tea leaves, or attach weight to the predictions of gurus who are believed to have privileged access to knowledge of future events.

So it is not just the mathematical expression of the concept of probability that is recent, but the *concept* of probability itself as the quantitative expression of the likelihood of one of a number of possible outcomes. Even in the eighteenth century, Edward Gibbon could write of Hannibal's crossing of the Alps, 'although Livy's narrative has more of probability, yet that of Polybius has more of truth' and (in relation to a claim that the army of defeated Emperor Jovian was supplied with provisions by the victorious Persians), 'such a fact is probable but undoubt-edly false'.[3]

What did Gibbon mean? The words 'prove', 'probable' and 'approve' have a common root. That relatedness is not apparent from the way we use these words today. But the relatedness was apparent to medieval writers – and to Gibbon – for whom 'prob-able' meant something like 'approved by most right-thinking people'. In an era in which truth was established by religious or secular authority, such right-thinking people might properly decline to look through Galileo's telescope on the grounds that the Church had decreed that what he claimed to see could not be there.[4]

When the Royal Society, Britain's premier scientific body, was founded in 1660, it took as its motto 'nullius in verba' – today translated informally as 'take nobody's word for it' – a forceful assertion of the primacy of experiment and discovery over argument from authority. The modern idea of probability was very much part of the development of scientific reasoning in the seventeenth century; such reasoning was a prerequisite for the Industrial Revolution and the unprecedented economic growth it generated. The advance of probability theory would contribute to that economic development through the creation of markets in risk.

The first venues for managing risk were the coffee shops of London. Coffee had recently been imported from Arabia to Europe, and gentlemen met to consume the newly fashionable drink, converse, and do business. In the historic City of London, the insurance market began in Tom's coffee house, while securities were traded in Jonathan's – today regarded as the origin of the London Stock Exchange. The restoration of the monarchy after the dull morality of the Puritans led to an upsurge in gambling.

Mrs White's Chocolate House, in St James's near the royal palaces, evolved into the first of London's gentlemen's clubs, and served principally as a gaming venue. (And it may not be coincidental that fashionable St James's is today the centre of London's hedge funds, while the more business-oriented financial activities are found in the City.) The most famous coffee shop of all was that of Edward Lloyd, where patrons speculated on the weather, the tides and the fate of ships at sea, and merchants could lay off some of the risks associated with foreign trade. Established in 1688, Lloyd's of London is still globally pre-eminent in marine insurance. History casts a long shadow.

Mortality tables and life insurance

As Pascal and Fermat were exchanging learned correspondence, an English cloth merchant, John Graunt, was trawling the records of the cemeteries of London. Graunt noted the reported causes of death and his data were used to observe, if not to prevent, the spread of plague. He compiled records of the incidence of death in different age groups, and his analysis is the precursor of the tables actuaries use today to compute appropriate prices for annuities and life insurance. Graunt worked with the assistance of his patron and friend Sir William Petty, whose *Statistical Account of England* foreshadowed the national accounts compiled today by statisticians and extensively used by economists.[5]

Anxious to develop Graunt's work, the Society identified the extensive records of births and deaths in the Polish city of Breslau (now Wrocław) as a unique and promising source of data. The analysis was entrusted to Edmond Halley, better known for the comet to which his name is attached that reappears at intervals of seventy-five to seventy-six years.[6] Halley constructed the first mortality table, from which it was possible to estimate life expectancies.

The Equitable Life Assurance Society was founded in 1761, and took the name because it was the first life insurer to base its premiums on scientific principles designed to achieve fairness between different policy-holders, using a mortality table compiled from records of deaths in Northampton, England.[7] Such tables represent one of the earliest attempts to take the application of probability beyond the gaming table and apply it to processes that are not the random product of chance events.

The ability to use data in this way depends on an assumption that the underlying determinants of mortality are stationary – that the incidence of causes of death varies little from year to year. From time to time, events upset this assumption, such as plague in the seventeenth century and Spanish flu and AIDS in the twentieth. Improvements in sanitation and public health, and advances in medicine, dramatically reduced mortality in the twentieth century. In recent times, life expectancy for the population has increased by around three months per year.[8] As we write, however, this improvement appears to have halted or even gone into reverse, in Europe as well as in the USA, although more publicity has been given to the latter.[9] Is this a blip in a continuing trend, or a fundamental change? A random deviation, or a shift or a shock? We cannot at present – or perhaps ever – say. There are things we do not know, and things we do not know we do not know. And sometimes things we do know that are just not so.[10]

Probability as frequency

Abraham de Moivre, another French mathematician, developed the mathematics of games of chance pioneered by Pascal and Fermat. Like many of his co-religionists, de Moivre fled to England during Louis XIV's persecution of Huguenots in the 1680s. There he met Halley and became familiar with his work on frequency distributions. De Moivre linked the probabilistic mathematics of his former compatriots with the experimental investigations of his new English friends. He posed the question 'What would be the frequency distribution of the outcomes of many games of chance?' For example, suppose you tossed a fair coin a thousand times. On average, you would expect 500 heads. But you would rarely see exactly 500 heads. What was the probability of 499, or 510?

The numerical answer was, de Moivre showed, described by a bell-shaped curve now known as the normal distribution. The probability of exactly 500 heads was 2.523% – about one in forty. If you tossed a coin a thousand times and counted the number of heads, and you repeated that exercise many times, the number of heads would be determined by the theoretical probability given by the normal distribution. Of course, no sane person would think of doing this, but today you could ask a computer or robot to do it for you. You would count exactly 500 heads in about one trial in forty. The probability of 499 heads is very slightly less at 2.517%, so you should also expect 499 heads in about one trial in forty, and the probability of 501 heads is the same. You will score between 485 and 515 heads about two thirds of the time, and if you only encountered 100 heads you would have experienced an event even more improbable than the one Mr Viniar supposed he had encountered. Or you might conclude, as Mr Viniar should have concluded, that things were not as they seemed to his modellers.

Wherever there is a stationary process – for example, the variation of temperature or rainfall over the year – some statistical distribution can generally be found to fit.[11] These observations of the capacity of an abstract theory to provide exact and accurate predictions are so remarkable that it is hardly surprising that subsequent generations have been prone to exaggerate the scope of these powerful ideas. By the early twentieth century, the value of probability theory was well established in understanding games of chance, and in the analysis of data which are generated by a stationary process. The achievements of the great classical statisticians of that era had provided tools useful in many areas of both social and natural sciences. Statisticians had a secure place within the scientific community. The probabilistic turn led modern economists and other social scientists to proceed firmly down the probabilistic road.

The problem of points

The question the Chevalier de Méré had put to Pascal, which led to the modern theory of probability, was 'the problem of points'. Suppose a game of chance in the Chevalier's salon is interrupted. What is a fair division of the stakes between the players, given the outcomes of the incomplete game? For example, two players contribute to a pot of 100 Louis d'or and agree that the winner of the most of seven games will scoop the pool. The Duke of A has won three games and the Marquis of B one. The Duke is summoned to see the King and the evening's entertainment is abruptly terminated.

Before Pascal, the widely accepted solution to this problem gave three quarters of the pot to the Duke of A, recognising that he had won three out of four of the games actually played. This solution had been elaborated in the late fifteenth century by the Italian mathematician Luca Pacioli, widely regarded as one of the inventors of accounting, and at first sight seems plausible and fair.[12] But the Chevalier was not convinced that Pacioli had reached the right answer, and the two great mathematicians confirmed his doubt. If play had continued, the Marquis would have needed to win all three remaining games to succeed. If the chance of either player winning each game is one half, then the probability that the Marquis will succeed in winning all three is only one eighth. It follows that the probability that the Duke would have scooped the pool was seven eighths. So, the argument went, the pot should be shared in these proportions.

The Fermat–Pascal solution introduces three notions which are fundamental to all subsequent work. There is the mathematical concept of *probability* itself – the chance of winning any particular game. There is the method of calculation of *compound probability* – the probability of winning three successive games is obtained from the probability of a single win, one half, raised to the power of three. And the solution introduces the idea of *expected value* – the amounts each player could have expected to win if the evening's events had been repeated many times. And today we could programme a computer to simulate that scenario of multiple repetition and verify that the calculated expected value does indeed describe what would have happened if the evening's events had occurred again and again. (And, in the Chevalier's salon, they probably did.)

The solution of the problem of points was an early indication of the power of probabilistic reasoning. Pascal's counter-intuitive answer is persuasive once you have understood his thinking. What matters is anticipating the future rather than analysing the past. If the Duke and Marquis had planned to play one hundred games, then the Duke's three to one advantage at an early stage of the evening would have counted for little. But if there were to be only five games, the Marquis would certainly have lost – the result of the fifth game would be irrelevant, and it might not even have been played.

It pays to go Bayes

The final step in the development of the new theory of probability was the achievement of an unlikely hero – an obscure eighteenth-century country Presbyterian clergyman in England. The Reverend Thomas Bayes is by chance buried in what is now the centre of London's financial district. Among his papers he left a theorem that is one of the most widely taught ideas in statistics today.[13] Unknown in life Bayes may have been, but his name is known today throughout the world with branches of statistics and economics named after him. The term 'Bayesian', which describes not just a statistical technique but a school of thought, is the intellectual legacy of one man working in the Kent countryside.

Bayes' theorem enables us to calculate *conditional probabilities*: what is the probability that A will happen, given that B has happened? Although Pascal and Fermat had not achieved the generality of the Kent clergyman's analysis, the Chevalier's problem of points is a problem of conditional probability.[14] It is hard to imagine an environment and company less congenial to the Reverend Bayes than that which he would have encountered in the salon of the Chevalier de Méré. But let us take a flight of imagination and place him there, keeping score on a 'Bayesian dial' above the elegant mantelpiece. On the clock face is a pointer which registers the probability that each would win the pot, and which can swing from the complete certainty of zero probability at one extreme to complete certainty of 100% probability at the other. Since the game is fair, the mark is initially set in the middle at 50%. When the Duke won the first game the dial swung in the Duke's favour – to about 67%, as the clergyman hurriedly made the calculations required by his theorem. And when the Marquis won the second game, the dial reverted to its initial 50–50 position. But then the Duke won the third and fourth games and the dial moved again, so that when the King interrupted the evening the reading registered 87.5% in favour of the Duke.

The Bayesian dial is a visual representation of what is known as Bayesian reasoning. We deal with uncertainties by attaching 'prior probabilities' to uncertain events. Since the odds at the Chevalier's gaming table were fair, the prior probability that each player would win was 50%. But then the players constantly update their prior probabilities in the light of new information. The dial's first move records the probability that A will win the match *given that he has won the first game*, and then subsequently adjusts to the probability that he will win overall *conditional on A having won the first game, but B having won the second*, and so on as the evening progresses.

Hall

The Monty Hall problem[15] is a famous illustration of the power of Bayes' theorem, loosely based on the 1960s American quiz show *Let's Make a Deal*, in which contestants would bid for prizes hidden behind curtains, and named after its host. The puzzle was originally posed by the American statistician Steven Selvin – and has been subsequently the subject of extensive correspondence and literature. The contestant is shown three boxes, and in one Monty has placed the keys to a car which the contestant will win if he or she chooses that box. The other two boxes are empty. After the contestant has made a selection, Monty opens one of the other boxes, which is empty. He offers a choice. The contestant can stick with the original choice, or switch to the other box.

The intuitive answer is that initially the keys were equally likely to be in each of the three boxes; and now, with only two boxes to choose from, it is equally likely to be in either of those that remain. So there is no reason to switch. But untutored judgement is wrong. Monty knows which box has the car keys. If the keys are in the box you chose initially – probability one in three – it does not matter which of the other boxes he opens. But if you made a wrong choice – probability two out of three – Monty must be careful to select the one remaining box which is empty, and the keys will be in the box he chooses not to open. So it is more likely (with probability two out of three) that the keys are in that unopened box than that they are in the box you chose (with probability one out of three). Monty has unknowingly given you vital information which tells you that the probability that the keys are in the other box is two thirds, and you should therefore switch.

If you find this hard to believe – and almost everyone does – then imagine that there are not three boxes, but one hundred.

Once you have made your choice, Monty opens ninety-eight boxes, all of them empty. It is still possible that the car keys are in your chosen box. But far more likely that they are in the one remaining box which Monty did not open. And if you are still not convinced, there are several websites on which you can play the Monty Hall game against a computer.[16] You will soon learn that it is best to switch. The problem of points and the analysis of the Monty Hall show are illustrations of the value of probabilistic mathematics. Each offers wholly convincing arguments for unexpected results.

The Indifference Principle

The solutions to the problem of points and the Monty Hall game rely on what has become known as the Indifference Principle – that if we have no reason to think one thing more likely than another, we can attach equal probabilities to each. We assumed that the Duke and Marquis were equally likely to win each of the remaining games, and perhaps there was a frequency distribution of past results of similar games to guide our conjecture. In the Monty Hall problem, we judged that if there were three identical boxes the probability that the keys were in any one of them was one third.[17]

John Maynard Keynes is known to everyone for his many contributions to public policy in Britain and internationally during the inter-war period and the Second World War. Before the Great War, however, Keynes had completed a fellowship dissertation – in effect, his doctoral thesis – at King's College, Cambridge. That work became the basis of *A Treatise on Probability*, published in 1921. It contains a chapter on the Indifference Principle. Keynes' conclusive rejection of the more general application of the principle can be summarised in a single illustration:

If, to take an example, we have no information whatever as to the area or population of the countries of the world, a man is as likely to be an inhabitant of Great Britain as of France, there being no reason to prefer one alternative to the other. He is also as likely to be an inhabitant of Ireland as of France. And on the same principle he is as likely to be an inhabitant of the British Isles as of France. And yet these conclusions are plainly inconsistent. For our first two propositions together yield the conclusion that he is twice as likely to be an inhabitant of the British Isles as of France. Unless we argue, as I do not think we can, that the knowledge that the British Isles composed of Great Britain and Ireland is a ground for supposing that a man is more likely to inhabit them than France, there is no way out of the contradiction.[18]

If we know nothing about world geography, the only reasonable answer to the question 'What is the probability that a man is an inhabitant of France?' is, 'I do not know'.

Keynes wrote of the Indifference Principle: 'No other formula in the alchemy of logic has exerted more astonishing powers. For it has established the existence of God from the premiss of total ignorance.'[19] Keynes certainly had in mind the famous 'wager' of Pascal, the founder of probability theory: 'God is, or He is not. Reason can decide nothing here . . . you must wager. It is not optional . . . Let us weigh the gain and the loss in wagering that God is. Let us estimate these two chances. If you gain, you gain all; if you lose, you lose nothing. Wager, then, without hesitation that He is.'[20] Pascal's was the first calculation which brought together probabilities with a subjective evaluation of possible outcomes, in the face of the most radical of all uncertainties.

Both the problem of points and the Monty Hall game are puzzles – completely specified problems with known rules and clear-cut answers. We are told, for example, how many hands the Duke and Marquis intended to play, and we know or infer that Monty Hall knew which box contained the car keys. The answers to puzzles are often – as in this case – highly sensitive to problem definition. The Monty Hall result depends on the (sometimes unacknowledged) premise that Monty knows which box contains the keys. If he does not, the problem is quite different. Monty might then have opened the box which unlocks the car, and presumably the contestant would then have left empty-handed. And if Monty does not know what each box contains, it is only chance that leads him to open an empty box: the judgement that each closed box is equally likely to contain the keys is then correct. But the fun from watching the game was the anguish of the participants facing the choice – to switch or not, with members of the audience shouting out their advice. (In *Let's Make a Deal*, raucous audience participation was an essential part of the show's now difficult to understand appeal to its viewers.)

But once everyone understands the problem, then how can the show sustain its interest? Can the viewers be confident that the original rules are still being applied? Real worlds are always complex. Many commentators and teachers use the Monty Hall problem to emphasise that a puzzle, or model, can only be 'solved' if the assumptions made are completely specified. And this observation is correct. But in a world of radical uncertainty, problems are rarely completely specified. The mathematics of probability requires that the sum of the probabilities of all possible events adds up to 1. So if we know that the car keys are equally likely to be in one of two boxes, the probability that they are in any one is 0.5; if three boxes, the probability becomes one third. And if the keys are twice as likely to be in one box as the other – *and must be in one or other of the two boxes* – then the respective probabilities are two thirds and one third.

But what if, in a radically uncertain world, we are unable to describe all possible events, far less judge their relative probabilities? In subsequent chapters, we will show how significant this problem is for the wide application of probabilistic thinking.

Bayes in the consulting room

The Monty Hall problem is light entertainment, but the diagnosis of cancer is a matter of life and death. Campaigning organisations urge screening for breast and prostate cancer. These tests are inevitably imperfect, sometimes giving unwarranted reassurance – false negatives – and sometimes raising unjustified concerns – false positives. Suppose mammography detects breast cancer in 90% of women with the disease (this figure is called the sensitivity of the test) and also correctly confirms that women are cancer-free in 90% of cases where there is no disease (this figure is called the specificity of the test). These figures are at the high end of estimates of the effectiveness of mammography.[21]

Of course, most women do not have breast cancer. If the overall incidence in the female population is 1%, what is the probability that a woman, whose mammogram tests positive, does in fact have breast cancer? The answer surprises most people – including most physicians. In a population of one thousand women, ten can be expected to have cancer, of whom nine will be identified by the test. Of the remaining 990 women, however, 99 – one in ten – will receive positive results. So there will be a total of 108 positives, nine of which correctly identify cancer, while 99 do not. The conditional probability that a woman who tests positive has the disease is one in twelve; a positive test correctly diagnoses cancer in only one in twelve cases.[22]

This calculation is based on an example used by the German

psychologist Gerd Gigerenzer, who has for more than a decade conducted his own campaign *against* campaigners for routine screening. Random screening for breast and prostate cancer may do more harm than good because overdiagnosis of these conditions leads to needless worry and unnecessary invasive procedures. In order to be effective, screening should be limited to those who have a higher probability of disease than the population at large. Or we need tests with better specificity and sensitivity. Gigerenzer has accumulated evidence that medical practitioners, ignorant of Bayes' theorem, seriously exaggerate the risks to their patients and the validity of these tests.[23] One life saved through early diagnosis is far more salient in their minds than the much larger number of patients who are victims of treatment they do not need.

Gigerenzer displayed judgement and experience in his analysis of the effectiveness of breast cancer screening. His example deploys a model in which the calculation of the incidence of cancer could be treated as a puzzle and solved. Of course, Gigerenzer did not suggest that he had measured the true incidence of breast cancer, or the statistical validity of test results. But his analysis shows, powerfully, that the opinion of experts who understand medicine but not probability can be gravely misleading.

We can rarely be confident in generalising our models to the world – it is easy to think of reasons why women who are more susceptible to breast cancer are more likely to seek mammograms than women who are not. In games of chance, such as the wagers that prompted the Chevalier de Méré to contemplate the problem of points or the Monty Hall problem, everything is either known or unknown, deterministic or random. But that dichotomy does not exist in most real worlds. We know something, but never enough. That is the nature of radical uncertainty.

In his analysis of random screening for cancer, Gigerenzer did not make the mistake of supposing that a probability derived from a thought experiment was a probability which could be applied to the real world. He did not claim that he had calculated the probability that any actual person had contracted breast cancer. But, as we saw in chapter 1, Mr Viniar *did* make that mistake when he claimed to have observed a 25 standard deviation event. He confused a probability as calculated within a model with a probability in the world of which the model claimed to be a representation.

To make a statement about probability in a real world it is necessary to compound the probability derived from the model itself with the probability that the model is itself true. And there is no means of knowing whether the model is true; indeed it is difficult even to attach meaning to the concept 'the probability that a representation of the world *is* the world'. This failure to distinguish 'bad luck' – an unlikely event within the confines of the model – from the failure of the model itself is widespread, as we will see in later chapters. We shall call this problem of model failure the Viniar problem, in honour of the former Goldman Sachs executive.[24]

5

·———·———·

A FORGOTTEN DISPUTE

This is what I see and what troubles me. I look
on all sides, and I see only darkness everywhere.
Nature presents to me nothing which is not matter
of doubt and concern ... The true course is not to
wager at all.

—BLAISE PASCAL, *Pensées*[1]

By the early twentieth century, the uses of probability were well established in understanding games of chance, such as cards, roulette, or *Let's Make a Deal*. The theory had also proved valuable in the analysis of data generated by a more or less stationary process, such as mortality, for which extensive frequency data were available. As states, and private bodies such as insurers, began to record information in systematic form it was no longer necessary, as John Graunt had done, to peruse gravestones in search of knowledge. And when the processes generating outcomes were stationary and well understood, such as tossing a fair coin, frequency distributions could be deduced from probabilistic reasoning.

From the earliest days of probabilistic thinking, attempts were made to apply such reasoning outside the domain of the observable frequencies of games of chance and human mortality, to use probabilistic language and mathematics in the description of unique events such as the Yucatán asteroid or the bin Laden raid. And from the earliest days of probabilistic thinking, such extension was resisted. Opponents of extension for long had the upper hand. In his 1843 *System of Logic*, the British philosopher John Stuart Mill criticised the French mathematician Pierre-Simon Laplace for applying probability theory 'to things of which we are completely ignorant'.[2] Another French mathematician, Joseph Bertrand, went further.[3] He lambasted his countrymen for making absurd assumptions in the application of probabilities to problems outside the domain of games of chance. We believe that the sun will rise tomorrow, he said, because of 'the discovery of astronomical laws and not by renewed success in the same game of chance'.[4] Even this belief depends on the astronomical laws remaining stationary. If we cannot rely on the stability of such laws then it is impossible to use past frequencies to infer probabilities of future events. Bertrand was mindful of what David Hume had written more than a century earlier: 'That the sun will not rise tomorrow is no less intelligible a proposition, and implies no more contradiction, than the affirmation, that it will rise. We should in vain, therefore, attempt to demonstrate its falsehood.'[5] And it may have been in response to that famous formulation of the problem of induction by the irreligious Hume that the Reverend Bayes picked up his pen to describe conditional probabilities and to suggest that inferences could be made from data even if the underlying processes were not fully understood.[6]

Subjective probabilities

By the late nineteenth and early twentieth century, the development of the mathematics of probability by great statisticians such as R. W. Fisher, Jerzy Neyman and W. J. Gossett had created a corpus of understanding and knowledge so powerful that the pressure to extend its application was hard to resist. So some users of probabilistic reasoning sought to apply it to unique events – such as the result of the Kentucky Derby – which were not the outcome of any stationary process. Or to use probabilities to navigate wide-ranging uncertainty such as the risk exposures of Goldman Sachs. And this was necessary if Bayesian reasoning was to have much application outside the gaming room.

If I think Dobbin is very likely to win the Kentucky Derby, I might say that I think the probability that Dobbin will pass the winning post first is 0.9. What does this statement mean? One interpretation is that if the race were to be run one hundred times in identical circumstances of weather and track conditions, and with exactly the same runners and riders, then Dobbin would win on ninety occasions. But in any year, the Kentucky Derby will be run only once, and in earlier and subsequent races there will be different runners and riders, different track conditions, and different crowds cheering their favourites. So the statement 'the probability that Dobbin will win is 0.9' is not a claim about frequency, an assertion that Dobbin will win the race on 90% of the occasions on which the Kentucky Derby is run; it is a statement of the speaker's belief that Dobbin is a strong contender.

When 'John', the CIA representative at the White House meeting, said 'The probability that the man in the compound is bin Laden is 95%,' he was not saying that on 95% of similar occasions bin Laden would be found there. And when people say of an historic but imperfectly understood event 'I am 90%

certain that the Yucatán asteroid caused the extinction of the dinosaurs', this is not a claim that on 90% of occasions on which the dinosaurs became extinct the cause of their extinction was an asteroid landing in the Gulf of Mexico, but an expression of their confidence in their opinion. These assertions of confidence or belief – 'the probability that Dobbin will win is 0.9', 'the probability that the man in the compound is bin Laden is 95%', 'I am 90% certain that the Yucatán asteroid caused the extinction of the dinosaurs' – are today described as statements of subjective, or personal, probability. In this book we will use the term subjective probabilities throughout. The adjectives 'subjective' or 'personal' acknowledge that the assessment is not objective but a matter of individual judgement, and that different people may attach different probabilities to the same past, present or future event, both before and after it has occurred.

The triumph of subjective probability

As we described in chapter 1, John Maynard Keynes and Frank Knight emphasised the significance of radical uncertainty, and denied that probabilities could be applied outside the realm of known or knowable frequency distributions such as games of roulette or observations of mortality or weather. There could hardly be a sharper contrast of personalities than that between these two, both flag bearers for radical uncertainty and opponents of the application of subjective probabilities.[7] Keynes was a liberal scion of the English upper middle class, who moved effortlessly between the intellectual and agnostic world of Cambridge and the bohemian literary milieu of Bloomsbury; Knight had graduated from a small Christian college in Tennessee before attending the state university, and then completed a PhD at Cornell before taking a teaching post in Iowa. Politically conservative, he moved to the University of Chicago in 1927. Knight is often described as the founder of the Chicago School of Economics, with its resolute focus on individual rational choice and free markets.

But there was a contemporary of comparable stature who took a different view. Frank Ramsey, a philosopher and mathematician who also made contributions to economic theory, was a friend and colleague of Keynes at King's College, Cambridge.[8] His brilliant career was cut short by his death from postoperative complications at the age of twenty-six. Although notions of personal probability had been implicit for many years, Ramsey was the first to describe 'subjective probability' in a more formal way.[9] Ramsey further proposed that the mathematics which had been used for the analysis of probabilities based on frequencies could be applied to these subjective probabilities. Similar analysis was developed independently by Bruno de Finetti, an Italian statistician who bizarrely linked his academic work on probability to his personal support for fascism.[10]

Ramsey and de Finetti won, and Keynes and Knight lost, that historic battle of ideas over the nature of uncertainty. The result was that the concept of radical uncertainty virtually disappeared from the mainstream of economics for more than half a century.[11] The use of subjective probabilities, and the associated mathematics, seemed to turn the mysteries of radical uncertainty into puzzles with calculable solutions. And it would be at the University of Chicago that the triumph of subjective probability over radical uncertainty would be most enthusiastically celebrated.

Many great economists contributed to the creation of the Chicago School, but the figure best known to a wider public was Milton Friedman, Professor of Economics from 1946 to 1977 and one of the most influential economists of the twentieth century. Friedman's *Price Theory – a Provisional Text* may be regarded as the primer of the doctrines of the Chicago School. In it he wrote:

in his seminal work, Frank Knight drew a sharp distinction between risk, as referring to events subject to a known or knowable probability distribution, and uncertainty, as referring to events for which it was not possible to specify numerical probabilities. I've not referred to this distinction because I do not believe it is valid ... We may treat people as if they assigned numerical probabilities to every conceivable event.[12]

Friedman's followers distanced themselves – at least in this respect – from Knight's legacy. They even explained that the revered founder of the school could not have meant what he said. In an article published in 1987 in the *Journal of Political Economy*, the house journal of the Chicago School, Stephen LeRoy and Larry Singell explained: 'The received interpretation of Knight's classic risk-uncertainty distinction – as concerning whether or not agents have subjective probabilities – constitutes a misreading of Knight. On the contrary, Knight shared the modern view that agents can be assumed always to act as if they have subjective probabilities.'[13] It is impossible to accept this assertion given Knight's description of uncertainty and entrepreneurship. LeRoy and Singell argue that 'to deny the existence of subjective probabilities is to deny that agents are able to choose consistently among lotteries'.[14] But that is exactly what Keynes and Knight did deny. And with good reason, as we will now see.

The probability of an attack on the Twin Towers

'We may treat people as if they assigned numerical probabilities to every conceivable event.' So what was the probability that terrorists would fly passenger planes into the World Trade Center on 11 September 2001? Nate Silver, a well-known political pundit in the United States and a devotee of subjective probabilities and Bayesian reasoning, has attempted to answer that question. According to Silver, 'most of us would have assigned almost no probability to terrorists crashing planes into buildings in Manhattan when we woke up that morning . . . For instance, say that before the first plane hit, our estimate of the possibility of a terror attack on tall buildings in Manhattan was just 1 chance in 20,000.'[15] But what is the question to which this number is the answer? Is it the probability of an attack that morning? That day? That year? At all? There should be very large differences in the answers to these distinct questions; the probability of an attack on the morning of 11 September must be much lower than the probability that an attempt to conduct such an attack will be made at *some* time. And are we estimating the probability of 'terrorists crashing planes into buildings in Manhattan' or 'the possibility of a terror attack on tall buildings'? There are many forms of terror attack on tall buildings not involving planes, such as the 1993 bomb in the basement of the North Tower. Without a clear problem specification, there is no reason to anticipate meaningful, consistent or useful answers to questions about probability.

Silver goes on to specify the probability of a plane hitting the World Trade Center by accident: 'This figure can actually be estimated empirically,' he asserts, putting the chance at 1 in 12,500. He reports two accidents prior to 2001 involving planes colliding with Manhattan buildings, in 1945 and 1946 respectively. So there were around 25,000 days between 1946 and 2001 on which no planes crashed into New York skyscrapers. During this time, aircraft movements increased by several orders of magnitude, but air traffic control advanced beyond recognition. We do not know how one can conclude from the data cited that the probability of such an accident on any particular day is 1 in 12,500, although we understand the calculation Silver made. He divided 25,000, the number of days between 1946 and 10 September 2001, by two, the number of air accidents involving high buildings in Manhattan between 1945 and 10 September 2001.[16]

The two-child problem

In the absence of any other information, the probabilities that a child is a boy or a girl are more or less equal. So, in the absence of any other information, the probability that the first child in the Smith family is a boy is one half and that the first child is a girl is also one half. And, in the absence of any other information, the probabilities that the second child in a two-child family is a boy or a girl are also equal and each is one half. These assertions are not based on 'the indifference principle' but on the findings of biological research, confirmed by observed frequencies. Two-child families are very common in modern developed economies and the frequencies of the sequences BB, GG, BG and GB – where the first letter identifies the gender of the first child and the second letter the gender of the second child – are more or less the same. This is a matter of biology making the gender of successive children in a family more or less independent, again supported by observation.

Boys and girls are born in more or less equal numbers. And although the numbers of births in England and France are also similar – about 700,000 annually – the probability that the first child in a two-child family is English and the second is French is very low, much lower than the probability that both children are English or French. EE and FF are very common, FE and EF are not. This obvious point illustrates why it is always dangerous to talk about probabilities without understanding the processes which generate the observed data, as many were surprised to discover in the global financial crisis.

Now suppose that you are told that the Smiths have two children and you know that one is a girl. What is the probability that the other child is also a girl? This problem seems to have been first posed in 1959 by Martin Gardner, the American mathematics journalist and puzzle compiler, and has remained controversial – and unresolved – ever since, 'notorious' in the view of one author.[17] As the Wikipedia entry on the subject notes, almost everyone who has written about the problem remains convinced that their different answers are right.

There are four equally probable sequences of births: BB, GG, BG and GB. One – BB – is ruled out by the information that one child is a girl. The other three remain equiprobable. In only one of the remaining three does the girl have a sister (GG). So the relevant probability is one in three. This seems compelling.

But look at the issue in a different way. Suppose you had been told nothing about the gender of the first child. Then it would be easy to agree that the probability that the other child was a girl was one half. But since a child is equally likely to be a boy or girl, and the gender of the second child is independent of the first child, the information that one of the two children is a girl tells you nothing about the probability that the other child is a girl. Hence the relevant probability is one in two. This argument also seems compelling.

But at most one of these propositions can be right. So is the probability that the girl has a sister one in two or one in three? The answer may depend on precisely how the information that one child is a girl was obtained. Without such knowledge the problem is insufficiently defined. You invite the new neighbours, the Smiths, round for tea and they tell you they will bring their two children. The first child to run up the path is a girl. In the absence of any other information, it is reasonable to assume that this observation tells us nothing about the gender of the second child, just as the gender of the first-born tells us nothing about the gender of the second-born. So the answer to the question is one half, the known frequency of female children.

But suppose you are recruiting for the Boy Scouts or Girl Guides. You attend a Girl Guide meeting and invite those girls present who have exactly one sibling to approach her, if the sibling is a girl, about membership. What is the probability that the girls have a sister to recruit? You are now looking only at two-child families with at least one girl, which rules out the inclusion of any BB households. In the absence of any other information, the probability is one third. But the problem is not fully specified. GG households may be over-represented. Do girls join the Guides to get away from their brothers, or their sisters, or because they have heard good reports from their siblings? Does one effect offset the other? Perhaps. Or perhaps not. We simply do not know. And what if you meet the child on some unplanned occasion? This might be similar to seeing the first child up the path – or it might not. Perhaps fathers are more likely to take their sons to a football match, and mothers their daughters on a shopping expedition. Or perhaps not. In conditions of radical uncertainty, subjective probabilities are necessarily sensitive to trivial information and details of problem specification, and it therefore makes little sense to formulate or act on them.

You never have to swing

'To deny the existence of subjective probabilities is to deny that agents are able to choose consistently among lotteries,' write LeRoy and Singell. The idea – which has been present, often implicitly and sometimes explicitly, since subjective probabilities were first employed – is that an observer can deduce subjective probabilities by presenting people with the opportunity to bet on various outcomes. The term 'pignistic probability' was coined by Philippe Smets to describe the process of claiming to deduce subjective probabilities from observed gambling behaviour.[18] The phrase is derived from the Latin word *pignus*, meaning a wager. 'I think that the probability that Dobbin will win the Kentucky Derby is 0.9' means that I will bet on Dobbin if the odds are better than that and against Dobbin if the odds are worse. Some readers may be surprised that anyone who thinks Dobbin will win the race would bet against Dobbin, and even more surprised at the suggestion that it might be irrational for them to decline an opportunity to do so. This is a first indication that many people do not think naturally in terms of subjective probabilities and that the meaning of 'rationality' is contested.[19]

The Kentucky Derby is America's most famous horse race, held every summer at Churchill Downs near Louisville with exactly twenty runners. But in February 2019, the authors were approached by a devotee of Milton Friedman seeking to establish our subjective probabilities of every conceivable event. 'What is the probability that Dobbin will win this year's Kentucky Derby?' he asked. When we demurred he became more insistent. Would you back Dobbin to win at 5 to 1? No, we responded, but then he offered 50 to 1. When we accepted, he lowered the odds, and so the dialogue continued until he established the price – odds of 20 to 1 – at which we were exactly indifferent between accepting and refusing. Starting from this figure he used the pignistic method to deduce our subjective probability of Dobbin's victory – in this case 0.047.[20]

Neither we nor he knew the entire list of potential runners but he went through some other possibilities. What about Hercules at 100 to 1? he enquired. And so the discussion went on until he had established our subjective probability for every conceivable runner in the race. At that point, he pulled out a spreadsheet and added up all the subjective probabilities he had computed. As we had hoped, he was able to confirm that they totalled exactly one.

Ramsey and de Finetti would have been proud of us, or at least relieved. The winning argument which Ramsey provided to counter Keynes was that anyone who did not attach a consistent set of subjective probabilities to all uncertain events would be certain to lose money if they bet at those probabilities.[21] If the total of the probabilities which we had attached to the prospects of Dobbin, Hercules and all the other runners in the Kentucky Derby had been either less than one or more than one, our interlocutor from Chicago would have been able to make money out of us. If the total had been less than one, he could have *placed* a bet with us on every horse in the race and been certain to win more than he had staked. If the total had been more than one, he could have *accepted* our bets on all runners and again been certain to make a profit. But since they added up to exactly one, he was able only to congratulate us on our rational adherence to a consistent set of personal probabilities.

Of course this exercise did not actually occur. And like most people we know, we would have shown the inquisitor the door long before he had been able to compile his spreadsheet. Far from demonstrating the power of Ramsey's concept of rational behaviour in the face of uncertainty, the thought experiment reveals the absurdity of the suggestion that people act as if they attach probabilities to every conceivable event. Rational people will decline to participate in any proposed wager when their information is imperfect and may differ from that held by other people. Pascal may have been right to observe that when the issue was the existence of God, to wager was 'not optional'. But betting on the Kentucky Derby *is* optional. We have no relevant knowledge of the names of the runners in the forthcoming Kentucky Derby, or their form, and no interest in pursuing the matter further. It is extremely unlikely that our subjective probabilities would add up to one because we have no reasonable basis on which to formulate such probabilities and no intention of obtaining any such basis.

'I give you two to one that the Smiths have two girls.' 'No, but if you offer five to one we have a deal.' 'You are a betting man, Mr Churchill' – he was, in fact, a regular and unsuccessful player of games of chance – 'so I wager you a sovereign that Germany will win the war.' It is not likely that Churchill's reaction to the proposed wager would have been polite. We would expect few takers if we opened a book on the composition of the Smith family. These are not the kind of transactions in which people engage, except in jest.

And one of the several reasons why this sort of wagering is not normal or acceptable social behaviour is relevant to the use of this kind of analysis in financial markets. The people who are willing to take the other side of such bets are likely those who have different, and better, information than we do, and in daily life we regard it as discreditable that they exploit that advantage for financial gain. Or else the gamblers are fools who believe they know more than they do, or have unwarranted confidence in their judgement. Even Sky Masterson and Nathan Detroit, the inveterate gamblers of *Guys and Dolls*, declined to bet on the sales of Mindy's cheesecake and the colour of Nathan's tie. As Sky's father had warned him, 'you're going to wind up with an earful of cider' if you gamble when information is unequally distributed.[22]

We gamble with our lives when we overtake the vehicle in front, board an aircraft, or influence our metabolism by swallowing a pill. But we do not make these choices with the aid of some consistent underlying structure of subjective probabilities, which can be illuminated by offering a variety of bets. Households and businesses cope with radical uncertainty by formulating the context within which we make observations or decisions. Households piece together their knowledge of the Smith family, statesmen and historians their understanding of the evolution of the Second World War. And they do not act until they have sufficient confidence in the narrative they have constructed. There is no Bayesian dial.

If many experienced and well-informed observers give very different answers to the same question – is the man in the compound bin Laden? – then any honest person who had no additional specific information would respond 'I do not know'. Neither of us has ever heard anyone say something like 'the probability that the Smiths have two boys is 0.6' and we never expect to. We have, however, often heard them say things like 'I think their child is a girl' or 'I don't know whether their child is a boy or a girl'. If that question matters there is usually a simple means of resolution, which is to make further enquiry. And if for some reason this is impossible, and the answer still matters, the appropriate course of action is one which is robust to both possibilities. If we have to entertain the child tomorrow, we find a toy or a video appropriate to either gender.

The notion that observing how people gamble gives insight into rational behaviour under uncertainty is strange. After all, bookmakers and casinos consistently make money at the expense of their customers. Most people wager only occasionally for cheap amusement. They enjoy an afternoon at the racecourse, they support the raffle at the village fete, they like to dream that they might win the National Lottery. Prudent investors buy and sell only a very small proportion of the universe of available securities, for the sensible reason that they do not feel sufficiently well informed about the characteristics of most of the securities in that universe to take a view. And when intelligent investors do buy or sell, they require what Benjamin Graham christened a 'margin of safety' between price and their assessment of value.[23] Graham was the British-born American investor who through his writings made famous the strategy of investing based on long-term fundamental values. His follower, Warren Buffett, the most successful investor in history, put it more colourfully: 'I call investing the greatest business in the world ... because you never have to swing. You stand at the plate, the pitcher throws you General Motors at 47! U.S. Steel at 39! and nobody calls a strike on you. There's no penalty except opportunity lost. All day you wait for the pitch you like; then when the fielders are asleep, you step up and hit it.'[24]

And that is why when Buffett was asked how he responded to auctions of businesses conducted by investment banks, he replied with the musical words of George Jones: 'when your phone don't ring, it'll be me'.[25] If 'we can treat people as if they attached numerical probabilities to every conceivable event', and if such probabilities formed the basis of their economic decisions, then you *do* 'have to swing' and people would indeed be willing to take one side or the other of every possible bet. But the prediction that people routinely engage in such transactions is plainly false, and no prudent individual would even think of behaving in that way.

A very few professional gamblers are successful because they have observed anomalies, or studied the processes of apparent games of chance particularly carefully – Edward Thorp and the Ritz patrons – and the organisers of gambling establishments are anxious to identify them and exclude them from their casinos. But most regular gamblers are sad people, some in the grip of addiction, some suffering from persistent delusions about their own skill. It is true that when experimental subjects are asked to come up with subjective probabilities using these pignistic methods they can sometimes be persuaded to do so, usually with the aid of pressure from their professors and modest financial compensation for their cooperation. However this politeness in the face of silly requests provides no reason to believe that the numbers derived from such experiments bear any relation to an underlying set of consistent subjective probabilities. And as we shall see in chapter 7, the empirical evidence is that they do not.

Once it is acknowledged that most people do not bet on most things, and that it is simply not true that everyone would be willing to take one side or another of any proposed lottery, the argument deployed by Ramsey against Keynes simply fails. In a world of radical uncertainty, most people do not choose among lotteries, far less enter them, and for good reasons. They do not stake their fortunes on the fall of the cards, the throw of a die, or the spin of a roulette wheel. They shun randomness. They are reluctant to make commitments in situations they do not understand, especially when others may have a better understanding of them. Shrewd business people appreciate the importance of radical uncertainty. Of course, there are people who will take a bet on anything, but that is a mark of weirdness, not rationality. Enrico Fermi, the brilliant physicist whose work was central to the Manhattan Project, supposedly opened a book on whether the July 1945 test explosion in the desert would ignite the atmosphere and if so whether it would destroy only New Mexico or the whole world. It was not the Nobel Prize winner's finest moment.[26]

6

———— • ————

AMBIGUITY AND VAGUENESS

'When I use a word,' Humpty Dumpty said, in rather a scornful tone, 'it means just what I choose it to mean – neither more nor less.'

—LEWIS CARROLL, *Through the Looking-Glass*, 1871[1]

Golf is a popular sport across the world. In 2019, a new rulebook was introduced which aimed to simplify the regulations and speed up play.[2] Several of the new rules require that an event is 'virtually certain'. For example, 'You will be found to have caused your ball to move only if that is known or virtually certain (that is, it is at least 95% likely that you were the cause)'. What does this number mean? The rulebook states that 'virtually certain means that ... all reasonably available information shows that it is at least 95% likely that the event in question happened'. This amplification adds nothing. As the BBC's golf correspondent commented, 'This is 100% subjective.'[3] Either you moved the ball or you didn't.

The Royal and Ancient Golf Club had fallen into a common and modern trap of bogus quantification. The authors of the rule believed that attaching a number to their judgement gave it an objectivity and scientific precision which a qualitative assessment would have lacked. Chicago's Frank Knight, who understood radical uncertainty well, took a different view:

The saying often quoted from Lord Kelvin[4] ... that where you cannot measure, your knowledge is meagre and unsatisfactory; as applied in mental and social science is misleading and pernicious. This is another way of saying that these sciences are not science in the sense of physical science and cannot attempt to be such without forfeiting their proper nature and function. Insistence on a concretely quantitative economics means the use of statistics of physical magnitudes, whose economic meaning and significance is uncertain and dubious ... In this field, the Kelvin dictum very largely means in practice, if you cannot measure, measure anyhow!'[5]

Knight can hardly have failed to notice, though he refrained from mentioning, that Kelvin's dictum was engraved on the building which houses the social science faculty of the University of Chicago.

The new rules of golf conflated two ideas – the confidence of the adjudicator in his judgement, and the likelihood that the judgement is correct – and described the result as a probability. Discussion of uncertainty involves several different ideas. Frequency – I believe a fair coin falls heads 50% of the time, because theory and repeated observation support this claim. Confidence – I am pretty sure the Yucatán event caused the extinction of the dinosaurs, because I have reviewed the evidence and the views of respected sources. And likelihood – it is not likely that James Joyce and Lenin met, because one was an

Irish novelist and the other a Russian revolutionary. My knowledge of the world suggests that, especially before the global elite jetted together into Davos, the paths of two individuals of very disparate nationalities, backgrounds and aspirations would not cross.

In the context of frequencies drawn from a stationary distribution, probability has a clear and objective meaning. When expressing confidence in their judgement, people often talk about probabilities but it is not clear how the numbers they provide relate to the frequentist probabilities identified by Fermat and Pascal. When they ask whether Joyce met Lenin, the use of numerical probability is nonsensical.

Harrisburg or Philadelphia?

Is Philadelphia the capital of Pennsylvania? Which city, San Antonio or San Diego, has the larger population? About two thirds of respondents in a recent survey opined that Philadelphia was indeed the capital of Pennsylvania.[6] And about two thirds of those respondents expressed 100% confidence in their answer. The minority who thought that Philadelphia was not the capital of Pennsylvania were similarly confident – two thirds of them were certain that they were right.

There were two significant differences, however, between the group which answered yes and the group which answered no. Those who thought Philadelphia was the capital believed that most other people would agree with them. Those who disagreed did not expect that others would share the same view. The second difference is that those who answered 'no' gave the correct answer. Although Philadelphia is the largest town, and economic hub, of Pennsylvania, the state capital is Harrisburg. Presumably many of those who answered 'no' knew this, or at least had some reason for believing that the 'obvious' answer was wrong. When the same people were asked whether Columbia was the state capital of South Carolina (it is), once more two thirds of respondents answered yes. Both yes and no voters were less confident, however, and yes voters were a little more inclined to think that others would agree with them.

Rather more seriously, the same study asked dermatologists to assess whether lesions were malignant or benign. About two thirds of answers were correct. But weighting opinion by the degree of confidence expressed by the dermatologist added nothing to the accuracy of the judgements. Dermatologists who thought their colleagues would give a different opinion were slightly more likely to be correct in their own diagnosis. People who disagree with the obvious answer may do so because they are better informed, or more thoughtful; but perhaps they are simply making a mistake.

And does San Antonio have a larger population than San Diego? (It does: about 1.5 million people live in the Texan city against 1.4 million in the Californian one.) Asked to judge which of a selection of paired US cities was bigger, there was little difference between the performance of US and German students (who presumably knew less about US geography), and the same was true when paired German cities were used.[7] Small amounts of information made little – or sometimes perverse – difference to the quality of answers.

In these experiments, respondents were not allowed to give what would have been for most of them the appropriate answer to questions like 'What is the capital of South Carolina?' or 'Is San Diego larger than San Antonio?' which is 'I don't know: if it matters I will look it up'. For issues such as these, of course, it doesn't matter. But it matters very much to the patients of dermatologists whether their lesion is malignant or benign, and whatever his or her provisional opinion, a competent doctor would order a biopsy of any suspicious lesion to permit further and more conclusive judgements. Intelligent people do not make important decisions on matters about which they are ignorant when additional data are readily available. And any bar-room conversation, or presidential tweet, will remind you that the degree of confidence with which a proposition is expressed is not the same as the probability that the proposition is true.

Thus there is a difference between probability and confidence. I am more confident that Paris is the capital of France than that Dobbin will win the Kentucky Derby, but what could it mean to say I am 50% more confident? And, in everyday language, likelihood means something different still. It is unlikely that Joyce and Lenin met, but the presence of both in Zurich in 1917 is central to Tom Stoppard's play *Travesties* (Joyce was writing *Ulysses* in the sanctuary of neutral Switzerland while Lenin was waiting for the train to the Finland Station). Perhaps this further information shifts the reading on the Bayesian dial from one in a million to one in a thousand; perhaps both Joyce and Lenin used the same newsagent and with these additional data the Bayesian dial might swing to one in a hundred. But Joyce smoked heavily and Lenin detested the habit – the dial swings again.

But the exercise is ridiculous. And the numbers are arbitrary – why not a probability of 1 in 123,456 or 1 in 1,387? – and hence meaningless. And the statement 'the probability that Philadelphia is the capital of Pennsylvania is 0.7' is absurd. Philadelphia is either the capital of Pennsylvania or it is not, and the correct answer is a matter of ascertainable fact. But someone ignorant of US politics and geography might reasonably think and say, 'It is likely that Philadelphia is the capital of Pennsylvania', applying the general rule that the capital of a country or region is often its principal city; Paris is the capital

of France, Munich the capital of Bavaria, and Boston the capital
of Massachusetts, although New York is not the capital even of
New York state, far less of the United States. And our knowledge of the world would lead us to think it more likely that
Lenin met Rosa Luxemburg (the leader of the German communist revolution of 1918) than that he met James Joyce (if you
are interested, Lenin and Luxemburg did meet when Lenin and
his wife changed trains in Berlin in 1908).[8] Philadelphia is not
the capital of Pennsylvania, and anyone who offers odds on the
answer to such a question is a knave (and anyone who accepts
them a fool). You will wind up with an earful of cider.

The 'Linda problem' is one of the most frequently reported
experiments in behavioural economics. In his bestseller
Thinking, Fast and Slow, Daniel Kahneman describes it thus:
'Linda is thirty-one years old, single, outspoken, and very
bright. She majored in philosophy. As a student, she was deeply
concerned with issues of discrimination and social justice, and
also participated in anti-nuclear demonstrations. Which of the
following is more likely? "Linda is a bank teller" or "Linda is a
bank teller and is active in the feminist movement".'[9]

The most common answer (given by 85% to 90% of undergraduates in major universities)[10] is that Linda is more likely
to be a feminist bank teller than a bank teller. That answer is
wrong in terms of probabilities because the probability of two
events A and B occurring together cannot exceed the probability of A occurring alone. Since some bank tellers are not
feminists, feminist bank tellers are necessarily observed less frequently than bank tellers. But, to the surprise of Kahneman and
his colleagues, many people continue to assert that the second
description is the more likely, even after their 'error' is pointed
out. Our experience is that even audiences of actuaries, whose
professional background is in the application of probabilities,
do this. They do not acknowledge their alleged 'irrationality'.

What is going on here? The subjects were not asked about probabilities but about likelihood, and they answered the examination question Kahneman asked rather than the one he thought he was asking. When we ask whether it is likely that Joyce met Lenin, or that Philadelphia is the capital of Pennsylvania, they do not reason probabilistically but interpret the question in the light of their broad contextual knowledge. That was the lesson Sky Masterson's father had conveyed to his son, and it is one well understood by Kahneman's respondents. People do not think of the Linda problem in terms of frequencies, or as an exercise in probabilistic reasoning. They see the description of Linda as a story about a real person, and the biography of Linda which ends only by identifying her as a bank teller is not, without more information, a satisfactory account. Faced with such a narrative in real life, one would seek further explanation to resolve the apparent incongruity and be reluctant to believe, far less act on, the information presented. In later chapters we will describe the central role which narrative and contextual reasoning rightly plays in managing uncertainty.

'Jabberwocky'

The first lines of the poem 'Jabberwocky', from Lewis Carroll's *Through the Looking-Glass*, raise difficult questions of probability:

> 'Twas brillig, and the slithy toves
> Did gyre and gimble in the wabe:
> All mimsy were the borogoves,
> And the mome raths outgrabe.[11]

What is the probability that toves are nocturnal? What is the probability that they are mammals? But there is only one sensible answer to questions about the nature and habits of toves, which is 'I do not know'. 'Jabberwocky' is generally described as nonsense verse, although any imaginative reader will come away with some sense of meaning, which is why the poem has remained popular for more than a century. Even if the words are not intelligible, they are more than a random arrangement of letters; indeed, it has been claimed that they are drawn from a private language from Carroll's childhood.[12]

We anticipate that serious-minded colleagues will berate us for drawing lessons for the methodology of social science even from such an enduring source of delight for children as *Alice in Wonderland*.[13] We disagree; in creating a simple, self-contained world which resembles life but parodies it, Carroll was conducting an exercise very similar to the recent development of economic models. Here is Robert Lucas, the Chicago-based father of modern macroeconomics, describing the exercise in which he believed he and his colleagues were engaged:

> We are storytellers, operating much of the time in worlds of make believe. We do not find that the realm of imagination and ideas is an alternative to, or retreat from, practical reality. On the contrary, it is the only way we have found to think seriously about reality. In a way, there is nothing more to this method than maintaining the conviction . . . that imagination and ideas matter . . . there is no practical alternative.[14]

The creation of this completely specified analogue world directly parallels the exercise undertaken by Lewis Carroll, or by Tolkien in describing Middle-earth (or by the modern producers of *Game of Thrones* or the creators of computer games such as *Fortnite*). By inventing their own language and characters, Carroll and Tolkien left their readers in no doubt that any relationship between their models and the real world could only be one of analogy; indeed children can enjoy these books without making any such connection. But by using words such as 'output', 'inflation' and 'money' which appear to have real counterparts, rather than 'toves' and 'borogoves', Lucas and his followers elided this distinction between their artificial world and the complex real world, and many users of their analysis were misled.

Mathiness

The belief that mathematical reasoning is more rigorous and precise than verbal reasoning, which is thought to be susceptible to vagueness and ambiguity, is pervasive in economics. In a celebrated attack on Nobel Prize winner and *New York Times* columnist Paul Krugman, the Chicago economist John Cochrane wrote, 'Math in economics serves to keep the logic straight, to make sure that the "then" really does follow the "if," which it so frequently does not if you just write prose.'[15] But there is a difficulty here which appears to be much more serious in economics than it is in natural sciences: that of relating variables which are written down and manipulated in mathematical models to things that can be identified and measured in the real world. This is an aspect – perhaps the principal aspect – of a problem which Paul Romer, 2018 Nobel laureate, has described as 'mathiness'.[16] Romer points to concepts such as 'investment specific technology shocks' and 'wage markup' which are no more observable, or well defined, than toves or borogoves. They exist only within the model, which is rigorous only in the same sense as 'Jabberwocky' is rigorous; the meaning of each term is defined by the author, and the logic of the argument follows tautologically from these definitions.

In *Through the Looking-Glass*, Alice sensibly concluded that she needed to know more if she was to understand her situation, and had the good fortune to have an oracle close to hand:

'You seem very clever at explaining words, Sir,' said Alice. 'Would you kindly tell me the meaning of the poem "Jabberwocky"?'

'Let's hear it,' said Humpty Dumpty. 'I can explain all the poems that ever were invented – and a good many that haven't been invented just yet.'

So Alice begins reading.

'That's enough to begin with,' Humpty Dumpty interrupted: 'there are plenty of hard words there. "Brillig" means four o'clock in the afternoon – the time when you begin broiling things for dinner.'

'I see it now,' Alice remarked thoughtfully: 'and what are "toves"?'

'Well, "toves" are something like badgers – they're something like lizards – and they're something like corkscrews.'

'They must be very curious creatures.'

'They are that,' said Humpty Dumpty: 'also they make their nests under sun-dials – also they live on cheese.'[17]

If Alice had fallen into the world of personal probabilities, she would have brought to it assessments of prior probabilities of the habits of toves, and her Bayesian dial would swing back and forth in the light of Humpty Dumpty's advice. If brillig means four o'clock in the afternoon, it seems unlikely that toves, which are reported to be gyring and gimbling at that time, are indeed nocturnal creatures. It is less clear how Humpty Dumpty's explanation helps her decide whether or not toves are mammals; indeed the implausibility of his description casts doubt on the veracity of all information supplied by Mr Dumpty. We know that many students of economics today experience similar confusion as their professors describe the internal logic of a model tenuously related to any real world.

Inevitable ambiguity

But not all instances of mathiness are as extreme as Romer's examples. For example, output is a variable, often the principal variable, in many macroeconomic models. The empirical counterpart to aggregate output is generally assumed to be GDP, gross domestic product.[18] GDP is a very different kind of measure from, say, temperature or velocity, which are empirical facts which can be observed with the aid of suitable instruments, and in respect of which any competent observer will come up with the same answer.[19]

There is no such thing as aggregate output. What statisticians record as aggregate output is the sum of the output of individual goods and services, weighted by the market price of these goods and services. An obvious difficulty is that for many goods and services no such market price exists. Police and fire services, defence provision, and local roads are everywhere provided without charge to most beneficiaries, as are modern services such as Facebook, Google and Spotify. In many countries health and education are provided outside the market. It has been recognised since the earliest days of national income accounting that financial services pose a particularly serious problem.

One of the largest quarterly *increases* (this is not a misprint) on record in the reported contribution of the financial sector to UK GDP occurred in the fourth quarter of 2008, when the sector was rescued from collapse.[20] Moreover, the composition of output changes, sometimes dramatically, from year to year, and this means that the growth rate of an economy's GDP, to which much attention is devoted, is the product of a further calculation of an index number calculated at base quantities and prices.[21]

Central banks around the world target measures of inflation. But what is inflation? Statistical agencies measure, each month, the cost of buying a prescribed basket of goods and services.

That basket represents an average of everyone's consumption, based on surveys of household expenditure. But everyone buys a different bundle of goods. Both rich and poor people have very different consumption patterns from the average.[22] Every year, sometimes more often, the basket must be revised to reflect current consumption patterns. It didn't include smartphones but now it does. Of necessity, the basket always lags behind changing patterns of consumption.

Money is a fundamental economic concept. But central banks report many different quantitative measures of 'the money supply' and the expression M in a mathematical model is as imprecise as the confused references to 'money supply' in much popular writing. And what is meant by 'money' is temporally and geographically specific. Money is dollars in the US, and euros in Europe. Not so long ago, money was gold and silver. For the inhabitants of Yap in the Caroline Islands, money was Rai, heavy circles of limestone with a hole in the middle. Some people think that crypto-currencies such as Bitcoin and Ethereum are 'money'. Numbers are essential to economic analysis. But economic data and economic models are never descriptive of 'the world as it really is'. Economic interpretation is always the product of a social context or theory.

Expressing uncertainty

When we are wondering whether the man in the compound is bin Laden or what happened to the *Mary Celeste*, whether the second Smith child is a girl or whether Joyce met Lenin, probabilities are unhelpful. Any expression of probability is a claim to a knowledge of the underlying issue which, by the nature of the uncertainty surrounding these problems, the speaker cannot have. In these circumstances, it may often make sense to describe the degree of uncertainty in non-probabilistic ways.

It is intelligible to say 'it is likely that Philadelphia is the capital of Pennsylvania' even though it is not, and intelligible to say 'this evidence made it more likely than before that bin Laden was the man in the compound' although we know, after the relevant decision was made, that bin Laden was the man in the compound. And it is intelligible to say 'I would not be surprised to learn that Philadelphia, or Pittsburgh, or Harrisburg, or one of many other towns, was the capital of Pennsylvania, but I would be surprised to learn that San Francisco was the capital of Pennsylvania'. Or 'I am not confident that the man in the compound is bin Laden, but confident that he is not Elvis Presley'. Or 'I am virtually certain that the crew of the *Mary Celeste* was not eaten by sea monsters'.

These descriptions of likelihood, confidence, surprise and certainty are often used in everyday language, interchangeably with probabilities. But they are not probabilities. They give us rankings, representing an ordering rather than a numerical scale. When Bo Derek bowled over Dudley Moore in the film *10* (he rated her '11'), she demonstrated the fatuously arbitrary nature of Moore's schema for appraising female beauty. Moore could judge one woman more lovely than another, but no more.

Vagueness and ambiguity

Many practical problems are ill defined. Information needs to be interpreted in the light of the context in which that information is obtained. Different people may reasonably arrive at different interpretations of the same question, even in extremely simple cases such as the two-child problem. Perhaps the most serious difficulty this raises for economists is the meaning of 'expectations'. In an uncertain world the expectations of households and firms, not to mention participants in financial markets, play a key role in defining economic outcomes. 'Expectations' therefore are central to many economic models. But what exactly are expectations? How are they measured? How are they determined? In chapters 19 and 20 we discuss the less than satisfactory answers economics offers to these questions.

Language is a useful means of communication only when its terms command the same meaning to the speaker and the hearer. Whether something is intelligible is itself uncertain. 'What is the probability that bidh e sileadh seo feasgar?' The only sensible answer is 'I do not know' – unless you are among the infinitesimal proportion of the world's population which speaks Scottish Gaelic and can respond that there is a high probability that it will rain this afternoon. A problem can be understood only in the light of what you already know or believe.

If, as in the two-child problem, people can continue to dispute the description of a situation – whether that description is verbal or numerical – even though they agree about the known facts of that situation, the formalised description fails to add to our knowledge. In contrast to the Monty Hall problem, in which you can verify the 'correct' answer by repeating the game many times – and derive an objective, frequentist, probability – there is no means of resolving the dispute between protagonists in the two-child problem. The seeming precision of any numerical estimate is illusory. In the absence of further information, the only satisfactory answer to the question 'Is the Smiths' other child a girl?' is 'I do not know'. Of course, you could always ask Mr or Mrs Smith, or raise with Linda questions about her role in the bank and interest in feminism.

There is often vagueness or ambiguity in the description of future states of the world. Concepts are called vague when the 'law of the excluded middle' – either it is so, or it is not so – is not satisfied. Either it is Saturday, or it is not Saturday. But we are less confident whether it is warm, or not warm. Such vagueness is not necessarily a matter of loose or sloppy reasoning. Many descriptions are useful, but necessarily vague in this sense. 'War' or 'recession' are useful concepts but they are intrinsically ill defined, in that the states of war and not war, or recession and not recession, are not capable of precise definition. The Vietnam War was not a war declared by the US Congress in the manner required by the US constitution (the Gulf of Tonkin Resolution, approved following an attack on the American naval ship *Maddox* which may never actually have occurred, gave the President authority to use armed force to resist aggression), but few would dispute the label of war.[23] But are the conflicts in Ukraine or Syria 'wars'?

Vagueness can be reduced or eliminated by exact definition, but such definition is itself arbitrary. The World Bank distinguishes 'high-income' from low- and middle-income economies.[24] But from time to time it changes that definition (at the time of writing it was annual gross national income per capita of more than $12,056), and many people would be surprised to find that Barbados, Poland and the Seychelles are 'high-income' countries along with Norway, Switzerland and the United States. Although the term 'ambiguity' is often employed to describe many kinds of uncertainty, we prefer to limit its use to genuine linguistic ambiguity. The word 'bank' has a different meaning depending on whether the context is fishing or financial regulation. Henry Kissinger's 'there is only one China and Taiwan is part of that China' is a clever illustration of the diplomacy that means whatever the listener wants to hear. St Athanasius gave a truthful but misleading answer when his pursuers asked him 'Where is the traitor Athanasius?' and he responded, 'Not far from here.'

Ambiguities of language would be unimportant in the present context were it not for the ambiguities associated with the words used in economics. The word 'ambiguity' is itself ambiguous, and so is the term 'random' – its meaning depends on a precise specification of the population from which the random selection is made, which is why the meaning of a 'randomly selected' child is unclear. But whether the issue is vagueness or ambiguity, it is impossible to converse intelligently about subjective probabilities in the absence of a shared understanding of the state of the world under discussion and the language in which it is described.

Vagueness and ambiguity may be observed not just in the terms used in describing a problem, but in the connection between actions and outcomes. The Monty Hall problem has a definite solution which can be identified clearly once the implicit as well as the explicit rules of the game have been spelt out (and hence made capable of replication by a computer). And a computer (or a human) can deduce the rules of chess, given a sufficient number of completed games. It can do so because the rules of chess are precisely defined and objectively agreed. The computer, and the human, also have the option of reading the manual. But President Obama's problem had no analogous rules. It was inherently underspecified. As were the strategic options facing Ken Olsen or Steve Jobs. There was no rulebook.

Behind these efforts to escape radical uncertainty is the belief that there is a scientific truth – a description of 'the world as it really is' – waiting to be discovered as new information gradually becomes available. Data can help us update an initial, or prior, probability distribution into a new 'posterior' probability distribution. But that prior distribution is by its nature subjective; so, therefore, must be the posterior distribution. As Edward Leamer, the distinguished American econometrician, has emphasised, 'statistical inference is and must forever remain an opinion'.[25] Deciding which information is relevant to a decision is a matter of opinion – or, as we would prefer to describe it, judgement.

Communicating uncertainty

People want to know what the weather will be tomorrow, but the weather is uncertain. Modern weather forecasters make statements of the kind 'there is a 40% probability that it will rain tomorrow' and this is sometimes useful information. But what people really want to know is whether they should carry an umbrella or plan a picnic. The repeated experience of both authors is that many people are unwilling to accept that precise knowledge of the future is simply not available, and rather than be told 'on the one hand, on the other', they would prefer to consult the charlatan who 'knows' the answer, and who will certainly have an explanation of why events turned out differently.

Climate systems are complex and non-linear. An 80 mph wind is more than twice as damaging as a 40 mph wind. And outcomes are very sensitive to initial conditions, which will never be known exactly. These properties create what is known, appropriately, as a chaotic system for which truly accurate forecasts will never be possible; 40% is essentially a statement of frequency, best interpreted as 'on 40% of occasions on which respected meteorologists say this, it will rain'.[26] The weather forecast is the product of experience, confidence and judgement.

There is, however, a further problem. The statement 'it will rain' is 'vague', and for meteorologists means that at some point in the relevant area to which the forecast applies there will be some precipitation during the relevant time period. The UK Met Office explains: 'by "any precipitation" we mean at least 0.1mm, which is about the smallest amount that we can measure'.[27] But to be told, even with certainty, that somewhere in the UK tomorrow there will be rain – possibly an amount so small that you would not even notice it – is not a basis for deciding whether to take an umbrella or cancel your daughter's wedding.

If it matters (and we often have occasion to use the phrase 'if it matters' in this book) you can assemble a group of people – event planners, weather forecasters, the mother of your prospective son-in-law – who will advise on the best way to proceed with your daughter's wedding. Obama assembled relevant and complementary experts in planning the Abbottabad raid. And the nervous father of the bride can even insure against a disastrous downpour. But he cannot eliminate uncertainty. Nor would it solve his problem to characterise it probabilistically. He can protect against the adverse consequences of uncertainty, and hope to enjoy the unanticipated pleasures which arise from imperfect knowledge of the future. He hopes that the event will go as planned. Actually, he hopes that it will be better than planned. But the thoughtful wedding planner relies on a robust and resilient adaptation strategy rather than a forecast.

Is the weather like the economy?

Like climate systems, economic and social systems are non-linear. As a result, the evolution of the economy, like the climate, is difficult to forecast. And economic forecasting is necessarily harder than weather forecasting because there is a stationarity in the underlying physics of weather systems which is missing in the underlying structure of economic systems. There are no fixed laws of motion governing the path of the economy.

Weather forecasts matter because decisions by farmers and prospective fathers-in-law depend on their expectations. And if weather forecasts are as good as they have now become, the expectations of farmers and others will broadly equate to the predictions of meteorologists. Economic expectations affect the behaviour of businesses, households and governments. But economic agents, rightly, attach rather little weight to economic forecasts. We cannot therefore work on the basis that expectations reflect 'the consensus forecast' – if indeed there is such a thing – and need to measure expectations directly or model the process by which they are formed.

Although the quality of economic forecasts remains poor, planning for the economic future is necessary. Businesses must take investment decisions. Central banks need to take decisions today on interest rates, the effects of which will become apparent only with a lag. Today's decision must be based on a judgement about the likelihood of different future out-turns. In days gone by, central banks would often say as little as possible about their reasons for decisions – indeed, before 1994 the US Federal Reserve did not even announce its decisions. But today communication, not only of decisions but of the reasons for those decisions, is accorded great importance. The behaviour of financial markets depends on expectations about how the central bank will respond to future events. That communication takes many forms. Minutes of the decision-making body and speeches by its members create a narrative within which outsiders interpret decisions on interest rates.

Like the Met Office, a central bank must convey inescapable uncertainty to people who crave unavailable certainty. The Bank of England was the first central bank to employ a visual method to display its judgement about the degree of uncertainty surrounding the impact of its decisions on its target – the annual inflation rate of consumer prices. The aim of the Bank's Monetary Policy Committee (MPC) was to set interest rates in order to keep inflation as close as possible to its target of 2% a year. For a given level of interest rates, the uncertainty about the resulting path of inflation was displayed in a 'fan chart' – the figure below depicts the chart from the Bank of England's *Inflation Report* of May 2013.

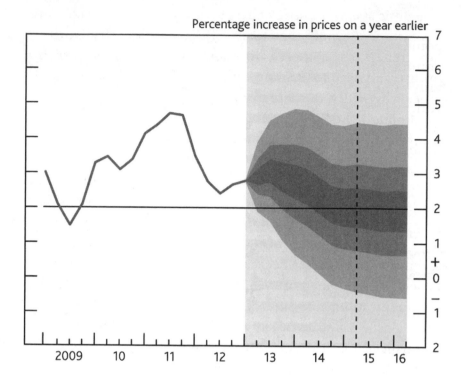

Percentage increase in prices on a year earlier

The Bank's description of the fan chart was, in terms of frequencies, similar to the Met Office's description of its own expression of probabilities:

> If economic circumstances identical to today's were to pre-vail on 100 occasions, the MPC's best collective judgement is that inflation in any particular quarter would lie within the darkest central band on only 30 of those occasions. The fan chart is constructed so that outturns of inflation are also expected to lie within each pair of the lighter red areas on 30 occasions. In any particular quarter of the forecast period, inflation is therefore expected to lie somewhere within the fan on 90 out of 100 occasions.[28]

The aim of the fan chart was to shift attention away from point forecasts ('next year inflation will be 2.3%') which had dominated macroeconomic forecasting and to introduce a narrative of uncertainty. During the financial crisis, the fan was widened to communicate greater uncertainty even though there was no basis for quantifying precisely by how much. Quite deliberately, the fan charts did not contain a line for a central forecast – the aim was for the reader to come away with a visual impression of the degree of uncertainty. And at least initially fan charts were used by the financial press, and even television, to emphasise the uncertainty about future economic events. Provided fan charts are interpreted as a way of telling a story through a picture rather than a statement of numerical probabilities, they form a useful way of communicating uncertainty (as it is perceived by central banks) to a wider audience.

Probabilities are used today in economic, scientific and general conversation. Yet radical uncertainty is not well captured by probabilistic reasoning. As Keynes put it: 'It is difficult to find an intelligible account of the meaning of "probability", or of how we are ever to determine the probability of any particular proposition; and yet treatises on the subject profess to arrive at complicated results of the greatest precision and the most profound practical importance.'[29] A century later, Keynes would have been astonished by how many such treatises there were.

7

PROBABILITY AND OPTIMISATION

Many candid persons, when confronted with the results
of Probability, feel a strong sense of the uncertainty of
the logical basis upon which it seems to rest.

—John Maynard Keynes[1]

From the beginnings of probability theory, mathematicians
realised that a further logical step was necessary to translate
that theory into advice as to when to gamble and when to keep
your money in your pocket. The concept of *expected value* was
part of the Pascal–Fermat solution to the problem of points.
If the pot contained 100 Louis d'or, and the probability that
the Duke would win at the moment of termination was seven
eighths, the expected value of his winnings was 87½ Louis d'or.
When the values and probabilities of all possible outcomes are
known, one can compute the 'expected value' of a bet. And
this is a starting point for judging its attractiveness. If a gamble
entails equal chances of winning $200 or losing $100, the

expected value is the sum of 0.5 × $200 and 0.5 × minus $100, which amounts to $50.

Problems with expected value

You are offered the choice of two envelopes and are told that one contains twice as much money as the other. You make your choice, open envelope one, and find that it contains $100. The referee asks if you would prefer envelope two. Since one envelope contains twice as much money as the other, but you do not know whether you have chosen the larger or the smaller, you know that the second envelope contains either $200 or $50, so you stand to gain $100 or lose $50 by switching from envelope one to envelope two. If you apply the Indifference Principle, and judge each of these outcomes equally likely, this sounds a good deal – expected value of $25 – so you switch.

But suppose you had initially chosen envelope two, which contains either $50 or $200. If it had contained $50, you would have stood to gain $50 or lose $25 by switching. If $200, you would either gain $200 or lose $100. In both cases, the possible gain is twice the possible loss. So if you had chosen envelope two, you would now want to switch to envelope one. Yet this conclusion cannot be right. Your initial choice is random, and it cannot be the case that if you selected envelope one you will always want to switch to envelope two – while if you chose envelope two you will always do better to switch to envelope one. But no one has ever come up with a clear and simple explanation of why the recommendation to switch is wrong. The hidden assumption is that there is a 50–50 chance of gaining or losing by switching irrespective of the amount in the envelope. But is that right? Who is putting the money in the envelope, and what are their financial resources? There appears no coherent way to identify the possible states of the world that characterise the problem, and hence no sensible basis for assigning probabilities. And this is true even though the rules of the puzzle appear to have been fully described.

The question could be tackled by making assumptions which would completely define the problem. For example, one might assume that the larger amount was between $1 and $1 million with all amounts in between equally probable. However there is no reason other than mathematical convenience to make these assumptions. There are no limits to the range of possible outcomes, and no reason to think that all possible outcomes are equally likely. Stick or switch? We simply do not know. The two-envelope problem is a striking illustration of the difficulty of applying probabilistic reasoning when the range of possible outcomes is not known completely, i.e., when there is radical uncertainty.

And there are other good reasons why decision-makers might not focus on expected value. Paul Samuelson posed to a colleague the wager which offered a 50% chance of winning $200 and a 50% chance of losing $100. The colleague replied that he would not take the bet, but would be interested if Samuelson promised to repeat the offer one hundred times. From the perspective of expected value, this response is a mistake – the colleague is turning down a wager with an expected value of $50.

But it is easy to understand why someone might respond in the manner of Samuelson's colleague.[2] The single wager involves a 50% chance of losing $100. We do not know whether $100 was a large sum for the individual concerned, though we would speculate that it was unlikely that such a loss would deprive the family of Samuelson's colleague of their supper. If you accept the multiple bet however, you might lose

$10,000 − $100 × 100 − which most people would certainly regret. However, such an outcome is very unlikely − nearly a 25 standard deviation event. The expected value of your winnings over the hundred trials is $5000 and there is a less than 1% chance that you will lose any money at all. The single wager and the multiple wager are entirely different propositions. One entails a high probability of an immediate but manageable loss. The other involves a large probability of gain, a low probability of any loss, and an extremely small probability of substantial loss at some time in the future. Is accepting one and rejecting the other really irrational? Attitudes towards risk should not be judged by their consistency with a particular set of arbitrary axioms. An extremely small probability of loss is not the same as no risk or loss, and a very high probability of winning is not the same as certainty. People may, and do, differ in their attitudes towards such gambles.

Before we judge Samuelson's colleague irrational we would need to know a great deal more about the context and the individual. George Shackle − an English economist whose writings on uncertainty defied the American consensus of the post-war period − tells of the palace guard pondering whether to join the revolution, knowing that he faces likely death if he discharges his duty and the revolution succeeds, but that he will also die if he joins the insurgents and the coup fails. But to defend the palace and see the coup fail may give rise to large rewards. Knowledge of the frequency of successful revolutions is of little help.[3] Only *this* revolution matters.

The choices we make between uncertain events are typically far more complex than those observed in elementary games of chance. The Viniar problem − the mistake of believing you have more knowledge than you do about the real world from the application of conclusions from artificial models − runs deep.

The triumph of 'the American school'

Nineteenth-century economics was developed in the context of the utilitarianism of the English philosophers Jeremy Bentham and John Stuart Mill. Individuals sought to maximise their utility and moral actions served to maximise the sum of such utilities – 'the greatest happiness of the greatest number'. The Oxford economist F. Y. Edgeworth, a pioneer of the use of mathematical reasoning in economics in the late nineteenth century, visualised the 'hedonimeter' which would measure pleasure and pain as objectively as a thermometer would measure temperature. These writers went too far, and no one today believes in the possibility of hedonimeters, or that shoppers peruse the aisles using their smartphones to make calculations which maximise their utility.

But analysis of an essentially utilitarian kind came into modern economics from a different source. It was shown – most effectively by Samuelson – that if households made choices among goods in accordance with a set of plausible axioms which were claimed to be definitive of rationality, then they were acting *as if* they were maximising some objective mathematical function which one might as well call utility. Consistency of choices was critical among these axioms. This approach proved fruitful in the understanding of many real-world problems. It allowed economists to analyse many questions concerning how changes in prices, reflecting changes in supply conditions or economic policies, would affect the allocation of resources in a market economy. And economics textbooks are full of examples of the successful application of such techniques. Several leaps were required to extend this thinking from consumer choice between goods to decision-making under uncertainty. Samuelson at first resisted, but then applauded, such extension. And that change of heart was how he was able to criticise his reluctant-to-wager colleague for his inconsistency. Consistent behaviour requires that if you accept (or reject) a gamble once, you should accept (or reject) the same gamble every time it is offered. Just as consistent behaviour requires that if you prefer today to travel to work by car rather than train, you will choose the car today, and tomorrow, and the day after.

The analogy between commuting patterns and wagering is not very convincing. Nevertheless, this development of the axiomatic approach to 'rational' choice won wide – eventually almost universal – acceptance, with little recognition of the fundamental implausibility and empirical irrelevance of the assumptions involved. Supermarket shoppers filled their trolleys *as if* they maximised their utility. And decision-makers faced with radical uncertainty behaved *as if* they maximised their subjective expected utility.

This extension of the axiomatic approach from the analysis of consumer choice to decision-making under uncertainty was the result of the work of several US-based scholars. John von Neumann was a polymathic genius who worked on the Manhattan Project and subsequently helped to develop the hydrogen bomb. In their classic work *The Theory of Games and Economic Behavior*, von Neumann and his Princeton colleague Oskar Morgenstern sought to establish that probabilistic reasoning could provide a coherent and rigorous framework for rational decision-making in a world of uncertainty. Jimmie Savage, who had been a research assistant to von Neumann, went to Chicago in 1946 and held a chair of statistics there from 1954 to 1960.[4] He developed most fully the conditions under which axiomatic reasoning could be equated with the maximisation of expected utility, conditions which rely heavily on the analogy with a world of certainty.[5] As a young academic at Chicago he met the equally youthful Milton Friedman and together they authored an article, described as written by Friedman on the basis of ideas generated by Savage, which is seminal in the treatment of uncertainty in economics.[6]

In Savage's world we are invited to see the future as a collection of gambles, or lottery tickets. But the lotteries were not just private wagers or games of chance. Whether the decision-maker is anticipating next week's weather, the progress of a career, the economic rise of China, or the advance of technology, he or she visualises all possible outcomes and attaches probabilities to them. Savage knew that, as a description of behaviour in real worlds, this was absurd. In his own classic work *The Foundations of Statistics* published in 1954, he described such analysis of the future as the 'look before you leap' principle and wrote:

> Carried to its logical extreme, the 'look before you leap' principle demands that one envisage every conceivable policy for the government of his own life (at least from now on) in its most minute details, in the light of a vast number of unknown states of the world, and decide here and now on one policy. This is utterly ridiculous ... because the task implied in making such a decision is not even remotely resembled by human possibility. It is even utterly beyond our power to plan a picnic or to play a game of chess in accordance with the principle, even when the world of states and the set of available sets to be envisaged are artificially reduced to the narrowest reasonable limits.[7]

Savage's intention was to explore a basis for the existence of personal subjective probabilities without implying that the method had universal or even general relevance to decision-making. Indeed, he emphasised that it applied only to 'small worlds'.[8] The distinction between a small world in which people can solve problems by maximising expected utility and the large world in which people actually live is crucial, and we shall refer to it frequently in later chapters. Savage went on to explain that he believed his approach might be used 'to attack relatively simple problems of decision by artificially confining attention to so small a world that the "look before you leap" principle can be applied there'.

Savage was careful not to claim that his analysis could be applied outside the narrow confines of his 'small worlds'. The problem of points and the Monty Hall problem both relate to small worlds – games of chance which are repeatable and repeated. Savage's caution over the scope of his analysis was not shared by economists who have since been happy not only to adopt the assumption that in a world of uncertainty individuals optimise by maximising their expected utility, but to claim that the resulting models have direct application to policies appropriate for large worlds.

The collaboration with Savage defined Friedman's views on the appropriate tools for analysing risk and uncertainty, views which proved influential among his colleagues and students. While Savage was initially modest about the scope of his approach, Friedman had few doubts on this – or almost any other – matter. We have described Friedman's *Price Theory – a Provisional Text* as the primer of the doctrines of the Chicago School. Friedman went on to explain there: 'just as we can suppose that an individual acts as if he attached a definite utility to every possible event if it were to occur, so we can suppose that he acts as if he attached a definite probability to each such event. These "personal probabilities" are assumed to obey the usual laws of the mathematics of probability.'[9]

But Friedman was following neither the letter nor the spirit of Savage's analysis, which employed restrictive assumptions relevant only to 'small worlds'. Yet Savage himself must share responsibility. In his own writings Savage was clear about the limitations of probabilistic reasoning, but in dealing with his colleagues he pushed subjective probabilities and Bayesian analysis to the point where 'if one were not in substantial agreement with him, one was inimical, or stupid, or at the least inattentive to an important scientific development'.[10] Personal relationships between Savage and his colleagues deteriorated and in 1960 he left Chicago for Michigan. And Friedman's followers distanced themselves – at least in this respect – from Savage's reservations.

When Milton Friedman retired from Chicago in 1976, Gary Becker acquired the mantle of academic leader of the Chicago School. And Becker's aspirations for the application of his ideas were as ambitious as Friedman's. 'All human behavior', he wrote, 'can be regarded as involving participants who maximize their utility from a stable set of preferences and accumulate an optimal amount of information and other inputs in a variety of markets. If this argument is correct, the economic approach provides a unified framework for understanding behavior that has long been sought by and eluded Bentham, Comte, Marx, and others.'[11] This was ambitious indeed.

From expected value to expected utility

In the eighteenth century, Daniel Bernoulli[12] sought to resolve the 'St Petersburg paradox' which had been formulated by his cousin Nicolaus[13] and so named because his solution was first published in the proceedings of the Imperial Academy of Sciences of St Petersburg. Imagine a gamble in which a coin is tossed again and again until it shows a head. You win $1 if the head occurs on the first toss, $2 if the first head appears on the second toss, $4 if three tosses are required – and so on. How much would you pay to play?

Simple arithmetic shows that the expected value of this

game is the total of: the prize if heads appears on the first toss, multiplied by the probability of that happening ($1 \times \frac{1}{2} = 0.5$); plus the prize if the head appears on the second toss ($2 \times \frac{1}{4} = 0.5$); and so on. The prize is increasing at the same rate as the probability of winning that prize is falling, so the answer to every similar sum is 0.5. The number of such calculations is infinitely large, and therefore so is the expected value of your winnings. The calculation of expected value includes a small probability of winning absurdly large amounts: thirty-one tosses would make you a billionaire, forty the richest person in the world – and the potential winnings escalate from there. But there is a 50% chance that you will end up with only $1 and a 75% probability of $2 or less. Nevertheless, if your only concern was to maximise the value of your expected winnings, you 'should' be willing to pay almost any amount for an opportunity to play the game. But no one would in reality pay more than a small sum. The attractions of the remote prospect of astronomical wealth are far outweighed by the near certainty of loss. No rational individual would, in our judgement, trade their entire resources, or very much at all, for such a gamble.

In general, the more you have of something, whether money, food or viewings of your favourite movie, the less is the pleasure you derive from an additional unit. Few people would imagine that Jeff Bezos[14] is a hundred times happier than an ordinary billionaire, or enjoys a hundred thousand times the pleasure of a common-or-garden dollar millionaire. If utility increases less rapidly than wealth – the relationship is non-linear – then gains will be valued less than losses of similar monetary amount are resented. Bernoulli's resolution of the St Petersburg paradox was that a gamble is worthwhile if and only if it maximises expected utility rather than expected wealth. And so decision-making using probabilistic reasoning came to be equated with maximisation of expected utility. Pascal, with his wager on the existence of God, had foreshadowed the idea of deciding on a gamble by multiplying the gain or loss, measured in terms of happiness rather than money, by the chance of that gain or loss occurring.

In secular choices, the difference between expected value and expected utility may depend on how wealthy you are. You might not accept a bet with equal chances of gaining $200 or losing $100 if you cannot afford to lose $100. A rich man might happily take the wager, but a poor man might not bet if the potential loss meant his family would starve. The affluent Duke regarded gaming winnings as a mere trifle, and for him there was little difference between the two concepts. But perhaps the impecunious Marquis, who had contributed 50 Louis d'or to the pot, could not easily afford to go home empty-handed.

Some individuals are greedy, others less so. St Francis's happiness was complete if he had sufficient clothes to conceal his nakedness and a crust of bread to eat. The extra happiness he obtained from an increase in his worldly goods declined rapidly. But for a rapacious banker who finds fulfilment only in the size of his bank balance, expected wealth and expected utility are the same. The difference between the expected utility and expected financial gain from a wager is described as a measure of *risk aversion* – the greater the risk aversion, the more reluctant a gambler will be to take on a bet.

Yet even in small worlds the model of subjective expected utility maximisation seems to be a poor guide to how we *do* behave. In the experiments of behavioural economics, the subjects – mostly American students – are induced to enter artificially created small worlds by monetary payments or in order to please their professors. And they break the rules of subjective expected utility. Repeatedly and persistently.

The Bayesian dial in the classroom

In 2016, Michael Woodford and colleagues at Columbia University published the results of an exercise to determine how students respond to new information.[15] The students made random draws from a box containing both green and red rings. The proportion of green and red rings in the box changed over time. Participants in the experiment were told that from time to time there would be a change in the underlying probability of drawing a green rather than a red ring. They were asked to estimate the probability that the next ring to be drawn would be green and report their draw-by-draw estimate using a mouse to adjust a slider on a computer screen. The most important finding of the experiment was, perhaps, the extraordinary patience of the student participants in submitting to a pointless task for an extended period for meagre return.[16] But the students failed to live up to Woodford's expectations. The slider should, Woodford thought, have moved back and forth with each draw of a ring, in line with each twitch of the Bayesian dial. But it did not. 'Our subjects depart from the optimal Bayesian benchmark in systematic ways ... but [they] usually leave their decision variable unchanged for periods of time, despite the receipt of many new pieces of information in the meantime. We conclude that their failure ... reflects imperfect attention, limited memory or related cognitive limitations.'[17] Woodford simply assumed that the ideal benchmark is the Bayesian solution, and an auxiliary hypothesis of human failure (described by Woodford as 'rational inattention', a failing with which we find it easy to sympathise) was required to reconcile the model with the experimental results.

The philosopher Anthony Appiah coined the term 'cognitive angels' to describe idealised agents who can maximise expected utility correctly, and contrasted them with real people who take time to compute and make errors in the process. Richard Thaler, winner in 2017 of the Nobel Prize in Economics, similarly distinguished 'econs' and 'humans'.[18] We do not regard the pursuit of expected utility maximisation – in a world of radical uncertainty – as characteristic of an angel. It is unlikely that the students at Columbia were angels in any sense of the word; they were human. They learnt about Bayesian reasoning in the classroom but did not apply it in their lives because it was rarely useful – in planning their lives and their careers they simply did not have the information needed to compute their expected utilities.[19] And Woodford was not able to point to bad decisions made by his 'rationally inattentive' students; he could only criticise their method of reasoning. They should, he thought, have steered by the Bayesian dial.

The Bayesian dial in the Oval Office

And so we might envisage President Obama sitting at his desk in the Oval Office, beneath a Bayesian dial. When the meeting begins, the dial is arbitrarily set at 50%, on the misguided grounds that, in the absence of any information at all, the probability that bin Laden is in the compound is 0.5.[20]

As the intelligence reports come in, the reading on the dial swings to and fro. Some agents are confident, others are not; some are more convincing than others. Finally, time is up and the meeting must end. All heads, including the President's, look up at the dial. The prior probability of one half has been replaced by a new posterior probability. Perhaps it is 31%, or perhaps it is 72%.

And now the President asks his advisers to judge how the Pakistan military will respond to the arrival of American helicopters in the city which is their centre of operations. The Bayesian dial is reset at 50% for this new puzzle. As divergent views on this new uncertainty are expressed the dial swings back and forth. For each reaction, there are many possible American responses.

And what, the President asks, if some of the equipment malfunctions? – the problem which had defeated Jimmy Carter's attempt to free the Tehran hostages. The tree of possibilities sprouts more branches and aides bring in a large whiteboard to record the ever-multiplying array of possible outcomes. And once all the combinations of possibilities have been identified, the President must attach his subjective expected utility, or his estimate of the social welfare of the American people, to each possible outcome. This done, a quick calculation generates an expected value for the outcome of the mission.

Of course, it was not like that at all. No one has ever enjoyed so much access to data, and so much expertise to tell him what he might need to know, as is available to the President of the United States. But even with such resources, an exercise of this kind is impossible. Obama was not optimising. He was not maximising his subjective expected utility, or that of the nation. He could not conceivably have held the information which would have enabled him to do so. How could he, in the face of so many ill-defined uncertainties?

Steve Jobs was not watching a Bayesian dial: he was waiting until he recognised 'the next big thing'. And Winston Churchill also played a waiting game as he saw the United States gradually dragged into war – and did his utmost to accelerate American entry. We do not know whether Obama walked into the fateful meeting with a prior probability in his mind: we hope not. He sat and listened to conflicting accounts and evidence until he felt he had enough information – knowing that he could expect only limited and imperfect information – to make a decision. That is how good decisions are made in a world of radical uncertainty, as decision-makers wrestle with the question 'What is going on here?'

In contrast, bank executives relied on the judgements of their risk professionals, who in turn relied on Bayesian techniques, and the results were not encouraging. Woodford's students, even though they were familiar with the principles of Bayesian reasoning, did not approach their task in this way – even though the experiment was designed to stimulate them to do so. Woodford's students were not making bad decisions. They simply did not use Bayesian reasoning to process new information. An alternative interpretation of the experimental results is that the students were developing a sequence of narratives, and challenging and revising the narrative at discrete intervals as they went along. Far from being systematically biased, the students were systematically struggling to come to terms with radical uncertainty in the manner in which thoughtful people normally come to terms with it. (Or, perhaps, waiting for the session to end and to collect their $10.)

When we express doubt about the practical relevance of the Bayesian dial, we are not for a moment suggesting that people should not modify their views in the light of new information. We think they should manage radical uncertainty as President Obama did – listening to evidence, hearing pros and cons, inviting challenges to the prevailing narrative, and finally reaching a considered decision. And Obama might have been forced, as Carter had been, to change his decision when he learnt of problems in the execution of the agreed plan which had not been anticipated. In the fortunate event this proved unnecessary.

The meaning of risk

The Oxford Dictionary defines risk as 'the possibility that something unpleasant or unwelcome will happen', and this is the meaning which would be understood by the board of J. P. Morgan, a typical household, a racing driver or a mountain climber.[21] Risk in its ordinary meaning concerns unfavourable events, not beneficial ones.

Risk is asymmetric. We do not hear people say 'there is a risk that I might win the lottery' because winning the lottery is not something they would describe as a risk. They do not even say 'there is a risk I might not win the lottery' because they do not realistically expect to win the lottery. The everyday meaning of risk refers to an adverse event which jeopardises the realistic expectations of the individual household or institution. And so the meaning of risk is a product of the plans and expectations of that household or institution. Risk is necessarily particular. It does not mean the same thing to J. P. Morgan as it does to a paraglider or mountain climber, or to a household saving for retirement or the children's education.

In 1979, Daniel Kahneman and Amos Tversky, the two Israeli psychologists working in America who were popularised in Michael Lewis's bestseller *The Undoing Project*, offered 'prospect theory' as an alternative account of behaviour under uncertainty to the conventional 'rational' view based on the Friedman–Savage axioms. Uncertainty was 'coded' relative to some reference point around which gains were valued less than losses of similar amount were resented. However, Kahneman and Tversky introduced the further concept of 'decision weights'. Low-probability events command an importance greater than their probability would suggest. This explains why people enter lotteries they have a negligible chance of winning. Yet there are similarly low-probability events which play no part whatever in our decision-making. The authors have taken no precautions against falling asteroids.

Very often, the risks that concern us are not risks to the status quo, but risks to our plans to change that status quo. We formulate business strategies and plans for retirement. We invest our savings or undertake new projects, from holidays to building works. And we do all these things with expectations as to the outcome – expectations which take a narrative rather than probabilistic form. We have never heard anyone say there is a 70% chance that this year's holiday will be worth £100 more than they have paid for it; we have often heard them say that they expect this year's holiday to be their best ever, or tell us when they come back that they were disappointed.

The reference narrative

We believe the best way to understand attitudes to risk is through the concept of a *reference narrative*, a story which is an expression of our realistic expectations. For J. P. Morgan, the overarching reference narrative is one in which the bank continues profitable growth. A large corporation will have many strategies for achieving that overarching objective in particular areas of its business and there will be a reference narrative relating to each business unit. Some of these business unit reference narratives may be very risky, but the corporation may tolerate such risks provided they do not endanger the reference narrative of the organisation as a whole.

Households will similarly have high-level goals of happiness and security, and many subsidiary narratives – in which they buy a house, pay for the children's education, enjoy a comfortable retirement. For the Formula One world champion, risk may be the things that would prevent him winning the race; but for a less accomplished driver, risk would be failure to achieve a decent place, and for the authors, risk would be spinning off the track at the first bend. And the risks faced by the mountain climber are the events that would prevent him or her reaching the summit. The meaning of risk is specific to the individual, household or institution concerned.

A reference narrative governed the meeting at which

President Obama ordered the SEALs to Abbottabad. The helicopters would land in the compound, the men would fight their way into the building. We suppose, but do not know, that the unspoken premise was that bin Laden would be killed in the attack. Dead or alive, he would be flown out of Pakistan in US custody. That reference narrative describes, more or less, what actually happened.

But many things might have derailed that narrative. The operation might have suffered the equipment and logistical failures which had grounded the 1979 mission to rescue the Tehran hostages. Bin Laden might not have been in the compound, because US intelligence was faulty or because he was absent at the time of the raid. The President and his advisers debated these risks and discussed appropriate responses. The most difficult issue was how to handle a situation where the operation was quickly detected by the Pakistani military authorities and confronted with an armed response. The overriding objective was to ensure that the reference narrative was robust and resilient. The key to managing risk is the identification of reference narratives which have these properties of robustness and resilience.

And since different people start with different reference narratives, the same risk may be assessed by different people in different ways. Risk may not be the same for those who work in an organisation as it is for the shareholders of that organisation. The relevant risk for the IBM executives who resisted the development of small computers in the 1970s was that their personal reference narrative, which was based on the corporation's established business model – and hence their own positions and expertise – would be devalued.

Risk is failure of a projected narrative, derived from realistic expectations, to unfold as envisaged. The happy father anticipating his daughter's wedding has in mind a reference narrative in which events go ahead as planned. He recognises a variety of risks – the prospective bridegroom has cold feet, a torrential downpour drenches the guests. There is an implied *measure* of risk in such assessment – an outcome can fall short of expectations by a narrow margin or a wide one. The scale of that risk may or may not be quantifiable, before or after the event. But this interpretation is very different to the view that has come to dominate quantitative finance and much of economics and decision theory: that risk can be equated to the volatility of outcomes.

Risk aversion and risk appetite

One reason why this view of risk as volatility has been popular among economists is that it fits well with the notion that the difference between expected utility and expected wealth is a quantitative measure of risk aversion. Risk as volatility can be compounded with risk aversion to yield a monetary value of the cost of risk. This calculation enables risk to be priced as a commodity, and bought and sold between people who have different preferences for risk, just as fruit can be bought and sold among people who have different preferences for apples and pears.

The difference between expected utility and expected wealth does provide an explanation of some aspects of behaviour in the face of uncertainty. It elucidates why a rich person might invest in a speculative enterprise while someone less wealthy would not. Or why you should insure against your house burning down: the expected disutility – the financial and emotional loss you will suffer from the conflagration, multiplied by its admittedly low probability – is larger than the cost of the premium. So the expected *utility* of the transaction is positive even if its expected *value* is negative. Conversely, the expected value to the insurer is positive and by pooling risks – the equivalent of repeating Samuelson's game one hundred times – the company achieves a high probability of making a profit overall.

But this explanation seems to offer only a partial account of behaviour towards risk. Friedman and Savage had struggled to explain why people who insured would also gamble.[22] Another problem is that the explanation of insurance works only for losses which are large relative to the existing wealth of the insured. Otherwise there is virtually no difference between expected utility and expected gain or loss. It follows that it makes no sense to insure something you could afford to lose. Yet many people who could afford to replace their holiday luggage or their mobile phone choose to take out insurance against possible loss. British electrical appliance retailers made extraordinary profits from selling insurance against repairs to the products they sold until they were effectively banned from doing so.[23] And well-off households were as likely to buy these policies as poor families which might struggle to meet the costs of repairing their washing machine. Inexpensive insurance policies which carry a large excess, or deductible, ought to be popular with optimising households, but insurance companies have found such policies difficult to sell. And our experience is that none of our friends are convinced to modify their behaviour by our economic explanations of their irrationality. One of us struggled unsuccessfully for forty years to persuade his college not to insure its silver. The college could afford to lose the silver and would not and probably could not replace it if it did.

Insurance is based not on calculations of expected value, but on the desire to protect the reference narrative of the insured. The reference narrative is one in which we arrive on holiday with all our luggage, the mobile phone is in our pocket, the washing machine is working and the College silver is available for feasts. And those who gamble are also thinking about narratives rather than probabilities and expected utility. They may be entertaining the dream of winning the lottery; or they may be among the sad people we see tethered to slot machines or hopefully clutching slips in betting shops. Wholly rational individuals like to think about the idea that they might win millions, even if they do not really expect to do so, and they know that their dream cannot materialise if they do not buy a ticket. Entering the lottery may be part of a social ritual, as is buying a raffle ticket, whether at the village fete or at the black-tie dinners favoured by hedge fund managers. There may be some confusion at work in these transactions – we suspect that some people do not recognise that the insurer does not return their bags when they are lost in transit, but only pays for the purchase of a new set of clothes. Yet the motivation behind the insurance is easy to understand. Purchasers of such costly policies are not buying additional expected utility but some protection against derailment of their reference narrative.

And insurance often protects the reference narrative of employees rather than the organisation they work for. The members of the College Finance Committee knew they would be blamed if uninsured silver was stolen, but not thanked for saving the cost of the premium. One of us recalls discussing with executives of a very large British company the rationale for corporate insurance policies since the company's balance sheet was larger than that of most insurance companies. The response was that insurance gave the company some protection against a knee-jerk reaction by directors and shareholders in the event of disaster hitting the business. Not enough, as it subsequently transpired; the business in question was an oil company with interests in the Gulf of Mexico. The primary purpose of risk management is often to protect the reference narrative of individuals within the organisation rather than the organisation itself.

Risk aversion

The account of human behaviour towards risk provided by expected utility theory is an impoverished one. Oscar Wilde gambled with, and sacrificed, his social position and literary career by not only seeking the services of rent boys but by prosecuting the Marquess of Queensberry for denouncing his immoral behaviour. Wilde's folly is only one of many examples of successful people who court danger in low life. The pleasure that some derive from mountain climbing and paragliding cannot be the product of cogitation beneath a Bayesian dial. And this type of risk-seeking seems domain-specific. Some people seek risks on mountain tops, others in fast cars, some on the trading desk. And knowing that someone drives racing cars may not give useful information about their investment goals.

Expected utility theory tells us that St Francis, whose wants are easily satisfied, would be very risk averse; the money-obsessed banker far less so. Yet most people would think it highly risky to relinquish worldly goods and rely on the benevolence of strangers. And they would be right. Eric Blair, who was educated at England's leading public school, chose to live as a tramp and a dishwasher in Paris restaurants under the persona of George Orwell. He nearly died on two separate occasions from illnesses contracted in these unhealthy environments, narrowly escaped death first on the battlefield and then by execution during the Spanish Civil War, and finally succumbed to tuberculosis at the age of forty-six. Orwell sought risk, and in doing so enriched his own understanding and that of others. But St Francis may have felt secure in the reference narrative established by his belief that his actions were in accordance with the will of God.

Those greedy bankers, by contrast, may be insatiable in their demands for personal wealth but cautious in assuming personal risk. The senior executives who led financial institutions towards collapse in 2008 largely walked away from the wreckage as rich men. But their bonus plans pale into insignificance beside that of Elon Musk, of Tesla and SpaceX, who demanded and received from the car company a scheme which could net him $55 billion – his current wealth is estimated at $20 billion, enough for most people. But Musk is the greatest business risk-taker of our age – and with his own money as well as other people's.

Anticipating risk

In a world of radical uncertainty, there are limits to the range of possibilities we can hold in our minds. We cannot act in anticipation of every unlikely possibility. So we select the unlikely events to monitor. Not by some meta-rational calculation which considers all these remote possibilities and calculates their relative importance, but by using our judgement and experience. Sometimes this selection reflects the salience of the events: every week we hear about new lottery winners; we do not often read about victims of falling asteroids, and there is probably not much we could do about them anyway. Such behaviour can be described as acting *as if* the relevant probabilities were higher or lower than they may objectively be – if, indeed, there is any basis for calculating these objective probabilities. But this interpretation fails to recognise the rational explanation that rational people derive benefit (the dream of the lottery win) or incur disutility (the fear of the asteroid) from events which do not in fact occur. That is how terrorists have been able to impose costs far greater than the actual physical damage they inflict – and they know it.

There is much more to our attitudes to risk than can be explained by expected utility. The 'risk as feelings' perspective of George Loewenstein – an American who is one of the few economists to have made empirical studies of risk-taking behaviour and may be regarded as a founder of neuroeconomics, the study of responses in the brain to economic choices – emphasises the hopes and fears that individuals experience at moments of anticipation and decision. The dream of a lottery jackpot. The exhilaration mixed with trepidation as the mountain climber tackles the notorious (Sir Edmund) Hillary step, the last major obstacle in the ascent of Everest. The complex mixture of feelings experienced by Fermi and his Los Alamos colleagues as they awaited the first nuclear explosion in the New Mexico desert. As we take the Hillary step (neither of us has or intends to) there is the present fear of failure, or worse, and the prospective exhilaration of reaching the summit. Fermi and his colleagues experienced one set of emotions as they set in train events of literally world-shaking significance, and expected another when they knew the outcome. Risk is something all of us feel emotionally, and we will see in chapter 9 that there are good evolutionary reasons for this.

Once we move away from the small worlds of repeated events, known frequency distributions, and pay-offs which are small relative to existing wealth, there is simply no basis for the claim that rational decision-makers should maximise subjective expected utility. Radical uncertainty is fatal to the attempt to draw an analogy between consumer choice and decision-making under uncertainty. We cannot define all possible future outcomes. Our knowledge of present and future states of the world is imperfect and even if we attached probabilities to them we would be foolish to act on these probabilities when it is likely that others have better information and understanding. The optimising model of behaviour under uncertainty does describe some common aspects of human behaviour. In 'small worlds', such as simple games of chance, maximising expected utility can be a useful guide to how we *should* behave. But even in such worlds individuals might reasonably have objectives other than the maximisation of their expected utility from their winnings. The Duke of A found gaming an agreeable way to spend a spare evening. The Marquis of B frequently derived pleasure from the hope that on this occasion he would win. And buyers of lottery tickets enjoy the thought of receiving a life-changing jackpot even though they do not seriously expect to receive it. The exchange between Samuelson and his colleague was not capable of being settled by any demonstration that one answer was 'better' or more rational than another.

If some of the examples we have cited seem extreme, and they are, they reinforce that central Knightian insight into the links between radical uncertainty and creativity. If St Francis and George Orwell and Elon Musk defy the precepts of rationality as described by expected utility theory, we might reasonably wish there was more such 'irrationality'. At a more mundane level, people we like and admire buy lottery tickets, drive fast cars and climb mountains; they insure their bags against loss, the College silver against theft, and their oil wells against blowout. We hesitate to describe them as irrational. And that invites the more general question – what is the meaning of rationality in a radically uncertain world?

Part III

Making Sense of Uncertainty

8

———•———

RATIONALITY IN A LARGE WORLD

One of the greatest reasons why so few people
understand themselves is that most writers are always
teaching men what they should be, and hardly ever
trouble their heads with telling them what they
really are.

—BERNARD MANDEVILLE, *Fable of the Bees*[1]

The approach to decision-making under uncertainty developed by von Neumann and Morgenstern and elaborated by Friedman and Savage in the 1940s sets out a definition of 'rationality' based not on observation or introspection, but on a set of a priori axioms. This way of thinking we will describe as 'axiomatic rationality'. It has the logical consequence that there is something which might be described as 'subjective expected utility' which individuals who are 'rational' are maximising. Obedience to these axioms, it was claimed, defined 'rational' behaviour. This is not a particularly obvious way to define 'rationality' and it is certainly not the only possible approach. It is, however, one which has come to dominate economics.

But a few lone souls disputed that view from the beginning. In the early 1950s, the French economist Maurice Allais went on to the attack. Suspicious of the growing domination of economics by US scholars, Allais published his findings as 'a critique of the postulates and axioms of the American school'.[2] Allais presented his critique in 1953 in *Econometrica*, then as now a major economics journal, but he wrote in French. His article is preceded (very unusually) by a note (in English) from the Norwegian editor, Ragnar Frisch. Frisch, along with Jan Tinbergen of the Netherlands, is often described as the founder of econometrics and the pair were recipients of the first Nobel Prize in Economics in 1969.[3] Frisch commented:

> One evening (at the Paris colloquium in May, 1952) when a small number of the prominent contributors to this field of study found themselves gathered around a table under the most pleasant exterior circumstances, it even proved to be quite a bit of a task to clear up in a satisfactory way misunderstandings in the course of the conversation. The version of Professor Allais' paper, which is now published in ECONOMETRICA, has emerged after many informal exchanges of views, including work done by editorial referees. Hardly anything more is now to be gained by a continuation of such procedures. The paper is therefore now published as it stands on the author's responsibility. The editor is convinced that the paper will be a most valuable means of preventing inbreeding of thoughts in this important field.[4]

Allais presented the others at the colloquium with a number of different lotteries, and showed that their choices among them violated the assumption that his distinguished colleagues were maximising their expected utility. Allais and Frisch had been joined at that Paris colloquium by Bruno de Finetti, who may by then have regretted his admiration for Mussolini, and by the Americans Milton Friedman, Paul Samuelson and Jimmie Savage, at what must have been a remarkable occasion (described more fully in the appendix). And, for a moment, the arguments of Allais caused the proponents of the 'American school' at least to stop and think.

The school had critics even on its home turf. At Harvard in the early 1960s, Daniel Ellsberg observed what he called 'ambiguity aversion' – people might prefer certainty to maximising subjective expected utility. (Ellsberg later acquired much greater fame as the former Defense Department official who passed to journalists the 'Pentagon Papers', which revealed much of the hidden truth about the Vietnam War to the *New York Times* and *Washington Post*.)[5] And in 1978, the American cognitive scientist and pioneer of artificial intelligence at Carnegie Mellon University Herbert Simon received the Nobel Prize in Economics for 'his pioneering research into the decision-making process within economic organizations'. Simon indeed pioneered ways of making decisions in a world of radical uncertainty. But as we will see below, only a seriously misinterpreted version of his work was incorporated into mainstream economics (although George Loewenstein, whose work in neuroeconomics we introduced in the last chapter, holds the chair at Carnegie Mellon named after Simon).

While Ellsberg was ferrying purloined documents to the *Washington Post*, Kahneman and Tversky were beginning their joint programme of research. Michael Lewis would claim, almost fifty years later, that this collaboration 'changed the world'. This assertion is a considerable exaggeration, although the collaboration did change academic economics. But after Kahneman was awarded the Nobel Prize in Economics in 2002

(Tversky had died, aged fifty-nine, six years earlier), the work of the pair received far wider attention. Many more economists studied what became known as 'behavioural economics', which offers a list of widely observed 'biases' in people's behaviour. These studies claim that we suffer from optimism and over-confidence, and we overestimate the likelihood of favourable outcomes. We are guilty of anchoring: attaching too much weight to the limited information we hold when we start to analyse a problem. We are victims of loss aversion: treating losses with a concern not given to equivalent gains. And so on.

While Allais, Ellsberg and Simon regarded their observations as a rebuttal of the view of decision-making under uncertainty put forward by Friedman and Savage, the approach pioneered by Kahneman and Tversky adopted a markedly different stance. The subject of their critique is the decision-maker, not the model of decision-making. If the world does not conform to the model, the failure is not a failure of the model but a failure of the world, or to be precise, of the people the model is intended to describe.

Rational behaviour

'Biases' can be identified only when contrasted with a coun-terfactual of unbiased or 'rational' behaviour. Since the word 'rationality' is powerful, it should be used with great care. But what does it mean to act rationally? Ordinary usage suggests two characteristics of rational judgement or action. First, the judgement or action would be based on beliefs about the world which were reasonable. Not necessarily correct beliefs – as we have seen, in a world of radical uncertainty we may not know even after the event what the true state of the world was. But a belief that a bus will arrive at a stop within the next ten minutes is a reasonable belief, even if it proves to be wrong.

A second requirement of rationality is an element of internal logic or consistency. The judgement or action is appropriate given the beliefs about the world which give rise to it. This proposition requires care in interpretation. It may be difficult to distinguish errors in reasoning from mistakes in belief. The Dutch-American decision theorist Paul Schoemaker[6] tells the probably apocryphal story of the man who won 'El Gordo', the world-famous Spanish lottery, after dreaming of the number seven seven times and concluding that seven times seven – forty-eight according to him – was therefore his lucky number. But even if he had recalled the seven times table correctly, his action would have been irrational.

It is possible to disagree with our interpretation of 'rationality', although it is consistent with a line of thought which can be traced back two millennia to Aristotle's characterisation of practical rationality as deliberative excellence.[7] But that very possibility of disagreement makes an important point. The axioms of choice under uncertainty do not enjoy any monopoly on the term 'rationality'. Maurice Allais' companions at the Paris dinner reported by Ragnar Frisch revealed preferences incompatible with those axioms. On what basis can we conclude that the men who attended the Paris symposium, among the cleverest people on the planet, were failing to act 'in accordance with reason or logic'? Rational behaviour is not defined by conformity with a set of axioms set down even by such distinguished thinkers as John von Neumann and Milton Friedman.

Styles of reasoning

At the end of the nineteenth century, Charles Sanders Pierce, a founder of the American school of pragmatist philosophy, distinguished three broad styles of reasoning.

Deductive reasoning reaches logical conclusions from stated premises. For example, 'Evangelical Christians are Republican. Republicans voted for Donald Trump. Evangelical Christians voted for Donald Trump.' This syllogism is descriptive of a small world. As soon as one adds the word 'most' before either evangelical Christians or Republicans, the introduction of the inevitable vagueness of the larger world modifies the conclusion.

Inductive reasoning is of the form 'analysis of election results shows that they normally favour incumbent parties in favourable economic circumstances and opposition parties in adverse economic circumstances'. Since economic conditions in the United States in 2016 were neither particularly favourable nor unfavourable, we might reasonably have anticipated a close result. Inductive reasoning seeks to generalise from observations, and may be supported or refuted by subsequent experience.

Abductive reasoning seeks to provide the best explanation of a unique event. For example, an abductive approach might assert that Donald Trump won the 2016 presidential election because of concerns in particular swing states over economic conditions and identity, and because his opponent was widely disliked.

Deductive, inductive and abductive reasoning each have a role to play in understanding the world, and as we move to larger worlds the role of the inductive and abductive increases relative to the deductive. And when events are essentially one-of-a-kind, which is often the case in the world of radical uncertainty, abductive reasoning is indispensable. Although the term 'abductive reasoning' may be unfamiliar, we constantly reason in this way, searching for the best explanation of what we see: 'I think the bus is late because of congestion in Oxford Street'. But the methods of decision analysis we have described in earlier chapters are derived almost entirely from the deductive reasoning which is relevant only in small worlds.

Rational people sometimes make mistakes. But we would expect that rational people would normally agree that their judgements were mistaken when errors in either their beliefs or their logic were pointed out to them. We have considerable sympathy with the concept of irrationality put forward by the Israeli economist Itzhak Gilboa: 'A mode of behavior is irrational for a decision-maker, if, when the latter is exposed to the analysis of her choices, she would have liked to change her decision, or to make different choices in similar future circumstances.'[8] Someone who was waiting for a bus in the belief that the normal timetable was operating would probably agree that they had been unfortunate or even foolish once it was explained that today was a public holiday with no service. But if they remained at the stop after learning this, they would be irrational.

Yet even in small worlds, subjects are often slow to rethink their positions. The Monty Hall problem continues to perplex; debate over the 'correct' answer to the two-child problem remains unresolved. Martin Gardner and others have made careers out of devising such puzzles. Some puzzles are interesting and challenging because we know there is a definite answer on which everyone will agree if only we can work it out. Others, such as the two-child problem, are difficult because they are not sufficiently well defined to admit of an agreed solution. Most problems we confront in life are typically not well defined and do not have single analytic solutions.

But logic derived from reasonably maintained premises can only ever take us so far. Under radical uncertainty, the premises from which we reason will never represent a complete description of the world. There will be different actions which might properly be described as 'rational' given any particular set of beliefs about the world. As soon as any element of subjectivity is attached either to the probabilities or to the valuation of the outcomes, problems cease to have any objectively correct solution.

The invisible gorilla

The American psychologists Daniel Simons and Christopher Chabris conducted a famous experiment in which subjects were asked to watch a short video of two groups passing a basketball, one group wearing white and the other black.[9] They were asked to count the number of passes made by the group wearing white shirts. We recommend you watch the video and count the passes, being careful to ignore the activity of the black-shirted players.[10]

Did you see the person dressed in a gorilla suit who enters the picture, walks slowly across the screen, thumps her chest, and moves off screen after about nine seconds? If you did not, you are not alone – about 70% of the subjects in the experiment did not notice the appearance of the gorilla. And most were astonished to discover that they had missed the gorilla when the video was replayed to them. Kahneman argues that the experiment reveals that humans are 'blind to the obvious, and we are also blind to our blindness'.[11] But how should we interpret this result? Is it the result of a human failing? Or a human strength? Surely it is sensible when asked to carry out a specific task to blot out any extraneous observations irrelevant to that task, and the experiment demonstrated the power of human capacity for concentration.

When confronted by the challenges of living in a complex world, we know that there are many stimuli that we would do well to ignore in order to concentrate on the matter at hand. Indeed, the phenomenon of 'blindness', far from being a failing, may be regarded as a positive virtue. The Hungarian-American psychologist Mihaly Csikszentmihalyi has found that individuals are happiest when in 'flow', completely focused on difficult but rewarding activities.[12] Participants in high-level sport use the phrase 'in the zone'. The former England cricketer Michael

Brearley, now a leading psychoanalyst, has spoken about this experience: 'Absorbed in the moment, we feel freed from everything insignificant and petty, from the shackles and complexities of our own personality and of a flustered everyday life, from extraneous thinking'.[13] Brearley was an outstanding captain of the England team in part because he was not watching the crowd, wondering what he would have for supper, thinking about his impending visit to his mother-in-law, or reviewing Margaret Thatcher's radical economic policies. He was dealing – brilliantly – with the task at hand. He had limited his focus to the immediate problems his exceptional talents could solve.

Biases in context

The claim to identify biases in human behaviour presupposes knowledge of what unbiased behaviour looks like. The behavioural economist claims to know the right answer, which his inept subjects fail to identify. But only in small worlds are right and wrong answers clearly identified. Most of the observed 'biases' in behavioural economics are not the result of errors in beliefs or logic, although some are. Most are the product of a reality in which decisions must be made in the absence of a precise and complete description of the world in which people live, in contrast to the small worlds in which the students whose choices are studied in experimental economics are asked to participate.

In those latter exercises, there is always something which the experimenters think is the 'right' answer. Kahneman uses as an example of bias a drawing similar to the image on page 142.[14] His subjects are asked to judge which of the three figures on the page is the largest, and most choose the one furthest back. Of course, the figures are drawn so as to be the same size on the page. But almost everyone can understand why almost everyone makes this mistake. We engage in a sophisticated interpretation of a two-dimensional picture as a three-dimensional reality, in spite of the injunction not to, because this is what we do in the large world of life. What may seem to be cognitive illusions in one context represent a reasonable response in another. There are many similar optical illusions, almost all of which are the result of context and which can mostly be dispelled by changing context. And economists who label certain types of behaviour as cognitive illusions may be missing the point that the people they observe are not living in the small world which they themselves inhabit (or the small world they model).

The problem of how we move between the small world of two-dimensional representation and the real three-dimensional world has a long history. The Greeks and Romans, capable geometers, understood perspective; the Egyptians, and medieval painters before the Renaissance, did not. They drew objects in line with their physical nature rather than how their eyes actually perceived them from a particular vantage point. In the early fifteenth century, Brunelleschi and other Renaissance artists and architects rediscovered perspective. Brunelleschi's sketch of his plan for the church of Spirito Santo in Florence was an early illustration. The church was built to his design and five centuries later, after the discovery of photography, we can recognise how faithfully his drawing anticipated what we see when we walk through the doors. And we appreciate the scale of Brunelleschi's insight by understanding how the effect is achieved: the pillars seem smaller as they recede; narrower as they rise; and appear to lean slightly outwards. But it required communication between artists of genius to achieve a full appreciation of the complex reality of visual perception.

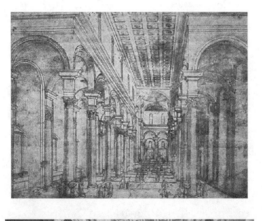

When subjects are asked to read out loud the text in the following triangle:

A
BIRD
IN THE
THE HAND

many people fail to spot the repetition of the word 'the'. But who is really making the mistake here – the experimenter or the subject? Making sense of slightly erroneous text is something we do all the time. The rational response to seeing the text depends entirely on the context. If you are auditioning for a play, and see a repetition of the definite article, it is likely that you spotted a typographical error. You should ignore the repeated word to maintain the sense of the text and your own chances of getting the part. If, however, you have been asked by an optician to read the text hanging on the wall in order to test your eyesight, it would be sensible to read that text literally. Opticians display nonsense text for precisely that reason. In a behavioural experiment, where the context is unclear, the experimenter is no more able to decide what is right or wrong than the participant. Human failure is in the eye of the beholder and the context determines the appropriate response.

Kahneman reports answers which he and Tversky obtained to the following question about words in the English language: 'Consider the letter K. Is K more likely to appear as the first letter in a word or as the third letter?'[15] According to Kahneman, most people wrongly respond that K appears more often as the first letter. It is easier to think of words that begin with a particular letter than to acknowledge words that have that letter in the third position. Kahneman and Tversky christened this the 'availability heuristic'. It uses the simplest memory search to come up with an answer.

But the experiment did not provide any serious motivation for answering the question, or even for defining properly the question being asked. Most people might reasonably answer 'I don't know, but if it is important I will try to find out'. And then they might ask, 'Before I do that, would you define the question more precisely?'

It is not at all obvious what is meant by an English word. Kaama, sometimes caama, is the English rendering of the Bantu term for a variety of hartebeest found in South Africa, but rarely encountered in most parts of the English-speaking world. Did the questioner mean the number of words in a dictionary, or the frequency of words in a text, which would be weighted by the extent of use? The claim to know the relative frequency of the letter K in words turns out to be based on an article published in 1965 which listed the frequency of letter placement in twenty thousand English words.[16] With the aid of modern search techniques, the website BestWordList, based on a compilation of Scrabble dictionaries, has twice as many words which begin with the letter K as have that letter in third place – the opposite of Kahneman's claim.[17] Our answer to Kahneman's ill-defined question remains 'we don't know'. Just as rational individuals governed by reason and logic decline to take part in most gambles, rational individuals governed by reason and logic avoid giving answers to such questions in real life if they do not know the answer.

But the subjects of the Kahneman–Tversky experiments were not allowed to say that they knew too little about the content or context of the set puzzles to solve them; they were instructed to tick a box on a questionnaire. There wasn't any context to the problems posed in the experiments, or none that made sense. And most exercises in behavioural economics do not explain why the subject is being asked to answer the question. The experimenters did not really want to know how many English words had K as the third letter. It is hard to imagine why anyone, even Scrabble players, would want to know that. Devoid of a meaningful context, these experiments tell us little about large worlds.

In large worlds, behaviour is driven by the purpose of the activity. Am I counting the basketball passes or searching for a gorilla? Is this test designed to measure my knowledge of English or my eyesight? Why do I want to know how many words have K as their third letter? When Kahneman ascribes to human failure the fact that his subjects fail to follow literally the ridiculous instructions given in the problem of the three figures illusion or in the 'bird in the hand' experiments, he is failing to disclose the relevant background, which is 'I am going to pose some silly problems designed to show that people often apply their sophisticated abilities to infer context (to make a three-dimensional interpretation of a two-dimensional representation, or to understand the writer's intention from the misspelt text) rather than doing exactly what they are told'. The subjects are – reasonably – assuming that they are being asked to interpret a cartoon or make sense of a text rather than to adhere literally to bizarre instructions.

Such behaviour is not irrational if rationality is defined by reasonable beliefs and internal consistency. Kahneman and Tversky describe their findings as documenting systematic errors in the thinking of most people which, they argue, contradict the assumptions of social science in the 1970s that people are generally 'rational'. But they do not present a definition of 'rationality' relevant to large worlds, in which problems have no well-defined solutions. Although Kahneman and Tversky acknowledge that normal human behaviour is often guided by intuition, impressions and emotions, they regularly return to versions of the observation that 'there are distinctive patterns in the errors people make. Systematic errors are known as biases, and they recur predictably in particular circumstances.'[18] The fact that such deviations are said to be widespread and predictable should make us sceptical of the claim that they are errors.

We are constantly engaged in abductive reasoning, using our knowledge and experience to make sense of complex situations. Sherlock Holmes claimed to have been the master of deductive reasoning – the website which accompanied the BBC series *Sherlock* used to be titled 'the science of deduction'. But it was Aristotle, not Arthur Conan Doyle, who wrote the book on deduction – logical reasoning from stated premises. Holmes was actually skilled in abduction, filtering disparate evidence in search of the best explanation. We use abductive reasoning when we judge perspective and make nonsensical text intelligible. That skill has enabled humans to make the leaps of imagination involved in tackling ill-defined problems which constitute scientific discovery or the artistic innovation epitomised by Brunelleschi and his contemporaries.

Behavioural economics has contributed to our understanding of decision-making in business, finance and government by introducing observation of how people actually behave. But, like the proselytisers for the universal application of probabilistic reasoning, practitioners and admirers of behavioural economics have made claims far more extensive than could be justified by their findings.

Kahneman offers an explanation of why earlier and inadequate theories of choice persisted for so long – a 'theory-induced blindness: once you have accepted a theory and used it as a tool in your thinking, it is extraordinarily difficult to notice its flaws'.[19] We might say the same about behavioural economics. We believe that it is time to move beyond judgemental taxonomies of 'biases' derived from a benchmark which is a normative model of human behaviour deduced from implausible a priori principles. And ask instead how humans do behave in large worlds of which they can only ever have imperfect knowledge.

Nudge

Failure to appreciate the fact that people are struggling to know what it is to be rational in a world of radical uncertainty leads to the conclusion that their 'mistakes' should be corrected by policy interventions, and recommendations of this kind have been suggested by Richard Thaler. Thaler was careful in his use of the word 'rationality'. His Nobel lecture contained only a handful of references to 'rational' or 'rationality' whereas the citation by the committee that awarded the prize used the words forty-seven times.[20] But Thaler was clear what he meant by rational behaviour – he urges his students in his MBA class to 'maximize expected utility' and avoid the biases of those who require to be nudged into more appropriate choices.

Some of his suggested interventions to 'nudge' people towards more appropriate behaviour appear sensible. For example, automatically enrolling people into pension schemes, and allowing them subsequently to opt out, rather than the other way round, may be helpful in simplifying what might otherwise seem an overly complicated decision and help people avoid big mistakes.[21] We have sympathy with such policies – up to a point. Most people who are asked whether they should be saving more, taking more exercise, and eating and drinking less, will give the answer they think is expected of them, although it is not clear what we learn from such enquiries.

We are inclined to apply the Gilboa test: would people agree that the actions into which they are 'nudged' are indeed in their best interests, and that their un-nudged behaviour was irrational, once the 'right' decision is explained to them? It is likely that many people would acknowledge that they should eat more vegetables, or wear safety helmets when they cycle, even if they find it difficult, un-nudged, to act on these perceptions. But a philosophy of nudging carries the risk that nudgers claim to know more about an uncertain world than they and their nudgees do or could know. As we explained in chapter 1, it is extremely difficult to assess how much any particular individual should invest in a pension plan. And the prescriptive tone of much of what is written in behavioural economics makes apparent the reality of the danger of well-meaning illiberalism. Tversky was interested in what he called 'natural stupidity', and prone to find it in those who disagreed with him.

Bounded rationality

Building on the observation that complexity makes it impossible to evaluate the consequences of all possible outcomes and select the most advantageous, the economist Herbert Simon introduced the concept of 'bounded rationality'.[22] We cannot possibly assess the consequences of all conceivable choices. The hypothetical exercise which set Obama beneath the Bayesian dial and in front of a whiteboard depicting endlessly branching arrays of possibilities could only ever be a fantasy. The problem of making good decisions in large worlds is generally not the difficulty of calculating the logical consequences of agreed premises and a well-defined set of alternative actions – a task a computer can now perform better than humans. It is the problem of context – the impossibility of knowing all the feasible choices and the full detail of the environment in which these choices will take effect. The human brain is not a computer implementing an axiomatic decision-making process, and as a result is a better decision-maker in many complex situations.

Simon recognised that radical uncertainty prevented people from behaving in the optimising manner defined by a priori axioms. And so he argued that 'more than minor tampering with existing optimization theory is called for'. He was anticipating, but not preventing, the subsequent development of a large literature based on such minor tampering.[23]

Simon was interdisciplinary in his interests and research, and was also a pioneer of artificial intelligence. He suggested that one way in which people might approach decisions in a radically uncertain world was to use a rule of thumb to search for a 'good enough' outcome. Such behaviour was described as 'satisficing', and in practice can deliver superior outcomes to actions selected by optimising behaviour. The reason is that to pretend to optimise in a world of radical uncertainty, it is necessary to make simplifying assumptions about the real world. If these assumptions are wrong – as in a world of radical uncertainty they are almost certain to be – optimisation yields the wrong results, just as someone searching for their keys under the streetlamp because that is where the light is best makes the error of substituting a well-defined but irrelevant problem for the less well-defined problem he actually faces. As Mr Viniar had done, along with most of the financial services industry and its regulators.

Economists have adapted the phrase 'bounded rationality' to mean something very different from Simon's description as the consequence of radical uncertainty. They have instead used it to describe the cost of processing information, which then acts as an additional constraint in an optimisation problem. Bounded rationality, in this sense, adds to the optimisation calculation the costs and benefits of obtaining the information which we choose not to have. Of course, this is not what Simon meant. Nor, indeed, does it make much sense as a description of any process with practical application. The implications of bounded rationality are not represented by adding computational costs to an optimisation problem. Bounded rationality as proposed by Simon reflects the challenges of making decisions governed by reason and logic under radical uncertainty in which no computable solution is available. Simon is reported to have joked that he should take legal action against his successors who misused his terminology and neglected his insights.[24]

Gary Klein is an American psychologist who began his career with the US Air Force and subsequently studied the behaviour of experienced, practical decision-makers. His subjects were military personnel, firefighters, paramedics: people who are called upon to make decisions, usually under pressure, often with little time to spare. In such activities, there are people whose abilities are recognised as exceptional – the commanders you want to lead you into battle, the fire chiefs whose judgements are venerated by their crews, the paramedics you hope will attend when you suffer an accident. Klein's central finding is best summarised in his own words:

> With experienced decision-makers, the focus is on the way they assess the situation and judge it familiar, not on comparing options. Courses of action can be quickly evaluated by mentioning how they will be carried out, not by formal analysis and comparison. Decision-makers usually look for the first workable option they can find, not the best option. Since the first option they consider is usually workable, they do not have to generate a large set of options to be sure they get a good one. They generate and evaluate options one at a time and do not bother comparing the advantages and disadvantages of alternatives.[25]

Klein describes the reality of decision-making in complex situations, which require the search for a workable solution rather than a process of optimisation. Both of us have experience of the academic committee which cannot reach a decision because it is always possible that there *might* be a better option than the one which is on the table: 'the best is the enemy of the good'. Real people do not optimise, calculate subjective probabilities and maximise expected utilities; not because they are lazy, or do not have the time, but because they know that they cannot conceivably have the information required to engage in such calculation. Nevertheless good decision-makers, like Klein's firefighters and paramedics, or Warren Buffett or Steve Jobs, are rightly respected for their judgement. Simultaneous with the work of Kahneman and Tversky, but to less public attention or acclaim, the German psychologist Gerd Gigerenzer has led a group of researchers at the Max Planck Institute in Berlin.[26] Gigerenzer and his colleagues are focused less on 'biases' than on the ways in which real people make actual decisions on the basis of necessarily limited information. The group has emphasised the value of simple heuristics – or rules of thumb – in enabling us to resolve situations characterised by radical uncertainty. Gigerenzer and his colleagues have promoted a toolbox comprising 'fast and frugal' heuristics.

Evolution has helped humans develop and apply different skills relevant to coping with a radically uncertain world, and we are fortunate that this is so, because radical uncertainty is today more extensive than ever. The choice of heuristic depends both on the context of the problem faced and also on the results of evolution in selecting heuristics which are successful. Bounded rationality, in this way of thinking, can be seen as ecological or evolutionary rationality – a method of coping with radical uncertainty that improves our chances of survival. Natural intelligence is not described by optimisation capabilities, but is the result of an evolution of the traits necessary to tackle complex and ill-defined problems. Experts who optimise using complex models often fail when confronted with a new challenge whereas ordinary humans do better. Long Term Capital Management collapsed but Berkshire Hathaway became the largest investment company in the world. It seems that ecological rationality has performed better than optimising rationality. Why is this so?

9

———— • ————

EVOLUTION AND DECISION-MAKING

Computation is not thinking ... You are much more
like your house cat than you are ever going to be
like Siri.

—BRUCE STERLING[1]

Behavioural economics has identified a raft of ways in which
humans depart from axiomatic rationality. These behaviours are described as 'biases', signs of human failure. The claim
is that the highly developed cognitive abilities of our species
exhibit common and pervasive deficiencies. It is as though God
had given us two legs so that we could run or walk, but made
one leg shorter than the other so that we could not run or walk
very well. An intelligent creator would not do that, and evolution did not.

There is an alternative story to that told by behavioural
economics. It is that many of the characteristics of human reasoning which behavioural economics describes as biases are in

fact adaptive – beneficial to success – in the large real worlds in which people live, even if they are sometimes misleading in the small worlds created for the purposes of economic modelling and experimental psychology. It is an account which substitutes evolutionary rationality for axiomatic rationality.

Coping with uncertainty in all its dimensions has been an important part of human evolution. Over thousands of years of radical uncertainty humans have learnt many coping strategies and developed a capacity to make decisions in the face of imperfect knowledge of worlds that they encounter for the first time, and may never encounter again. To cope with the world as it is, we have developed thought processes to deal with problems that are ill defined, ambiguous and radically uncertain. Human minds approach problems in ways that are markedly different from those of computers. In particular, whereas computers are efficient in solving well-defined puzzles, humans excel at finding ways to cope with open-ended mysteries. And the human capacity for, and pleasure in, storytelling is a central element of that ability.

We cope with the future by organising our lives around reference narratives. These reference narratives are not necessarily worked out in specific detail but they provide a basis for planning and a framework for day-to-day choices. Like Klein's firefighters or Woodford's students, we change the reference narrative in response to disconfirming events, but infrequently and discontinuously. And we do not construct these narratives in isolation. We discuss them with family and friends. We take advice from professionals. We benefit from the collective intelligence accumulated and readily available in the various communities in which we live. We are not defective versions of computers trained to optimise in small-world problems, but human beings with individual and collective intelligence evolved over millennia.

Evolution is smarter than economists

The discovery of the theory of evolution was a seminal moment in human thought. But throughout the century that followed the publication of Charles Darwin's work, the application of evolutionary theory in biology, and even more outside it, lacked rigour. Only in the 1960s were the mechanisms of biological evolution more adequately described, after Francis Crick and James Watson unravelled the structure of DNA and scientists such as W. D. Hamilton and John Maynard Smith developed more sophisticated mathematical models of evolutionary processes. Evolution was the result of mutation, selection and replication of genes. Genetic mutations which enhance the ability of the gene to replicate itself would spread through the population. Richard Dawkins' inspired metaphor of the 'selfish gene' thrust such thinking into popular consciousness.

It is the gene, not the individual, which is selfish in Dawkins' metaphor, and the difference is important. Obviously, the gene has no consciousness or direction, but evolution leads to the results which would be observed if the gene were able to promote itself selfishly. 'The selfish gene' is an illuminating 'as if' hypothesis.[2] Because we share genes with our offspring and our relatives, kin selection prompts us to help them, even at a cost to ourselves. Hamilton set out the mathematics of the selfish gene and suggested in a tongue-in-cheek exposition of the implications of his theory that: 'we expect to find that no one is prepared to sacrifice his life for any single person but that everyone will sacrifice it when he can thereby save more than two brothers, or four half-brothers, or eight first cousins'.[3] But as kinship becomes more distant, genetic relatives will be less and less supportive of each other.

Altruism, kinship and mutuality

You find yourself in an unfamiliar location, unsure of how to find your destination. You ask a stranger for help. You expect the stranger will give you directions, and this expectation is generally fulfilled.[4] If it is not, the usual reason is that person does not know the way either. Why are strangers so ready to guide us? After all, it is unlikely that we will ever see that individual again, far less that he or she will be able to benefit from our reciprocation of their assistance. How does spending time to provide guidance to unrelated and unknown individuals help us? People who are not economists do not find the explanation of this behaviour troubling. The common sense answer is that most human beings are nice and helpful, and it is more pleasant to live in a society where people help each other in this way. So long as the cost of providing assistance to people you do not know is not very great, you will generally provide it.

But reconciling this everyday observation with the underlying evolutionary theory has been found to be problematic. How does this niceness assist our genes to reproduce themselves? If the biological mechanism of genetic selection were the only mechanism of evolution, then evolutionary theory would seem to provide some support for economic models based on populations of rational individuals independently maximising their own utility. It seems only a short stretch from the selfish gene to the selfish individual. And from the beginnings of evolutionary thinking it was obvious that the idea had many applications beyond the development of biological variety which was the subject of Charles Darwin's book *On the Origin of Species*. The social philosopher Herbert Spencer, now almost forgotten, was a leading intellectual figure in the late nineteenth century. Spencer coined the term 'survival of the fittest', and his ten-volume 'System of Synthetic Philosophy' attempted to explain how evolutionary concepts could be applied to almost every discipline. A modern application of evolutionary theory to economics came in the early 1950s from Armen Alchian, a member of the Chicago School, who claimed that firms will behave *as if* they maximised profits, even if they had no intention of doing so.[5] Survival of the fittest was, he argued, inherent in a competitive market. The observation that there are mechanisms of evolution other than the biological, and that competitive markets may be one such evolutionary mechanism, was correct and important.

The discreditable history of eugenics, a pseudo-science adopted by Nazis, white supremacists and other racists, means that even today those who offer evolutionary accounts of social behaviour encounter fierce resistance. The biologist E. O. Wilson, whose scientific career has been devoted to the study of social insects such as ants and who argued for unity between biological and social sciences,[6] experienced opposition to his theories so extreme that demonstrators waved a swastika and poured water over his head as he delivered a lecture.

The reconciliation of biological evolution with human niceness is that the gene may propagate itself in a population 'as if' the gene were selfish, but that need not imply that individuals are selfish. A group of people who are nice to each other might prosper relative to a group who were nasty to each other. And so the genes for niceness would spread. But the British mathematical geneticist John Maynard Smith showed that sometimes nastiness rather than niceness might flourish within groups.[7] Events in the 2007–08 financial crisis illustrate the problem, while also hinting at its solution. Investment banking groups Bear Stearns and Lehman Brothers made money for the nasty (their employees) at the expense of the nice (their customers), until nastiness within the groups themselves, and their earlier nastiness towards other groups, led to their collapse when they received little sympathy or support in their hour of need.[8] And numerous other firms would not have survived the 2007–08 financial crisis if survival of the fittest had not been so weakly applied to financial institutions. Nasty individuals prospered, and their actions brought about the near collapse of both the nasty and the nice. Since humans operate in groups, success within and relative to other groups will influence the outcome of the biological process of gene replication. Once we acknowledge that individuals operate within organisations, which range from Lehman Brothers to closed monasteries devoted to the worship of God, then we must also acknowledge that the measure of 'fitness' which human evolution favours is much more broadly defined than success in procreation.

We are human animals, distinguished from other species by our capacity for communication and language, and that social interaction changes the bleak picture of individualistic behaviour implied by simple interpretations of the selfish gene. Children of English-speaking parents tend to speak English, and the children of French-speaking parents French, for reasons that have nothing to do with their DNA. The economic advantages of cooperating in groups are so large that traits which are conducive to success in group interaction – such as the 'language instinct', or an inclination to be helpful to other members of the group – are favoured by both genetics and culture.

Paleontologists speculate that social kinship groups – mutually supportive clusters of people who need not be closely related to each other – came into being in the Upper Paleolithic period, between 30,000 and 50,000 years ago.[9] The advantage of being better able to cope with radical uncertainty was one of the primary drivers of the emergence of unreciprocated altruism in these societies; their cultures evolved to expect nice behaviour and punish nasty behaviour. The larger and more diverse the pool of people who might provide help, the less vulnerable are individuals and households to unanticipated events.

Our knowledge of the behaviour of Paleolithic groups is obviously limited and our best insight comes from anthropological studies of those remote tribes whose lifestyles differ little – at least until recently – from those of our distant ancestors. The Maa-speaking people of East Africa manage uncertainty through a system of risk-sharing which is distinct from, though related to, modern conceptions of debt or insurance. Their *osotua* framework is based on a reciprocal commitment to help one another in future unspecified circumstances, and these obligations are inherited:

> Osotua relationships are started in many ways, but they usually begin with a request for a gift or a favor. Such requests arise from genuine need and are limited to the amount actually needed . . . Once osotua is established, it is pervasive in the sense that one cannot get away from it. Osotua is also eternal. Once established, it cannot be destroyed, even if the individuals who established the relationship die. In that case, it is passed on to their children.[10]

The implicit contract of the *osotua* relationship is enforced by the norms of the community, which are designed to increase the security of the reference narratives of households. Radical uncertainty – imperfect knowledge of future states of the world and of the consequences of actions – means that contracts contingent on all possible outcomes could not be written even if there were mechanisms for formulating and enforcing them. The economic benefits derived from extending kinship beyond close genetic relationship are large. Reductions in the costs of managing risk not only offer direct benefit but facilitate innovation, since every innovation involves risk. The ability to conduct productive activity in larger groups yields greater opportunities for the division of labour through specialisation and exchange. The rest, as they say, is history – the modern world has taken innovation, the pooling of risks and the division of labour to levels unimaginable by any previous generation. Since 1800, national income per head in the US has risen more than twenty-five-fold and in Britain almost twenty-fold, and life expectancy has doubled.[11] Economic and social life has been transformed. None of that would have been possible without the collective intelligence which has produced constant advances in technologies and business processes and extended the division of labour; none of it possible without better public and private health care and the social risk-sharing which helps people survive personal and natural catastrophes. Modern humans rely on social kinship networks to buffer many risks: serious illness, redundancy, relationship breakdown. And since Bismarck's creation of social insurance in late nineteenth-century Germany, the state has been there to help manage these risks, extending much further the size of the group which provides reciprocal assistance.

Thus the association of evolution with far right causes, including racism and extreme market fundamentalism, and with the aggressive selfishness which tramples others underfoot to make way for ourselves and our offspring, could hardly be further from the mark. Human evolution gave us the capacity – exceptional among species – to communicate with each other, learn from each other, persuade each other. Humans typically function in groups. Other primates which form groups exhibit some of the traits of altruism, cooperation and empathy which axiomatic descriptions of 'rational' behaviour struggle to explain. Up to a point; the primatologist Richard Wrangham has described how even among chimpanzees males are aggressive and selfish and only the sexually promiscuous bonobos display the degree of niceness which prompts humans to show strangers the way.[12] But the capacity of humans to communicate with each other through language is one of the factors – perhaps the most important factor – distinguishing us from other species. This emphasis on communication reinforces the notion that what may be 'biases' in individual problem-solving behaviour in well-defined puzzles are actually advantageous in the group resolution of the ill-defined problems posed by uncertainty.

The Socratic dialogue is a long-established method of seeking truth by exposing the competing arguments of protagonists. The objective in all these processes is to find, through group interaction, a narrative to which all can subscribe – and to set a course of future action in the light of that narrative. The observations of participants contribute to that narrative, and the meaning of these observations is derived from the context in which they are made.[13] Evolution gave us a capacity to reason which, as a 2017 book by two French researchers in cognitive science, Hugo Mercier and Dan Sperber, explains, 'is not geared to solitary use'.[14] Evolution has produced the collective intelligence and social norms and institutions which are 'the secret of our success'; these social capabilities provide the reason that humans dominate the planet.[15]

Multiple levels of evolutionary selection

If social groups developed the division of labour and the mutualisation of risk-sharing, and subsequent millennia took these socio-economic innovations to unsurpassed levels, the outcome was equally unsurpassed levels of prosperity. And the emergence of broadly defined kinship groups had many other economic and social advantages. Much of modern life would be difficult without a degree of trust, and economic life would be almost impossible. The World Values Survey shows a strong positive correlation across countries between per capita income and answers to the question 'Do you think that most people can be trusted?'[16] Recognition of the importance of social and cultural evolution long precedes Darwin; it certainly can be found in the work of the thinkers of the Scottish Enlightenment. 'Nations stumble upon establishments, which are indeed the result of human action, but not the execution of any human design,' wrote Adam Ferguson in 1782.[17] And Adam Smith's contemporaneous observation that 'man is led by an invisible hand to promote an end which was no part of his intention' is widely quoted today by people who know nothing else of economics.[18] These eighteenth-century Scottish Enlightenment figures had realised that social and cultural practices were themselves the product of evolutionary processes.

Societies have established moral codes or religious practices to discourage non-cooperative behaviour. They have created institutions, from social ostracism to prisons, to reinforce sanctions against non-cooperators. And businesses, and many other institutions and organisations, succeed if and only if their characteristics are conducive to their survival. Competitive markets – and even religions and moral codes operate in competitive markets – display the processes of modification, replication and selection which are the characteristics of evolution, although such evolution has nothing to do with our genes.

There are, therefore, many different kinds of evolution, and outcomes are the product of natural selection at many levels. We observe co-evolution, in which different mechanisms of evolution operate in parallel. For example, even though most adults find milk difficult to digest, lactose tolerance is widespread among populations living in areas where dairy farming is common, because genetic predisposition and cultural practice have evolved together. Although the reasoning that says 'since I am a New Zealander and New Zealand has more cows than

people then it is advantageous for me to be lactose tolerant'
is correct, such reasoning is not the explanation of why most
New Zealanders are lactose tolerant. Most New Zealanders are
descendants of European immigrants. As a result they inherited
the genetic mutation which facilitates lactose tolerance and
brought with them the practice of dairy farming. And when
they realised how favourable the country was for dairy farming they brought the ancestors of New Zealand's five million
cows. Among New Zealanders of Polynesian or Asian descent,
lactose intolerance is still relatively common.[19] But over time,
intermarriage and natural selection will erode these genetic
differences.

Evolution creates predispositions – to consume a diet rich in
dairy products or to trust other people – which influence behaviour. Such predispositions can be overcome with greater or lesser
difficulty by conscious effort, as the parable of the scorpion and
the frog relates:

> A scorpion asks a frog to carry it across a river. The frog
> hesitates, afraid of being stung, but the scorpion argues that
> if it did so, they would both drown. Considering this, the
> frog agrees, but midway across the river the scorpion does
> indeed sting the frog, dooming them both. When the frog
> asks the scorpion why, the scorpion replies that it was in its
> nature to do so.[20]

People of European genetic origin drink milk, and people
everywhere try to help strangers, because 'it is in their nature to
do so', not because of any calculation that it is in their interest to
do so. And they construct and teach moral codes and penalise
people who violate those codes for similar reasons. Most behaviour is the product of both nature and nurture. The biological
determinism that it is 'all in our genes', and the behaviourist

claim that the mind is a 'blank slate' on which anything can be written, are both untenable.[21]

The difference between doing something because it is in one's self-interest and doing the same thing because it is 'in one's nature' is material. 'If you can fake sincerity you've got it made', but the act of fake sincerity is difficult to sustain.[22] More to the point is Archbishop Whately's comment that 'honesty may be the best policy, but he who adopts that policy is not an honest man'.[23] The wife-and-husband psychologist and anthropologist Leda Cosmides and John Tooby claim that we have specific cheater-detection mechanisms designed to identify fake sincerity and feigned honesty. Their proposition remains controversial.[24] But most of us have learnt to escape the life insurance salesman and to mistrust the used car dealer. When we refuse the sales pitch, or trust that our colleagues will not steal our wallet, we are acting in ways that are typically, but not necessarily always, in our best interests. In a radically uncertain world we do not know whether such actions are or are not optimal – the life insurance salesman might on this occasion be proposing an irresistible offer, or one of our colleagues might be desperate to feed his gambling habit or her drug addiction. Uncertainty is radical everywhere. And the irrational 'biases' identified by behavioural economists as being 'in our nature' are not, in any ordinary meaning of the term, irrational. They are traits that are advantageous outside the 'small worlds' of the casino and the psychology laboratory. And they have evolutionary origins.

Loss aversion

Evolution has fitted humans to deal with the many kinds of radical uncertainty encountered in large worlds. Different attitudes to uncertainty influence the chances of survival of individuals and groups. In some environments, such as business and sport, to play safe is to relinquish the possibility of success. It may even be an advantage to overestimate one's chances of success. In other environments, it may make sense to avoid risks. One reason why the human species has survived is that our ancestors were not eaten by predators, and the authors were able to write this book because they were not knocked down while crossing the road. In the modern world we don't often need to escape lions and tigers; but the reactions which prompt us to avoid dark streets, jump out of the way of oncoming vehicles, and flee from terrorist attackers are generally sound. There are chemical and neurophysiological bases for these responses. They were reinforced from an early age by the warnings delivered to us by our parents. A predisposition to avoid large losses is a useful attribute.

These actions are not the result of any calculation. Not just because we don't have the time, or the information, to make any calculation of subjective expected utility, although it is relevant that we don't. But also because, as Taleb has emphasised, evolution favours those who survive, and they are not necessarily those who maximise expected value.[25] Perhaps rational economic man dies out because no one would want to mate with him.

If we lived in simple, stationary, small worlds, then optimisation and skill in solving the puzzles of small worlds would be the key to evolutionary success. But we do not, mostly, live in small worlds. In the real world, extreme events – the tails of distributions – are relevant to survival. When crops fail or plague is endemic, only the very fittest survive; but in ordinary dull life only the most unlucky or careless fall victim to plane crashes or murderous partners. The average person died in the Black Death[26] but does not die in a road accident.

Evolution has given us the traits and institutions which enable us to survive, mate, and pass the same traits and institutions on to our children. And sometimes this need for survival directs us to find the best possible outcome, sometimes the best on average, sometimes to avoid the worst. And most often to muddle through. The firefighters whose accomplishments Klein admired did not find optimal solutions, but again and again found solutions which were good enough. And Roosevelt and Churchill succeeded in the same manner.

For an individual, choosing the strategy most likely to succeed maximises expected winnings. But a group made up of such optimising individuals is eventually wiped out by infrequent calamities. As a result, the groups whose genes come to dominate are those who apply 'mixed strategies', varying their habitat.[27] The American political scientist James Scott describes the reality of this in the history of 'scientific' forestry. Planting the 'best' trees led to monocultures which were in due course wiped out by previously unknown parasites.[28] The Irish potato blight was able to devastate that country's agriculture – leading to at least a million deaths from disease and starvation and to substantial and prolonged emigration from the island – because the potato had been identified as the optimal crop for that country's conditions and so the country's food production was poorly diversified.[29] Humans are all better off because we are all different, and because there is no single way to be rational; we give thanks for our current state to St Francis and Oscar Wilde and Steve Jobs and to millions of people who became skilled at their own specialist but routine tasks.

Confidence and optimism

To adherents of axiomatic rationality and behavioural economists alike, optimism is a 'bias', leading to errors in calculations of subjective expected utility. We are not so sure. Admiral James

Stockdale, the American naval officer who was imprisoned and tortured in Vietnam,[30] attested effectively to the evolutionary value of confidence and optimism. Prisoners of war with no knowledge of what was happening in the outside world experienced the mental anguish of radical uncertainty along with the physical anguish of their ill treatment. He observed: 'You must never confuse faith that you will prevail in the end – which you can never afford to lose – with the discipline to confront the most brutal facts of your current reality, whatever they might be.'[31] Stockdale contrasted his own survival with the fate of those who imagined specific outcomes that would lead to their release. Their morale was crushed by the failure of their predictions to materialise.

As Britain was faced with the threat of a German invasion in 1940, Winston Churchill told Parliament in one of his most famous speeches: 'We shall go on to the end. We shall fight in France, we shall fight on the seas and oceans, we shall fight with growing confidence and growing strength in the air, we shall defend our Island, whatever the cost may be. We shall fight on the beaches, we shall fight on the landing grounds, we shall fight in the fields and in the streets, we shall fight in the hills; we shall never surrender.'[32] Like Stockdale, Churchill was suffused with optimism but unable and unwilling to define the basis of that optimism. Churchill's ringing defiance in the face of adversity was the product of his relentless confidence and self-belief, not the outcome of considered reasoning. Sometimes, but only sometimes, this self-assurance was justified. It led to his hair-raising exploits in the Boer War, his enthusiasm for disastrous policies such as the Gallipoli expedition, and his persistent, unsuccessful resort to the gaming tables. And excessive self-confidence can be a dangerous trait in a political leader. But in the right circumstances – those of 1940 – Churchill's optimism and confidence were vital.

Steve Jobs similarly failed to conform to the conventional depiction of 'rational' behaviour under uncertainty. Just as Churchill became premier with no specific plan for how the war would develop, Jobs returned to Apple content to wait for 'the next big thing'. Jobs's biographer, Walter Isaacson, writes of his subject's 'reality distortion field'. The phrase was adopted from *Star Trek* by one of Apple's first software designers, who identified his CEO's approach as 'a confounding melange of a charismatic rhetorical style, indomitable will, and eagerness to bend any fact to fit the purpose at hand' – characteristics similar to those identified by Churchill's biographers.[33] Strikingly, however, the first half of Isaacson's book, which deals with the period prior to Jobs's 1997 return to Apple, contains sixteen references to the 'reality distortion field', the remainder contains only three. As the *New York Times* commented after Jobs's death: 'Before he was forced out in 1985, Mr Jobs was notoriously hands-on, meddling with details and berating colleagues ... in his second stint at Apple, he relied more on others, listening more and trusting members of his design and business teams.'[34]

Evidently, optimism is productive, but more so when contained and channelled. Overconfidence is generally a disaster at the gaming table but vital to the leader inspiring team-mates, business colleagues or troops. Churchill's great 1940 speech was an expression of his own personality and his own views. But it was delivered to Parliament and to a much wider audience. At that crucial juncture, Churchill's achievement was to persuade his Cabinet colleagues that it was both necessary and possible to continue the war, to provide the British public with the inspiration to do so, and to assure other countries – both hostile Germany and sympathetic America – of British resolve.

Richard Branson, the ebullient founder of the Virgin Group, was a more successful gambler than Churchill. According to unauthorised biographer Tom Bower, Branson's initial venture was on the verge of financial failure – he was not interested in the nuts and bolts of cash flows and budgets.[35] Branson and a colleague took £500 from the till of their Notting Hill record shop and spent the night at the Playboy Club, a Park Lane casino. Branson's claim to have a successful system seemed unfounded until, at 5 a.m., he placed their remaining chips on a final bet and won back substantially more than the pair had lost. And so a business empire was born.[36]

Certainly, Branson's behaviour was reckless, Churchill's bravado often foolish, and Jobs's career included repeated failures. But neither they nor the world would have been better off if they had learnt to control their 'biases' and suppress their 'irrationality'. And that observation exposes the limitations of the concept of axiomatic rationality. Churchill, Jobs and Branson lived in a large world, not the small world in which rational behaviour can be reduced to a mathematical calculation in the context of a well-defined problem and complete knowledge of the environment. Their achievements remind us of the insight which Frank Knight described a century ago, too long forgotten; the connection between radical uncertainty and entrepreneurship. As Keynes observed, the spirit of enterprise dies when mathematical expectation takes over. Risk-taking behaviour which might appear inconsistent with axiomatic rationality is the central dynamic of a capitalist society – a key part of 'the secret of our success'.

Dual systems

Daniel Kahneman, the towering figure in behavioural economics, has written of 'system one' and 'system two', differentiating intuitive reaction from the rational process of conscious thought. The 'biases' of behavioural economics arise when system one leads us to results which the more considered judgement of system two would reject. There is a widespread belief in folk psychology about the different influences of left brain and right brain. It is not clear whether the distinction between system one and system two is intended as metaphor or as a description of actual mental processes. Modern neuropsychology largely rejects these theories of duality.[37] Different parts of the brain appear to play different roles in our thinking and decision-making; some become more active when we take risks, others when we make love. But there is a single process of cognition, engaging not only brain but body; in the 1980s the neurophysiologist Benjamin Libet established that we begin to act – as in removing our hand from a hot stove – even before we begin the cerebral activity which directs the action.[38] The brain is an entity, not a committee.

In a famous study, the neuroscientist Antonio Damasio reported on a patient whose brain damage rendered him effectively unable to experience emotion.[39] The outcome was not that the subject was a hyper-rational denizen of a large world – he could function only in a small world. In everyday life he was unable to make any decisions at all. He would agonise for extended periods over matters of no real importance, such as the time of his next appointment. His problem was that there is a more or less unlimited amount of information potentially relevant to any decision. Trying to process all this information led to paralysis in his decision-making.

All of us potentially face a similar problem. If we try to analyse all possible outcomes of all possible actions that we might take we will decide nothing, because radical uncertainty means that the branches on the tree of Bayesian reasoning multiply indefinitely. What will the weather be like next Wednesday? Will the bus arrive on time? And that is even before we start to ask what will be the level of stock prices in 2025, or the state of relations between China and the United States in 2030. Such is the nature of radical uncertainty, and why humans have evolved ways of making choices that differ from the systematic evaluation of all possible outcomes.

We use words like reflex, instinct, emotion and intuition to describe what we do when we pull our hand away from the hot stove, rush to the aid of a distressed child or injured stranger, mistrust a potential new employee or business partner. These are not 'irrational' responses we would be well advised to suppress, but behaviours which evolution has honed for us and social learning has reinforced in us to enable us to cope with a radically uncertain world. Humans benefit from *evolutionary* or *ecological* rationality, which is different from axiomatic rationality, and more relevant to the large worlds in which we all function.

Still, there is some validity in the system one/system two distinction. We will come back to that in chapter 15, in which we distinguish *evolutionary* rationality – which is the basis of our judgements and actions – from *communicative* rationality, the language we use to explain our judgements and actions to other people. Humans are distinguished from other mammals by their capacity for communication and coordination.[40] This propensity towards cooperation is not limited to humans, but its scale and extent are rare in the natural world. 'Eusociality' describes behaviour in which animals practise a communal division of reproductive and nurturing labour, with multiple generations living together and working to rear the collective young. Eusociality leads to the division of labour, whose critical importance to economic development Adam Smith recognised in the very first pages of *The Wealth of Nations*. Eusocial species are highly productive, able to undertake complex tasks, and build elaborate artefacts.

Eusociality has emerged down two distinct evolutionary pathways. Manifestations of eusociality are found among humans, and to a much smaller extent in some other mammals, and is the product of communication. In humans, the development of highly sophisticated language abilities brought about an order-of-magnitude change in the capacity to achieve the division of labour. Eusociality is also found in some insect species, notably ants, termites, and some bees. In an ant colony, all workers are related to the queen, who specialises in reproduction; thus the genetic mechanisms are entirely different from those of mammals, but the division of labour is extensive. Fertilised eggs are taken to dormitories where they are cared for, and where the larvae they become are fed by workers. Other workers gather or manage resources, and soldiers defend the common nest from enemies.

Human versus machine intelligence

Evolutionary rationality gave us the capacity to make computers, but not to be computers. Computers can perform calculations far more accurately, and more quickly, than even the most numerically agile of humans. Such computers can now play chess, or the Asian game Go, better than any human player. And they can implement profitable trading strategies in financial markets – with the aid of highly skilled programmers – and read many diagnostic scans better than most radiologists. For all of these problems there is a large existing database from which the computer can learn: all the games of chess and Go which have ever been recorded, the mass of data on securities market prices, and the thousands of scans which have already been made and for which the ultimate outcome is known.

Artificial intelligence (AI) engages computers which can learn from experience. It is the means by which many believe that eventually all mysteries will become soluble puzzles. DeepMind, an AI company, put together a program which beat the reigning champions of Go – a game which has more potential combinations of board positions than there are atoms in the universe. It did so by allowing the computer to create a massive database of games constructed by playing against itself. DeepMind's computer did not need access to any historic data. But this was possible only because Go is a problem which, although immensely complex, is comprehensively and precisely defined by its rules. The DeepMind computer which taught itself to play Go had access to the rules of Go and knew, at the end of each of the many thousands of games which it played with itself, which side had won. All the successes of artificial intelligence to date have been based on the ability of the computer to train itself in this way, and its speed of calculation means that a computer can very quickly play more games of chess or Go than an individual could in a lifetime.

The problem President Obama faced was altogether different. The information to which he had access was unavoidably limited. The consequences of his decision depended on many knowns and unknowns, and there was little if any basis for attaching probabilities to them. No rulebook governed the response of the men in the compound, whoever they were, or of the Pakistani government or military. The situation was unique, and the President could not train himself by making that decision thousands of times and seeing the result. At best, he could utilise loose analogies to situations he and other political leaders had encountered. But any historical analogy would be strained. Anthony Eden, who had resigned from Chamberlain's Cabinet in 1938, lost office as Prime Minister in 1957 after making the mistaken analogy between Hitler and Nasser and launching an unsuccessful invasion at Suez. Obama did at least have the opportunity to learn what the proximate consequences of his decision were, which is often not the case in major political or business decisions. But his problem was not one of computation.

We do not think it is simply a failure of our imagination to say that we find it difficult to understand what a computer acting as President of the United States would actually begin to do in that situation.

And even the chess- and Go-playing computers are not pro-grammed to optimise. As Herbert Simon had envisaged in the 1950s (when he greatly underestimated the time it would take to build a machine which could defeat a grandmaster), these machines satisfice. They find not the best move, but a move that is good enough. There is, in principle, a 'best' way of playing chess – a perfect game in which no move by either white or black could be improved on. This would be the 'solution' to the game of chess (which economists in characteristic style describe as the subgame perfect Nash equilibrium). But we do not have, and perhaps never will have, computers powerful enough to find that game.[41] If neither Magnus Carlsen (in 2019 the world champion) nor Deep Blue can play a perfect game of chess, it stretches the imagination to suppose that ordinary people and businesses could optimise the game of economic life.

Kahneman argues that in understanding human behaviour, noise – randomness – is even more important than 'biases'. He looks forward to the day when artificial intelligence will elim-inate our natural stupidity: 'it's very difficult to imagine that with sufficient data there will remain things that only humans can do'.[42] As a result he suggests that it would be a good idea to 'replace humans by algorithms wherever possible'.[43] In this way, the biases and noise that allegedly represent the systematic and random deviations of human from axiomatically rational behaviour can be avoided.

But mathematical reasoning applies only to a small world and not to the large world in which we actually live, and it is not clear how the computer would learn what was 'rational' in that world. Computers can perform many tasks more quickly and reliably than humans, and we should use them for those tasks. But a computer would not have resolved the issues faced by Napoleon and Obama, and gave the wrong answer to the Viniar problem. For too long, the type of intelligence that is necessary to cope with a world of radical uncertainty has been underestimated and undernourished. The concepts of biases and noise, which underpin much of behavioural economics, are, when taken to the lengths of a general theory, inconsistent with radical uncertainty, with evolution, and with the collective nature of much human decision-making.

Judgement cannot be avoided in a world of radical uncertainty. Remember the old adage: only do what only you can do. We need to apply that to human reasoning in worlds of radical uncertainty. We have no need to fear computers; we should use them. To do that requires judgement. Good judgement cannot be summarised in twelve rules for life, seven habits of effective people, or even twenty-one lessons for the twenty-first century.

Human intelligence and artificial intelligence are different, and the latter enhances rather than replaces the former. No computer has yet come within even close distance of writing a poem or a novel which anyone would want to read. The portrait *Edmond de Belamy* which was created by a computer and sold at Christie's in 2018 for $432,500 achieved that price because of its curiosity; it is neither good nor original. Even computer language translation fails in fully maintaining the sense of the original, far less its style, because computers do not 'understand' the context to which the text refers.[44] Our actions reflect both the context within which we act and our shared narratives about that context. And it is because they lack that context that computers are not capable of negotiating with Chinese diplomats or building a strategy to defeat a terrorist insurgency. And that is why the 'singularity' — the time at which artificial intelligence will supersede the product of natural, cultural and social evolution in humans — is no more than a distant pipe dream. Artificial intelligence offers the prospect of ever faster ways to solve complex puzzles, but it will not resolve mysteries.

The forces that designed the universe equipped us to acquire most easily and most rapidly the capabilities which are crucial in our lives, including the ability to cope with unanticipated and unique events. If the ability to do very extensive calculations rapidly were a vitally important characteristic required in the real 'large' world, then evolution would probably have helped humans develop that capacity. Instead, we humans have acquired other skills. Skills such as the ability to synthesise both quantitative and qualitative information in order to make sense of ill-defined and complex situations. Skills such as the capacity to stimulate our own and other people's thinking about human behaviour, and about future possibilities, through insightful and imaginative essays and stories.

10

THE NARRATIVE PARADIGM

The narration itself doth secretly instruct the reader, and more effectually than can possibly be done by precept.

—THOMAS HOBBES,
Of the Life and History of Thucydides[1]

Humans acquire knowledge through communication and learning. Chimpanzees and even bonobo apes do not go to school. In chapter 1 we described how Dick Rumelt, Professor of Business Strategy at University of California Los Angeles, would invite his classes to tease out 'what is going on here'. The case-study method of the MBA class requires students to prepare for each weekly session by reading material about a decision in a company of which they have no prior knowledge. Much of the work in determining 'what is going on here' has already been done by the teaching assistant who prepared the case. The class debates the material and, with the aid of the professor, forms a view of 'what is going on here', and moves towards a recommended course of action. The cases are rarely live – the company has already, for better or worse, moved on.

To observe that any decision starts from the question 'What is going on here?' seems obvious and even trivial. But as Rumelt, with decades of relevant experience, immediately recognised, it is not. That mode of analysis is certainly very different from the approach of the Bayesian dial, in which lone decision-makers begin from a set of prior beliefs and watch the dial move back and forth as new information becomes available to them. The student who begins the course with prior probabilities derived from one or two previous experiences, or picked from one of the shelves of trite business books in the airport shop, will quickly see these demolished in a well-conducted MBA class. Intelligent views about actions, and the range of possible actions, are expressed at the end, not the beginning, of the process of ascertaining 'what is going on here'.

We have both had the good fortune to see in action good and bad decision-makers – in business, in politics, in finance. And to observe that having prior opinions about everything is one of the principal characteristics distinguishing the bad decision-maker. Victims of ideology or arrogance, often talking more than they listen, such people fail to acknowledge that on almost every subject, someone else knows more than they do. They do not recognise the limits of knowledge – both the limits of their own knowledge, and the limits of *all* human knowledge of complex and evolving situations. They believe themselves capable of ranking all possible uncertain bets. Unlike Buffett, they are always ready to swing on every pitch.

Good decision-makers, by contrast, listen respectfully, and range widely to seek relevant advice and facts before they form a preliminary view. And when they do arrive at a view, they invite challenge to it, before drawing the discussion to a conclusion. Well conducted, the case method of the business school is an exercise in teaching future executives to think in this way. And similar exercises are part of the curriculum of law schools and of the apprenticeship phase of medical training.

Rumelt's students were fortunate to sit in front of one of the finest professors. Most are not so lucky. And others, recruited by consulting firms, are supplied with a collection of priors – a PowerPoint pack of which only the title need be changed from presentation to presentation. The reality of what is called strategy formulation in business is often depressingly different from the process of ascertaining 'what is going on here'.

The strategy weekend

The strategy weekend is a ritual in which senior management decamps to a country hotel in the expectation that, stuffed with fine food and lubricated by good wines, the team can contemplate the future of their company with an especial detachment. One of us was sitting at a refectory table in a panelled room hung with old paintings of dubious authenticity. On opposite sides of the table were the planning manager and the chief executive of one of the company's main operating businesses. The chief executive picked up the bulky strategic plan and lost his temper with the planning manager. 'We have spent three man-years providing information for this document,' he said, 'and I can't think of one occasion on which we have referred to it. What do the numbers in it mean? Are they forecasts? Are they targets?' By this time, the planning manager was equally angry. 'You are now in charge of a business of twenty thousand people,' he snapped. 'You can't go on running it by the seat of your pants.' As they later acknowledged in the bar, they were both right. The chief executive did need a broader sense of where the business was going than his day-to-day considerations; but the document presented to him, by those who were charged with responsibility for planning, was not meeting his needs.

Another time, another place: a company with a very different image of itself that was reflected in the conduct of the proceedings. The location was not the peaceful English countryside, but close to a major airport. The room was full, not of antiques, but of audio-visual equipment. This company had flown someone described as a 'facilitator' from the United States to orchestrate the day's proceedings. He was strutting on the platform trying to elicit attention, reminiscent of a pimp trying to attract customers into a risqué nightclub. 'We've got to ask ourselves,' he said, 'what sort of company we want to be. Do we want to be Europe's leading firm in our industry, or not?' The audience contemplated this. 'Let's take a vote on it.' By this time some people were looking to the floor in decent embarrassment. The vote proceeded, and the reader can guess which way it went.

But no sooner had the firm embarked on planning the implementation of its decision to become Europe's leading firm in its industry than it hit a snag. The firm had only 2% of the German market. An earlier attempt at German entry had not been successful. It was agreed that Europe's leading firm in that industry needed to have at least 15% in Germany. That clearly meant a German acquisition. There were only two firms that were available and large enough to fill this gap. The choice was quickly narrowed down to one.

Within half an hour, this firm had effectively made a decision to make an acquisition in Germany – one it subsequently implemented. At no time had it discussed what such an acquisition would cost, what the likely returns from it would be, or what value it could add to the relationship. That company exemplified a dominant tradition of business thinking of the 1980s. An approach based around visions and mission statements – a wish-driven strategy, founded not on a sense of what the company is but on what it would like to become, reminiscent of children debating whether to become a brain surgeon or an engine driver.

Another strategy weekend, another company. The audience was watching a video entitled 'Quality is Free'. The video explained that better quality led to higher demand. That implied lower unit costs and greater revenue, leading to increased profits, enabling quality to be improved still further. This virtuous circle would continue for ever. The firm concerned was a water supply company. At the end of the presentation one of the authors approached the consultants who had shown the video with what he thought were constructive criticisms. He pointed out that what people generally mean by quality in the water industry is drinking water quality. But less than 2% of all the water consumed is drunk – most is used for washing, flushing, in industry or agriculture, or in protecting golf courses and the courts at Wimbledon.[2] So even if improvement in drinking water quality led to a doubling in demand for drinking water, it would increase total consumption by less than 2%. Even that increase seems optimistic. People rarely say, 'I'll have another glass of your tap water, please, it's so good.'

Moreover, higher volumes do not lead to lower unit costs in the water supply business, rather the opposite. A water company makes use of the cheapest and most accessible sources first. That is why water charges are higher, and rising, where demand is growing. And the majority of that water supply company's customers, and practically all their drinking water customers, were on tariffs under which what they pay is independent of the amount they consume. Thus, not only could there be no lower unit costs from better quality, there would be no increased revenues for that company. Whatever businesses the circle of quality might apply to, the water supply industry was not one of them. The model was simply not relevant to the issues the company faced.

But the consultants were unwilling to engage in the argument on those terms. They did not dispute the assertions about costs or demand or revenues. They regarded the author as a tiresome pedant. What was being presented were metaphors, inspirational messages. They were not intended to be literal statements about that company or indeed about any company. By treating them as assertions about the real world, subject to appraisal and verification, the author had misunderstood the nature of the exercise.

And so had the executives present. These companies had paid substantially for what they supposed was the best advice. They were earnestly seeking knowledge, but what they were receiving was, at best, of no value to them. They were victims of three of the most common errors, not only in the formulation of business strategy, but in analysis and problem-solving more generally.

The first company, sitting beneath the bogus ancestral portraits, had mistaken quantification for understanding, and confused forecasting and planning, in a manner which provided little help but encouraged the proliferation of invented numbers. This was a common approach to business strategy in the 1970s, and most companies have now moved beyond it, just as states have moved beyond the five-year plan. But the public sector is instead awash with models and metrics, and the mantra that what can be counted counts – and hence that only what is counted counts and what counts can and must be counted – has infected all areas of public and business policy.

The second company, embarking on the acquisition of a German firm, had confused aspirations with strategy. That confusion naturally leads to the complaint that formulating strategy is easy: implementation is the problem. There are many worse examples of the practice than the one above. At least that debate was a spur to action, even if a poorly reasoned one. It is today almost obligatory for organisations, small or large, private or public, to adopt some vacuous statement of vision or mission. You have read them and passed them by, but do not underestimate the time wasted debating their wording. Or, more seriously, the extent to which that wasted time has substituted for serious discussion of the character and purpose of the organisation and the development and achievement of that character and purpose.

And the third company, whose directors had spent half an hour watching 'Quality is Free', oblivious to its irrelevance to the water industry, had failed to recognise the difference between motivational proselytisation to employees – for which there is a role – and boardroom debate. Winston Churchill was an inspired orator in his speeches to Parliament and public, but it is hard to imagine that his Cabinet colleagues would have reacted well to similar bombast when confronting the endless practical difficulties of fighting alone against an all-conquering opponent.

Diagnosis

Rumelt describes the process of asking 'What is going on here?' as one of diagnosis, the term drawn from medicine. Jerome Groopman, writer and practising physician, has attempted to discover *How Doctors Think* in a book with that title. Groopman describes mistakes he and his colleagues have made in diagnosis, attributing many to the standard list of 'biases' familiar to readers of behavioural economics. But most are in fact the result of excessive attention to prior probabilities – 'he looked healthy when he walked into the surgery', 'there's a lot of it about', 'most of my patients with symptom x have disease y'.

The good doctor listens, tests, asks questions, and only then arrives at a provisional diagnosis, treading a fine line between correctly identifying the symptoms which support a provisional diagnosis and being too quick to identify what he or she expects to find. That is why good doctors discuss difficult cases with their colleagues, and many groups of clinicians institutionalise that practice.

Which of us would wish to consult a doctor who did not demonstrate both confidence and caution in reaching a diagnosis? Or one who sat beneath a Bayesian dial which swung back and forth during the consultation? With an initial setting that read either 'I don't know' or 'most people get better in a few days anyway', even though both statements are likely true. Or a doctor who was unwilling to share, perhaps selectively, the diagnostic reasoning? Communication is central to the skills of the good doctor. And we suspect that many people will be reluctant to be treated by computer, just as they are reassured by the sight of the uniformed pilot even though the computer is actually flying the plane. When a skein of geese takes out the engines, the passengers recognise that humans may cope more effectively than computers with radical uncertainty.

Computers and the algorithms they use can effect large improvements in medical care. Billions of people seek treatment every year and the training base on which artificial intelligence can learn is huge. And as with the machine that plays chess or Go, the progress of patients provides feedback on how well the program is performing, although such feedback is never as rapid or as clear as in these games. A computer can maintain and search the entire corpus of medical knowledge better and more quickly than the most distinguished of medical academics. The power of these methods will improve and speed up the process of diagnosis and may even displace the doctor in many well-defined 'small world' problems.

But we expect that it will be highly skilled and experienced doctors, aided by algorithms and data-driven treatment protocols, who will continue to attract patients. One of the authors is still alive because the old-fashioned, intuitive but experienced doctor – whom he initially viewed sceptically – pursued the question of 'What is going on here?' and identified an issue which the accurate but incomplete diagnosis of the younger, more scientifically trained doctor had missed.

Historical narratives

As we recounted in chapter 4, Gibbon said of Hannibal's passage of the Alps that the account of Livy 'has more of probability, yet that of Polybius has more of truth'. The comment not only illustrates the changing meaning of probability, but different approaches to history. Livy set out to write a comprehensive history of Rome, weaving into a whole the legends which had contributed to Roman identity and culture. And he did so in a literary masterpiece which is still studied by students and scholars two millennia later. It is perhaps unlikely that Livy really believed that Rome was founded by, and named after, one of twins who had been abandoned to the Tiber river and rescued and nurtured by she-wolves. But for Livy's purposes it did not matter whether the story was an accurate account of events which had actually occurred.

Ethnicities are based on mixtures of myths, legends and selective accounts of real historical events: Alfred burnt the cakes; Harold was pierced in the eye at the Battle of Hastings; and Magna Carta is the founding document of democratic institutions. Perhaps. The Scottish history one of us learnt at school elevated skirmishes between groups of thieving raiders into victorious battles against the English enemy, but made no mention of the Scottish Enlightenment; that seminal event in the history not just of Scotland but of the world contradicted rather than reinforced the prevailing ethnic narrative of romantic and heroic nationalism. And the other author learnt that after the English had resisted the savage and uncivilised Scots for centuries, the collapse of the Scottish economy at the beginning of the eighteenth century paved the way for the pacification of the Highlands and allowed the creation of a peaceful, prosperous, democratic United Kingdom.

In *The Second World War*, Winston Churchill wrote in his characteristic style, 'the supreme question of whether we should fight on alone never found a place upon the War Cabinet agenda. It was taken for granted and as a matter of course ... we were much too busy to waste time on such unreal, academic issues.'[3] Contemporary records now available demonstrate that this statement is completely false: the decision to fight on was the subject of heated debate in the War Cabinet.

Polybius had a very different objective from Livy – or Churchill. Polybius was one of a few classical authors – Herodotus another – to emphasise material evidence over authority. Churchill was composing inspirational narrative in the style of Livy, not history in the style of Polybius. By the time of the Enlightenment, the lives of French kings still comprised the greater part of Voltaire's historical writings, but he went far beyond chronicling their victories and celebrating their fecundity. Voltaire was interested in the economics, culture and society of the eras he described. And Gibbon himself set the model for a very different style of history in his *Decline and Fall of the Roman Empire*.

In the early nineteenth century, the German historian Leopold von Ranke famously set out the objective of modern historical scholarship – to describe 'wie es eigentlich gewesen ist', often translated into English as 'how it really was'. Georg

Iggers, Ranke's modern editor, emphasises that this rendering fails to capture adequately the spirit of the original German. Setting Ranke's observation in context, he writes, 'It is not factuality, but the emphasis on the essential, that makes an account historical.' Iggers argues that 'wie es eigentlich gewesen ist' is equivalent to 'determine what is going on here' rather than 'explain the world as it really was'. Iggers continues: 'Ranke belonged to the tradition of 19th-century German thinkers who stressed that the historical and cultural sciences dealing with values, intentions and violations were fundamentally different from natural sciences and required unique methods aiming at concrete understanding of historical phenomena rather than abstract causal explanations.'[4]

From this perspective two distinctions are important. First, the emphasis on values, intentions and violations invokes concepts which are more difficult, though not necessarily impossible, to express in mathematical language. Second, and more importantly, history is primarily concerned with unique events. As Shackle emphasised, the frequency distribution of the outcomes of revolutions was not relevant to the palace guard. He could be executed only once. There are board games which represent great and closely fought historical battles, such as Gettysburg and Waterloo, and these games would not command continued attention if General Robert E. Lee and Napoleon could not plausibly win them. And, perhaps, if these battles had been fought many times, and we could construct a frequency distribution of the outcomes, as we can for the board games, we could infer from that a probability that Lee or Napoleon would have won. However, on the single occasions on which Gettysburg and Waterloo did take place, Lee and Napoleon were defeated, and so American slavery was ended and Britain is not a French-speaking nation.

Anthropology

A group of economists met with anthropologists to see what they could learn from each other. The differences were quickly apparent. The anthropologists had undertaken fieldwork in Papua New Guinea, the Amazon basin, and English police stations. The economists found the idea of visiting a factory or trading floor amusingly exotic. The anthropologists watched and listened; the economists asked for the figures. The anthropologists took the fieldwork home afterwards and wrote a narrative. The economists had sketched a model even before encountering the data set. Still, as former Florida Republican governor (now Senator) Rick Scott put it, 'How many degrees in anthropology does Florida need for a healthy economy?'[5]

The group adjourned to the pub, and someone bought a round of drinks. The conversation naturally turned to the origins and rationale of this social phenomenon. The anthropologists saw it as an example of ritual gift exchange, which cemented social relationships and anticipated reciprocity. They cited not only the *osotua* practices of those Maa speakers in Africa, but the potlatches of native tribes in the American north-west (ceremonies involving massive and sometimes destructive exchanges of gifts), and the modern American – and European – practice of marking a proposal of marriage with a costly engagement ring. The economists found an altogether different explanation for a round of drinks. The practice minimised transaction costs, reducing the number of occasions on which money needed to be handed across the bar, and the frequency with which the bartender made change. They drew an analogy with Ronald Coase's famous analysis of when it made sense to deal through markets and when it was better to internalise the transaction within the firm.[6]

It was an economist, of course, who proposed an empirical

test of the alternative hypotheses. What happened if you bought more drinks than had been bought for you? The anthropological explanation suggested that you should feel pleased, as does the happy groom-to-be when his gift is accepted, in anticipation of future mutual exchange of favours. The economist feels regret at having spent a sub-optimal evening.

But the test proved inconclusive. The anthropologists felt as anthropological studies predicted; the economists' reactions were consistent with their economic theory. One lesson, perhaps, is that anthropologists – and perhaps others – should not socialise with economists; the economists will feel pleased but the anthropologists' expectations that their generosity will be returned in future are likely to be disappointed. 'Economists Free Ride, Does Anyone Else?' was the title of a widely noted study.[7] (The economist who relies on others to buy him drinks is known to his colleagues as a 'free rider' – non-economists may apply less neutral language.) The authors concluded that non-economists did not mainly free ride, but that economists did; when the authors sought to explore the reasoning of both groups they found that 'Comparisons with the economics graduate students are very difficult. More than one-third of the economists either refused to answer the question regarding what is fair, or gave very complex, uncodable responses. It seems that the meaning of "fairness" in this context was somewhat alien for this group.'[8]

Reciprocity and exchange

The evening led the authors to realise that anthropologists and economists are not really so far apart. Adam Smith began *The Wealth of Nations* with the observation that 'the propensity to truck, barter and exchange is common to all men'.[9] The classic anthropological study of reciprocity in human relationships is

Marcel Mauss's 1925 essay *The Gift*. Mauss asked, 'What power resides in the object that causes its recipient to pay it back?'[10] 'The objects are never completely separated from the men who exchange them.'[11] Mauss's thesis would be summarised in the popular adage 'there's no such thing as a free lunch', which fifty years later would be the title of a book by Milton Friedman.

When a doting grandparent gives a present to a grandchild, there is an expectation that the child will return the favour, but no expectation that the returned favour will be of equivalent value. Everyone understands that gift-giving is part of the process of establishing and cementing social relationships, and that these relationships serve economic as well as social purposes. (Except, perhaps, a few economists: Joel Waldfogel's short article in the *American Economic Review* on 'The deadweight loss from Christmas' showed that the monetary value recipients attached to gifts was significantly less than their cost. This was assumed, at least by the present authors, to have been written with tongue in cheek until Waldfogel followed it up with a book developing the thesis at much greater length.)[12]

As Mauss explained, gifts generally entail some notion of reciprocity. But the more remote the ties of community or kinship, the greater the need for some sort of equivalence in exchange. Until one reaches the purely commercial exchange, in which the transaction becomes an anonymous one between parties who cannot have any other relationship with each other because they do not know who they are. Such exchanges require some sort of accounting system, in which credits and debits are recorded. Animals groom each other, but, as Smith went on to observe, 'Nobody ever saw a dog make a fair and deliberate exchange of one bone for another with another dog.'[13] The ability to calculate and render precise accounts, which is a creation of modern commercial life, enables lengthy chains of transactions between parties far apart.

But few transactions in a modern economy are anonymous. We buy trusted brands and rely on recommendations from friends or reviews on websites. Our supermarket, as well as our doctor, tries to build a relationship with us. Even in the most monstrous excesses of modern capitalism, social ties and reciprocity are important. In Tom Wolfe's defining novel of 1980s New York, *The Bonfire of the Vanities*, a chapter is entitled 'The Favor Bank' and Tom Killian, attorney for the bond-trading anti-hero, assures him, 'Everybody does favors for everybody else. Every chance they get, they make deposits in the Favor Bank.'[14] The egregious email correspondence between the traders involved in fixing LIBOR and other London securities markets is replete with comments such as 'I owe you'.[15] Even as they engaged in fraud, the participants engaged with each other through what an anthropologist would recognise as gift exchange. No one who has seen *The Godfather* would be surprised.

Such loose reciprocation within social groups is particularly important because radical uncertainty makes impossible the actuarial calculation of fair prices for risks based on frequentist probability distributions. In practice, we deal with most risks through mechanisms of loose reciprocation involving family and friends, affinity groups and other mechanisms of mutualisation, and state institutions based on some concept or other of social insurance.

Unique events and multiple explanations

We have described how students of business, historians and anthropologists approach the question 'What is going on here?' Their accounts are eclectic and pluralist. They require what the anthropologist Clifford Geertz, following Gilbert Ryle, called 'thick description': the need for multiple levels of explanation of social – including economic – phenomena. The doorbell rings. It rings because an electrical circuit is completed causing a hammer to strike metal. It rings because someone pressed the bell push. It rings because an anthropologist neighbour wishes to invite us for drinks. All these are valid components of explanation.

The economic and anthropological theories of the practice of buying rounds of drinks were complementary, not competitive. Studies of gift exchange are plainly relevant to the nature of social interaction among friends in a bar. Yet if the practice of the round were inefficient, it would be less likely to survive. In 1884, the Canadian government made the holding of potlatches a criminal offence. It believed that the economies of the tribes which held them were severely damaged by the practice. Franz Boas, widely described as the father of modern anthropology, protested vigorously that even if the law were appropriate, the practice was too deeply embedded in tribal culture for the prohibition to be enforceable.[16] Both the government and Boas had a point.

And Waldfogel also had a point when he described the deadweight loss from Christmas. We have both received – which adult has not? – presents we did not really want, and silently regretted the expense the donor had incurred. But we would not favour the criminalisation of the exchange of Christmas presents, or even suggest that people should be 'nudged' into abandoning the practice. The transfer of value from giver to recipient is only a small part of 'what is going on here'. A thicker description is required.

'Thick description' is needed to understand economic events, such as the 2007–08 financial crisis. Any explanation of these events which does not include an anthropological appreciation of the dysfunctional culture of the securities trading activity of the time fails to elucidate why financial institutions behaved in ways so damaging to both their balance sheets and their reputations. And it is also important to allow room for an explanation of why macroeconomic developments permitted excessive expansion of bank lending and trading to occur.

Whether we are dealing with potlatches, Christmas, family life or financial crises, a proper response begins with an assessment of 'what is going on here'. This diagnostic phase takes different forms in different fields. People visit doctors because they believe they are ill. Engineers are consulted on a specific project. A historian typically studies one period or aspect of history; often the interests of their PhD supervisor will have set the course of their career. An anthropologist similarly hones his or her professional skills on a specific, unique, piece of fieldwork. Aeronautical engineers undertake a project – to put a man on the moon, or to build an aircraft which will take five hundred people to Australia.

The participants at the strategy weekend were susceptible to bullshit because they did not really believe they had a problem; the offsite debate was no more than a required observance of the modern corporation. Like the readers of self-help books, the attendees planned to return to their offices on Monday morning to get on with their work. Business leaders have often told us 'we want someone like you to challenge our ideas'. Our experience is that the statement is almost never true. Need, sometimes; want, rarely.

Law is slightly different. Clients who consult a lawyer may not have a problem – although they often do. They have an issue. In many colleges, students of law are taught to follow a structure described as IRAC: issue, rule, analysis, conclusion.[17] The impressive skill of a top lawyer is to identify the issue; to give structure to an array of amorphous facts, frequently presented in a tendentious manner – that is, to establish 'what is going on here'. Once the diagnostic phase is accomplished, the remaining stages follow logically. Rule – establish the relevant legal principles. Analysis – how does that set of legal principles relate to the facts of this particular case? Conclusion – what should the client do, or the court decide? And the lawyer should do this in a dispassionate, unemotional manner.

IRAC is a useful acronym for anyone engaged in the search for practical knowledge. In the legal context it leads naturally to the two next stages of effective practical reasoning – communication of narrative and challenge to the prevailing narrative. Some of the most important and skilled storytellers are trial lawyers in the courts.

11

·

UNCERTAINTY, PROBABILITY AND THE LAW

The hardest thing about thinking like a lawyer is overcoming the very desire to be rational in the face of uncertainty.

—JEFFREY LIPSHAW[1]

For thousands of years, courts of law have been required to reach decisions under conditions of radical uncertainty. King Solomon delivered what may be the earliest recorded legal judgment, in the case of the two harlots; both claimed to be mother of the same baby. In modern times, it has been argued that lawyers have much to learn from probabilistic mathematics and Bayesian reasoning. There is some validity to this view, but more to its opposite – that devotees of probabilistic reasoning have much to learn from the accumulated wisdom of the practice of law.

Sally Clark and O. J. Simpson

Sally Clark, a British solicitor, was tried in November 1999 for the murder of her two sons. Clark's first son died suddenly within a few weeks of his birth in September 1996, and in December 1998 her second son died in a similar manner. The prosecution introduced statistical evidence presented by a consultant paediatrician, Professor Sir Roy Meadow. Meadow explained that the observed frequency of 'sudden infant death syndrome' (SIDS) in a family of Clark's social background was 1 in approximately 8500 and so the chance of two deaths was 1 in (8500 × 8500), or about 1 in 73 million. Meadow repeated the aphorism 'one sudden infant death is a tragedy, two is suspicious, three is murder'.[2]

Using Meadow's evidence, the prosecution claimed that the odds of two cot deaths in the same family were so low as to be expected only once a century. Given the complex and conflicting medical evidence, it would be surprising if that striking and simple statistic had not played a role in helping the jury come to its verdict of guilty. Clark was sentenced to life imprisonment and her reputation shredded by the British press. In 2003, she was released from prison after winning an appeal – albeit largely on procedural grounds rather than as a result of the misuse of statistics at her trial. Nevertheless, the Royal Statistical Society formally expressed its concerns about the misuse of statistics in such trials.[3] Sadly, as a result of her ordeal Clark suffered severe psychiatric problems and died from alcohol poisoning in 2007.

As a result of Clark's and several other similar cases, Professor Meadow was struck off the medical register for serious professional misconduct by the General Medical Council in 2005 (although he was reinstated by order of a court in 2006, which decided that his mistake in misunderstanding and misinterpreting the statistics had not amounted to serious professional misconduct).[4] We return below to key aspects of this case, which the journalist Geoffrey Wansell described as 'one of the great miscarriages of justice in modern British legal history'.[5]

O. J. Simpson, an American football legend, failed to surrender to police investigating the murder of his wife Nicole and was arrested following a car chase which was relayed live on CNN. His subsequent televised trial and acquittal may represent the most widely followed criminal proceedings in modern history. The most memorable moment of the trial was when the prosecution invited Simpson to try on the bloodstained glove found at the scene of the crime. 'If it doesn't fit, you must acquit!' interjected Johnnie Cochran, Simpson's flamboyant defence attorney. It didn't fit.

But the case seemed to hinge on DNA evidence. Although the forensic use of DNA was then in its infancy, the court was told that the probability that two randomly selected people have a DNA match is around one in five million. The prosecution used this figure to argue that the presence of Simpson's DNA at the crime scene demonstrated his guilt beyond reasonable doubt. The defence pointed out that 30 million people lived in the Los Angeles area and therefore six people in Los Angeles alone were potentially implicated in the murder. How should the jury have assessed such claims?

Legal reasoning

When probabilistic reasoning was developed in the seventeenth century, many mathematicians and philosophers at the forefront of the new approach felt strongly that their ideas could and should be applied to the law. Indeed, legal problems – such as the interpretation of contracts, the credibility of witness testimony and the design of panels of judges – were among the principal applications of the new theory of probability.[6] Nicolaus Bernoulli – originator of the St Petersburg paradox, whose proposed resolution by his cousin Daniel was described in chapter 7 – wrote a dissertation on the application of mathematical probability to the law.[7] And three famous French statisticians and probabilists, Condorcet, Laplace and Poisson, devoted much effort to producing theories of how the legal system should operate based on explicit probabilistic reasoning.[8] Inspired by evident injustices, such as the infamous case of Jean Calas, a Protestant merchant from Toulouse, who was tried, tortured and executed in 1762 for the murder of his son (for religious reasons he had tried to cover up his son's suicide) and later exonerated after a campaign led by Voltaire, these figures of the Enlightenment believed probabilities could be used to reform the French legal system.

Condorcet, in an annotated translation into French of Bernoulli's dissertation, set out to show how the risk of judicial error could be minimised by appropriate numerical targets for the size of judicial tribunals and the majority required for a guilty verdict. His criterion was that the probability of an innocent person being convicted should be no higher than the chance that someone going about their daily business should suffer an unexpected fatal accident; a probability which Condorcet estimated, on the basis of statistics on such phenomena as fatalities during Channel crossings, to be 1 in 144,768. By assuming that each judge made a correct decision with probability 0.9, Condorcet calculated that a tribunal should consist of thirty judges, with twenty-three 'guilty' votes required for conviction.[9]

Such finely tuned proposals had little impact on the administration of justice. During the French Revolution Condorcet was an important Girondin figure, author of their draft constitution and for a time secretary of the National Assembly. Accused of treason for criticising the alternative constitution drawn up by the now controlling Montagnard faction, he wisely decided not to trust the revolutionary courts, went into hiding but was apprehended, and is believed to have committed suicide to escape execution. Although the probabilists saw the legal system as a fruitful application of their science, their approach proved more problematic than at first appeared.

Compounding probabilities

Condorcet calculated the optimal size of a judicial tribunal by assuming that all his thirty judges made decisions independently without reference to colleagues or their opinions. Similarly, Professor Meadow's calculation of compound probabilities by multiplying 8500 by itself to arrive at 1 in 73 million requires that the two events are independent of each other. Condorcet's calculations were fanciful, Meadow's assumption implausible. Whatever the environmental or genetic causes that contribute to cot death, it is plausible that they are common to children of the same parents in the same household. In England and Wales in the late 1990s, a baby in a family with a previous cot death was ten to twenty times more likely to suffer the same fate than a baby in another family.[10] It is also likely that a mother who is capable of murdering one of her children is more than averagely capable of murdering another. We simply do not know the relative strengths of the two sources of persistence. And yet Meadow's claim that 'two is suspicious, three is murder' depends on a judgement that murderous intent is more enduring than other contributors to infant death. But no evidence on this was before the court, and such evidence would be hard both to find and to interpret. We simply do not know. Despite the cases in which Meadow gave evidence, against not only Mrs Clark but also other bereaved mothers, little is known about why infants sometimes die in their cots without any sign of illness or accident. There was no database from which reliable information could be ascertained.

In the Simpson trial, both prosecution and defence submissions on probability were seriously misleading. The prosecution claimed that the presence at the crime scene of DNA which matched Simpson's demonstrated his guilt; the defence argued that Simpson was only one of six people in the Los Angeles area alone who might have committed the crime and left their DNA at the scene. Neither calculation incorporated the critical fact that OJ was the husband of the dead woman. The forensic evidence needed to be linked to recognition that most women who are murdered are murdered by their husbands or partners – especially if, as in this case, there is a history of domestic abuse. The jury might have considered the question, 'What is the probability that Nicole Simpson was murdered by someone with the same DNA as her husband, but who was not her husband?' And since that probability is very small, the defence's suggestion that the blood at the scene might have come from an assailant other than Simpson did not constitute a reasonable doubt.[11] The DNA match permitted the decisive rejection of one line of defence, but could not, without other evidence, have been a basis for conviction.

Other lines of defence argument cast doubt on the handling of forensic material in police custody. European police forces spent years seeking a hypothetical international serial killer whose DNA had been found at over forty crime scenes before establishing that the DNA belonged to an employee of a facility which had manufactured contaminated swabs.[12]

The prosecutor's fallacy

Professor Meadow, the lawyers who deployed his evidence, and the judge who allowed it to go before the jury made numerous errors in the trial of Sally Clark. The most fundamental of these mistakes, however, was one made so often that it has acquired the label of 'the prosecutor's fallacy'. The prosecution argued that the defendant must be guilty because the probability of two accidental cot deaths is very low. But it is also true that the probability that a mother would successively murder her two sons is very low.[13] To ignore this second statement and argue that the first statement implies guilt beyond a reasonable doubt is a mistake of statistical reasoning. Fortunately, the probability that any event occurs which gives rise to criminal proceedings is very low.

Once the probabilities associated with every element of a narrative are multiplied together, as the mathematics of probability requires, the probability that the particular sequence of events described in the narrative will occur steadily diminishes. If you crumple a piece of paper, it makes some shape; but the probability that it would make that particular shape is infinitesimally low.[14] It would be absurd, or at least trivial, to conclude that one has observed a 25 standard deviation occurrence. Crimes are rare and unique events.

In chapter 5 we saw Nate Silver fail to make sense of the question 'What is the probability that an unlikely and unique event would occur?' when we know that the event has *in fact* happened. Silver was writing in the context of the attack on the World Trade Center; David Viniar struggled similarly in relation to probabilities in the global financial crisis. We can say that the probability that the fair coin which *has* just fallen heads *would* have fallen heads is one half, because tossing a coin is the subject of a well-defined and stationary frequency distribution. But most events are not random drawings from a well-defined and stationary probability distribution. So Silver's calculation of probability was meaningless; Viniar's statement may have been true within the Goldman Sachs model, but was not true of the ill-defined non-stationary world of complex financial instruments. And no similar statement of probability can be made for most issues that are the subject of contested legal proceedings.

Probabilistic reasoning and Bayes' theorem are helpful, even indispensable, when a narrow issue in a legal case can be expressed as a small-world problem – as in dismissing Simpson's claim that some other perpetrator left at the scene of the crime DNA which happened to be an exact match for his own. But the use of probabilities in court is frequently confused and confusing, and has on occasion, as in the application of the prosecutor's fallacy to Sally Clark, been disastrous.

Nevertheless, some devotees of probabilistic reasoning continue to suggest that lawyers should actually make elaborate calculations of compound probabilities. In the wake of the Sally Clark case and other misuses of probabilities in legal cases, the Royal Statistical Society in consultation with experienced lawyers prepared a series of reports describing how statistical expertise should be used in courts.[15] But the eminent authors of these reports simply assume that personal probabilities and Bayesian reasoning are the appropriate means of handling a wide range of uncertainties. Implicitly, they treat the problem as one of judicial ignorance of the relevant mathematics.

Their analysis treats the issue before the court as one of determining the relative probabilities of two mutually exhaustive and exclusive claims – on the one hand, that the prosecution or claimant's submission is true, on the other, that the defence submission is true. The Monty Hall problem has that exhaustive and exclusive structure. The keys are in one box or the other, and the contestant, with or without the aid of Bayes' theorem, assesses the relative probabilities. It is difficult to see how the amorphous submissions of both prosecution and defence in the Simpson trial could have been framed in this way. Indeed, Simpson's defence took advantage of its right not to propose any alternative explanation but simply to cast doubt on the plausibility of the prosecution version of events. In the Sally Clark case the issue might have been posed in terms of relative probabilities: given that Mrs Clark's two sons both died in unexplained circumstances, what is the probability that she murdered them (the prosecution case) relative to the probability that both suffered cot deaths (the defence case)?[16] Alternatively, the court which tried Mrs Clark might have framed the question as one of conditional probability: 'Given the improbable fact that both her infant children died, what was the probability that Mrs Clark had murdered them?' But these calculations are fraught with difficulty. There are many explanations other than murder for the death of infant children. And 'sudden infant death syndrome' is not an explanation of death but an admission of absence of explanation. We simply do not know enough to be able to sensibly frame such a discussion in probabilistic terms.

But at least these are the kinds of question, like the Monty Hall problem, in which a knowledge of Bayes' theorem is helpful. The decision is presented as a 'small world' problem to which there is a definite solution. Such an approach can be useful in organising thinking about certain aspects of a case – the relevance of DNA evidence for example – but not in understanding the case as a whole. As Adso, the novice monk turned detective in *The Name of the Rose*, discovered, 'logic could be especially useful when you entered it but then left it': an overarching narrative will always be necessary in making legal decisions.[17] The job of the court is always to establish 'what is going on here' in a unique case. And that is a narrative, not a statistical question.

The differences between probabilistic and legal reasoning

Court proceedings are the most systematic process we have for reaching decisions under conditions of imperfect knowledge – partial ignorance of the past, greater ignorance of the future. And these proceedings follow a style of reasoning very different from the methods of classical statistics.

The courts of England, the United States and some other countries operate under 'common law' systems. These jurisdictions have different standards of proof in civil (private disputes between parties) and criminal cases. The civil requirement is to demonstrate the merit of a case on 'the balance of probabilities' (in England) or 'the preponderance of the evidence' (in the United States), formulations generally assumed to have essentially identical meanings. In a criminal case, however, the guilt of the defendant must be demonstrated 'beyond reasonable doubt'.

For people – like us – who studied economics and statistics at university, there appears to be an obvious interpretation of these phrases. 'Balance of probabilities' means that it is more likely that the proposition is true than that it is not. The probability that it is true must exceed 50%. But to demonstrate a proposition 'beyond reasonable doubt' is to establish its truth to some very high degree of probability – perhaps at a level of 95% or beyond. Yet conversations with lawyers establish that things are not really like that. Indeed when US judges were asked what probability was required to meet the requirement of 'preponderance of the evidence', not only did they offer a wide variety of answers, but most answers were higher – sometimes much higher – than 50%. US jurors' estimates differed by more.[18]

And when delivering judgments or advising juries, judges in common law jurisdictions have resolutely declined to give juries any numerical answer to the question of how much uncertainty constitutes 'reasonable doubt'.[19] The standard of criminal proof is demanding because the injustice from punishing the innocent is perceived to be greater than the injustice of freeing the guilty. Greater, but how much greater? In Genesis 18, Abraham asks God to establish how many righteous must be found in Sodom for the city to be spared. While Abraham bargains the number down to ten, it seems that only the four members of Lot's family met the criteria of righteousness, and Sodom was destroyed. God was required to balance the 'type one' error of rejecting the true hypothesis against the 'type two' error of accepting the false hypothesis, and the modern statistician faces the same problem. Medical testing similarly distinguishes the sensitivity (avoidance of false negatives) and significance (vulnerability to false positives) of its procedures, and attempts to measure them – see Gigerenzer's critique of mammography in chapter 4. Why do lawyers resist similar quantification?

One explanation, favoured by many economists and statisticians, is that lawyers simply lack adequate understanding or knowledge of statistical methods. And there is some truth in that. Courts have often struggled to resolve satisfactorily cases in which statistical evidence plays an important role, as the Clark and Simpson cases illustrate. Often, as in these cases, the statistical evidence presented is itself confused and confusing. Judges do not have, and juries certainly cannot be expected to have, statistical expertise. But those who denounce the innumeracy of lawyers fail to recognise the powerful reasons why probabilistic arguments have only a limited role to play in legal judgments.

The English and American systems offer both prosecution or claimant, and defence, an opportunity to present their cases, but they do not determine the outcome by reference to the likelihood ratio: the relative probabilities of the truth of the alternative contentions. The 'rodeo problem' set by Oxford philosopher Jonathan Cohen in 1977, or the similar 'blue bus' problem described by the American legal scholar Laurence Tribe, poses the issue.[20] There are 1000 seats at the rodeo and 499 tickets are sold. But there is a hole in the fence and the arena is full. The rodeo organiser sues each of the 1000 attendees and wins every case on the balance of probabilities.

But no court would make such a ruling, and we imagine few people believe that it should – though legal scholars have debated the issue for forty years.[21] As Cohen observed, 'the advancement of truth in the long run is not necessarily the same thing as the dispensation of justice in each individual case. It bears hard on an individual like the non-gatecrasher at the rodeo if he has to lose his own particular suit in order to maintain a stochastic probability of success for the system as a whole. So if the system exists for the benefit of individual citizens, and not vice versa, the . . . argument fails.'[22] Tribe makes a similar point: 'tolerating a system in which perhaps one innocent man in a hundred is erroneously convicted despite each jury's attempt to make as few mistakes as possible is in this respect vastly different from instructing a jury to *aim* at a 1% rate (or even a 0.1% rate) of mistaken convictions'.[23]

The limits of statistical reasoning

The issue identified by Cohen and Tribe has wider signifi-cance than its – important – application to the judicial process. 'Statistical discrimination' is the term used to describe the practice of judging people by reference to the overall character-istics of the group to which they belong. For example, the once common practice of redlining – charging more for services, such as credit, to people who live in a particular area without regard to their own specific credit history – was outlawed in the United States by the Community Reinvestment Act of 1977.

Injustice to individuals is inherent in any application of statistical discrimination. Even if it is true that the redlined district displays higher rates of default than the general population, some, perhaps many, individuals who live there could be relied on to pay their debts. Moreover, redlining certainly had the effect, and may have had the intention, of discriminating against African-Americans. Statistical discrimination may in practice be a mechanism for indirectly implementing policies which if instituted openly would be illegal or otherwise unacceptable. We may wish the police to be more effective in clearing up crimes, but don't want them to do this by 'rounding up the usual suspects'.[24] A civilised judicial system treats people as individuals, not as drawings from a statistical distribution.[25]

The availability of big data, which enable us to learn far more about correlations – although not necessarily about causation – creates new opportunities for statistical discrimination and new dangers from its use.[26] Related issues arise from the development of machine learning – computers trained on historic data will develop algorithms reflecting past patterns of selection which may no longer be either appropriate or acceptable.[27] Even if the explicit use of information such as gender or race is prohibited, the algorithms may have that consequence – without conscious intention for such discrimination on the part of anyone at all.

And yet it would be impossible to abandon statistical discrimination. Employers need to select job candidates from hundreds of applications; universities choose students from thousands who would wish to attend. They identify CVs on the basis of criteria that have in the past been correlated with success. Employers look for relevant experience, universities for high examination grades. Profiling and stop and search techniques in policing have undesirable consequences, but no one could reasonably quarrel with the need to focus police resources on locations where crimes are likely to be committed.

One of us recalls listening to the complaint – made in a university of course – that it was discriminatory to advertise for a qualified accountant. It was not too difficult to secure agreement with the proposition that people with an accounting qualification were more likely to have the relevant skills for an accounting position than people who did not, even though some qualified accountants are incompetent and there are people without accounting qualifications who are nevertheless knowledgeable about accounting. Most of us prefer to consult a qualified doctor rather than interview a random selection of individuals to assess their medical knowledge. We benefit from prior selection by people who are better qualified to administer a test of professional knowledge and competence than we are, although that begs the question of how the people who administer these tests are in turn selected. Discrimination is unavoidable, and the issue is how to prevent inappropriate discrimination. But what is and is not appropriate is controversial and may change over time.

So it proved harder to deal with the argument that people with accounting qualifications are not representative of the population as a whole in respect of gender, ethnicity, age and other characteristics. They are not, and there is a history, now mostly behind us, of inappropriate discrimination in the selection of those who were *trained* to become qualified accountants. But to omit what should have been an uncontroversial requirement for an accounting position would have been to waste the time of those making the appointment and of many unsuccessful applicants. And an intention to exclude minority groups was not remotely in the minds of those who drafted the advertisement. There is little alternative to a pragmatic approach which evaluates cases on their merits. Statistical information and probabilistic reasoning will often be relevant to those merits, though they do not absolve us from the overriding requirement to ask 'What is going on here?' We return to these issues in discussing the implications of radical uncertainty for insurance in chapter 18.

There is no Bayesian dial above the head of the judge in a court of law. A judge who walks into the court on the first day of a trial with a prior probability in his or her mind is a bad judge, and juries are explicitly warned to disregard any prior probabilities they may hold. And these juries are often enjoined not to make up their minds before they have heard the whole of the evidence and the respective submissions of the parties. For compelling reasons. Courts wish to exercise control over the nature of the arguments used to determine the outcome of a case. And thoughtful decision-makers in other fields of life should do the same.

And a reasonable prior probability of the defendant's guilt is high since people do not usually find themselves in the dock without cause. But following the principle that justice should be administered in an individual not a statistical manner, the law adopts the presumption of innocence. This is very different from the idea that before the evidence is heard one should attach equal prior weight to guilt and innocence. Indeed, a presumption of innocence cannot be translated into any particular numerical probability of guilt going into the case, including zero. The case must be decided on its merits. The principle of Bayesian updating of a prior probability of guilt is incompatible with an initial presumption of innocence. Or with the requirement in civil proceedings that the claimant discharge the burden of proof.

Best explanation

Because justice is administered not on average but in individual cases, bare statistical evidence, in the absence of a narrative, is never enough. Most women who are murdered are murdered by their domestic partners. That may be a reason for the police to investigate the whereabouts of the partner – we doubt if many people would regard such enquiry as an inappropriate application of statistical discrimination. But, whatever frequencies might tell us about probabilities, such statistics cannot, without a narrative context, form a basis for a conviction. We need a story. Narratives are the means by which humans – as judges, jurors or people conducting the ordinary business of life – order our thoughts and make sense of the evidence given to us.[28]

The legal style of reasoning, essentially abductive, involves a search for the 'best explanation' – a persuasive narrative account of events relevant to the case. The great jurist and US Supreme Court Justice Oliver Wendell Holmes Jr began his exposition of legal philosophy with the observation that 'The life of the law has not been logic; it has been experience ... The law embodies the story of a nation's development through many centuries, and it cannot be dealt with as if it contained only the axioms and corollaries of a book of mathematics.'[29] The search for best explanation begins by imposing the burden of proof on the prosecution or claimant, who must provide an account of the relevant events, and demonstrate that the account would, if the court finds it convincing, meet the requirements of the law in establishing guilt or liability. The defence may offer an alternative account, challenge the validity of the narrative presented, or simply deny that the burden of proof has been satisfied.[30] Narrative reasoning is therefore at the heart of legal decision-making. The prosecution or the claimant is required to present an account of relevant events. The outcome depends on the quality of that explanation. In civil proceedings, the narrative must be a good one, better than any alternative narrative. If so, the claimant succeeds on the balance of probabilities. In criminal proceedings, the narrative must be sufficiently compelling that no materially different account of events could be seriously entertained – the prosecution case is established beyond reasonable doubt.

A 'good' explanation meets the twin criteria of credibility and coherence. It is consistent with (most of) the available evidence, and the general knowledge available to judges and jurors. They know that people rarely choose to impale their chest on a knife, or enter houses at night to return mislaid goods to their rightful owners. (Although judges tell juries that they must reach their verdict on the basis of the evidence alone, the application of such 'common sense' knowledge of context is central to the rationale and operation of trial by jury.) A good explanation demonstrates internal coherence such that, taken as a whole, the account of events makes sense. The best explanation can be distinguished from other explanations and is not compatible with these other explanations. Statistical reasoning has its place but only when integrated into an overall narrative or best explanation.

Radical uncertainty means that it is rarely possible to know the complete set of possible explanations. If the 'best explanation' is difficult to reconcile with the evidence, even if it is the best available explanation, then a legal case, whether civil or criminal, cannot succeed. The further requirement of 'balance of probabilities' or 'preponderance of the evidence' is then that the best explanation is significantly better than any alternative explanation. And the meaning of 'beyond reasonable doubt' is then that no other plausible explanation of events remains in the mind of the jury.

Reasoning by elimination is sustainable only if the complete set of possibilities is known. Thus Sherlock Holmes's dictum that 'when you have eliminated the impossible, whatever remains, however improbable, must be the truth' cannot provide a basis for a decision in a court of law.[31] Nor, for that matter, is it wise to use that maxim in other real-world situations. Only a few minutes after Holmes uttered his dictum the great fictional physician

Sir James Saunders revealed that the true explanation of the puzzling events was another, and happier, one; a medical diagnosis of a malady of which Sherlock Holmes was not aware. 'Are there not subtle forces at work of which we know little?' Sir James opined.[32] Sir James was alive to the notion of radical uncertainty.

An appreciation that 'best explanation' is the basis of legal reasoning resolves an issue that has puzzled scholars of comparative law. Civil law jurisdictions in France and Germany do not acknowledge the distinction between civil and criminal burdens of proof which is critical in the common law systems of England and the United States. From a probabilistic standpoint, this apparent difference of procedure makes no sense: everyone agrees that a higher standard of evidence is needed to convict a murderer than to resolve the disputed terms of a contract. And this is as true in France or Germany as it is in England or the United States. Common law jurisdictions are focused on an adversarial process, in which the parties provide competing narratives, and challenge the narrative provided by the other, and the judge plays a relatively passive role listening to these pleadings before adjudicating between them or inviting the verdict of the jury – which the great English jurist Sir William Blackstone described as 'a tribunal composed of twelve good men and true'.[33] This practice is still maintained in English and American law. Civil law countries give judges an investigative and inquisitorial role. The depth of investigation and inquisition which the judge will think appropriate will depend on the gravity of the issues. In France, for example, juries are empanelled only in the most serious criminal cases; and when they are consulted they sit together with three professional judges. In civil law countries, therefore, the meaning of 'burden of proof' is altogether different as between a contractual dispute and a murder trial.

At risk of considerable oversimplification, we might sum up

by saying that in common law jurisdictions the claimant or prosecuting party provides an explanation and the court determines
whether it meets the requisite standard; in civil law jurisdictions,
the judge seeks to construct the best explanation. As might be
expected, the practical differences between these two types of
process are less marked than the differences in their institutions
might seem to imply.

In a powerful address to her Princeton students, Anne-Marie
Slaughter, a distinguished American international lawyer who
served in the Obama White House, argued:

> Thinking like a lawyer also means that you can make argu-
> ments on any side of any question. Many of you resist that
> teaching, thinking that we are stripping you of your personal
> principles and convictions, transforming you into a hired
> gun. On the contrary, learning how to make arguments
> on different sides of a question is learning that there are
> arguments on both sides, and learning how to hear them.
> That is the core of the liberal value of tolerance, but also the
> precondition for order in a society that chooses to engage in
> conflict with words rather than guns. It is our best hope for
> rational deliberation, for solving problems together not based
> on eradicating conflict, but for channeling it productively and
> cooperating where possible.'[34]

In that process of rational deliberation, statistical reasoning
can assist, but never replace, narrative reasoning. We develop
narratives and use them to convince others of our point of view.
A world of radical uncertainty is one governed not by statistical distributions but by unique events and individuals. Justice
requires a process of legal reasoning which respects that unique-
ness. The courtroom is a place for stories to be told, evaluated,
and judged. But certainly not the only place.

12

———— • ————

GOOD AND BAD NARRATIVES

No one ever made a decision because of a number. They need a story.

—DANIEL KAHNEMAN[1]

When we described the twists and turns of the Second World War and the ups and downs of tech entrepreneurs in the computer industry, we told of these events not in the probabilistic terms used by statisticians, but in the narrative manner employed by historians. Probabilistic reasoning is a relatively recent tool, only a few centuries old. Narrative reasoning, by contrast, has been around for tens of thousands of years. And is very much with us today. There is truth in literature as well as in mathematics and science. As Michael Lewis concluded when trying to explain the implications of the experimental findings of Kahneman and Tversky, 'the stories we make up, rooted in our memories, effectively replace probability judgements'.[2]

In chapter 9 we described how extended social kinship groups developed in Paleolithic times. From the very beginnings of cooperative human action, hunter–gatherers formed groups to provide self-protection and exploit the division of labour. And as humans began to communicate they clustered round camp-fires to tell stories – we see the beginnings of narratives twenty thousand years ago in cave paintings such as those at Lascaux. Upper Paleolithic tribes would elaborate epics of heroism and invent fantastic mythologies to explain natural forces they did not understand. The anthropologist Polly Wiessner has compiled meticulous records of the conversations of the !Kung Bushmen, the modern communities whose practices are believed most to resemble those of Paleolithic societies. During the daytime, one third of communication relates to economic matters (and a similar amount of time to bickering – the typical modern office is much the same). But 'After dinner and dark, the harsher mood of the day mellowed . . . The focus of conversation changed radically as economic concerns and social gripes were put aside. At this time 81% of lengthy conversations involving many people were devoted to stories; these stories were largely about known people and amusing, exciting, or endearing escapades.'[3]

Storytelling is how humans normally try to interpret complex situations. And such storytelling is universal. The Bushmen gather round the fire, and Manhattanites and Londoners fight for tickets to the musical *Hamilton*. Humans are natural storytellers. And humans use these stories in reaching decisions by using analogies, in testing argument and understanding of both processes and facts, and to elicit the cooperation of others in arriving at and implementing good decisions. Narratives aid both understanding and persuasion. And most people are more comfortable with the concrete than with the abstract. As young teachers, or more seasoned speakers, it did not take us long to learn that we could grip an audience with a good story and lose the room with a few statistics or a single equation.

What makes a 'good' narrative? Quality of presentation makes the most immediate impression on us. Among the Bushmen, 'Both men and women told stories, particularly older people who had mastered the art. Camp leaders were frequently good storytellers, although not exclusively so. Two of the best storytellers in the 1970s were blind but cherished for their humor and verbal skills ... Those who listened were entertained while collecting the experiences of others with no direct cost.'[4] And in the West, it is brilliance of execution and performance that attracts us to the novels of Jane Austen, and leads us to admire the Royal Shakespeare Company and the performers in *Hamilton*. Johnnie Cochran, who led the defence of O. J. Simpson, was only the latest in a long line of eloquent and flamboyant litigators. But the power of a narrative ultimately rests on its capacity to help us make sense of a complex and confusing world. Cochran's grasp of probability may have been weak but his success was obtained before the mainly black jury by placing the Simpson case within a larger narrative of sustained hostility between the Los Angeles Police Department and the African-American community.

Performance enhances narrative, but even when performance might seem to be everything, as with a work of art, the narrative context is key to a full appreciation. Even in a school production, *As You Like It* is a great play. Credibility is the consistency of the narrative with real or imagined human experience. Credibility in this sense is not the same as truth; *Pride and Prejudice* is not true but is credible. *Through the Looking-Glass*, obviously not an account of possible events, derives a certain credibility from the relationship of Carroll's fantasies to real phenomena; the Red Queen, who must run faster to remain in the same place, is a powerful economic metaphor, and 'Jabberwocky' is not meaningless even though we appropriately call it nonsense verse. Credibility is closely related to coherence: a story is coherent if its components are internally consistent. The damsel hanging over a cliff edge at the end of chapter 5 must be rescued in chapter 6 before she reappears in chapter 7. Shakespeare ties the loose ends in Act V. We reach the end of the narrative satisfied, because we feel we know 'what is going on here'. Credibility and coherence are the hallmarks of a compelling explanation.

Narrative is not simply a synonym for verbal communication. Nor is verbal communication less 'scientific' than algebraic or other symbolic communication. To cope with radical uncertainty we try to form a coherent and credible answer to the question 'What is going on here?' This effective use of narrative is in sharp contrast to the idea that narratives are a recourse of ill-informed and 'biased' agents who prefer storytelling to computation.

A mystery to many may be a soluble problem for a few, as with NASA's mission to Mercury, or in *The Adventures of Sherlock Holmes*. All the clues needed to solve the puzzle in the classic crime novel are embedded in the text, but only the great detective can distinguish the clues from the false scents and solve the puzzle. The crime novel is, like a crossword, an artificial construction devised by a compiler. The reader knows that the author will provide a solution at the end of the book – unless, as Tony Hancock found in the BBC radio series, you reach the end and discover that the last page has been torn out.[5] But many problems we face, as individuals in our daily lives or collectively in public policy, do not promise a resolution in the final chapter. The last page has not yet been written and we may never reach it.

The impossibility of capturing narrative complexity with subjective probabilities is illustrated by *Through the Looking-Glass* but applies equally in the real world. Faced with similarly unique but rather more momentous issues than encounters with imaginary creatures, Roosevelt failed to anticipate Pearl Harbor and Stalin was blindsided by the German invasion, even though both had been supplied with specific intelligence that attacks were imminent. These failures in forecasting by Roosevelt and Stalin reflect not misjudgements about probabilities but weaknesses of imagination about what the future might hold. Lord Kelvin could not envisage the existence of aeroplanes. Leonardo da Vinci had conceived of manned flight, but Kelvin, the down-to-earth scientist, could not see how it might be achieved. Science fiction is an outlet for imaginary voyages into the future and no one can sensibly impute probabilities to the events these speculations describe; they illustrate how narratives can be used to challenge existing ideas about how the world works.

Metaphors we live by

Our need for narratives is so strong that many people experience a need for an overarching narrative – some unifying explanatory theme or group of related themes with very general applicability. These grand narratives may help them believe that complexity can be managed, that there exists some story which describes 'the world as it really is'. Every new experience or piece of information can be interpreted in the light of that overarching narrative.

Even at the cutting edge of science, in theoretical physics, the search for a unified theory of everything has preoccupied the field for two decades around the contested narrative of string theory.[6] The idea that physics might provide a comprehensive description of 'the (physical) world as it really is', while controversial, is not ridiculous. But applied to human behaviour, the claim is patently ridiculous.

False narratives may nevertheless be socially beneficial. The Kalahari Bushmen, like the people of many pre-scientific cultures, believe that thunder and lightning express the anger of the gods. But at worst, this belief acts as a restraining influence on behaviour of which the gods might disapprove. And in almost all pre-scientific cultures which have been studied, superstitious and often extended narratives are used to 'explain' natural phenomena which are not understood. The belief in life after death, like the need to propitiate deities to avoid adverse weather, has been, in the main, a beneficial influence on behaviour and provides comfort to the dying and their friends and relatives. But the narrative of a better life to follow can do immense damage when elaborated into a claim that jihadi suicide bombers will be greeted in paradise by welcoming virgins.

Religion has been the source of an overarching narrative in most societies. And for many people it still is, and today is mainly a benign force, providing a moral code and a sense of direction for its adherents. In the geographies and segments of societies in which religious beliefs have declined, the space left by the receding tide of religious faith was filled for many, first by Marxism, and more recently by market fundamentalism and environmentalism. George Eliot memorably caricatured the narrative of the pompous and pedantic Edward Casaubon, who imagined he had found the Key to All Mythologies.[7]

Our individual lives are often centred on personal narratives – 'metaphors we live by'.[8] The term 'narrative paradigm' originates with the American communication scholar Walter Fisher. In his seminal work on the role of narratives the central works are Arthur Miller's *Death of a Salesman* and F. Scott Fitzgerald's *The Great Gatsby*. Each of these works ranks among the greatest products of twentieth-century American literature, and both describe the collapse of the false narratives which their central characters had constructed for themselves.[9] And both the play and the novel illustrate the desolation which followed that collapse. The same theme is poignantly developed in Kazuo Ishiguro's novel *The Remains of the Day*.

Good judgement

The American political scientist Philip Tetlock accumulated the forecasts of purported experts over two decades, mostly in relation to geopolitical events, and judged their accuracy. This appraisal requires that the question posed to the forecaster is specific and tied to a timescale; otherwise the forecaster will easily find excuses for his or her failure in confounding factors. Failed gurus claim that their prognostication was essentially correct although it might appear otherwise to us; or they tell us that the date at which their thesis will be confirmed has not yet arrived. That is why Tetlock sets questions whose outcomes are binary and quantifiable, such as 'Will the number of registered Syrian refugees reported by the United Nations Refugee Agency as of 1 April 2014 be under 2.6 million?'[10] As we observed in chapter 2, this requirement for definitive validation excludes many of the questions to which we crave answers. Tetlock argues that, by answering many small – and often uninteresting – questions like this, we can form a view on the questions we really care about. But answers to big questions, such as what should be America's response to the geopolitical fallout of the Syrian civil war, are more than the sum of the answers to small questions.

Tetlock's assessment of the accuracy of historical forecasts provides useful insight into what characterises reliable and unreliable predictors. Few readers will be surprised that Tetlock learnt from his initial work that the forecasters in his sample were not very good; little better than a chimpanzee throwing darts.[11] What is, perhaps, most surprising is that he found that the principal factor differentiating the good from the bad was how well known the forecaster was. The more prominent the individual concerned, the more often the forecaster is reported by the media, the more frequently consulted by politicians and business leaders, the less credence should be placed on that individual's prognostications.

Tetlock's intriguing explanation draws on the distinction, first made by the Greek poet Archilochus, developed by Tolstoy and subsequently popularised by Isaiah Berlin, between the 'hedgehog' and the 'fox'. The hedgehog knows one big thing, the fox many little things. The hedgehog subscribes to some overarching narrative; the fox is sceptical about the power of *any* overarching narrative. The hedgehog approaches most uncertainties with strong priors; the fox attempts to assemble evidence before forming a view of 'what is going on here'. We both have the experience of dealing with researchers for radio and television programmes: if you profess an opinion that is unambiguous and – for preference – extreme, a car will be on its way to take you to the studio; if you suggest that the issue is complicated, they will thank you for your advice and offer to ring you back. They rarely do. People understandably like clear opinions but the truth is that many issues inescapably involve saying 'on the one hand, but on the other'.

The world benefits from both hedgehogs and foxes. Winston Churchill and Steve Jobs were hedgehogs, but if you are looking for accurate forecasts you will do better to employ foxes. Tetlock's current good judgement project, intended to create teams who are not only good at forecasting but who become better with experience, is designed to educate foxes.

Narratives of the future

The Frenchman Pierre Wack, a former journalist and student of eastern mystics, was an unconventional oil company executive. In the 1960s, he built a team at Shell which constructed alternative scenarios of the company's future operating environment. Famously, in early 1973 he presented senior management with a scenario in which Middle East oil producers formed a cartel to exert monopoly power. In October of that year the Yom Kippur war broke out between Israel and its neighbours. Arab states imposed an oil embargo on the United States and other western countries which were perceived as supporters of Israel. Oil prices rose sharply and continued to rise even after the embargo was relaxed the following year.

Wack and his team were credited with having helped Shell anticipate the 'oil shock'. Since then, scenario planning has been central to Shell's strategic thinking, and other companies have undertaken similar exercises. Shell scenarios make extensive use of quantitative data and emphasis is placed on their internal consistency but they are, essentially, narratives. A useful narrative may be turgid prose rather than literary masterpiece – a washing machine instruction manual rather than *Pride and Prejudice* – but Wack's unusual background helped gain attention for his thinking.

Scenarios are useful ways of beginning to come to terms with an uncertain future. But to ascribe a probability to any particular scenario is misconceived. We have both had the experience of describing alternative future economic scenarios and being asked, 'So which do you think is going to happen?' The questioner is unprepared for the correct answer – 'I think it very unlikely that any of these scenarios will unfold in the manner I have described'. Scenario planning is a way of ordering thoughts about the future, not of predicting it.

Anyone establishing a new business will be expected to have a business plan. That plan will set out, typically for five years, expected costs and revenues. If you are looking for finance from a bank or from 'business angels' they will insist on seeing such a document. Commercial spreadsheets will guide you in filling in the numbers. Accountants and business advisers will be pleased to assist.

Business plans are represented as forecasts, but they are not. We have rarely seen a business plan for which the out-turn even slightly resembled the numbers on the spreadsheet. The purpose is not to forecast, but to provide a comprehensive framework for setting out the issues with which any business must deal: identifying markets, meeting competition, hiring people, premises and equipment. Even though the business plan is mostly numbers – many people will describe the spreadsheet as a model – it is best thought of as a narrative. The exercise of preparing the plan forces the author to translate a vision into words and numbers in order to tell a coherent and credible story. The budding entrepreneur who cannot put together a coherent and credible business plan does not deserve, and generally will not receive, support.

Learning from fiction – il n'y a pas de hors-texte[12]

A narrative need not be true to yield insight. The dog that did not bark in the night is a metaphor of such wide significance, especially in science, that it has become a cliché:

> INSPECTOR GREGORY: 'Is there any other point to which
>   you would wish to draw my attention?'
> HOLMES: 'To the curious incident of the dog in the
>   night-time.'
> GREGORY: 'The dog did nothing in the night-time.'
> HOLMES: 'That was the curious incident.'[13]

Conan Doyle made a thought-provoking observation which had nothing to do with dogs or detectives. Jane Austen provided a pared-down description of the lives of her fictional characters which has informed millions of people who would never read academic accounts of social history. *Pride and Prejudice* is true to life in a profound sense, but the visitor to England who asks 'Can I visit the house where Mr and Mrs Bennet lived?' is a victim of misapprehension.

And the tourists who queue outside 221b Baker Street in London to visit the rooms of Sherlock Holmes are not victims of a misapprehension that the great detective is to be found there, but participants in an amusing fantasy. The Australian philosopher Mark Colyvan poses the question 'What is the probability that Sherlock Holmes walked down Goodge Street exactly seven times?'[14] Since Sherlock Holmes is a fictional character, there is no fact about the frequency with which he walked down Goodge Street which could be ascertained. The only knowledge of Sherlock Holmes we have or could have is contained in the text of the stories about Sherlock Holmes written by Conan Doyle, although this is complicated by subsequent authors recounting other supposed activities of Sherlock Holmes.

Among scholars of English literature, the problems which arise from mistaking the work of fiction for 'the world as it really is' were caricatured almost a century ago by Lionel Knights in his famous essay *How Many Children Had Lady Macbeth?*[15] Shakespeare's play provides insight into the nature and limits of ambition, but is not an account of Scottish history (of which it is a travesty), still less the domestic arrangements of the Macbeth family.

When we read a novel, watch a Shakespeare play or listen to a parable, we can try to understand 'what is going on here' in multiple, complementary ways. The autistic child prodigy Jedediah Buxton, when asked what he thought of *Richard III*, observed (correctly) that the play contained 12,445 words.[16] Some readers might look for allegories in the text which could speak to broader points outside the book, consider how the text fits into the overall web of literature of which they are aware, and simply think about how it makes them feel. Going deeper, they might examine the context of the work: the life of the author; the historical conditions at the time; the ideas which others claim to have extracted from it. Interpretation is always personal, always dependent on context.

The Irish literary critic Denis Donoghue explains how this works: 'Theory . . . has an air of speculation about it . . . we use a theory for what it is worth, and we drop it when it has served its day.'[17] Franz Kafka's *The Trial* is one of the most influential novels of the twentieth century. It recounts the experience of Josef K., who is arrested without being given a reason, and his struggle to resist and understand his conviction. Is the story a commentary on the opaque bureaucracy of the Austro-Hungarian empire; an expression of Kafka's difficulties with, and fear of, life; or simply a darkly absurdist tragicomedy? The novel can be read as all of these things, and each reading gives us new ways to appreciate the text without any of them being what it is 'really about'. Gabriel García Márquez said that reading Kafka's *The Metamorphosis* changed his own view of writing: 'I thought to myself that I didn't know anyone was allowed to write things like that. If I had known, I would have started writing a long time ago.'[18] The measure of the quality of a fictional narrative is not whether it is true but whether it is illuminating. And as with any other work of art, interpretation is a matter for the beholder, not just the compiler. We judge *Macbeth*, in the first instance, by the quality of the language and stagecraft, and then, more reflectively, by the insights we derive about the causes and consequences of ambition. We know that whatever the events described in a political novel, such as George Orwell's *Nineteen Eighty-Four* or Ayn Rand's *Atlas Shrugged*, the quality of the work depends in the first instance on the perceived elegance of the narration and thereafter on the effectiveness and persuasiveness of the implicit argument.

Narratives and emotions

Humans are not computers. We make decisions using judgement, instinct and emotions. And when we explain the decisions we have made, either to ourselves or to others, our explanation usually takes narrative form. As David Tuckett, a social scientist and psychoanalyst, has argued, decisions require us 'to feel sufficiently convinced about the anticipated outcomes to act'.[19] Narratives are the mechanism by which conviction is developed. Narratives underpin our sense of identity, and enable us to recreate decisions of the past and imagine decisions we will face in the future. Emotions and human cognition are not separate processes. In developing his concept of conviction narrative theory, Tuckett suggests that a decision-maker must manage the 'emotions evoked during narrative simulation' in order to develop sufficient conviction about a proposed decision.[20] Tuckett's thesis was formulated after listening to participants in financial markets describing at length how they did in practice make the decisions. The Reverend Bayes was rarely discussed.

Successful businesses are built around narratives. Bill Gates and Steve Jobs resisted Olsen's scepticism that anyone would want a computer in their home, and developed a fresh narrative around personal computing; Jobs successfully embraced – and Steve Ballmer, Gates' successor, rejected – the later narrative which took the computer from the phone to the cloud and the pocket. Sam Walton, who founded the Walmart chain of stores, recalled that 'I have concentrated all along on building the finest retail company we possibly could. Making a personal fortune was never particularly a goal of mine.'[21]

Bill Allen, a modest man who was dragged to the CEO's office against his will, understood the inspirational power of narrative.[22] He made Boeing the world leader in civil aviation by choosing to 'eat, breathe and sleep the world of aeronautics'.

When his company embarked on a project to build the world's largest commercial plane, the 747, a non-executive director who asked for financial projections was told that some studies had been made, but the responsible manager could not remember the results.[23] Allen's tenure was followed by that of Phil Condit, who emphasised the need for a 'value based environment', allowed Airbus to become a formidable rival, and created no value for his shareholders.[24] Under Allen, Boeing also introduced the 737, which became the best-selling plane in aviation history. Struggling fifty years after that launched to compete with the more modern Airbus A320, Boeing chose not to design a new plane but to fit fuel-efficient engines to its ageing blockbuster. This modification proved more difficult than anticipated, requiring complex adjustments to the aircraft's handling, and the two crashes of the 737 Max in 2018 and 2019 were uncannily reminiscent of the Comet disasters of 1954 – the result of unforeseen consequences from the decision to adapt an earlier design to new circumstances. Unk-unks are inevitable in aviation, and understanding of systems does not necessarily keep pace with their complexity.

We have observed the 'business plans' of startups in the dotcom madness of 1999, and again in Silicon Valley today, which describe ventures whose purpose is to raise funds from investors rather than revenues from customers. These business plans rarely extend beyond later funding rounds and these businesses rarely survive that far. And a persuasive narrative makes all the difference. The young, attractive and charismatic Elizabeth Holmes secured funding of $750 million, and briefly appeared to be a personal billionaire through her company Theranos. Its product could supposedly detect many illnesses from a pinprick of blood. Theranos offered its services through pharmacies, and commanded a peak market capitalisation of $9 billion. But the technology did not exist. In 2018 Holmes settled securities fraud charges filed by the SEC with a hefty fine and an agreement not to serve as director or executive of a public company; Theranos was wound up.[25] Holmes still faces criminal prosecution for false claims about the efficacy of the corporation's tests. For a decade, the narrative went unchallenged by board members, investors and regulatory agencies and unravelled only when a *Wall Street Journal* investigative reporter persisted with penetrating questions. Successful narratives survive continual challenge and unsuccessful ones are displaced – sometimes not soon enough.

Narratives and financial markets

The modern financial world is full of noise. Tom Wolfe notoriously described the roar of the trading floor as 'the sound of young white men baying for money'.[26] Everywhere there are screens, their constant flicker announcing the arrival of new data. Across the bottom a moving ticker announces what is described as news. Above it, talking heads make assertion and counter-assertion. 'Interest rates will rise in the third quarter.' 'They will remain unchanged through the end of the year'.

The dominant characteristic of modern finance is the constant interplay of competing narratives. The role of the economist in an investment bank is to provide stories with which salesmen can regale their clients, and with which clients can be entertained over lunch. In the worst, but not uncommon, excesses of the use of narratives in finance, traders propagate false narratives in schemes such as 'Dr Evil' and 'Darth Vader' with the aim of disrupting bona fide transactions in bonds and electricity to their advantage. Narratives, true and false, play a central role in financial markets. The American economist Robert Shiller has recently documented the importance and contagious nature of narratives in financial markets, and Tuckett's 'conviction

narrative' account of the behaviour of traders is based on extensive interview material.[27]

Narratives in finance and business may be true or false,
damaging or benign, but are rarely innocuous. The false beliefs
that thunder had a supernatural explanation and that the solar
system revolved around the Earth did not affect stock prices,
or have much effect on any other economic phenomena. But
financial markets have their analogues of the evil imams who
propagate false narratives for their own ends. Shiller gives
many illustrations of trivial or false narratives which have nevertheless received widespread attention. Such false narratives
may circulate for a time. There were no witches in Salem, the
recession in the American economy in 1920 was not caused by
war profiteers, and American democracy was not threatened
by a wide-ranging communist plot in the 1950s. But the fact
that some people believe that the attack on the Twin Towers in
2001 was orchestrated by the US government should not blind
us to the more important observation that the most common
reason why narratives are contagious is that they are consistent
with evidence and experience. Reasonable people now believe
that the Earth revolves around the sun, that AIDS is caused
by a virus transmitted through contaminated blood, and that
racial segregation is not only unjust but based on false science,
although many reasonable people once believed otherwise. And
prevailing opinion about these matters – 'probability' in the
sense employed by the ancient Greek rhetoricians – has altered
because there is a marketplace for ideas in which there is a tendency, not always sufficiently rapid, for valid new ideas to drive
out older, erroneous ones. Knowledge is itself the subject of an
evolutionary process.

In a world in which to list all possible outcomes and their
probabilities would be impossibly complex, narratives are an
essential part of how we reason. But they are not just a way in

which we provide ourselves with the 'best explanation'. They play a crucial role in how we communicate with each other, and how we reach collective decisions. Narratives change and evolve over time, and need to be constantly challenged. In the chapters that follow, we discuss the processes by which we create and present narratives and the ways in which narratives evolve, are challenged, and change.

13

TELLING STORIES THROUGH NUMBERS

Today's scientists have substituted mathematics for
experiments, and they wander off through equation
after equation, and eventually build a structure which
has no relation to reality.

—NIKOLA TESLA, 'Radio Power Will Revolutionize the
World' in *Modern Mechanics and Inventions* (July 1934)

Probability has developed our understanding of things
humans always – loosely – knew. The first mortality tables,
such as those of John Graunt, were constructed by assembling
many observations of age at death, from which the probability
of dying at any particular age and the probability of living to
any particular age could be calculated. The remarkable discovery was made that a relatively few mathematical formulae were
capable of describing many different observed phenomena. If
you knew a little about the distribution, and the appropriate

formula for that class of distribution, you could use that information to calculate the whole of the distribution. De Moivre's bell-shaped 'normal' distribution, introduced in chapter 4, gained that name because it was encountered so frequently.[1] The first applications were in physical sciences, such as astronomy, but in the nineteenth century the Belgian Adolphe de Quetelet showed that many social phenomena also followed a normal distribution.[2] It is no exaggeration to say that this discovery opened up the social sciences to the application of the quantitative methods which had been the basis of natural sciences.

Half of all American men born between 1977 and 1987 are over 5ft 9½in in height, and 5ft 9½in is also the average height of American men born in that decade. The normal distribution describes the height of American men. It also approximates to the distribution of daily percentage movements in stock prices (though not well enough for purposes of risk management since the normal distribution performs poorly in describing the extremes, or 'tails', of financial outcomes). And when quantum mechanics was developed in the twentieth century, the normal distribution played an important role in understanding the position and momentum of elementary particles.

How do we know that the average height of American men is 5ft 9½in? We don't. No single person or agency has measured all Americans, and to do so would be impracticable. The methods of classical statistics, developed during the late nineteenth and early twentieth centuries, enabled the properties of a population to be deduced from the properties of a sample. The Bureau of the Census derives an estimate of the distribution of the heights, and many other characteristics of the American population, from the National Health and Nutrition Examination Survey (NHANES) which provides a comprehensive medical check for around five thousand Americans each year.

Almost everyone introduced to statistics is surprised by the confidence with which estimates are made on the basis of small samples. In any year, only one in sixty thousand Americans will take part in the NHANES, so that it is not only unlikely that any individual will ever take part but unlikely that he or she will know anyone who has taken part. Yet provided those chosen are a random selection of the population – and it is difficult not only to achieve this but to verify that it has been achieved – the error in the calculation of the average height is negligible.

Such statistical analysis makes it possible to estimate not just the average height, but the distribution of error in the estimate of the average height.[3] The height of American men is the result of the aggregation of many factors – the height of parents, the length of pregnancy, and early nutrition. The Central Limit Theorem of probability states that if a variable is the sum of a large number of factors which are themselves random and independent of each other, the resulting distribution of that variable will be normal. The assumption of independently additive influences describes the process of determining height sufficiently well that the distribution of heights of Americans is approximately normal.[4]

Only 20% of American men are more than 6ft tall and another 20% are less than 5ft 7in in height. The average, or mean, of the distribution is 5ft 9½in and the standard deviation – a measure of variability – is 2¾ inches. These two parameters tell you everything you need to know about the distribution of heights of that population.[5] With the aid of tabulations of the distribution you can then estimate what proportion of the population will be above or below any particular height. Two thirds of men are within one standard deviation of the average – a property of the normal distribution. The number of men taller than 6ft 4in or shorter than 5ft 3in is too small for the sample conducted by the US Bureau of the Census to give a reliable estimate of the population proportion. These extremes represent the tails of the distribution. If you saw a man 11ft 6in tall (you won't) you would have observed a 25 standard deviation event, as rare as Mr Viniar's observation of movements in financial prices.

But the normal distribution was only the most common of the family of statistical distributions which were developed in the nineteenth century. The Russian statistician Ladislaus Bortkiewicz analysed the distribution of deaths from horse kicks in fourteen different corps of the Prussian army in the two decades from 1875 to 1894. As Bortkiewicz had anticipated, he could use the Poisson distribution – a different formula, named after the French mathematician Siméon-Denis Poisson – to match the overall number of deaths. On average, in a corps there were 0.7 deaths a year from horse kicks and no deaths only one year in two. From knowledge of the size of a corps, his analysis enabled Bortkiewicz to predict the incidence of deaths by year for each individual corps.[6] For many students – including the authors – analyses such as this were a life-changing revelation of the potential of social science. Even the most banal of human affairs could, it seemed, be addressed by the methods of science; the vagaries of the Greek gods had been tamed.

Statistical distributions are the product of an interaction between deductive and inductive reasoning. The methods of deduction describe the process that gives rise to the observed variable – the height of American men, the number of Prussian officers killed. The methods of induction examine such data, and form hypotheses about how the data were generated. The hypothesis may predict the distribution, and be validated by observation of it, or be derived following observation of it. In either case, the applicability of the analysis depends on the continuing validity of the underlying model.

The model Bortkiewicz used ceased to have relevance after 1918. The defeated Prussian army disappeared, and insofar as there is a successor – the army of the Federal Republic of

Germany – that army no longer relies on cavalry and its officers are very unlikely to be victims of horse kicks. Perhaps those who emphasised the whims of the gods had a point after all. The relevance of models to human affairs is more contingent, more transitory, than their relevance to natural phenomena. Physicists rely on stationarity – physical laws remain unchanged for century after century. Economic and social phenomena are not similarly stationary. The two great wars of the twentieth century altered society in many ways, among which the disappearance of Prussian cavalry regiments was only one, and not the most significant. These fundamental changes in world economies represent what economists call a shift or structural break.

Power laws

The most common word in the English language is 'the'. In this book, that word is used 9742 times and accounts for about 7% of the total words in the book. The second most commonly used English word is 'of', followed by 'and'. The words 'gadzooks', 'valetudinarian' and 'antidisestablishmentarianism', although accepted by our spellchecker, do not otherwise appear at all in the book, or in any other book or article either of us has written.

The American linguist George Zipf studied word frequencies long before computers could take over such tasks, and formulated what is known as Zipf's Law.[7] When word frequency is plotted on a logarithmic scale, the result is more or less a straight line, with a stable relationship between the popularity of a word and the number of words of similar popularity. The nth most frequently used word appears with frequency $1/n$ times that of the most frequently used word. And the number of words is not limited to the number in Microsoft's dictionary, or even to the listings of the *Oxford English Dictionary*. There are many words which have very rarely been used, like kaama, and new words are being invented every day.

This type of distribution is known as a power law, yet another widely applicable mathematical formula, and one which has markedly different characteristics from the distributions of classical statistics. In the normal distribution, the mean (average), median (middle) and mode (most frequently observed) outcomes are the same. These measures of *central tendency* will differ somewhat if the distribution is lognormal, but the basic pattern in which most observations cluster around the centre is common to all. But the properties of power law distributions are significantly different. In particular, extreme outcomes are much more frequent, and the average value of some power law distributions cannot be calculated.[8] If height was distributed in a similar way to word usage, most men would be dwarfs (the majority of words are hardly used at all) but a few would be hundreds of feet tall (the human equivalent of 'the' and 'of').

Power laws have much wider application than word frequencies. The Australian Don Bradman was the greatest batsman in the history of cricket, and the fitted power law enables us to estimate how many batsmen there would have to be before there was another as good as Bradman, how many batsmen are as bad as the authors, and even to conjecture how good Bradman was relative to other fine players of other sports (stunningly good).

The normal distribution has many applications. It can be fitted to the heights of batsmen. But not to their prowess – if it could then there would never have been a player of Bradman's calibre, nor millions of ingenue cricketers who would be dismissed by the first ball bowled by a competent opponent. Nor could a normal distribution describe earthquakes; if it could there would never have been an earthquake like that which hit Valdivia in Chile in 1960, the largest measured by modern recording equipment. Earthquakes follow a power law – there are many small earthquakes, so small they pass unnoticed, every day. And so do asteroids – the Yucatán crater was created by the largest of which we have knowledge, but Earth is regularly hit by objects from space. The nineteenth of October 1987, on which the principal American stock indices fell by around 20% during the day, is the financial analogue of the Valdivia earthquake. Extreme events are common with power laws and rare in normal distributions.

The application of power laws to economics was pioneered in the early 1960s by the Polish-French-American mathematician Benoit Mandelbrot. He established that movements in cotton prices could be described by a power law.[9] Power laws have a property of 'scale invariance'. If you look at a snowflake under a powerful microscope, the shape of every small part you see is the same as the shape you see with the naked eye. The property which creates this beautiful structure is called fractal geometry. The graph of securities price movements in every minute looks very similar to the graph of securities price movements on every day. Power laws do better than normal and lognormal distributions in picking up the extremes of market fluctuations, which is important for controlling risk and understanding long-run patterns of returns. Power laws might even be relevant to understanding the frequency of use of the letter K.

Despite the apparent wide scope of power laws, and the aesthetic appeal of the underlying mathematics, this type of analysis has received far less attention from economists and statisticians than the traditional distributions of everyday statistics, such as the normal.[10] Too much intellectual capital has been invested in assumptions which, although adequate most of the time, fail in situations which give rise to financial crises and other extreme, and hence important, outcomes. The growing ability to obtain and manipulate very large amounts of data may provide a stimulus to the application of fractal mathematics and power laws to provide a common description of both normal and extreme outcomes.

But although power laws describe the frequency and magnitude of earthquakes well, they contribute almost nothing to telling people what they really want to know – when and where will the earthquake happen, and how bad will it be? These questions can only be answered with a knowledge of the science and chemistry of subsurface geology, and a capacity to observe what is going on under the Earth's crust, which is beyond the current scope of the relevant science. And the same is even more true of earthquakes in technology, business and finance. Observation is of little value without understanding of the processes which give rise to these observations, and knowledge of the processes similarly limited without theoretically driven observation.

Why opinion pollsters stumble

Probabilistic mathematics has proved a powerful tool for the description of many economic and social phenomena. Surveys such as the NHANES of the health and nutrition of a small group of people give us valuable information about the characteristics of 300 million Americans. We know the data are of good quality because the results do not vary much from year to year, and the nature of the variations makes sense – average height increases over time, but not by much. And the data are consistent with information derived from other sources.

The Bureau of the Census works hard to ensure that the NHANES respondents are a random sample of Americans. But what exactly does one mean by 'Americans'? Citizens? Residents? People who are in America on a particular day? There is no single comprehensive register of any of these things. And since no one can be obliged to respond to an invitation to submit to this medical examination, even if the population invited is chosen at random the Bureau cannot expect that the examined population will be one in which every American is equally likely to be represented. The procedures of NHANES appear to be vindicated by results. But estimates of populations drawn from samples are only as good as the methods employed to construct those samples. Random sampling from a large population of individuals is used for many other purposes, of which opinion polling to predict election results has been the most recently controversial example.

When polling began, the scale of these sampling difficulties was not well understood. One of the greatest fiascos in polling history was the *Literary Digest* prediction of the result of the 1936 US presidential election. The magazine anticipated a landslide victory by the Republican candidate, Alf Landon; its prediction was based on a survey of the voting intentions of 2.3 million electors. The result was indeed a landslide: incumbent President Franklin Roosevelt won every state in the Union except Maine and Vermont. The magazine had sent out questionnaires to about ten million people, using its own subscription list and records of phone subscribers and automobile owners. But, especially in the aftermath of the Great Depression, these groups were not representative of the American population. And Roosevelt had been a polarising figure. The 2.3 million people who responded to the *Literary Digest* enquiry included many more of those who were outraged by his New Deal policies than those – typically poorer households – who supported them.

The landslide buried the *Literary Digest*, which closed soon after. But at the same time it established the reputation of the then little-known George Gallup, who correctly predicted the result by using the methods of 'quota sampling', and within a couple of decades the name Gallup was almost synonymous with political polling. Quota sampling seeks to match the characteristics of respondents to known characteristics of the

American population as a whole. Starting from the responses of the people the pollsters do contact successfully, quota sampling uses a model to estimate from the answers which *are* received what the answers would have been if the people giving answers *had* been a random selection from the population. Modern pollsters, who often experience low response rates, know that their sample is not in any sense random, and now use sophisticated and complex models to adjust for their failure to achieve randomness. But this confronts the pollsters, and those who want to use their results, with the Viniar problem: the probability derived from the model has to be compounded with the probability that the model is itself true. We can usefully say things like 'the pollsters are very experienced', or 'the model has worked well in the past' – as we could of Nate Silver before 2016. But these are judgements, not statements about probabilities. It is thus very difficult to justify the attachment of a statistical confidence interval to an opinion poll result.

Nor is this the last of the problems. The answer to a question about voting intentions needs to be translated into a prediction of voting behaviour. People give more honest answers to some questions than others; aggregate sales statistics reveal that they are much more reliable at reporting their consumption of milk than their consumption of alcohol.[11] And then there is also the requirement to transform predicted shares of the popular vote into an anticipated electoral outcome. For a referendum – such as the UK vote on Brexit in June 2016, in which all that mattered was the vote count on each side – this translation from votes to outcome is straightforward (albeit that many pollsters got their estimates of votes wrong). But when a President is selected by an electoral college, or the composition of the government depends on results in individual constituencies, an additional modelling exercise is required. In two major elections of 2016 – the US presidential election and the Brexit referendum – the failure of the pollsters to anticipate the result was the consequence of the failure of their models to translate their raw data into an accurate prediction – a manifestation of the Viniar problem.[12]

After the 2015 UK General Election, in which the Conservative Party defied predictions and won an outright majority, and the unanticipated outcome of the Brexit referendum, many pollsters in Britain tweaked their models further, recognising in particular that their procedures had underestimated Conservative strength. The result was that during the 2017 General Election campaign, there was an unusually wide spread of predictions by different polling groups. In the end only two firms – YouGov and Survation – came close to getting it right. YouGov correctly judged that the adjustments to models which would have improved the pollsters' performance in 2015 were very different from those required by the different circumstances and different issues of 2017, when student and other young or cosmopolitan voters turned out in unexpectedly large numbers to vote against Theresa May's Conservative Party. Survation, by contrast, had made less adjustment to their original 2015 model than their competitors, and came closer than any other polling group to the final result.[13] It is evident that any prediction relies on some underlying model, and both the validity of the prediction and the confidence to be placed in it depend on the empirical relevance of that model. Even when a problem appears to be purely statistical – as many pollsters believed – radical uncertainty and its implication of non-stationarity intervene to make forecasting anything but statistical.

False stories and bogus statistics

In March 2015, the British tabloid newspaper the *Daily Express* ran the headline 'Chocolate accelerates weight loss; Research claims it lowers cholesterol and aids sleep'.[14] Similar stories appeared in other media. They were based on an article published in the *International Archives of Medicine*, which describes itself as a peer-reviewed open access journal – one of many such journals, some reputable, some less so, which have emerged in the era of digital publication. The report was based on research, of sorts; the authors had indeed established that a group they selected which had followed a low-carb diet supplemented by chocolate had lost weight relative to a similar group denied the chocolate. The weight loss was described as 'statistically significant'; beneficial effects on cholesterol and sleep had also been observed, but were below the levels which classical frequentist statistics regards as significant.

The study did report its results accurately, but was in fact a spoof created by German scientists and journalists to expose the low standards of peer review operated by some supposedly scientific journals and the gullibility of newspapers and their journalists and editors.[15] And their credulousness exemplified, in extreme form, the widespread abuse of probabilistic reasoning in science and economics. What was meant by 'statistically significant' in this 'research' was that the probability that the weight loss observed in the study would be the product of chance was less than 5%. But, as we have shown above, any claim about a probability is derived from a model which describes how the observed data were generated, and the validity of the claim depends on the validity of the model. What is the model here?

The experiment was a poorly conducted example of what is known as a 'randomised controlled trial' (RCT), considered the 'gold standard' of research to judge the safety and efficacy of new drugs. RCTs are now also increasingly fashionable in economic research.[16] The objective is to select two groups of people who differ in only one respect – in this case, the amount of chocolate they eat. It is very difficult to make sure that the groups are identical in all other respects, although clinical researchers go to extreme lengths to try to achieve this result – for example, they insist on 'double blind' trials in which neither patients nor doctors know who is receiving the drug and who is treated with only a placebo.

Even in the best-designed randomised controlled trials, there will be many inescapable differences between the subjects of the trial and the control group. The researchers noted that the chocolate-guzzling subjects slept better; perhaps this was a result of their greater chocolate consumption, but probably not. Perhaps they were just, on average, more relaxed individuals. The implicit assumption is that the two study groups were identical in all relevant respects other than their chocolate consumption, where 'relevant' means anything that might affect their weight gain or loss. If that assumption were true then the observed difference would be registered in only one out of twenty such trials. But it is hard to imagine that this assumption was true, or how one would know that it was true.

And there have been many, perhaps less formal, trials in which people have eaten lots of chocolate and failed to lose weight. None of these made headlines in the *Daily Express*. Researchers tend to report only positive results because negative results are not interesting, and this is true of more serious scientific research than the chocolate 'study'. Just as newspapers do not publish accounts of safe streets and accident-free roads, academic journals do not accept papers that demonstrate that eating chocolate does not make you thin. Research chemists understandably highlight studies which show positive effects of the compounds they study, and pharmaceutical companies have powerful incentives to publicise the effectiveness of their products while burying, literally and metaphorically, their failures.

The chocolate 'study' is a reminder that even if the drugs are entirely useless and the study truly randomised, a 'statistically significant' result will be obtained, on average, in one trial out of twenty. Unless *all* trials are reported, the claims of statistical significance are meaningless. And no one will ever report all trials, because people do not waste time and money pursuing to the end lines of research that do not even appear promising.

In response to criticism of this kind, some pharmaceutical companies have agreed to much more extensive publication of negative as well as positive results of clinical trials. This greater openness helps to alleviate the problems, but does not eliminate them. A paper a decade and a half ago by John Ioannidis, who holds chairs in both Medicine and Statistics at Stanford University, was entitled 'Why Most Published Research Findings Are False', and has become one of the most widely cited scientific papers.[17] Ioannidis asserted that the claims made in a majority of papers in academic journals had proved incapable of being replicated in subsequent studies.

While Ioannidis' work primarily concerned medicine and related subjects, his critique is equally valid for similar work in finance and economics. Economists frequently derive their findings from large data sets. One major study was able to replicate fewer than one half of published results, even with assistance from the authors and use of the same data employed by these authors.[18] A smaller study of experimental findings in economics found that around 60% of results could be replicated.[19] But experimental economics, unusually, is economic research under laboratory conditions; it involves asking subjects questions like 'How often does the letter K appear in a text?' The percentage of results that would have been reproduced successfully would certainly have been much lower if the same conjectured 'bias' had been investigated in a different experiment. And the growing use of proprietary data sets means that the problem of replication is likely to worsen.

The chocolate diet, and the 'research' on which it was

based, are obviously worthless; but the spoof only manifested in extreme form issues which pervade more serious scientific research. Another study, published in a major psychology journal, showed that University of Pennsylvania undergraduates became younger when they listened to a recording of the Beatles playing 'When I'm 64'.[20] Of course, the authors did not for a moment believe that such an effect actually existed. But they had followed a standard protocol for reporting results in that well-respected journal. The basic idea, common in economics as well as psychology, is to identify the variable one is trying to explain, and then list factors that might influence that 'dependent variable'. Age was the dependent variable and the 'explanatory variables' were factors likely to be relevant to the age of the student – such as the age of the student's father – and others which were not, like whether the student had just listened to that Beatles song. They then undertook statistical tests of the contribution of the different explanatory variables to the dependent variable – the age of the students. They established that the coefficient on the music was material and, in terms of standard statistical tests, significant – exposure to the recording lowered age by more than a year.

If the underlying model the researchers had used had been valid – i.e. age really was a linear function of the list of factors the researchers had specified including the music one had recently heard – then the authors would correctly have concluded that one year was the best estimate of the age-reducing effect of 'When I'm 64'. But the model was, as the authors well knew, nonsensical. Claims about statistical probability are only as good as the models from which these probabilities are derived, which are often – as in the chocolate diet and 'When I'm 64' cases – poorly articulated or not articulated at all. In other cases, as with the Goldman Sachs risk models, the model has not been empirically validated but simply deduced from a series of assumptions analogous to, but less precise than, the axioms of choice under uncertainty.

A century ago, the founders of classical statistics developed methods of inference for problems of small worlds analogous to games of chance. Some of these methods, it was hoped, could be used to improve decisions in everyday life. These optimistic ambitions for the scope of probabilistic reasoning have not been entirely dashed. There is a limited class of problems in which stationary processes generate an observable frequency distribution, and in such cases statistical methods are powerful. But these achievements have led to many inappropriate applications of seemingly similar techniques.

14

TELLING STORIES
THROUGH MODELS

All models are wrong, but some are useful.

—GEORGE BOX[1]

I n 1950, Albert Tucker, chair of the Mathematics Department
at Princeton University, was asked to give a seminar to a general audience of social scientists. Tucker was collaborating with
Melvin Drescher and Merrill Flood of the Rand Corporation
on the foundations of game theory. Realising that his listeners would not welcome a blackboard covered with equations,
Tucker invented the story of the Prisoner's Dilemma, a fabricated account of two felons incarcerated in separate cells.[2] Only
by trusting each other not to spill the beans could the criminals
hope to avoid a long jail sentence. Without that trust, the best
strategy was to confess in the hope of a more lenient sentence.
Today, millions of people who have forgotten, or never knew,

the names of Drescher, Flood and Tucker remember the story of the cunning sheriff. And subsequent theorising has made the Prisoner's Dilemma one of the most insightful and fruitful of economic models.

The objective of this kind of modelling is to turn a mystery into a puzzle – to find a problem which is much simpler, which has a defined solution and yet bears sufficient resemblance to the substantive problem to yield insight and illuminate the best course of action. Following Savage, we describe these as 'small world' models. From its very beginnings, useful economic theory has generally been of this kind. Adam Smith began *The Wealth of Nations* by illustrating the concept of the division of labour through a stylised description of a pin factory. There is no evidence that he was describing a real pin factory. In the early nineteenth century, David Ricardo proposed a model of international trade based on comparative advantage which continues to be among the central insights of economics.

Two hundred and fifty years before Donald Trump's presidency, Adam Smith had refuted the mercantilist view of foreign trade as a zero sum game in which one country gained at the expense of a weaker or foolish partner – trade could benefit both parties.[3] Ricardo developed Smith's argument to show that a country that was more efficient than another country in producing everything could still benefit from trade with the less efficient country, and vice versa.[4] In the style of his times, he illustrated his thesis with a story based on a numerical example.

Suppose, Ricardo hypothesised, Portugal could produce a certain quantity of wine with the labour of eighty men, while ninety Portuguese men could manufacture a number of bales of cloth. In England, where the climate was wetter and less sunny, the same quantity of wine required the labour of a hundred and twenty men, but the equivalent volume of cloth could be produced by a hundred men. Although in this example England was less productive than Portugal in both the wine and the textile sectors, both countries would benefit if Portugal specialised in wine and England in cloth.

At first sight, the proposition that it is beneficial to trade with less efficient countries might seem counter-intuitive – as does, at first sight, the proposition that it is possible to trade with *more* efficient countries. But Ricardo's model showed that trade can bring significant benefits whenever there are differences in capabilities either between individuals or between countries. A country's absolute advantage in producing different goods and services was less important than its comparative advantage: in which sector or sectors was the country relatively more productive? The model does not enable us to forecast the volume of trade, but does help us understand why, in the absence of artificial impediment, trade has flourished between countries at very different stages of economic development. And how untutored intuition can mislead.

Even those without any formal training in economics understand that prices are set by the interplay between supply and demand. If goods remain unsold, then a fall in the price should stimulate demand and clear the market. But in some markets things don't seem to work that way. One reason is that sellers may know far more about the quality of the goods they are selling than do the buyers, and buyers recognise that fact. In 1970, George Akerlof showed that in the presence of this 'asymmetric information' it may be difficult to find *any* price at which trade occurs.[5] Potential buyers of second-hand cars do not know whether a particular vehicle is of high or low quality. They are perhaps willing to pay a particular price for a car of average quality. But the only sellers who would accept such an offer are those who own cars of lower than average quality – 'lemons'.[6] Realising that, potential buyers lower their offer price. That leads owners of better-quality cars to drop out of the market, and only cars of even lower quality are on sale, a process known as adverse selection. As this process continues, the market may collapse altogether. The difference in information between buyers and sellers means that no price can bring about a balance between supply and demand.

Adverse selection may arise in many markets. Health insurance depends on pooling risks, but the healthy will seek to drop out and the less healthy will be anxious to obtain coverage. In practice, health insurance works well only when there is some compulsion to join. Like many good ideas, the problem of adverse selection may seem obvious when explained but the idea has proved immensely helpful in understanding a range of markets, and explaining why some of these markets do not function well.

Models such as those of Ricardo, Tucker and Akerlof are based on readily understandable accounts which illustrate fundamental economic ideas. These models may be presented as equations, numerical examples or amusing stories, and have proved particularly fruitful in economics. While not providing comprehensive or quantitative answers to economic problems, they help us frame arguments to understand better the nature of the mystery, by drawing analogies with a small world in which a puzzle has a determinate answer.

Ricardo, Tucker and Akerlof changed the way people thought about the operation of markets by telling stories to which their audience could relate: the trade between England and Portugal in cloth and wine; the fanciful encounter in the sheriff's office; the unsatisfactory market in second-hand cars.

Truth and falsehood in models and narratives

None of these stories are, in the ordinary sense of the word, true. As a matter of fact, England was far more efficient than

Portugal in textile production in the early nineteenth century. The sheriff in the Prisoner's Dilemma no doubt committed numerous breaches of the constitutional rights of the two criminals. And we can recount an experience of explaining the Akerlof model to a general audience, only to be faced with an outraged response from a representative of the Retail Motor Federation (the trade association for British used-car dealers) who claimed that it constituted a libel on his honest members. But Tucker was not talking about the US criminal justice system, nor Akerlof impugning the integrity of members of the Retail Motor Federation. And no information about the production costs of textile mills refutes Ricardo's exposition of the principle of comparative advantage.

The efficient market hypothesis is one of the most controversial models in economics – so controversial that in 2013 Eugene Fama, who developed the model, shared the Nobel Prize with Robert Shiller, who has worked to refute it. The essential insight is that publicly available information is incorporated in securities prices. The explanation of the seemingly contradictory accolades – it is hard to believe that a similar award would be made in the natural sciences – is that it is a mistake either to believe that the hypothesis is true or to assert that it is false. Most public information is incorporated in securities prices, but not always or perfectly, and that latter fact makes it possible to design successful investment strategies. Both supporters and critics of the efficient market hypothesis appear to make the mistake of believing that such a model describes 'the world as it really is'. The efficient market hypothesis is the archetype of a model which is illuminating without being 'true'. Like great stage plays, such as *Macbeth*.

A small-world model is a fictional narrative, and its truth is found in its broad insights rather than its specific detail. 'The representative agent', 'the consumer' or 'the firm' in an economic model is not an actual person or business, but an artificial construct, every bit as much a conceit of the author as is Sherlock Holmes. And any expectation such an agent might hold is an assumption of the model, not a property of the world, just as the adventures of Sherlock Holmes are inventions of Arthur Conan Doyle, not a description of any real world. Economics began with simple models which were expressed as narratives, sometimes populated with hypothetical numbers, as in Ricardo's description of comparative advantage. The author of *The Wealth of Nations* was chided by the economic historian John Clapham, who wrote, 'It is a pity that Adam Smith did not go a few miles from Kirkcaldy to the Carron works, to see them turning and boring their cannonades, instead of to his silly pin factory which was only a factory in the old sense of the word.'[7] The Carron works, which were in fact a day's trip from Kirkcaldy, were one of the first great factories of the British industrial revolution. Smith's Scottish contemporary, the poet Robert Burns, did make the visit and commented, 'We cam na here to view your warks, In hopes to be mair wise, But only, lest we gang to hell, It may be nae surprise'.[8]

Perhaps Clapham had a point; economists, ancient and modern, should get out more to see the things about which they write abstractedly. But not much of a point. Smith was not writing about the manufacture of pins, any more than Akerlof had been describing the activities of the members of the Retail Motor Federation, or Tucker the functioning of the American criminal justice system. They were using these models as illustrations of principles of much more general applicability.

Economics subsequently made advances through a whole series of small-world models of this type. Two decades after Smith, Thomas Malthus provided a notorious model of population and growth, which we discuss further in chapter 20. In addition to his principle of comparative advantage, David

Ricardo developed a model of economic rent: the amount received by the supplier of an input in excess of the amount necessary to ensure its supply (many people in the sports and financial services industries would surely work there for lower rewards than they currently receive).

It is no longer fashionable to tell a story with illustrative calculations in the manner of Smith and Ricardo. More formal mathematical expression is required, and sometimes the maths can be sophisticated. In the early 1950s, an American, Kenneth Arrow, and a Frenchman, Gerard Debreu, used fixed point theorems (drawn from the latest advances in topology) to prove, under certain assumptions, the existence and efficiency of an equilibrium of a competitive market economy.[9] But although their mathematics is complicated, the conclusions are not; the authors provided a clear statement of the conditions under which a decentralised economy could successfully match supplies and demands, and offered a further expression of the conditions under which that equilibrium might be in a certain sense efficient. For many people, Arrow and Debreu provided the formal mathematical underpinning to Smith's narrative of the 'invisible hand'.[10]

More than lemons

Offensive though it may have been to the Retail Motor Federation, Akerlof's work was followed by the development of many models, some useful, some not, of markets characterised by asymmetric information. Michael Spence explained how the prices of complex goods did not simply equate supply and demand, but were used to signal information about product characteristics.[11] Joseph Stiglitz emphasised the inherent contradiction in the efficient market hypothesis: if all information was 'in the price', why would anyone invest in obtaining information in the first place?[12]

These models are small-world analogies which help direct us towards the key characteristics of larger worlds. One of us recalls the experience of trying, and failing, to dispose of the unexpired portion of a property lease. Chanting the economist's mantra of 'supply and demand', he insisted on reducing the price. When the lease failed to sell at the lower price, he switched model; perhaps price acted as a signal as well as a mechanism for equating supply and demand. Returning the price to the original level, a small incentive persuaded an interested purchaser to take the lease off his hands.

And Ricardo deployed his intellectual gifts to achieve practical success. His grasp of the importance of asymmetric information in financial markets was intuitive. He made a fortune in bond speculation, allegedly leading a group of traders who jettisoned bonds very quickly in order to promote market panic and then bought the bonds back at low prices in order to sell once the panic subsided.[13] In August 2004, a similar strategy, named Dr Evil, was adopted by Citibank traders. It led to a substantial fine from the Financial Services Authority and was described as 'knuckleheaded' by the bank's CEO.[14]

There are several ways of conducting auctions. The most common is to sell through open bidding, in which prices rise until only one prospective purchaser is left. eBay uses a variant of this method. A second is a sealed bid auction, often used in competitive tendering for public contracts, in which contenders submit their proposals and on a specified day the envelopes are opened and the lowest bidder is awarded the contract. An alternative sealed bid procedure gives the contract to the lowest bidder, but at the price offered by the runner-up. This means that bidders can reveal their true valuations without worrying that their bids might affect the price they will pay if successful. A fourth procedure, the 'Dutch auction', is so named because it is employed in the market at Aalsmeer near Amsterdam airport, one of the largest buildings in the world, where flowers from around the world are bought and sold. A large clock displays a gradually declining price until a bidder stops the clock by agreeing to buy (if in Amsterdam, get up early enough and you will be amazed by how quickly the clock disposes of an extremely large number of flowers). William Vickrey, Nobel laureate in 1996, demonstrated that under plausible assumptions all four methods would, on average, produce the same outcome.[15] If you think that obvious, ask yourself why a seller might earn just as much by accepting the second highest offer as by accepting the highest offer (the answer reflects the fact that the various methods lead to different patterns of bids).

Vickrey's approach was essentially deductive. But when the US government began to auction offshore oil blocks, rather than allocate them administratively, a group of petroleum engineers began to ask 'What is going on here?' They observed the low returns oil companies were making on fields to which they had bought the rights in auctions. The winner's curse model, an example of inductive reasoning – a general principle is deduced from experience of the particular – was first developed by three of these oil company employees.[16] In their model a field is worth a similar amount to most companies, but this value is hard to estimate before drilling begins. Before an auction, each firm commissions a survey to estimate the value of the field: if the surveys are unbiased, then their average should be close to the true value. But the estimates themselves will vary, perhaps widely. Companies know only their own estimates and the firm with the highest estimate is likely to bid the most and win the auction – only to discover that the oil field is, on average, worth less than they thought. The blocks they win are those on which their geologists have screwed up. This problem recurs in business and finance: in corporate takeovers, the bid most often succeeds because the bidder has paid too much. In 2007 two

British banks, Royal Bank of Scotland and Barclays, competed to see which would overpay the most for the Dutch bank ABN AMRO. When Barclays' share price fell as their shareholders became nervous, RBS won the bidding contest, and suffered the winner's curse and failed in 2008.[17]

Perhaps the best-known application of auction theory was in the spectrum auctions, in which the US and European governments derived extraordinarily large amounts of revenue from selling bandwidth to competing mobile phone operators. By this time, a generation of graduate students had developed complex variants on the core models. But disproportionate attention has been devoted to such model elaboration in artificial small worlds rather than to empirical study of how these processes work in actual large worlds. Paul Klemperer, who was involved in the design of spectrum auctions for mobile networks in Britain and other countries, observed that 'what really matters in auction design . . . is mostly good elementary economics. By contrast, most of the extensive auction literature is of second-order importance for practical auction design.'[18]

The only article on methodology

Friedman and Savage recognised that their approach differed from the ways in which successful generals, statesmen and business leaders described the processes by which they made their decisions. But, they argued, this seeming inconsistency between the theory and observation of decision procedures was not even a substantive objection, far less a fatal one. Friedman and Savage drew an analogy with expert billiard players. Although these experts manifestly did not compute or even know, far less understand, the complex equations necessary to determine the best shot, their decisions differed little from those they would have made if they had undertaken the required calculations.

Thus the observer who was a poor billiard player, but a whizz with differential equations, could accurately anticipate the play. Expert players act 'as if' they were rational maximising agents.

There are some problems with this analogy. Perhaps the most obvious is that the theory of billiards it presents is entirely useless in helping us to predict the result of a match. Although it is true that experts play more or less the ideal shots which the differential equations would predict, the reason that one player wins and the other loses is that both deviate slightly from those perfect shots in real play. These small imperfections are representative of the phenomenon which Knight had identified as critical to the functioning of a market economy. Although most profit opportunities have been taken, it is those that have *not* been taken which provide rewards to entrepreneurs and which drive innovation in technology and business practice. Paradoxically, the desire of the Chicago School to treat the economy as if markets were perfectly competitive left it blind to the earlier Chicago insight which emphasised the capacity for innovation arising from the search for profit in an uncertain and constantly changing environment. The innovative success of a market economy does not result from individuals or firms trying to 'optimise' but from their attempts by trial and error to navigate a world of radical uncertainty. In practice, successful people work out how to cope with and manage uncertainty, not how to optimise.

The 'as if' argument of the billiard table was further developed by Friedman, who asserted that it was inappropriate to regard the realism of assumptions as germane to the validity of a theory.[19] Instead, he claimed, 'the relevant question to ask about the "assumptions" of a theory is not whether they are descriptively "realistic," for they never are, but whether they are sufficiently good approximations for the purpose in hand. And this question can be answered only by seeing whether the theory works, which means whether it yields sufficiently accurate predictions.'[20] Friedman's argument was influential among economists, and claims were made for its application that extended far beyond choice under uncertainty.

The philosopher of science Daniel Hausman has described Friedman's article as 'the only article on methodology that a large number, perhaps a majority, of economists have ever read'; and for the authors of this book that was true for many years.[21] Hausman quickly demolished Friedman's argument, as many others have done, by pointing out that the premises of a theory are every bit as much predictions of that theory as deductions from those premises. Friedman's article appeared in a brief period of intellectual history in which a version of Popperian falsificationism – the idea that a hypothesis acquires scientific status only if there is a possibility that it might be refuted – was in fashion.

Falsificationism enjoyed its moment in (or rather out of) the sun in May 1919, when an experiment devised by Frank Dyson was conducted by fellow British astronomer Arthur Eddington on the island of Príncipe off West Africa during a total solar eclipse. Eddington established that Einstein's theory of relativity correctly predicted the path of light and Newton's view of gravitational fields did not. Einstein became an international celebrity, and two years later received the Nobel Prize in Physics.[22] But even in physics such conclusive tests are rare. Among other things, the experiment required that the rays of the sun be completely blacked out. And although Newtonian mechanics is not a description of 'the world as it really is', it is extremely useful in a wide variety of situations. It makes sense to live our lives under the assumption that physical laws hold and do not change, but it does not make sense to live our lives under the assumption that the world of human affairs is stationary.

The decisive rejection of this falsificationist view is encapsulated in what philosophers know today as the Duhem–Quine hypothesis: such refutation is rarely definitive, because any test requires a range of auxiliary assumptions, additional assumptions about the world, and it is always possible to argue that these assumptions have not been fulfilled.[23] Newton's law of the trajectory of falling bodies is falsified by observing the slow fall of feathers; but the application of his law depends on the object falling in a vacuum. So it is always possible to attribute apparent falsification to failure, not of the alleged law, but of the assumptions needed to illustrate the application of the universal law; in this particular case, the real world is plainly not a vacuum, although it is sufficiently close to a vacuum for Newton's equations to give good answers most of the time.

After the crisis of 2007–08, there were many explanations of why it was inevitable even though it was anticipated by few. Former Federal Reserve chairman Alan Greenspan was almost alone in observing that 'I discovered a flaw in the model that I perceived is the critical functioning structure that defines how the world works';[24] most people discovered that the crisis confirmed what they had been saying all the time. On many economic issues there will always be an explanation of why the anticipated outcome failed to materialise, and no means of disputing the explanation other than derision. Economists have repeatedly used this excuse, and received that derision. But variants of the falsificationist argument have enabled economists ever since to deflect criticism of their models for failing to confront the reality of how people behave, and to dismiss critiques of their predictive failures by reference to auxiliary hypotheses. Such a view is closer to religion than science.

The number is not the policy

One of us was shown a paper written by a well-known macroeconomist with considerable experience in central banks and finance ministries. The model showed that an inflation objective would be met, given the model, if the central bank announced today what interest rates would be at different dates for several years ahead.[25] The author of the paper was asked 'So what insight do we gain from this model?' The answer was that the numbers derived from the model should be the policy. That answer begins to make sense only if the economist believed that his model described 'the world as it really is'. But a small-world model does not do that; its value lies in framing a problem to provide insights into the large-world problem facing the policy-maker and not in the pretence that it can provide precise quantitative guidance. You cannot derive a probability or a forecast or a policy recommendation from a model; the probability is meaningful, the forecast accurate or the policy recommendation well founded only *within the context of the model.*

Other disciplines seem more alive to this issue. The bridge builder or the aeronautics engineer, dealing with a much more firmly established body of knowledge, will wisely be sceptical of a quantitative answer which is not consistent with his or her prior experience. And our own experience in economics is that the most common explanation of a surprising result is that someone has made an error. In finance, economics and business, models never describe 'the world as it really is'. Informed judgement will always be required in understanding and interpreting the output of a model and in using it in any large-world situation.

15

RATIONALITY AND COMMUNICATION

It must be remembered that the object of the world
of ideas as a whole is not the portrayal of reality – this
would be an utterly impossible task – but rather to
provide an instrument for finding our way about more
easily in the world.

—HANS VAIHINGER, *As If*, 1911[1]

B arack Obama made a good decision when he sent in the
SEALs to raid the bin Laden compound. Jimmy Carter
made a bad decision when he authorised the failed Delta Force
attempt to rescue the Tehran hostages. We know the outcomes:
in the 2011 action bin Laden was killed, there were no untoward repercussions, and all the US combatants returned safely;
in 1979, the Iranian hostages were not released, eight American
servicemen were killed when two helicopters collided, the US
reputation for military competence was severely dented, and
Carter was not re-elected to the presidency. But are we sure that

Obama made a good decision and Carter a bad one? Or was it just that Obama was lucky and Carter unlucky? We don't know. Many things could have gone wrong with the Abbottabad raid, and those that did were not fatal to the success of the operation; many things could have gone wrong with the Iranian raid, and those that did were fatal. In a world characterised by radical uncertainty, there are many things we don't know, even with hindsight. And others we know only with hindsight. But since we are reluctant to acknowledge the role that radical uncertainty – and luck – play in human affairs, we apply hindsight anyway. We congratulate Obama on his sound judgement, and criticise Carter for underestimating the risks involved.

Luck

Is poker a game of skill or a game of chance?[2] It is both, of course; the outcome depends on both the abilities of the players and the fall of the cards. Annie Duke describes how poker professionals talk of 'resulting' – the attribution of the quality of the result to the quality of the decision.[3] Poker is a small-world problem whose rules are completely specified and unchanging and in which computers are strong. Libratus, the poker-playing computer, is now on a par with leading professional poker players and the next generation of such machines is likely to be even better.

The England Test cricketer Ed Smith, now a journalist and cricket administrator, describes how players would say 'good luck' to batsmen who went out to face the opposition and 'bad luck' if they returned from early dismissal. But then his county team, Kent, employed a 'team builder' to help them agree a 'core covenant' which was worked out over several days spent away from serious training.[4] The 'core covenant' banned those expressions of encouragement or commiseration. It denied that luck was a contributory factor in sporting outcomes. Its philosophy was that radical uncertainty could be tamed by strength of will. Even at the time, Smith realised that this was nonsense, and on his retirement from cricket wrote a book entitled *Luck*, explaining how radical uncertainty was unavoidable, and luck played a major role not only in sport but in many other aspects of life.[5]

The Australian Don Bradman was, as we described in chapter 13, the greatest batsman of all time. He was supremely skilful, but also lucky: lucky that the Bowral team in rural New South Wales was a man short and gave the boy a chance to play; lucky that he chose cricket over tennis, though he might well have been the greatest tennis player ever; and unlucky that the Second World War deprived him of what might have been the best years of his career. Bradman's skill was reinforced by his extraordinary powers of focus and concentration. Few sports require and reward that skill to the same degree as cricket – each of Bradman's greatest innings, the triple century at Leeds in 1930 with which he introduced himself to an English audience, and his world record score of 459 for New South Wales, required him to bat for more than a day.

In chapter 8, we noted how another distinguished and literate cricketer, Michael Brearley, had described the experience of 'flow' – the exhilarating feeling of mastery of a well-defined (small-world) problem which Mihaly Csikszentmihalyi records as characteristic of so many outstanding exponents of practical skills.[6] One of the most important matches of Brearley's career was the World Cup Final at Lord's in 1979 in which he and Geoffrey Boycott – one of the most focused individuals ever to play any sport – successfully resisted the bowling of the formidable Barbadian fast bowler Joel Garner with a mixture of luck and skill and remained on the field for two thirds of England's allotted time. But their reluctance to take risks put pressure on England's remaining batsmen to score quickly and once the pair were out Garner ripped through the remaining English batting line-up and won the cup for the West Indies. Was Brearley's risk-averse strategy right or wrong? He – and we – will never know.

Reasoning and communication

Good decisions often work out badly, and bad decisions sometimes work out well. In 2019 Cardiff City, a newly promoted but struggling Premiership football team, turned to a talented Argentinian striker, Emiliano Sala, to boost their goal-scoring talent. In January 2019, Cardiff paid a club record transfer fee of £15 million for Sala. Two days later, Sala flew on a light aircraft from Nantes to Cardiff for a training session with his new club. The plane disappeared over the Channel Islands; Sala's body was later found in the wreckage on the seabed. Cardiff City was left with a bill for £15 million, no striker, and at the end of the season was relegated from the Premier League. But the Spaniard who won 'El Gordo' through a mistaken belief that seven times seven made forty-eight could afford to laugh at his error.

'Resulting' mistakenly judges the quality of a decision by its outcome. Owners of football clubs routinely sack managers after a few bad results. Resulting is all too common in financial markets – witness the absurd adage 'you're only as good as your last trade'. The petulant football club boss who sacks an able manager – such as the owner of Chelsea Football Club, Roman Abramovich, who peremptorily dismissed his world-class former manager José Mourinho – is generally making a mistake.

Better, it would seem, to assess the quality of the reasoning that lay behind a decision than to judge the quality of the decision by reference to the outcome. If I buy a lottery ticket because I think seven times seven makes forty-eight and win the jackpot, I might persuade myself that I made a good decision. But the reasoning behind that decision was faulty. You would be unwise to apply my experience to your own choices. Yet here too a slightly different form of resulting is common. Chess players – perhaps this is the only sport to make demands on concentration comparable to cricket – call the error 'analysing to the result'.[7] Assessment of the reasoning that led to a decision is determined by our knowledge of the outcome. A venture capitalist reviews the business plan of every prospective investment with care. But nevertheless expects that only a few of those selected will succeed. These failures do not, in themselves, discredit the methods of appraisal.

History, it is said, is written by the victors, and today's understanding of the past is interpreted in the light of knowledge of the events that followed. We confidently assert today that the political leaders of Britain and France in the 1930s were grossly negligent and complacent because we know, as they did not, what Hitler did subsequently. We take a much more favourable view of the debate in Churchill's bipartisan War Cabinet which led to the decision to fight on in the summer of 1940. But Nazi Germany might have achieved the rapid victory in Russia which had been accomplished in France, and the Japanese might not have attacked the United States at Pearl Harbor. In the event Germany did not, and Japan did. We laud Churchill as one of the great statesmen of the twentieth century, and disparage Hitler as an inept military leader as well as an evil man.

Our interpretation of history is heavily influenced by resulting. It is unlikely that Lincoln, Churchill and Roosevelt would have enjoyed the iconic status they hold if the Civil and World Wars had not occurred, if Pickett's charge had succeeded, or the D-Day landings had failed. But we also rewrite history to deny our culpability by attributing disasters to chance. The bankers who brought the global financial system close to collapse in 2008 assured us afterwards that no one could have anticipated that collapse; it was a 25 standard deviation event. Dick Fuld, who presided over the bankruptcy of Lehman Brothers, explained to a Senate committee, 'I wake up every single night thinking what would I have done differently?'[8] There are obvious answers to that question, but Fuld appears genuinely to have persuaded himself that he was victim rather than architect of his company's failure. What we mean by a good outcome is context-specific. And what is good for some may not be good for others. Fuld remained a very rich man, but Lehman employees lost their jobs and taxpayers were obliged to put their hands in their pockets. To judge decision-making under uncertainty we need to review the process of decision-making itself.

To act is not to explain, to explain is not to act

In 2001, England drew a crucial qualifying match against Greece to secure a place in the final stages of the football World Cup as a result of a remarkable goal scored by David Beckham in the last seconds of the game. Although he had missed several free kicks earlier in the match, as team captain Beckham decided to take the final opportunity himself. His curving shot under extreme pressure is one of the finest in soccer history. Dr Matt Carré of the Department of Sports Engineering at Sheffield University explained that the spin Beckham had imparted meant that the ball moved three metres laterally, from one side of the goal to the other, in the course of its forward progress. It then dipped into the top left corner of the goal towards the end of its flight because the airflow changed from turbulent to laminar mode, increasing drag by more than 100%. Carré observed that 'Beckham was instinctively applying some very sophisticated physics calculations to scoring that great goal'.[9] And in the previous chapter we saw Milton Friedman correctly noting that billiard players appeared to solve complex differential equations.

But we know that few billiard champions are experts in differential equations and that Beckham is not capable of undertaking sophisticated physics calculations. We also know that Dr Carré, who *is* capable of such calculations, would not have been capable of scoring that goal. Beckham could act effectively without properly understanding the explanation of his action; Carré could explain why the action led to a successful outcome but could not himself act effectively in that situation. As Nathan Leamon writes in his novel *The Test*, about life as a professional international cricketer, 'To play the perfect cover drive, it is not necessary to know how to play the perfect cover drive.'[10]

Yet to call Beckham's shot instinctive or intuitive is to demean the process which led to the effective action. Beckham's football prowess was the result of many years of experience, training and practice, as well as an extraordinary natural talent and, given his missed efforts earlier in the match, perhaps not a little luck. Learning a complex skill requires intensive practice; an evolutionary process of trial and error helps body and mind adapt to what is required. And as with other evolutionary processes, those undergoing it need not have much – or any – understanding of what is happening to them. Reasoning and decision-making are not the same thing. Reasoning is part of decision-making, but reasoning is not decision-making, nor decision-making reasoning. Decision-making describes the choice of actions, reasoning is how we explain those choices to ourselves, and to others.

We know that Beckham was a great player because he scored not just that goal, but so many others. We know for the same reason that Annie Duke is very good at poker. We judge the venture capitalist by the long-term record. Securities traders, unlike poker players, are not operating in a small and stationary world, and there is no equivalent basis for calculating probabilities, but opportunities for making similar decisions arise often, and the outcomes are clear. So it is possible to learn from long runs of successful results; hedge fund manager Jim Simons' trading algorithms have been – overall – very profitable. We may perhaps learn even more from long runs of unsuccessful results, although few traders are given the opportunity to establish these. But the calculation of 'alpha', a widely employed measure of fund manager 'skill', generally assumes, without justification, that investment returns are drawings from a stationary probability distribution.

Churchill, Lincoln and Roosevelt made many different decisions in the widest possible range of circumstances. Lincoln issued the emancipation proclamation; Churchill restored the gold standard in Britain and Roosevelt abandoned it in the United States. Keynes would write of Churchill's decision, 'he has no instinctive judgement to prevent him from making mistakes',[11] but of Roosevelt's that the President was 'magnificently right',[12] and subsequent experience would support both assessments. We are interested in both good decision-making and good decision-makers. It is not clear that Churchill would qualify as a good decision-maker, given his patchy career record, though his status as inspirational leader is beyond question; but Lincoln and Roosevelt, who did make some bad decisions and who learnt and recovered from them, would. And it is facile to judge either on the basis of the result alone.

David Beckham is not alone in finding it difficult to articulate the reasons for his choices. Malcolm Gladwell begins his book *Blink* with the signature example of the Getty kouros, a Greek sculpture whose provenance the museum believed authenticated, but which experts immediately identified as a fake.[13] As Gladwell describes it, the rationale of the expert judgements was vague – of the kind 'it doesn't look right'. But in time a similar sculpture was found which was conclusively identified as a fake and further investigation revealed that the documents describing the provenance of the Getty sculpture had been forged. The experts who queried its authenticity were genuinely expert, and Beckham one of the finest English footballers; their respective performances were the product of years of experience and training. But their expertise did not allow them easily to articulate reasons for their judgements.

Gary Klein has demonstrated how a skilled interviewer can tease out reasons, or at least explanations, behind good decisions.[14] Among many examples, he describes an incident towards the end of the 1991 Gulf War in which a British officer on the destroyer HMS *Gloucester* shot down an Iraqi Silkworm missile aimed at the ship. The sky was dense with American A-6 aircraft and for several hours the captain of the ship and other members of the crew were fearful that they had destroyed a friendly plane. But the officer stressed that he had been confident that he had identified a threat. His initial rationalisation – that the accelerating flight path described a missile not a plane – did not survive analysis. But a more elaborate explanation, which suggested that he was able to infer altitude although the radar signal did not give him this information directly, convinced others, and ultimately the officer himself.

We are not being fooled by randomness, or engaging in resulting, in giving these decision-makers credit for the results of their actions. David Beckham had shown himself to be a brilliant footballer on many occasions before the match between England and Greece. The art experts who pronounced on the Getty *kouros* had burnished their credentials over many years. The naval officer was an experienced and well-regarded sailor who saved his vessel. All these people were good at doing what they did even if they were not always able to explain why.

Communicative rationality

Had Klein discovered the reasons for the officer's decision? That seems at first sight to be an important question, and yet it's hard to know what it means. Or why it matters. When we touch a hot stove, we pull our hand away. Do we do so because it hurts, or because we will suffer tissue damage if we leave our hand there? The decision to down the Silkworm missile was good. In the heat of battle, the decision to fire, or not to fire, had to be made immediately. If there had been time for the officer to discuss the matter with his colleagues he would have been required to explain why he thought the object was a missile. His explanation might have been challenged, and the group might have reached agreement, or referred their continued disagreement to the ship's captain. The experts who assessed the Getty *kouros* did have such an opportunity to exchange views with each other, and arrive at a consensus, both as to their views and the reasons for their views. In the case of HMS *Gloucester*, this consultation took place only hypothetically, and long after the event, and 'resulting' allows us to congratulate the officer on his judgement. Rightly or wrongly. The process of reasoning is not the same as the process of decision-making.

The element of truth in Kahneman's 'system one/system two' distinction, which we described in chapter 9, is that there is a difference between the process by which we make decisions and the ways in which we describe these decisions to other people. We need such descriptions to justify our actions – to respond to the excited questions of sports interviewers after the match, to explain our actions to the captain of HMS *Gloucester*, to advise the Getty curators. We need such descriptions in the process of soliciting the views of other people and, if appropriate, modifying our own views in response. We need explanations of our actions to persuade others to cooperate with us in implementing the choices we have made. Most decisions, and virtually all important decisions, are made in a social context; we engage family and friends in our household decisions and work colleagues in our business decisions. Economic life is a cooperative process, and such communication is an essential part of human action. Different people will make different judgements faced with the same information because, given radical uncertainty, many different interpretations of the same data are possible. Good decision-making involves communication and exchange of views with others. Even if the final decision is the responsibility of one person, as it was in the White House, that individual will normally benefit from a wider discussion.

Coherence and credibility – the standards by which we judge all narratives – are the criteria by which we judge the quality of communication of the reasons for decisions. And in modern western culture we apply the test of rationality – consistency with logic and reason – to such communication. The narrative paradigm directs us to the *communicative* rationality emphasised by Hugo Mercier and Dan Sperber. Our actions are the outcome of evolutionary rationality; communicative rationality is the means by which we explain these actions to others. Beckham's goal and the survival of HMS *Gloucester* illustrate that these concepts are not the same – to act effectively is not necessarily to explain effectively, and to explain effectively is not necessarily to act effectively. But communicative rationality contributes to our evolutionary rationality.

Human intelligence is collective intelligence

Beckham appears an isolated figure as he runs up to the ball in front of a large crowd with England's hopes of qualifying for the World Cup finals resting on his shoulders. But his achievement was not a purely personal one; rather the culmination of a social process which involved contributions from team-mates and mentors such as his club manager Sir Alex Ferguson. Even in highly individualistic games, such as poker and chess, success depends on the ability to communicate with others and to benefit from that communication. Annie Duke describes the importance of exchanging knowledge and experience of poker with other skilled players. Magnus Carlsen works with Team Carlsen, supported by Microsoft, which has sponsored his career since he was thirteen. Carlsen's mentor has been Simen Agdestein, who teaches chess – and football – at Norway's elite sports academy, Norges Toppidrettsgymnas.

When Harold Abrahams won the gold medal in the 100m in the 1924 Olympics – the race immortalised in the film *Chariots of Fire* – his employment of the professional coach Sam Mussabini was regarded as little better than cheating. In a poignant moment in the film, Mussabini, excluded from the stadium, learns that his protégé has succeeded by hearing the notes of the British national anthem drift from the stadium. But in the hundred years since, advances in sports medicine, nutrition and engineering – the work done by Dr Carré and his colleagues and the activities of professional coaches – mean that the 100m which took Abrahams 10.6 seconds to run that day can now be covered by Usain Bolt in 9.58 seconds. And top professional coaches are now well-remunerated popular celebrities. Billy Beane, who brought statistics into baseball, not only achieved fame but the honour of being played by Brad Pitt in another movie celebratory of sporting success, *Moneyball*.

The sporting analogy is not simply a metaphor. Just as Beckham benefited from the contributions of sports experts and coaches, Obama was dependent on the assessments of intelligence agencies and the wisdom of his staff. Actors, mentors and analysts make their distinct contributions to good decision-making. And these are distinct skills.

Humans are a eusocial species, achieving things which are far beyond the capacity of any individual. The economic importance of this eusociality cannot be overemphasised. Other eusocial species, principally some insects, create complex artefacts, but by methods very different from humans. The queen bee does not actually rule, directing the actions of the hive; Woody Allen's *Antz* is an erroneous anthropomorphisation. Each individual insect follows genetically programmed behavioural rules. Agent-based modelling, which has found some applications in economics and other social sciences, seeks to replicate the behaviour of social insects in the understanding of human behaviour. And some lessons can be learnt from such models.

But we are not social insects; we are advanced primates, distinguished from others by our capacity for communication and cooperation. Michael Tomasello, an expert on chimpanzee behaviour, has pointed out that 'it is inconceivable that you ever see two chimpanzees carrying a log together'.[15] Chimps rival toddlers in spatial awareness, ability, understanding of simple computations, and comprehension of causality. Where toddlers score is in their capacity for social learning. And that is why adult humans are far more intelligent than toddlers, but grown chimpanzees no more intelligent than their young. Other species can solve small-world problems, sometimes better than humans. The children's game of rock, paper, scissors, which game theorists explain requires a solution in mixed strategies, is within the capacity of chimpanzees.[16] Pigeons can solve a version of the Monty Hall problem.[17] In some respects, intelligent non-human creatures correspond better than do humans to the representations of rational behaviour proposed by economists.

And pigeons can fly, whereas humans cannot. But humans are able to build the Airbus A380, with separate portions of the fuselage constructed in Britain, France, Germany and Spain;

they are able to mount an extraordinary logistics operation to bring the components together in an assembly plant at Toulouse; they are able to assemble crews and ground staff to operate the plane in conjunction with air traffic controllers around the world. No one individual could command even a fraction of the skills and knowledge to achieve this. No person knows how to build an Airbus, or to fly from London to Sydney, but a very large number of people working together do. Human intelligence is collective intelligence, and the ability to construct a complex artefact such as a commercial aircraft is the product of a collective intelligence built up over the more than two hundred years in which engines came to replace natural sources of power and the Wright brothers demonstrated that an entirely different technology from that used by pigeons would enable humans to take to the air.

The tens of thousands of people who have contributed to every Airbus flight do not know who the other contributors are; they communicate in small groups which in turn communicate with other small groups. To see economic life from any perspective other than that of the group is severely limiting – indeed is to miss the central point of how modern economies function.

How is the extraordinary feat of coordination which builds and flies the Airbus achieved? One view, which we might attribute to modern industrial organisation theory, identifies markets and hierarchies as mechanisms to achieve such coordination.[18] Entrepreneurs purchase the parts and skills needed to construct a jet plane. If they are uncertain about any aspect of the process – from how to assemble the components to how to land at Sydney airport – they deal with them by purchasing the appropriate contingent commodities. A second view relies on hierarchy to achieve coordination. Big Boss decides to build a jet plane, and delegates tasks to numerous Little Bosses – to one the wings, to another the fuselage, and so on. Big Boss hires consultants to advise on how to design appropriate incentive contracts for all the Little Bosses and their subordinates.

While there is some element of truth in both these caricatures, the task they set for the entrepreneur, or Big Boss, is plainly an impossible one. We can build aeroplanes only because we are not isolated individuals but a cooperative species. The Soviet Union, under the leadership of Big Boss, built civil aircraft, but very bad ones, and societies which lack any depth of social organisation adapted to productive activity such as Haiti or Nigeria cannot build aircraft at all.[19]

We have emphasised the need for a pluralism of models, and the same need for managed pluralism is obvious here. The Airbus consortium does not fit easily into the market/hierarchy dichotomy – it is less than a single firm but more than an array of independent firms contracting at arm's length. And when the market/hierarchy taxonomy was exported outside the United States, it struggled to account for structures such as the *keiretsu* of Japan, the *chaebol* of Korea,[20] or the clusters found in northern Italian towns and cities. We need help from another theory of the firm, which lays stress on capabilities.[21] Complex business organisations, whether consortia such as Airbus, the agglomeration of information technology-related activities in Silicon Valley, or diversified conglomerates such as General Electric, may most fruitfully be described as collections of capabilities. And businesses and economies advance by developing new capabilities, and by applying existing ones to changing markets and technologies. Such capabilities are bought, sold, exchanged, may be hierarchically ordered, but above all are simply available – 'the mysteries of the trade are in the air', in a phrase which Alfred Marshall coined to describe much more primitive levels of industrial organisation at the end of the nineteenth century.[22] And economists such as Paul Collier argue that these clusters of capabilities are both essential to reviving post-industrial cities and only feasible in the context of wide-ranging cooperation between governments and businesses.[23] Human intelligence is collective intelligence, and that is the source of the extraordinary human economic achievement. We can navigate radical uncertainty because we chart it together.

Individuals have different, and unavoidably imperfect, knowledge to contribute. And even when, as in the preparation for that White House meeting, they have exchanged that knowledge, they form different assessments of the same evidence. And make different judgements of the possible consequences of particular actions. Obama's decision was based not on a calculation of probabilities, but on weighing up the credibility and coherence of competing narratives. And he made a considered choice of action by spending time listening to and communicating with experienced and knowledgeable advisers. Communication is an essential part of developing a narrative.

16

·

CHALLENGING NARRATIVES

'Gentlemen, I take it we are all in complete agreement
on the decision here. Then, I propose we postpone
further discussion of this matter until the next meeting
to give ourselves time to develop disagreement, and
perhaps gain some understanding of what the decision is
all about.'

—ALFRED P. SLOAN[1]

When John F. Kennedy was inaugurated as President of
the United States in January 1961, he was the youngest
ever elected holder of the office. Within three months, the CIA
presented to him a plan to invade Cuba and overthrow Fidel
Castro, the firebrand who had ousted dictator Fulgencio Batista
two years earlier. The invasion was to be disguised as a coup
by elements of the Cuban military with support from exiled
opponents of the regime. The outcome was a fiasco. The exiles
who had been landed with the assistance of the US Navy were

quickly rounded up and killed or jailed. The lie that the Bay of Pigs landing was anything other than an operation planned and largely executed by the US government was soon exposed. Not only did the operation fail to oust Castro, it helped to consolidate his position and led him to seek external support from the Soviet Union. Fidel would lead Cuba for almost fifty years.

A decade later, the American psychologist Irving Janis popularised the term 'groupthink' for the process by which a group arrives at a bad decision because of the unwillingness or inability of its members to challenge the prevailing narrative.[2] One of Janis's signature examples was the proceedings which led to the approval of the Bay of Pigs landings (the failure to respond to the intelligence which foreshadowed Pearl Harbor was the other). After the event, the Joint Chiefs of Staff said that they had had reservations about the invasion plan but had felt inhibited in expressing their misgivings because they did not reflect the prevailing narrative of US supremacy. A new and inexperienced President presided over meetings in which challenge to that narrative was discouraged. Kennedy learnt from that experience, and was determined not to repeat it. His predecessor as President, Dwight Eisenhower, framed the key post-mortem question, asking Kennedy: 'Mr. President, before you approved this plan did you have everybody in front of you debating the thing so you got pros and cons yourself and then made your decision?'[3] When Cuba again became the principal issue on the presidential agenda, Kennedy managed the process of decision-making in a very different way.

On Tuesday, 16 October 1962, Kennedy was informed that a U-2 reconnaissance flight had produced evidence of Russian missile sites under construction in Cuba. The photographs were presented to a meeting in the White House by the CIA. Those present formed a group of senior Cabinet members and officials, later to be called the Ex-Comm, which met almost continuously for the thirteen days of what became known as the Cuban Missile Crisis.

The prospect of nuclear missiles based so close to the US mainland was unacceptable. How should the President respond? Rather quickly, the choices were narrowed down to two: a naval quarantine that would intercept further Russian ships en route to Cuba, or an airstrike on all military installations in Cuba followed by an invasion. Opinion among the group was sharply divided. The quarantine would not remove the missiles already in Cuba, and the airstrike ran the risk of an escalation to an all-out nuclear war. Forceful arguments were presented on both sides.[4]

Within Ex-Comm the debate continued day and night. The experience of the Bay of Pigs made Kennedy nervous of accepting advice without challenge. Before making his momentous decision, the President decided to follow two principles in seeking advice. First, recognising the significance of radical uncertainty, he feared the 'awful unpredictability of escalation' in ways that the military did not.[5] He made every attempt to avoid backing Chairman Khrushchev into a corner. He was conscious of the weakness of intelligence which earlier in 1962 had on four occasions advised him that Russians would not transport offensive weapons to Cuba, and cautious in interpreting intelligence and in accepting advice provided by the military.

Second, he ensured that the narratives he was receiving about the two courses of action were challenged. He did this by dividing Ex-Comm into two groups which were told to write papers to support their preferred option, and then to exchange documents and critique each other's narrative.[6] He also decided not to attend all the meetings of Ex-Comm. He did not want his presence to prompt the attendees to second-guess what he wanted to hear. He wanted to know what they really thought.

As Robert Kennedy, his brother and Attorney General, later wrote, 'the fact that we were able to talk, debate, argue, disagree, and then debate some more was essential in choosing our ultimate course . . . Opinion, even fact itself, can best be judged by conflict, by debate.'[7]

Concerned about the risk of escalation, Kennedy opted for the option of naval quarantine. Some of his military advisers preferred an airstrike. They agreed with the view of the well-known game theorist Thomas Schelling that 'there is just no foreseeable route by which the United States and Soviet Union could become involved in a major nuclear war'.[8] No rational leader would, they believed, permit a local conflict in Cuba to escalate into an all-out nuclear engagement. The crisis ended when Khrushchev realised that Kennedy wanted to avoid escalation, and, in return for a secret promise to remove US missiles from Turkey later, the missiles in Cuba were dismantled and returned to Russia. Documents subsequently released show how close the world came to a nuclear holocaust. Only then did the world discover that Russian commanders in Cuba had been authorised to use tactical nuclear weapons against a US invasion if communications with Moscow were severed.[9] One reason you are able to read this book is because President Kennedy made a good decision.

A year later, Kennedy was assassinated, and the lessons he had learnt seemed to have died with him. Modern historians debate, inevitably inconclusively, how America's disastrous entanglement in Vietnam might have evolved if Kennedy had remained President.[10] What we do know, however, is that 'groupthink' reasserted itself. And so did the narrative of US military supremacy. Challenges to the prevailing narrative of 'domino theory' were not welcomed. The reality that superior technology alone could not defeat a committed independence movement was not recognised. Even as the technocratic Secretary of Defense

Robert McNamara demanded evidence-based policy, evidence could always be constructed to support the predetermined policy. That was why the Pentagon Papers were suppressed. And why Daniel Ellsberg and those who helped his whistle-blowing faced the wrath of the US government. And challenge of key assumptions was sadly lacking when a later administration was planning the post-invasion future of Iraq forty years later.

Making decisions about an uncertain future is often a group activity. We rarely make major choices without seeking the opinions of other people, and are wise to do so. Communicative rationality is designed partly to persuade others, and partly to invite challenge. In wise hands, soliciting the opinions of other people is a genuine process of consultation and discussion. Less competent leaders may simply invite congratulations on their wisdom. Kennedy, with the assistance of the experienced Eisenhower, came to understand the difference. Not all his successors did, or found similar benefit in the advice of their predecessor.

Challenging narratives

For hundreds of years puerperal fever killed many mothers and their infants in childbirth. Rising rates of mortality in the new maternity hospitals in Europe in the seventeenth and eighteenth centuries reflected epidemics of puerperal fever in the very institutions designed to help mothers at childbirth. In 1795, the Scottish obstetrician Alexander Gordon published a treatise claiming that the disease was transmitted by midwives and doctors. The English doctor Thomas Watson in 1842 recommended that doctors wash their hands in a chlorine solution to prevent the transmission of infection from one case to another. And in 1843 Oliver Wendell Holmes Sr (father of the great jurist whom we met in chapter 11) published a paper in the *New England Quarterly Journal of Medicine* entitled 'On the Contagiousness of Puerperal Fever' also arguing that the cause of so many fatalities was the spread of germs by doctors. Perhaps the most systematic study of the causes and prevention of puerperal fever was made by the Viennese physician Ignaz Semmelweis. In 1847, he discovered that the incidence of the infection was much lower for women giving birth at home than in hospital and that it was greatly reduced if doctors had washed their hands in chlorinated water. Semmelweis did not really know why this was so – he reasoned, partly correctly, that the transfer of 'cadaverous particles' was responsible.[11]

All of these findings and advice were strongly resisted by the medical profession, for reasons that are easy to understand if not to sympathise with. Doctors resisted, indeed resented, the idea that they themselves caused the illnesses they were unable to treat. Angered ultimately to the point of derangement, Semmelweis died in a lunatic asylum. But his analysis was vindicated and today it is safer to give birth in a hospital than at home.

In 1854, Dr John Snow dramatically reduced the spread of cholera in London by removing the handle of the Broad Street pump in London's Soho district, forcing local residents to obtain water elsewhere. At the time, the prevailing narrative was that infectious diseases were spread by 'miasma' – noxious particles in the air. Given the vile smell which prevailed across London and other metropolitan areas at the time, this explanation was easy to believe. Like Semmelweis, Snow did not understand why his high-handed intervention was effective – he had simply observed the correlation between the incidence of the disease and the use of the Broad Street facility. After the epidemic subsided, the pump handle was replaced at the demand of users, who resumed their use of water. It was still contaminated by faecal bacteria, but the cholera epidemic was over.

Even in science, we rely on narratives; a good story can be

more compelling than publication of detailed research results. And this is still true in the twenty-first century. For many years, it was conventional wisdom among doctors that stomach ulcers were caused by stress and bad lifestyle leading to a build-up of acid in the stomach. Dr Robin Warren, an Australian pathologist, tried for many years to argue that ulcers were in fact the result of a bacterial infection. In the 1980s, together with fellow Australian Barry Marshall, he studied biopsies from a hundred patients and cultivated a bacterium which became known as *Helicobacter pylori* from some of these biopsies. They found that the organism was present in almost all the patients with gastric inflammations and duodenal and gastric ulcers. Yet it proved difficult to change the dominant narrative. Conventional treatment for ulcers required daily medication, possibly for life. Antacid drugs were therefore a major source of pharmaceutical company profits, but a course of antibiotics cost only a few dollars. So the industry, and the medical profession, were resistant to the idea that ulcers could be cured by antibiotics – in fact, most professionals denied that *H. pylori* was a pathogen at all.[12] So Marshall decided to swallow a solution containing the bacteria, and promptly came down with an attack of gastritis that often leads to ulcers. This drastic experiment changed the narrative. It is now accepted that most gastric ulcers are caused by *H. pylori*, often acquired in early childhood. Marshall and Warren were awarded the Nobel Prize in Medicine in 2005, and millions of people live less painful lives as a result of their tenacious challenge to the prevailing narrative.[13]

Knowledge does not advance through a mechanical process of revising the probabilities people attach to a known list of possible future outcomes as they watch for the twitches on the Bayesian dial. Instead, current conventional wisdom is embodied in a collective narrative which changes in response to debate and challenge. Mostly, the narrative changes incrementally, as the prevalent account of 'what is going on here' becomes more complete. Sometimes, the narrative changes discontinuously – the process of paradigm shift described by the American philosopher of science Thomas Kuhn. F. Scott Fitzgerald, describing his own mental breakdown, observed that 'the test of a first-rate intelligence is the ability to hold two opposed ideas in the mind at the same time, and still retain the ability to function'.[14] And the mark of the first-rate decision-maker confronted by radical uncertainty is to organise action around a reference narrative while still being open to both the possibility that this narrative is false and that alternative narratives might be relevant. This is a very different style of reasoning from Bayesian updating. Millions of people died and more suffered because doctors were slow to allow empirical observation to contradict the conventional narrative.

But we are only occasionally lucky enough to find those first-rate intelligences and first-rate decision-makers. As Paul Samuelson wrote: 'As the great Max Planck, himself the originator of the quantum theory in physics, has said, science makes progress funeral by funeral: the old are never converted by the new doctrines, they simply are replaced by a new generation.'[15] Planck (like Samuelson, a man who received a Nobel Prize for his contribution to paradigm shift) did not in fact say this, but he had expressed the sentiment in less pithy form.[16]

The displacement of the narrative of miasma by the narrative of germs took several decades and in particular required the patient experimental work of the French scientist Louis Pasteur. As he edged towards the truth, Pasteur wrote 'I am on the edge of mysteries and the veil is getting thinner and thinner', famously adding 'fortune favours the prepared mind'.[17] The willingness to challenge a narrative is a key element not only in scientific progress but in good decision-making.

Most central banks reach decisions on interest rates only after a lengthy committee discussion. The purpose of the discussion is to ask 'What is going on here?' (in the economy) and to develop a narrative both to reach and communicate a decision to those affected by a change in interest rates. As experienced by one of the authors, the benefit of the process is to challenge prevailing narratives about the state of the economy. Discussion within the Bank of England's Monetary Policy Committee helped all its members to challenge current views and float ideas. The striking observation is that although the policy decision was rarely unanimous, and was decided by majority vote of the nine-member committee, almost every member wanted to debate 'what is going on here' with other members. In almost twenty years, only one member said they would have been happy to forgo the discussion and email their vote to the Bank.

Business narratives

Alfred Sloan, author of the observation which began this chapter, was chief executive of General Motors from 1923 to 1946. The corporation grew during that time to become the world's largest industrial company. Perhaps no business organisation of that period has been studied as extensively as General Motors. Peter Drucker's 1946 *Concept of the Corporation* was the first best-selling business book and is still in print and widely read; Alfred Chandler's *Strategy and Structure* transformed business history from the hagiographic portrayal of companies and the heroic individuals who led them into the serious academic discipline it is today; and Sloan's own *My Years with General Motors* is one of the few autobiographies by a senior executive worth reading. Ronald Coase's depiction of the theory of the firm, for which he received the Nobel Prize in Economics in 1991, is a thinly disguised account of the General Motors of the inter-war period.

The essence of Sloan's management style was a mixture of a

closely knit senior executive group with considerable organisational decentralisation. On taking control of the corporation, Sloan replaced many of the senior executives with a group of his own choosing, and these individuals continued to be dominant throughout the heyday of the corporation. At the same time, however, divisions of the company – Buick, Cadillac, Chevrolet, Fisher Body etc. – continued to operate as autonomous units; there were no cars badged as General Motors. Sloan emphasised consultation, collegiality and concern to establish 'what is going on here': 'I never give orders. I sell my ideas to my associates if I can. I accept their judgment if they convince me, as they frequently do, that I am wrong. I prefer to appeal to the intelligence of a man rather than attempt to exercise authority over him.'[18]

Of course, these processes of engagement and review described the operations of the management cadre, not the organisation as a whole; the majority of General Motors employees worked on assembly lines and did what they were told. Drucker explained that 'the one definition I could obtain [*sic*] was considered an executive in General Motors was "a man who would be expected to protest officially against a policy decision to which he objects." Such criticism is not only not penalized; it is encouraged.'[19] Within the clearly demarcated boundaries between management and labour, challenge to prevailing narrative was welcomed. Such was the philosophy and to a degree the reality. And, for half a century, it worked.

If Alfred Sloan has a strong claim to have been the best CEO of the twentieth century, Eddie Lampert is establishing a claim to be the worst CEO of the twenty-first century. Lampert took control of the iconic US retailer Sears in 2005, merging it with a struggling downmarket Kmart. Lampert is a former hedge fund manager with no previous experience of retailing, or indeed of any non-financial business. He is notoriously averse to meetings, and issues instructions and reviews progress by video link from his homes in Florida and Connecticut. The headquarters of the companies are in Illinois and its stores are scattered across America.

Lampert is aware of the power of narrative reasoning. 'Dominant narratives develop and get defended primarily by repetition and secondarily by attacks on those who disagree with those narratives . . . They get repeated as if there were no alternative views or possibility of error in their thinking,' he told shareholders in 2010, as he lambasted regulation and government spending.[20] Perhaps that perception of dominant narrative was derived from introspection, since Mr Lampert has a reputation for not welcoming disagreement with his own narratives. A former business partner, Richard Rainwater, described Lampert to *Vanity Fair*: 'He's so obsessed with moving in the direction he wants to move that sometimes people get burned, trampled on, bumped into . . . I think he has gone about alienating himself from almost everyone who he's come into contact with.'[21] Lampert's spectacular 288ft yacht is named *Fountainhead*, after the Ayn Rand novel which is a paean to individualism and to sustained defiance of conformity and convention.

Mr Lampert's economic narrative, following that of Rand, is a libertarian one, and in that spirit he divided the company into separate profit centres competing with each other. These profit centres are not individual stores or regions; there are competing profit centres within the stores themselves.[22] Lampert's retail narrative is focused on a loyalty programme called Shop Your Way. 'From its inception, we envisioned Shop Your Way being the cornerstone of the Sears Holdings' transformation from simply selling goods to being the one stop destination for our members as they navigate everyday life.'[23]

We find ourselves little better informed by this narrative about the nature of the transformation Lampert claims to be bringing to the Sears business. And, it seems, Sears customers are similarly bemused. When Lampert took charge, the stock price was over $100; since then sales have fallen by half, and three quarters of its stores have closed. The lengthy disquisitions with which he addressed shareholders in an annual letter were discontinued. As we were completing this manuscript, Sears had entered Chapter 11 bankruptcy, only for its creditors to learn that the bidder who took over the assets of the failed chain was a group of Mr Lampert's funds.

America's least successful retailer's opinion of narratives contrasts with the opinion of Jeff Bezos, CEO of Amazon, and surely America's most successful modern retailer. Before each meeting at Amazon, executives read a six- to seven-page memo one of them has prepared – silently, for half an hour – before embarking on a discussion of it. These memos are 'narratively structured', with some taking the form of a press release for a proposed product.[24] Bezos believes that narratives are important, and not just because he has become the world's largest bookseller. The timeline for writing a high-quality memo is not a few hours, or even a couple of days, but a week or more. Outside of meetings, he notes that 'the thing I have noticed is that when the anecdotes and the data disagree, the anecdotes are usually right. There's something wrong with the way you're measuring.'[25] And these management practices have been instrumental in making Amazon, in just twenty-three years, one of the most valuable firms in the world.

It is our experience too that when data yield a counter-intuitive result, the most common explanation is that there is something wrong with the data. Not always, of course, and scientific progress from Galileo through Semmelweis and Pasteur to Einstein is the result of momentous experiments in which the data refuted the prevailing narrative. But every young researcher should be ready to ask the question 'Where do those data come from?' Both data and narrative must always be open to challenge.

Lincoln and Thatcher

Abraham Lincoln was sitting round the Cabinet table deliberating with his colleagues. The time came for a decision. Lincoln asked for a vote. All the Secretaries raised their hands in opposition. Then Lincoln raised his own and said, 'Gentlemen, the ayes have it.' Although widely repeated, the story is apocryphal. Yet a good deal of insight can be found in this fictional narrative. Lincoln sought challenge while accepting personal responsibility for the outcome.

Lincoln was elected President after he secured the Republican nomination as a compromise candidate in a convention deadlocked between powerful rivals. But he then appointed the most prominent of these rivals to Cabinet positions. Some, like William Seward, his Secretary of State, continued to believe they should be sitting in the President's chair. Lincoln took advantage of the talents which surrounded him, and responded to the challenges these individuals posed. Most fundamentally, he overcame his previous conviction that colonisation – the repatriation of freed slaves to Africa – should be the final outcome of the conflict, and was persuaded, even after he had been convinced of the need for emancipation, to delay its proclamation until 'the eagle of victory had taken flight'. There is no dispute that Lincoln was one of the greatest of American presidents and his administration one of the most effective.[26]

Margaret Thatcher remains a controversial figure. She achieved a transformation in British politics which no other figure of the time could have accomplished – the conquering of inflation and restoration of sound public finances, deregulation, limitation of the power of trade unions, a programme of privatisation, and the successful conduct of a campaign to regain the tiny Falkland Islands in the South Atlantic after an Argentinian invasion. But after her third election victory in 1987, her style became increasingly autocratic. According to her Employment Secretary, Norman Fowler, 'She was now determined to implement policies that more cautious voices had always argued against ... If a new minister were in any doubt about what was expected, Margaret Thatcher would indelibly mark his card. At one meeting she looked down at the departmental proposals that had been tabled and asked the other ministers, "Does anyone other than the Secretary of State agree with this paper?"'[27]

Fowler resigned from the Cabinet in early 1990 'to spend more time with my family' – a phrase that would subsequently become a cliché among departing executives who did not wish to give explanations for their departure from office (Fowler would again leave his family to become chairman of the Conservative Party under a new leader). Nigel Lawson, Chancellor of the Exchequer, had quit the Cabinet abruptly six months earlier. The resignation of Geoffrey Howe, Deputy Prime Minister, in October 1990 was followed by a blistering speech in the House of Commons in which he said, 'The time has come for others to consider their own response to the tragic conflict of loyalties with which I have myself wrestled for perhaps too long.'[28]

Reflecting four years later on Thatcher's conduct as Prime Minister, Howe observed: 'Her tragedy is that she may be remembered less for the brilliance of her many achievements than for the recklessness with which she later sought to impose her own increasingly uncompromising views.'[29] Howe's resignation speech led to a challenge to her leadership, and by the end of November 1990 Thatcher's tenure at Downing Street was over.

Of course, Thatcher operated in a democracy, and the consequence of her resistance to challenge was that her premiership came to a premature end. The same is true of business people who operate in a competitive market. The story of Sears under Eddie Lampert is one of constant decline, and it is virtually certain that he would have been deposed some years earlier if he had not held a controlling interest in the company. Autocratic leaders in regimes that lack such corrective mechanisms can inflict untold damage – to the careers and even lives of those who challenge the incumbent leader and to the policies of the countries they rule. The tenures of Hitler, Stalin and Mao ended only with the leaders' deaths.

Eisenhower and MacArthur

Eisenhower and MacArthur were the generals who led Allied forces to victory in the European and Pacific theatres respectively. Both harboured ambitions to be President; Eisenhower discreetly, MacArthur rather more publicly. One was courted by both parties to be their presidential candidate in 1952, and when he declared for the Republicans was elected to that office by an overwhelming majority.[30] The other was fired by President Truman for recklessly attempting to expand the Korean War into a potentially nuclear conflict with China.[31] And while MacArthur's initial barnstorming around the United States was greeted with some enthusiasm, this faded as audiences became less and less interested in his bitterness and recrimination.

Both were able commanders, but with very different leadership styles. Whereas Eisenhower sought out different perspectives, MacArthur avoided challenge and resisted bowing to the authority of others. The American soldier-statesman George Marshall once told him he had a court, not a staff; Truman said he didn't understand how the army could 'produce men such as Robert E. Lee, John J. Pershing, Eisenhower and Bradley and at the same time produce Custer, Patton and MacArthur'.[32] (Custer's 'last stand' at Little Bighorn led to the deaths of his entire detachment, and Patton's style was expressed in his notorious injunction to troops 'No bastard ever won a war by dying for his country. He won it by making the other poor dumb bastard die for his country.')[33]

General Montgomery, commander of the British land forces, despised Eisenhower, claiming 'he had no plan of his own ... Eisenhower held conferences to collect ideas; I held conferences to issue orders'.[34] Montgomery himself rivalled MacArthur in arrogance; Winston Churchill reportedly said of him 'in defeat, unbeatable; in victory unbearable'. Churchill selected Eisenhower among the American generals proposed as Supreme Commander (Europe) and even Montgomery acknowledged that he was the man to hold together the diverse group of generals who made up the top echelon of Allied command.

As President, Eisenhower was criticised for being controlled by his Cabinet, and in particular his Secretary of State John Foster Dulles. But Eisenhower was one of the most successful of modern presidents, his approach described by one historian as 'hidden hand leadership'.[35] MacArthur was a brilliant military strategist. His Pacific campaign in the Second World War was successful and he was a competent administrator of Japan. But he made errors in the latter part of the Korean War, and his warnings – that if that campaign was not fought to a victorious conclusion not only Asia but Western Europe would fall to the communists – proved wholly mistaken. His approach was in sharp contrast to the cooler judgement of Eisenhower, who considered escalating the Korean conflict but was persuaded otherwise, and who then successfully promoted and pursued the containment strategy of the diplomat George Kennan.

The result was a presidency of eight years of peace and

economic growth. Even when an armistice in Korea was concluded, few anticipated that the Cold War would remain cold
for another thirty-six years. And in his valedictory address as
President, Eisenhower would be the unexpected issuer of a
prescient warning against the growing power of the military-
industrial complex.

Protecting the reference narrative

The value of challenging narratives is not simply to find the
best possible explanation of what is going on. It is to test the
weaknesses of proposed plans of action, and to secure robustness
and resilience. Eisenhower led the Allied armies which invaded
France in June 1944 in the largest and most meticulously
planned logistical operation in history. On D–Day itself 160,000
troops were landed and three million men were available to support the invasion. Manoeuvres and phoney intelligence helped
persuade the Germans that the operation would take place at the
Pas de Calais and as a result German forces were spread thinly
along the Channel and Atlantic coasts. Eisenhower's approach
can be contrasted with that of Patton: 'We want to get the hell
over there. The quicker we clean up this goddamned mess, the
quicker we can take a little jaunt against the purple pissing Japs
and clean out their nest, too. Before the goddamned Marines
get all of the credit.'[36] Yet Eisenhower knew that many things
might go wrong. The day before the invasion, he prepared a
letter to be published in the event of failure.[37] We doubt if he
used a Bayesian dial to compute the probability that his letter
would be required. In the event, it proved unnecessary.

In pressing the case for probabilistic reasoning, Philip Tetlock
and Daniel Gardner, the appraisers of forecasting and architects
of the 'good judgment project', argue that 'For decades, the
United States had a policy of maintaining the capacity to fight

two wars simultaneously. But why not three? Or four? Why not prepare for an alien invasion while we are at it? The answer hinges on probabilities.'[38] No, it doesn't. There is no basis on which one can form probabilities of an invasion by aliens. The US maintained its 'two war' strategy for a different reason; the narrative which was uppermost in the minds of those who framed the policy was that of the Second World War, in which the country was obliged to fight a land war in Europe against Germany and a naval war in the Pacific against Japan at the same time. But over the subsequent decades the salience of that narrative faded, and it became apparent – not least after the lessons of Vietnam and Iraq had been absorbed – that the post-war era made different and more varied demands on the capabilities of the US military. When Donald Rumsfeld was appointed Defense Secretary by George W. Bush, he expressed scepticism about this two-war policy, and the strategy was finally abandoned under the Obama administration.[39]

The attempt to construct probabilities is a distraction from the more useful task of trying to produce a robust and resilient defence capability to deal with many contingencies, few of which can be described in any but the sketchiest of detail. Britain was taken by surprise when the Argentinians invaded the Falkland Islands in 1982 and the implications for Britain's defence capabilities have reverberated ever since. It is difficult to predict the outbreak or conduct of wars; if it were easier they would be less likely to happen. Military leaders instead undertake wargames in which they test their ability to deal with a variety of hypothetical situations, none of which they actually expect to happen – a process similar in philosophy to Shell's scenario planning. It is difficult to imagine what an alien invasion would look like. The novels and films which describe such an invasion demonstrate the limits of human imagination: neither the aliens nor their technologies are very different from the people and gadgets with which we are familiar. Given the variety of life forms which have evolved on Earth, who knows what intelligent life on another planet might be like? We are stretching the limits of radical uncertainty – but such uncertainty exists. There probably is life elsewhere, but the only honest answer is that we don't know.

There are concrete threats from Islamic terrorists, and unimaginable ones from outer space. But robustness and resilience, not the assignment of arbitrary probabilities to a more or less infinite list of possible contingencies, are the key characteristics of a considered military response to radical uncertainty. And we believe the same is true of strategy formulation in business and finance, for companies and households.

The supposed purpose of the off-site business meetings described in chapter 10 was to review the strategy of the business. If they had been better-facilitated events, they would have begun with a diagnostic phase in which the participants tried to establish 'what is going on here' and moved on to describe a reference narrative – 'to be pulled by the concerns out there rather than being pushed by the concerns in here', in the words of business strategist Henry Mintzberg, who continues 'we shall never really see it all. But we can certainly see it better' (a wise assessment of a world of radical uncertainty).[40] The effective business strategy is a reference narrative – a part qualitative, part quantitative scenario which defines the company's realistic expectations and describes the means of achieving them. Having proceeded in this way, the participants would then have considered and evaluated the risks to that business strategy or narrative, to establish whether it was robust and resilient to multiple (and possibly unknown) contingencies.

When Steve Jobs told Dick Rumelt that he would wait for the next big thing, he was not simply hoping that something would turn up. He knew that in the fast-moving world of consumer electronics at the turn of the century there would be exciting developments, but that it was hubristic to imagine that anyone could predict with any precision what they were going to be. He knew and understood his company's strengths relative to its competitors. He positioned the business to take advantage of a wide range of possibilities. Successful strategies involve matching the distinctive capabilities of the corporation to the (sometimes static, sometimes fast-moving) environment in which it operates.

When we plan a holiday, we begin from a reference narrative: the expectations we have of an enjoyable and relaxing experience. And then we recognise the possible risks – we might be delayed on the way to the airport, we might suffer a stomach upset from unfamiliar food – and we take steps to ensure that our reference narrative is robust and resilient to these specific risks. We leave home with time to spare; we put medications in our luggage. When we undertake a building project, we do the same – we discuss the plans in the schedule with the builder, and we try to describe the principal things which might go wrong. The nearest commonly used approximation to 'Bayesian updating' we have seen is the risk maps which it is almost obligatory to present to corporate boards. Typically these maps will consist of long lists of so-called 'risk factors', often accompanied by gradings of relative importance and illuminated with red or green traffic light signals. These documents follow a standard design, and are at best tenuously related to any statement of business strategy. The reports are typically received in near silence and the fact of their receipt minuted. The purpose is less to ensure that risks do not materialise than to provide evidence that the risks have been considered, or at least described – evidence which can be mobilised if these risks do materialise.

The better approach is to try to identify the small number of risks which might seriously derail the reference narrative, and to consider the contingencies which might be deployed to deal with them. If the Pakistani army intervenes, do the SEALs shoot their way out or wait for the President to negotiate a political solution? (Admiral William McRaven, who oversaw the operation, favoured negotiation, but was overruled by Obama, who feared the fresh risks which might ensue if another group of Americans was held hostage by a foreign power.)[41] If that list of material risks is not small, then its length calls into question the reference narrative itself; but this requires a judgement of materiality. In the real world, the list of everything that might go wrong, however slight and however unlikely, is more or less infinite.

Robert McNamara and his repentance

A willingness to change one's mind in the face of new evidence is a good thing. But the problem is to discern what constitutes new evidence. A belief that a coin is fair and that a head and tail are equally likely is challenged by a sequence of only heads. It is possible to calculate the odds of a particular sequence occurring. But the Vietnam War was not the one thousandth repetition of a game.

Robert McNamara was one of the 'whizz kids', young men who pioneered numerical operations management and transformed military logistics in the Second World War. In 1946, Henry Ford Jr, who had just taken over control of Ford Motors from his father, recognised the need to recruit fresh talent and hired the 'whizz kids' en bloc. McNamara, applying the techniques of operations management, quickly rose through the company and became its president. In 1961, John Kennedy appointed him Secretary of Defense – the two men were the same age – and McNamara continued to serve under President

Johnson until 1968. He was instrumental in the decision to deploy a naval blockade rather than an airstrike on Cuba.

But, obsessed with data, he reached decisions quickly with little external debate. His main challenge as Secretary of Defense was Vietnam, and his was the most influential voice on American policy after the President. In 1962, McNamara told one reporter, 'every quantitative measurement we have shows that we're winning'.[42] As the Vietnam War escalated, McNamara was the mainstay of this policy of pursuing military success. But by 1966 he was beginning to have doubts about America's ability to impose a military solution. In a memorandum that McNamara sent to President Johnson in May 1967, he wrote, 'the war in Vietnam is acquiring a momentum of its own that must be stopped'.[43] In 1968, just before leaving office to take up a position at the World Bank, he talked privately about the 'crushing futility' of bombing.[44]

The interesting question is why one of the most intelligent men ever to serve in a US administration allowed himself to be caught up in one of the worst policy disasters in US history. The historian Max Hastings poses the question of why there was so little debate and argument within the administration.[45] McNamara, long retired, observed that President Johnson did not encourage 'a full and open debate on issues that so sharply and clearly divided his most senior advisers'.[46] But in 1968 the debate exploded in public and Johnson was driven from the presidency. Reflecting on the Vietnam debacle, McNamara wrote in his memoirs that a major cause was 'over and over again ... we failed to address fundamental issues; our failure to identify them was not recognised; and deep-seated disagreements among the president's advisers about how to proceed were neither surfaced nor resolved'.[47] The Johnson administration adopted a narrative about Vietnam without genuine enquiry into what was going on, and resisted any challenge to the prevailing narrative. In his attempt to reduce the conflict to a quantitative appraisal of respective munitions stocks and body counts – the arithmetic of conventional warfare – McNamara failed to ask deeper questions about the nature and motivation of the enemy, in other words 'What is going on here?' Did America learn from its experience in Vietnam? In 2003, the United States invaded Iraq.

Part IV

Economics and Uncertainty

17

·

THE WORLD OF FINANCE

Things can be said in equations, impressively, even
arrogantly, which are so nonsensical that they would
embarrass even the author if spelled out in words.

—J. HOOVER MACKIN[1]

Thales of Miletus, a Greek philosopher, made important
discoveries in geometry and careful observations of the
frequency of natural events. His prediction of the solar eclipse in
585 BC was described by Isaac Asimov as 'the birth of science'.[2]
Thales also used his scientific knowledge to anticipate an especially plentiful olive harvest. He bought options on all the olive
presses in Miletus, and when demand soared he rented them out
at a substantial profit. According to Aristotle, Thales' motive
was not primarily pecuniary; he aimed to provide an answer to
the question so often thrown at philosophers and economists: 'If
you're so smart, why aren't you rich?'[3] It is unlikely that much
of this story is true but it is instructive, nonetheless. Careful

use of small models, well-structured narratives, and rationality based on reason and logic can be the source of worldly success as well as academic kudos.

Antonio, the Merchant of Venice, anticipated Paul Samuelson's discussion of the difference between single and multiple bets (recall that Samuelson was puzzled that a colleague might decline a wager with positive expected value if offered only once but accept if the proposal were repeated many times). Antonio explained the benefits of a diversified portfolio to Salarino, who worried about exposure to individual risks:

> My ventures are not in one bottom trusted,
> Nor to one place; nor is my whole estate
> Upon the fortune of this present year:
> Therefore my merchandise makes me not sad.[4]

And Antonio was confident of capital adequacy. Having stood as guarantor for Shylock's bond, he states:

> Why, fear not, man; I will not forfeit it:
> Within these two months, that's a month before
> This bond expires, I do expect return
> Of thrice three times the value of this bond.[5]

But Antonio's plans are thrown off course. First, the low compound probability of a sequence of adverse contingencies materialises. (In the event, the resulting mark to market valuation of Antonio's wealth, which damages his credit rating, proves too pessimistic; part of his argosy returns to port towards the end of the play). Second, radical uncertainty intervenes. An off-model event – the elopement of Shylock's daughter Jessica – leads the vengeful moneylender to seek enforcement of the bond despite the intervention of a lender of last resort with ample liquidity. Third, a further off-model event, the intervention of Portia, resolves the issue in Antonio's favour. But heedless of radical uncertainty, and over-influenced by his own probabilistic model, Antonio puts his life in danger. The narrative captures the essence of the model of diversification. And diversification is central to risk management in the face of radical uncertainty.

The meaning of risk and risk aversion

One of the authors attended a meeting between some business people representing major defence contractors, and a group of Treasury economists who had recently studied economics and finance before graduating from leading universities. The issue was the extent to which the contractors should be rewarded for assuming the considerable risks involved in major projects. Many such projects were by their nature unique. The economists argued that because the risk of overruns on an idiosyncratic project was uncorrelated with other risks to which the company and its shareholders might be subject, and the amounts were small relative to the total wealth of these shareholders, no compensation for such risk was necessary. Some even proposed that the appropriate rate of return was the yield on safe government bonds. The contractors, some of whom had recently made large losses on projects which far overran their budgets, looked incredulously at the economists as though they were inhabitants of another planet.

The two parties were unable to engage because they both used the word 'risk' but gave it entirely different meanings. For the economists, taught to view uncertainty through the lens of axiomatic rationality, risk was described by the variability of asset returns. For the contractors, risk meant that the project might not be completed as anticipated – that their reference narrative, in which the work was taken through to a successful conclusion, would not materialise in practice. They thought it unlikely that the project would proceed ahead of expectations, and such an outcome was certainly not what they had in mind when they talked about 'risks'. No doubt they also had in mind the risks to their own positions within the firm if the project went badly wrong. The meaning of risk depends on both the individual and the context. Both interpretations of risk are potentially relevant but the one maintained by the contractors reproduces the meaning of risk in ordinary language. And it is that interpretation – risk as failure to fulfil the central elements of the reference narrative – which we will continue to use, in this book and in our everyday lives.

In earlier chapters we described some risk lovers who have changed society – Richard Branson, Winston Churchill, Steve Jobs, Elon Musk, George Orwell. Ignaz Semmelweis, whose dogmatic conviction of his own rightness drove him to insanity but helped save the lives of millions of women. Barry Marshall, who changed medical practice and won a Nobel Prize by infecting himself with bacteria. None of this behaviour has anything to do with the utility of wealth functions of these individuals. And as we learn more about neurophysiology, we may come to understand such behaviour better by monitoring activity in the prefrontal cortex and the handling of the chemical dopamine than by proselytising for axiomatic rationality.

Risk-averse individuals are those who are reluctant to move outside the comfort zone of their established reference narrative. They seek certainties in a world of radical uncertainty by trying to limit themselves to a small, stationary world. They are people like Mr Stevens, the obsessively professional butler in *The Remains of the Day*, or Mr Banks in Disney's *Mary Poppins*. While the collapse of the East German state brought opportunities for many, others were disconcerted by the loss of the security offered by the constraints of its repressive regime. Risk lovers such as Musk or Orwell, by contrast, are constantly in search of new reference narratives – and through that search change, for better and worse, the reference narratives of everyone else.

Small-world models in a large world

The approach to risk we described above is in line with the thinking of those defence contractors. Risk is determined by the circumstances, and reference narrative, of individuals or businesses. Finance professionals, like those Treasury economists, think differently. In their world, risk is an impersonal, objective property of assets. A major contribution to such thinking originated in the work of Harry Markowitz at the University of Chicago in the 1950s.[6] His central idea was that one should judge the risk associated with an investment portfolio by looking not just at the risk associated with each individual asset, but at the relationship between the returns on different assets – the issue Antonio attempted to explain to Salarino. If the returns on different assets move closely together – the returns are highly correlated – then there is little benefit from diversification. But if the returns are uncorrelated then adding more assets reduces the variability of the portfolio as a whole. An 'efficient portfolio' is one that minimises the variability of the return on the portfolio for a given average rate of return.

Milton Friedman was one of Markowitz's examiners and reportedly was admiring of the work but concerned that it should be described as mathematics rather than economics.[7] In any event, Markowitz was awarded his PhD, developed a career in both academia and investment management, and in 1990 was awarded the Nobel Prize for his efficient portfolio model. That model remains today one of the pillars of modern financial economics, along with the capital asset pricing model (CAPM), which asks what a financial market equilibrium would look like if assets were priced in accordance with the efficient portfolio approach, and the efficient market hypothesis, described in chapter 14, which asserts that market prices reflect all available information.

The efficient portfolio model, the capital asset pricing model and the efficient market hypothesis are each good illustrations of how simple models can be used to illuminate complex problems. The critical insight of the portfolio approach is that risk is a property of a portfolio as a whole, and cannot be judged by simple addition of the risks associated with each element of that portfolio. Risk depends on context, and an action that is risky in one context may reduce risk in another. There is no such thing as a risky asset, only a risky collection of assets, a point which is still not well understood by many investors and financial advisers today. Markowitz's mathematics, not in fact very difficult, elegantly demonstrates and clarifies this insight.[8] The capital asset pricing model shows how the value of any financial asset depends on the properties of that asset relative to all other available assets, and provides a framework for understanding these relationships. Arbitrage – trade between assets with related but not necessarily identical characteristics – has been the basis of profitable strategies for many traders. And the CAPM makes a distinction between *specific* risk associated with a particular security – Will the defence contract be completed to time and budget? Will a drug pass clinical trials? Is an oil company's well productive? – and the *market* risk associated with general economic conditions relevant to all securities: if there's a recession, then we would expect the value of most securities to fall. Market risk is inescapable, specific risk diversifiable, and therefore market risk should be rewarded more generously than specific risk. This was the counter-intuitive argument of the Treasury economists.

The efficient market hypothesis is a powerful reality check. Everyone knows that Amazon is a successful retailer and that Apple products are attractive to consumers – and the stock price of these companies already reflects this. Anyone who is offered, or believes he or she has identified, an unexploited business or investment opportunity should ask themselves 'Why have other people not already availed themselves of that opportunity?' Of course, there may be a good answer to the question. But posing it can help you avoid expensive mistakes.

Portfolio theory, the capital asset pricing model and the efficient market hypothesis are useful, indeed indispensable, models, but none of them describe 'the world as it really is'. When people take these financial models too literally, populate them with invented numbers and base important decisions on them, the models become misleading, even dangerous. As they did in the global financial crisis. And on many other occasions. The large US hedge fund Long Term Capital Management collapsed in 1998 because the fund and its Nobel Prize-winning advisers, including Robert C. Merton, had too much faith in their models. (Merton was the son of the sociologist Robert K. Merton, whom we described in chapter 3 as the first social scientist to formulate the general issue of reflexivity – an issue which became highly pertinent as traders aware of LTCM's strategies positioned themselves to profit from the inability of the fund to maintain them.) The error is to mistake small-world for 'wind tunnel' models (see chapter 19) which replicate the large world in which we live.

We are glad we know about these small-world models and we think we are better investors for knowing about them. But we do not make the mistake of taking them too seriously, and we certainly do not believe that they describe 'the world as it really is'. Both Markowitz and Savage were well aware that their theories applied only to such small worlds, but their warnings have been largely ignored. Markowitz himself, asked about his own portfolio decisions in planning for retirement, responded: 'I should have computed the historical co-variances of the asset classes and drawn an efficient frontier. Instead, I visualized my grief if the stock market went way up and I wasn't in it – or if it went way down and I was completely in it. My intention was to minimize my future regret. So I split my contributions 50/50 between bonds and equities.'[9] Markowitz's description of his own behaviour corresponded to Loewenstein's model of 'risk as feelings' – his decision reflecting the hopes and fears he held in anticipation, rather than the maximisation of subjective expected utility implied in his own models.

Financial regulation

Those Treasury economists described above had been indoctrinated with the conventional wisdom of academic finance. Other graduates of the same courses had found employment in regulatory agencies. They equated risk with asset price volatility. Nowhere has the tension between different meanings of risk been more stark, and more damaging, than in financial regulation.

In the spring of 2007, the UK bank Northern Rock announced at its AGM that it was the best-capitalised bank in the United Kingdom, and would be returning 'surplus' capital to shareholders.[10] And according to the internationally agreed risk calculations embodied in the Basel regulations that had come into force at the beginning of the year, it was indeed the best-capitalised bank in Britain. The risk weights mandated by those new regulations assumed that mortgages were among the safest assets in which a bank could invest; however, if you stripped out the risk weighting, the liabilities of Northern Rock were eighty times its equity capital.

Worse, the very detailed regulations which defined 'capital adequacy' took no account of how the bank structured the liability side of its balance sheet — the bank's own borrowings which funded its mortgage lending. Under an ambitious young chief executive, Adam Applegarth, Northern Rock had moved far from the traditional building society it had been only ten years earlier, which took deposits from retail savers and lent them to home buyers. The bank now financed much of its lending from day-to-day borrowing in money markets before selling packages of securitised mortgages to other financial institutions. In August 2007 both the market for short-term borrowing and the market for re-selling packages of loans dried up and the bank simply ran out of money. Queues formed outside the company's branches as savers scrambled to get what was left in the tills. The panic subsided after the government guaranteed deposits and the Bank of England provided financial support. In February 2008, beyond rescue, Northern Rock was nationalised.

Clever people, sitting in Basel and drawn from around the world, had sought since the 1980s to set a global framework for bank regulation. But the approaches to risk which they had devised turned out to be misleading. They were wrong to believe that uncertainty could be encapsulated in fixed numerical risk weights loosely based on historical experience. The possibility that funding from wholesale markets would simply become unavailable, and that investor appetite for mortgage-backed securities would abruptly diminish, was not considered. Both commercial bankers and regulators believed that while retail funding might suddenly dry up, wholesale funding would always be available at a price. This reasonable assumption turned out to be wrong. Northern Rock was felled by an off-model event.

The abject failure of models in the global financial crisis

has not dented their popularity among regulators. European directives – known as Solvency II – have extended the use of similar models to the insurance sector, and a pension fund regime is likely to follow. But insurance companies rarely fail as a result of low-probability events described by risk models, but in consequence of off-model issues such as fraud or – as at Northern Rock – the realisation of narratives which had not been imagined by management or regulators.

Pension models

In 1991 the ebullient fraudster Robert Maxwell disappeared from his yacht in the Canaries and was found to have looted the *Daily Mirror* pension funds to support his crumbling business empire. Far more extensive regulation of occupational pensions followed. 'Defined benefit' schemes promise pensions based on past earnings rather than on past contributions. The UK 2004 Pensions Act requires these schemes to compute a 'technical valuation' of their liabilities. This requires a discounted cash flow calculation using projections of prices, earnings and investment returns over the life of the scheme, which by its nature will exceed fifty years. The trustees of the scheme must compare this number with the current assets of the scheme, and take steps to eliminate any deficit.

Of course, no one has any idea what prices, earnings and investment returns will be in fifty years' time. Unavoidably ignorant of all but a few of the numbers they need to complete their spreadsheet, the actuaries who advise these schemes invent all the numbers (technically the responsibility for verifying their assumptions lies with the scheme trustees, who have even less idea what the relevant numbers might be). They visit the client with a standard template loaded on their computer; this is essentially the same whether the client is a small employer with fifty staff or the whole university system of the UK. In chapter 20 we describe how widespread similar inventiveness in the face of inescapable ignorance has become.

The requirement to make plans to eliminate the 'deficit' shown by the 'technical valuation', enforced by the Pensions Regulator, was introduced in an attempt to ensure that if the scheme had to close, there would be sufficient funds to guarantee the pension promises. Laudable at first sight, that requirement now threatens to raise contributions to unaffordable levels. And it has already led to the closure of virtually all such schemes in the UK private sector. The regulatory regime seeks to reduce risk – in a world of radical uncertainty risk can never be eliminated – by prescribing a reference narrative so demanding and financially unattractive that no one will sensibly aspire to it. A combination of well-meaning but misguided regulation and the misuse of models has materially reduced the prospects of a secure retirement for a majority of the British population. Robert Maxwell inflicted more damage from the grave than in his discreditable life.

What could be more sensible than ensuring that pension schemes can meet their liabilities, or the requirement that banks issue enough equity capital to absorb likely losses? Yet the pensioners who worked for the *Daily Mirror* suffered not because contributions were too low but because Maxwell stole them. Equally, in the financial crisis risk-adjusted capital was a very poor predictor of which banks would fail, whereas simple leverage ratios were a better indicator. We do not believe, given past behaviour in the sector, that the financial services industry can be trusted to operate a banking system or to handle investors' money without strong regulation. But well-intentioned regulation has gone off the rails in creating an extraordinarily complicated and detailed rulebook. Such regulation cannot take into account all, or even many, relevant circumstances in a world of radical uncertainty. But the typical response to the demonstration of the inadequacy of such rules has been to write yet further rules. The recent experience of financial regulation illustrates the importance of avoiding the pretence of knowledge. We do not know when the next crisis will come, nor what it will look like. We need simple, robust principles to guide us, not tens of thousands of pages of detailed rules which elevate the duty of compliance over the spirit of proper stewardship of other people's money. We have made suggestions for such reforms in our own earlier writings. The more regulators attempt to define precise, detailed rules, which confuse more than clarify, the more likely is a counter-productive outcome. If only someone would stand back and ask 'What is going on here?' rather than tweak processes which have acquired their own seemingly irresistible momentum!

More narratives of finance

In chapter 12 we described how Robert Shiller has argued that swings in sentiment are important in understanding why large and disruptive changes in economic behaviour occur – whether stock market bubbles and crashes or sharp collapses in output during a depression.[11]

But Shiller's focus on narratives is rather one-sided. He uses the concept to explain behaviour which others have called 'fads and fashions'. In other words, he sees narratives as a departure from 'rational' optimising behaviour and therefore as irrational and emotional, despite their importance in explaining behaviour. In his words, 'among normal people, narratives are often somewhat dishonest and manipulative'[12] and 'economic narratives thus tend to involve ... actions that one might take for no better reason than hearing narratives of other people doing these things'.[13]

But the importance of narratives stems not from a weakness in human behaviour but from the nature of decision-making in a world of radical uncertainty. It is true that in certain financial markets narratives are occasionally 'dishonest and manipulative', but normal people make honest use of narratives to understand their environment and guide decisions under radical uncertainty. A narrative is needed to answer the question 'What is going on here?'

Contagious narratives often infect financial markets after some real events have genuinely altered economic fundamentals. Since the spread of the narrative is necessarily gradual, those who adopt it first may reap rich profits as latecomers climb on the bandwagon, and commentators exaggerate the speed and scale with which the consequences of economic developments will take effect. As has been widely recognised, people tend to overstate the short-run impact of a new technology and to understate the long-run impact.

The seminal work on financial bubbles is Charles Mackay's *Extraordinary Popular Delusions and the Madness of Crowds*. This book, written during the 1840s railway mania, traced an early history of contagious financial folly through the Dutch tulip craze of the 1630s and the South Sea bubble a century later. Recent scholarship is more sceptical about the nature and scale of the Dutch tulip craze, which seems to have been particularly silly. But the reference to delusion fails to recognise the kernel of truth commonly found in these narratives. No one can doubt that the growth of international trade from the eighteenth century, the construction of railways in the nineteenth century or the development of radio and commercial aviation in the 1920s were transformational economic events.

Similarly, investors were right to recognise that the successes of Japanese manufacturers in the 1970s and 1980s not only led to that country's emergence as a major economic power but were a precursor to a wider phenomenon of growth in emerging market economies. This did not, however, remotely justify the values attached to Japanese stocks and property as the asset price bubble inflated. The same overreach and reaction to it was repeated almost immediately in other emerging markets in the decade that followed, in the 'new economy' bubble of 1999, and during the convergence of interest rates across the Continent which followed the adoption of the euro. And in all these cases investors lost very large amounts of money as greater realism finally set in. The collapse of a narrative is a more rapid process than its transmission. And as we write, the financial press is full of perhaps the thinnest story since tulips to give rise to a bubble – the imagined future takeover of the world monetary system by crypto-currencies. Like other popular fictions, the Bitcoin phenomenon combines several perennial narratives – in this case, a libertarian vision of a world free of state intervention, the power of a magic technology, and the mystery of 'money creation'.

Round-up at Jackson Hole

In the 1980s, bond markets, once staid backwaters of the financial system, became the focus of an exciting new narrative based on securitisation. The idea was that lending institutions – banks, mortgage providers and finance companies – could package their loans into tradeable securities and sell them, mainly to other financial institutions. By doing so, they could supposedly offer more attractive combinations of risk and return than had previously been available in bond markets.

There were, and are, two possible rationales for such trade. One narrative saw securitisation as a mechanism enabling lenders to spread and diversify lending risks, thus lowering the costs of finance and – perhaps – allowing some of the benefits of these lower financing costs to be passed on to home buyers and small businesses. An alternative narrative was that securitisation provided the mechanism by which risks could be passed from those who understood or should have understood them – the original underwriters – to people who understood them less well.

But whatever the explanation, the immediate consequence was that a great deal of money was made by those who packaged and traded these securities. The volume of such products grew exponentially, and still more money could be made by those who built packages of securities from packages of securities (such as 'collateralised debt obligations squared'). And as the market grew, sales people searched more and more aggressively for new borrowers whose loans could be profitably securitised. They found them even among individuals with little or nothing in the way of assets and income, in what became the US subprime mortgage market.

Every year in late August, in Jackson Hole, Wyoming, among the splendour of the Grand Tetons, central bankers gather at the Economic Policy Symposium convened by the Federal Reserve Bank of Kansas City to discuss the latest ideas and challenges facing the world economy. In 2005, Raghuram Rajan, then the chief economist of the IMF and later Governor of the Reserve Bank of India, argued that financial deregulation and the rise of new financial instruments had increased the incentive for investors to take greater risks which they did not fully understand.[14] The warning was prescient, but not well received; most of those present were inclined to agree, some in vigorous language, with an earlier judgement of chairman Alan Greenspan that 'A major contributor to the dispersion of risk in recent decades has been the wide-ranging development of markets in securitized bank loans, credit card receivables, and commercial and residential mortgages. These markets have tailored the risks associated with holding such assets to fit the preferences of a broader spectrum of investors.'[15]

Referring to derivative instruments, Greenspan said, 'These increasingly complex financial instruments have been especial contributors, particularly over the past couple of stressful years, to the development of a far more flexible, efficient, and resilient financial system than existed just a quarter-century ago.'[16] The dominant and widely shared narrative was that efficient markets ensured that risks were being dispersed to those who best understood them and were best able to bear them. That narrative did not survive the shock of events in 2008.

The 2005 Jackson Hole meeting was a special occasion to say farewell to Alan Greenspan, who was about to retire from the Federal Reserve after eighteen years as chairman. Much unfair opprobrium has been directed towards Mr Greenspan since the financial crisis began just two years later; in his farewell address, Greenspan did warn that 'History has not dealt kindly with the aftermath of protracted periods of low risk premiums'.[17] In that, he was certainly correct.

The limits of finance theory

One of the authors spent more than a decade in business schools. He recalls describing the field of finance to potential supporters as 'the jewel in the crown' of business schools, and there was some justification for that claim. The subject was intellectually rigorous, its leading practitioners published in respected journals and consulted for financial institutions. Its students found little difficulty in obtaining interesting and remunerative jobs in government and finance. The subject appeared to combine academic substance and practical utility.

And yet in a wider sense the project with which the subject began fifty years ago, built on the contributions of Harry Markowitz, William Sharpe and Eugene Fama, has ended in failure. We note two very different demonstrations of that failure. One is that the models used by regulators and financial institutions, directly derived from academic research in finance, not only failed to prevent the 2007–08 crisis but actively contributed to it.

Another is to look at the achievements of the most successful investors of the era – Warren Buffett, George Soros and Jim Simons. Each has built fortunes of tens of billions of dollars. They are representative of three very different styles of investing. Buffett's investment company, Berkshire Hathaway, owns large, often controlling and in many cases 100% interests in a wide variety of businesses. Buffett's philosophy is to buy into businesses with strong competitive advantages, install outstanding managers – or in many cases find them within a company – and grant them almost total discretion. He has said that his favoured holding period for stocks is 'forever'. Soros, famous first for his bet against sterling as its peg to the European Monetary System collapsed in 1992, and most recently for his philanthropy (oriented towards the promotion of liberal democracy and recently towards new approaches to economics), relies on his capacity to distinguish between false and well-founded economic narratives. Simons, formerly a mathematics professor, employs brilliant (maths and physics) PhDs to devise algorithmic trading strategies to take very short-term positions in securities.

But there is more in common in the approaches of these men than appears at first sight. Their exceptional intelligence is one; they have responded to the challenge of 'if you're so smart why aren't you rich?' It is evident from Soros's writings that he has much in common with Thales of Miletus, and would prefer to be remembered for his ideas than his wealth. Buffett's letters – and all-day stage performances at the Berkshire Hathaway AGM in Omaha, Nebraska – dispense genuine insights in the guise of homespun country wisdom. Simons has published papers in top mathematical journals. Another common characteristic is a certain humility. Buffett and Soros repeatedly emphasise the limits of their knowledge. And Simons claims that he will never seek to override his algorithms.[18] He emphasises that he is a mathematician, not a student of market psychology, business strategy or macroeconomics.

And all ignore – are even contemptuous of – the corpus of finance theory based on portfolio theory, the capital asset pricing model and the efficient market hypothesis. Indeed that corpus of knowledge implies that they could not have succeeded as they have. These financial models emphasise points of which all investors should be aware – the benefits of diversification, the extent to which different assets offer genuine opportunities for diversification, and the degree to which information is incorporated in securities prices. But the lesson of experience is that there is no single approach to financial markets which makes money or explains 'what is going on here', no single narrative of 'the financial world as it really is'. There is a multiplicity of valid approaches, and the appropriate tools, model-based or narrative, are specific to context and to the skills and judgement of the investor. We can indeed benefit from the insights of both Thales of Miletus and Harry Markowitz, and learn from both of the contradictory narratives of the world of finance propagated by Gene Fama and Bob Shiller. But we must also recognise the limits to the insights we derive from their small-world models.

There are those in the finance sector who create programs which purport to define strategies that would maximise risk-adjusted returns. But these programs do nothing of the kind. Radical uncertainty precludes optimising behaviour. In the world as it is, we cope rather than optimise. The numbers which were used in these calculations are invented. Or they are derived from historic data series and assume a non-existent stationarity in the world. Struggling to cope with a large world which they could only imperfectly understand, the proponents of these calculations invented a small world which gave them the satisfaction of clear-cut answers. And financial regulators claiming to monitor risk in the financial system did the same. It is understandable that people who are given a job which they cannot do find instead a more limited task which they *can* do.

18

——— • ———

RADICAL UNCERTAINTY, INSURANCE AND INVESTMENT

What economists imagine to be rational forecasting
would be considered obviously irrational by anyone in
the real world who is minimally rational.

—ROMAN FRYDMAN[1]

The underwriters of the Lloyd's insurance market in the
City of London sit in a large room, each at their own cubicle, known as a box – as they have done for centuries. Brokers
walk around the room, attempting to place risks. One of the
authors sat at a box, listening to the process. The most interesting proposal was for insurance of a valuable private art collection
worth several hundred million dollars, stored in a highly secure
facility somewhere in Switzerland. The broker did not reveal
the identity of the owner, although only a handful of individuals
enjoy the necessary financial resources and artistic interests. The

underwriter, who specialised in this kind of insurance, made a shrewd, private guess as to the name of the client. Then he proposed a price. The broker moved on to several other boxes. The practice of the market is that if a respected underwriter accepts a risk – places his name on a slip – then others will give serious consideration to adding their own names, taking a share of the risk, at the suggested price.

The author asked the underwriter how he determined the price. There was no basis on which he could have calculated the probability of loss or the amount of loss. It was possible, but unlikely, that an intrepid thief might walk off with the collection; but more likely that one or two paintings would disappear, to be ransomed or sold to an eccentric who was content to enjoy possession, unknown to any but his most trusted crooked friends. The underwriter mused about these things but made no calculation. He explained that he just felt this was the right price for this kind of risk. Asked how he knew, he rather reluctantly explained that he had made adjustments up and down to the price which had been quoted for vaguely similar risks in the past. And pressed further, he acknowledged that if there had been recent claims in respect of art thefts, or even unusual claims which had nothing much to do with art, the price would have gone up. But this was not a Bayesian dial; the underwriter's mental processes were narrative rather than statistical. His assessment was a matter of informed judgement, but to describe it as gut feeling or intuition is an inadequate description of his capabilities. Only a handful of individuals are trusted by the insurance market to exercise such judgement.

At the end of that day, the underwriter explained that there were two things he and his colleagues could do well from their London location. They could underwrite highly idiosyncratic risks, such as the art collection. There was much experience in the market, and the decentralised organisation of Lloyd's meant that individual underwriters could make decisions without having to write complex explanations of their reasoning for risk committees. And they could underwrite very routine risks, such as motor accidents, where there were well-established databases they could analyse.

Until the 1990s, Lloyd's operated on the basis of unlimited liability accepted by 'names', rich individuals most of whom were not professionally involved in insurance or even finance. The names agreed to share the losses incurred by syndicates (underwriting groups) of which they were members and receive a corresponding share of the premiums. The costs of bearing risks were therefore pooled among a large number of relatively wealthy individuals. Effectively, the capital of the market was the resources of the English upper middle class. But from the 1970s the structure of social relationships which had sustained the financial system of the City of London broke down in the face of globalisation and meritocracy, and Lloyd's was brought to its knees through a combination of venality and incompetence. The residual losses of that era were assumed by Warren Buffett's Berkshire Hathaway in return for a large payment by Lloyd's. Buffett's company enjoyed both diversification and resources sufficient to meet any likely liability, and its simple decision-making structure was able, like that of the underwriter, to assume obligations too complex and difficult for more bureaucratic organisations to manage.

Lloyd's, and insurers generally, can operate at the two poles of near randomness and extreme radical uncertainty; the cases in between, of partial and asymmetric knowledge, are more difficult. Conventional insurers struggle with radical uncertainty, leaving the field to organisations such as Lloyd's or Berkshire Hathaway, which are sceptical of conventional financial wisdom.

Insurance as mutualisation

The mutualisation of risks by sharing them among socially connected groups long precedes the development of the formal practices which today we call insurance. The management of uncertainty among the !Kung involved no calculated relationship between the mutual exchange of favours and the expectation of return. Contracts of insurance of the kind we are familiar with today came into existence only in the seventeenth century.[2] But only for some risks. Commercial insurers covered risks such as fire, mortality and eventually motor accidents, but many even of those risks were managed in affinity groups in which a spirit of solidarity prevailed; people who worked in the same occupation or lived near to each other. The Scottish Widows Fund began in March 1812, when a number of Scots gentlemen gathered in the Royal Exchange in Edinburgh 'to establish a general fund for securing provisions to widows, sisters and other females'.[3] The vast majority of nineteenth-century insurers were mutuals – the owners were the customers. Only in the 1980s did mutuality begin to disappear from the insurance sector – and from finance more generally. In 2000, the Scottish Widows Fund was acquired by Lloyds Bank (which shares only a name with the Lloyd's insurance market) and became the bank's insurance and asset management subsidiary.

Some idiosyncratic uncertainties are insured through specially written contracts – the anonymous art collector could go to Lloyd's to insure his purchases. When the whisky producer Cutty Sark got cold feet about its promised reward of £1 million to anyone who produced the Loch Ness monster, it was also able to insure this 'risk' with Lloyd's.[4] If you must, you can insure against aliens landing on Earth before 2025.[5]

Great international reinsurance companies, such as Swiss Re and Berkshire Hathaway, which take over the risk of large losses from smaller or retail-focused insurers, effectively represent schemes of risk pooling and reciprocal assistance – mutualisation – managed on a global scale. They are the principal underwriters of idiosyncratic risk and we do not think it is an accident that, apart from the unique Lloyd's marketplace, the major reinsurers are based outside the financial centres of London and New York, where conventional probabilistically based risk management practices prevail.

In 1954, the Fourteenth International Congress of Actuaries met to consider the 'conditions that must subsist for a risk to be assurable'.[6] More than four hundred pages of rules and justifications were set out, and insuring the capture of the Loch Ness monster fell far outside them. Swiss Re claims that, for a risk to be reinsurable, 'it must be possible to quantify the probability that the insured event will occur'.[7] Nonetheless, Lloyd's assumed the monster risk. The great reinsurers employ armies of modellers. We cannot sensibly assign probabilities to many idiosyncratic risks – including many that Swiss Re assumes. But Frank Knight's observation 'if you cannot measure, measure anyhow' is as true in Zurich as in Chicago.

Obama shrewdly observed, when presented with a variety of estimates, 'what you started getting was probabilities that disguised uncertainty as opposed to actually providing you with more useful information'. The intelligence agencies did not know whether the man in the compound was bin Laden – but they did know a great deal. To say we cannot predict, or specify a probability distribution, is not to say we know nothing about the future. No reinsurer knows the probability that a category 5 hurricane will make landfall in Florida next summer. But that does not mean that models of climate and records of the damage caused by previous hurricanes have no role to play in their assessments, just that the underwriter must exercise good judgement. As he did in pricing the risk of the art collection. And the economist or banker or business strategist must do the same.

What makes commercial insurance possible is that the data-bases are good, but not too good. The outcomes for individuals are unknown but there is a well-documented and roughly stationary frequency distribution. Young men with sports cars will pay much higher premiums than elderly ladies with decades of unblemished motoring records. But within each class of risk, the question of which young men and which elderly ladies experience accidents is unknown. And this information is not known either by the insured or the insurer, otherwise the problem of adverse selection – only higher-risk individuals would seek insurance and only lower-risk individuals would be offered it – would prevent the emergence of an insurance market. Insurance is possible only when ignorance of specific future outcomes is considerable, and that ignorance is common to both insurer and insured.

The advance of big data means that this element of randomness will steadily diminish. Insurers can already obtain information through a device that monitors your personal driving behaviour, and the premium can mirror more and more exactly the losses which will result from that behaviour. As insurance becomes precisely tailored to the individual, and the element of randomness is reduced, it ceases to be insurance.[8] As more data for medical diagnostics become available we will progressively know more and more about the health prospects of any individual. And as Alexa reports back to her employers, more and more data about everything become available. When risks become certainties they cease to be insurable. For this reason, most countries, now including the United States, severely limit the ability of insurers to select their policy-holders or differentiate their premiums. This limits the scope for actuarial calculation of premiums based on probabilistic assessment of frequencies and returns insurance to a system of reciprocal assistance within the community.

Pensions

The bread which a retired person needs today was baked by someone working today. Pensions usually involve some implicit or explicit intergenerational sharing – a process of mutualisation which anticipates that reciprocal obligations will be passed down through generations. Through most of history, such provision took place primarily within the extended family – and the largest part of the burden of care of physical needs is still handled in this way today – although the community would commonly act as backstop. As communities became larger, these reciprocal obligations were stretched, and demanded formalisation. John Graunt, the London cloth merchant who pioneered the collection of mortality statistics, was a member of the Drapers Company, one of many organisations which regulated trade and provided mutual assistance. Those Scottish gentlemen gathered in Edinburgh to agree the basis on which they would provide for each other's widows. And the development of probabilistic mathematics allowed such obligations to be quantified. The Equitable Life Assurance Society, whose demise we observed in chapter 4, was founded in 1761 with the objective of determining subscriptions on actuarial principles. Tension between the twin principles of probabilistic reasoning and recognition of mutual obligations continues to be central to the evolution of insurance and pension provision.

Another change to the form of intergenerational risk-sharing came from the changing nature of employment. The aristocratic landowner understood that obligations to the estate worker lasted until that worker's death, and were inherited with the estate. The state, and large paternalistic employers such as banks and railways, took a similar view. These organisations took for granted that they would last for ever, and established trust funds to support their commitments. The benefits and obligations of pension provision can be mutualised in a variety of ways. They may be managed by a group of people who have shared social ties, as in early nineteenth-century Edinburgh. They may be largely assumed by the state, as in France. They may be managed by employers, either on an individual basis or as a group, which may relate to a particular industry, or be an affinity group of people who share a common interest or location. There are two conditions for such mutualisation to be effective. First, the group must be sufficiently large to share a variety of risks associated with investment returns, individual mortality experience, and the evolution of overall life expectancy. And second, there needs to be reason for confidence that the group which provides retirement security will remain in existence indefinitely.

If we look today at pension provision around the world, almost every possible combination of schemes can be found. A popular taxonomy identifies three pillars: a basic level of provision which is provided by the state; a second tier which is most often associated with employment; and a third level funded through the savings of individual households. The third pillar and possibly the second require investment decisions. As the evolution of the computer industry demonstrated, advances in technology mean that the life expectancy of companies is far from indefinite. So pension provision by individual employers is, in most cases, either an inefficient or a risky basis for pension provision. As a result, mutualisation will in future be based on other criteria, whether through the state or other collective entities.

Certainty is not the same as security

In the world of expected utility, if there is no uncertainty about outcome there is no risk. But certainty is not the same as absence of risk; the man who knows he will be executed tomorrow has certainty but his life is clearly at risk. Admiral Stockdale, while uncertain how he would survive his imprisonment in Vietnam, nonetheless never doubted that he would. The only reference narrative which allowed him to survive was one which envisaged his eventual release. In the context of pensions the search for illusory certainty has exposed millions to risk, depriving them of the opportunity to fulfil their realistic expectations of retirement security. Certainty is unattainable and the price of near certainty unaffordable.

A representative pension promise involves a commitment to a thirty-year-old, for example, to provide an amount of money, linked to the consumer price index, in fifty years' time when that person is eighty. How can such a commitment be guaranteed or underwritten? Government index-linked bonds with a lengthy maturity, which exist in many countries including the UK, US and Germany, appear to offer the possibility of such a guarantee. The credit risk associated with lending to these governments is extremely small, although it is talked up by ratings agencies and by advocates of curbs on government expenditure. These securities offer miserable returns. The situation in the UK is particularly extreme. The cost of buying a 2062 index bond in January 2019 was £208. That bond will be redeemed in 2062 for £100 (this is not a misprint) linked to the retail prices index. There is also an annual return of 0.2%, itself linked to the retail prices index. But since the terms on which this minuscule return could be reinvested are uncertain, if you want certainty it is best to set aside the full £208.

And the transaction is vulnerable to other political risks, including government interference with the compilation of the index. In 1974 the UK government introduced subsidies for products which were included in the index, with a clear intention of reducing the size of index-linked wage adjustments.[9] And in 2011 legislation was passed which altered references in many private contracts to the retail prices index to substitute an alternative measure, the consumer price index.[10] In countries with less independent statistical agencies, interference with indices is commonplace. Any pension provision entails the likelihood of further revisions to the taxation of pension funds either in the hands of individuals or of the funds themselves.

Thus liability matching can never be more than approximate. It is fair to ask, however, whether the volatility of the real value in 2062 of the 2062 bond is likely to be greater or less than the volatility of the real value of a portfolio containing a diversified range of physical assets. Such a portfolio might include a hotel on Sydney Harbour, an office block in California, agricultural land in England with development potential, and an apartment block in central Berlin. That portfolio would offer a yield substantially in excess of the indexed bond, and the probability that it would have lost more than half of its real value over the coming fifty years is minute. Unless there is a nuclear apocalypse.

The focus on extreme percentiles raises the more fundamental issue of the Viniar problem – extreme outcomes rarely come from 25 standard deviation observations, but from off-model events. The historic extremes of the UK and US stock markets were the falls of 1972–4 and 1929–33 respectively. These were not adverse drawings from some underlying stationary probability distribution. They occurred because in each period the narrative that the capitalist system was coming to an end gained currency, and not without justification. In the end, these fears were shown to be misplaced, and the markets recovered. An American investor who remained asleep from 1926 to 1936 or a Briton who suffered similar catalepsy from 1972 to 1982 would have noticed nothing untoward in his or her portfolio.[11]

But apocalyptic events of the kind which were feared at these times in Britain and the United States, but did not occur, did in fact occur in China, Germany, Russia and some other countries in the course of the twentieth century. There are no certainties in the world of business and finance. And such certainty as is available comes from achieving robustness and resilience through diversification rather than from committing to one 'safe' asset type. Risk is a personal experience, not a characteristic of an asset.

The sceptical financial economist

In the previous chapter, we described the three pillars of modern finance theory – efficient portfolio theory, the capital asset pricing model and the efficient market hypothesis. As we suggested there, the rational investor in a world of radical uncertainty must know these models, but should not take them either too literally or too seriously. The central insight of the Markowitz portfolio frontier model is that risk is the product of a portfolio as a whole and is not the sum of the risks associated with the individual investments within it. The importance of this observation for practical investment strategies can hardly be overstated. And this insight remains valid whether the meaning attached to the concept of risk is, as we prefer, based on a reference narrative, corresponding to the dictionary's definition as 'failure to meet realistic expectations', or the financial economist's definition of risk as 'variance of a probability distribution'.

Within portfolio theory, it is necessary to know the variance of the probability distribution of daily gains or losses on each of the securities in your portfolio, and also the *covariances* between these securities – whether a bad day for one is likely to be associated with a good or bad day for the other. In the analysis of covariances, 'beta' is the correlation between the movement of the stock price of a particular security and the movement of the market as a whole. Thus we would expect a consumer goods company selling to customers in developed economies to have a beta close to one. But if that business were to greatly increase its leverage, thus making its equity returns more volatile, its beta would exceed one, while a business whose activities were unrelated to the performance of the general economy might have a low beta. This was the argument that Treasury economists were using in their talks with the defence contractors, discussed in the previous chapter.

Looking at calculations of beta coefficients in practice reveals that very many are close to one, even if the activities and the leverage of the companies are very different. The reason is that beta coefficients are typically calculated over relatively short time periods, during which all stocks are influenced, positively or negatively, by changes in the prevailing market narrative. The growth figures are better than expected; the unemployment data worse. Extensive liquidity support given to markets by central banks has affected the prices of all assets, with the result that recent correlations between all assets appear to be high.

But radical uncertainty means that such calculations of correlations based on historic data sets represent a fool's errand. In most cases we simply do not know the variance of the relevant probability distribution, or the covariances. Returns on investment are not random drawings from a known and stationary underlying process. Yet much financial analysis and much financial regulation are predicated on the assumption that they are.

Perhaps that is why, although we know many people who construct efficient portfolio frontiers for their clients, we know none who use that approach to manage their own personal finances. Still, it is possible to do better than Markowitz himself, with his decision to put half his retirement fund in stocks and half in bonds. Pay attention to the fundamentals which are relevant to long-term performance of different kinds of assets. Understand that broad asset categories such as 'emerging market

stocks' and 'real estate' are convenient for the analysis of investment consultants, but are insufficiently granular to give insight
into the real impact of diversification. Over any but short time
periods, the factors that influence the performance of a retailer
in Vietnam and an oil services company in Brazil, or the returns
from an apartment block in Berlin and agricultural land in
Australia, are likely to be very different. Illustrative numerical
simulations may be illuminating, but are never a substitute for
asking 'What is going on here?'

Behind the efficient portfolio frontier and capital asset pricing
model lies the idea that individuals make similar assessments
of the underlying probability distribution. Since the model
assumes that everyone in this small world interprets risk in the
same way, differing only in their 'risk appetite', the proposition
that higher risk implies higher reward and vice versa follows
inexorably.

But risk means different things to different people. Risk
for the government is very different from risk for the defence
contractor, very different for someone saving for the deposit
on a house than for someone seeking to provide for a secure
retirement. Risk for an asset manager, whose reference narrative involves continued employment, is the risk of being fired
for underperforming compared to his or her peers. And for a
devotee of the capital asset pricing model, risk is the variance
of short-term stock price movements. If *your* concept of risk is
very different from that of the market as a whole, you can minimise your risk at other people's expense. Broad diversification
becomes 'a free lunch' reducing risk without cost. Once you
recognise that day-to-day price movements are not an indication of risk but a measure of meaningless noise in markets,
you can achieve your longer-term objectives at lower cost by
learning to ignore such fluctuations. There can be reward – not
without risk, but with little risk – through building a diversified

portfolio, turning off your computer, and thinking hard, though not necessarily frequently, about 'what is going on here'.

Broad diversification, involving building a portfolio which will be robust and resilient to unpredictable events, is the best protection against radical uncertainty, because most radically uncertain events will have a significant long-run effect on only some of the assets which you own. The kind of diversification which leads Silicon Valley titans to buy rural properties in New Zealand which they hope will survive the apocalypse – and which has become sufficiently popular to lead that country to impose restrictions on purchases of domestic properties by foreigners – is perhaps fanciful, but the style of thought is sound.[12]

Volatility is the investor's friend

Almost a century ago, Benjamin Graham, perhaps the first and most admired investment guru, and mentor to Warren Buffett, enunciated the proposition that the randomness of stock prices was a benefit rather than a problem for the intelligent investor. Graham used the metaphor of the volatile 'Mr Market', who would on a daily basis make random offers to buy and sell. In chapter 5, we described Buffett's different baseball metaphor: 'the pitcher throws you General Motors at 47! U.S. Steel at 39! and nobody calls a strike on you'.[13] And, he emphasised, you need not swing at all.

The metaphor assumes some ability to recognise over- and undervalued stocks, an ability which Graham and Buffett possessed in abundance. But Graham also identified and extolled the benefits of dollar cost averaging, the notion that an investor will benefit even if he or she knows nothing of the principles of stock valuation or the fundamentals of the company by simply investing a constant amount of money in the market on a regular basis. Even without any conscious intention or knowledge of investment strategy or corporate behaviour, this system buys more stock when prices are low and buys less when prices are high.

This approach to market volatility is precisely the opposite of the conventional view which has dominated finance theory for the last half century, which equates risk and volatility and shies away from securities with volatile prices. In Buffett's words, 'volatility is almost universally used as a proxy for risk. Though this pedagogic assumption makes for easy teaching, it is dead wrong.'[14] And similarly, the benefits of diversification are the result of elements of randomness in the distribution of investment returns. We are sometimes asked 'What is the cost of excluding particular kinds of investment from a portfolio?' For example, some investors may have principled objections to holding stocks in companies which trade in tobacco or armaments. But the answer must be 'we do not know'. If we did know, we would either exclude such stocks from our portfolio anyway, or invest in nothing else. But we do know that diversification reduces the risk that the reference narrative – the reliable emergency fund, the security of retirement, the continued growth of the college endowment – might not be realised.

The efficient market hypothesis, taken literally, implies that the investment success of George Soros, Warren Buffett and Jim Simons is impossible. Frank Knight, who recognised that radical uncertainty generates profit opportunities, has been vindicated by the extraordinary riches accumulated by these men. And the efficient market hypothesis is shown to be illuminating – an indispensable model – without being true. Buffett, history's most successful investor, was well aware of this. He wrote of proponents of the efficient market hypothesis: 'Observing correctly that the market was *frequently* efficient, they went on to conclude incorrectly that it was *always* efficient. The difference between these propositions is night and day.'[15] For Buffett, the value of that difference is $70 billion – the reward for taking advantage of Knight's insightful identification of the relationship between radical uncertainty and entrepreneurship.

19

---•---

(MIS)UNDERSTANDING
MACROECONOMICS

I have attended too many seminars, in some great
universities, which degenerated into a closed language
game played by a coven of initiates who prized obscure
self-referential congratulation over honest engagement
with reality.

—MICHAEL IGNATIEFF[1]

In 2003, the Nobel laureate Robert Lucas used his Presidential
Address to the American Economic Association to argue:
'My thesis in this lecture is that macroeconomics ... has succeeded: its central problem of depression prevention has been
solved, for all practical purposes, and has in fact been solved for
many decades.'[2]

After the financial crisis of 2007–08, the industrialised
world experienced the most severe downturn since the Great
Depression in the 1930s, and the decade following saw a

prolonged period of unusually slow economic growth. Financial crises, like wars, have occurred many times. But neither crises nor wars are the result of a stationary process; each is a unique event. The advances in economic theory lauded by Lucas did not prevent a major downturn in the world economy, nor did they give policy-makers the tools they required to deal with that downturn. The models he described assumed a stable and unchanging structure of the economy and could not cope with unique events that derived from the essential non-stationarity of a market economy.

'Wind tunnel' models in macroeconomics

When mathematical and statistical methods became widespread in economics in the post-war period, many economists believed it was possible to construct economic models of the 'wind tunnel' type. The models of the 1950s and 1960s were large but essentially mechanical – some literally so. The MONIAC (Monetary National Income Analogue Computer) machine, designed by a New Zealand engineer, Bill Phillips, studying at the London School of Economics, was a hydraulic model based on the ideas put forward in Keynes' *General Theory*. About a dozen such machines were constructed and used in economics departments around the world (one was magnificently rebuilt at the London School of Economics – it is now on display in the Mathematics Gallery of the Science Museum in London – and another working model is in the Engineering Department of Cambridge University).

As computers became more powerful, electronics eased out hydraulics, and Keynesian models were developed and run on computers. The approach of the Keynesian era was essentially pragmatic, supposing that simple relationships between economic aggregates would remain stable. And the 1950s and

1960s appeared to be a golden age of stability and growth in the global economy. But the foundations were much less secure than appearances suggested. Inflation accelerated slowly throughout much of the post-war period, and by the 1970s had challenged the complacent view that Keynesian demand management could eliminate economic instability. The Phillips curve (another invention of the creator of the eponymous machine) related wage increases to unemployment, and claimed to be a stable empirical relationship like the consumption function.[3] It implied a long-run trade-off between inflation and unemployment; the price of reducing one was to increase the other. But any idea that these observations were the outcome of a stationary process was discredited by the experience of steadily higher levels of both inflation and unemployment in the 1960s and 1970s.

One of the authors was employed on the Cambridge Growth Project to build one of the earliest econometric models of the UK economy. Such models usefully emphasise that different parts of the economy cannot evolve in totally separate ways. They capture accounting constraints which ensure that spending on consumption, investment, exports and by government must add up to total national income and output. The system of national accounts which was developed and adopted around the world from the 1930s to the 1950s still provides an indispensable framework for organising and understanding economic data. But the Cambridge Growth Project model could not explain changes in wages and prices, nor short-run movements in the level of total output. These depended upon expectations of future inflation and growth.

If Keynes had still been alive, he could have told his Cambridge colleagues that radical uncertainty was fundamental to understanding the economy, and that expectations about an uncertain future are not easily modelled by a computer. In

1939, Keynes published a review of the pioneering statistical study by the Dutchman Jan Tinbergen. That study was one of the foundations of the new subject of econometrics.[4] Keynes' main criticism of the new approach was that it assumed stationarity of relationships: 'the most important condition is that the environment in all relevant respects, other than the fluctuations in those factors of which we take particular account, should be uniform and homogeneous over a period of time'.[5] Keynes said of Tinbergen, 'The worst of him is that he is much more interested in getting on with the job than in spending time in deciding whether the job is worth getting on with.'[6] With prescience, Keynes foresaw temptations which subsequent generations would not resist.

The rational expectations revolution

The bridge builders had believed, with justification, that wind conditions on the east coast of Scotland or through the Tacoma Narrows would not be very different when construction was completed from those on which the plans had been based. But if the wind responded to the outcomes of the simulations, no such assumption could be made. And economies did react to forecasts and simulations. It was necessary to give expectations a larger role in economic models. The drive to achieve this was led by Lucas, also now in Chicago, whose 1976 'Lucas critique' was the death knell of the econometric macroeconomic models of the previous decade. If policies influenced expectations, policy-makers could not rely on the stationarity of underlying economic processes. The analogy with physical relationships, such as the impact of wind on structures, did not hold.

An obvious means of responding to the prior neglect of expectations would have been to undertake empirical work on the beliefs about the future which consumers and those

engaged in business and finance actually held, and the processes by which they established and changed such beliefs. But
little such research was undertaken. The new macroeconomic
theorists instead followed a different approach; Chicago economist Ronald Coase attributed a satirical description of it to the
English economist Ely Devons: 'If economists wished to study
the horse, they wouldn't go and look at horses. They'd sit in
their studies and say to themselves, "What would I do if I were
a horse?"'[7]

These theorists – Chicago was and remains a centre of their
thinking – followed the dominant paradigm of the universal applicability of subjective probability. Assumptions about
expectations were deductions about behaviour based on axiomatic rationality. The resulting theory of 'rational expectations'
requires that the expectations of all agents – firms, households
and governments – must be consistent not only with each other
but with the model which purports to describe it. This approach
assumed not only that there was a true model of 'the world as it
really is', not only that economists knew what the model was,
not only that everyone – from the titans of Wall Street to the
humblest of peasant farmers – knew what that model was, but
that they all formed consistent expectations on the basis of that
knowledge and acted on these expectations. In the words of
Thomas Sargent, whose 1979 text[8] literally 'wrote the book'
on the new thinking, 'There is a communism of models. All
agents inside the model, the econometrician, and God share the
same model.'[9]

Models based on the assumption of rational expectations may
have helped to shed light on some important issues – explaining
why, for example, attempts by governments to reduce unemployment to an unsustainably low level will lead not to higher
output but to accelerating inflation as expectations of wages and
prices increase. As in other areas, such 'small world' models can

be useful parables. But they do not describe the world as it is, and fail to help us understand depressions and financial crises. So we believe that economists *should* go and look at horses – observe the ways in which expectations are formed and how these expectations influence behaviour. And while the critics of the 1970s were right to·direct more attention to how individual choices affect aggregate outcomes, 'the secret of our success' as humans is that we benefit from both individual and collective intelligence. Humans are social animals and there is more to the behaviour of the group than the aggregate of independent individual decisions. Expectations need to be studied at both individual and aggregate level.

Completeness and the grand auction

Ever since the eighteenth century, when Adam Ferguson described 'spontaneous order' and Adam Smith supposedly lauded the 'invisible hand', the notion that decentralised markets might allocate resources more efficiently than central planning had been a theme of economic analysis. In the nineteenth century, Leon Walras, a French economist working at the University of Lausanne, attempted to express in a system of equations the idea that the uncoordinated decisions of millions of people might produce aggregate outcomes that were not only coherent but efficient.[10]

But Walrasian analysis only reached fruition when, as described in chapter 14, new and powerful mathematical tools were applied to economics by Kenneth Arrow and Gerard Debreu.[11] For some devotees of laissez faire, this was the analysis they had been waiting for – a rigorous mathematical demonstration of the maxim that 'you can't buck the market'. Building on Walras, Arrow and Debreu envisaged a 'grand auction', to which consumers brought their demand curves, workers and resource owners their supply curves, and producers their technical capabilities. In this 'grand auction' the price mechanism secured an equilibrium which reconciled all these demands and supplies and in which no one could be better off without making someone else worse off – all possible mutually advantageous trades had been realised.   ·

But in a radically uncertain world, markets are necessarily incomplete. There is no market in oil for delivery in 2075, for example, because there are so many uncertainties that no one is willing to trade. Even if airline companies would like to buy aviation fuel ahead of time to hedge their risks, they baulk at the risk of doing so if they cannot sell their tickets in advance. How many of us would contemplate buying a flight to a specified airport on 3 August 2030, contingent on the weather at that destination at that time and the political situation in that country in that year? There is no market for the services of an umbrella on a wet day in 2025 because the cost of setting up such a market far exceeds the benefits of doing so. And there was no present or future market in smartphones in 1997 because no one had thought of smartphones at the time. Arrow and Debreu recognised that they were describing an imaginary world akin to that of *Through the Looking-Glass*. And they interpreted that world as a rhetorical device, like those literary fictions, illustrative of propositions which might – or might not – be true in any real world. In a magisterial survey of that modelled world, written two decades later with another great economic theorist, Frank Hahn of Cambridge, Arrow described what he and his colleagues had been attempting to do: 'The immediate "common sense" answer to the question "what will an economy motivated by individual greed and controlled by a very large number of different agents look like?" is probably; There will be chaos ... Quite a different answer has long been claimed true ... In attempting to answer the question could it be true we learn a good deal about how it might not be true.'[12]

Earlier in his career, Lucas too had explained that we should not take such models literally: we should be engaged in 'the construction of a mechanical artificial world populated by inter-acting robots that economics typically studies'.[13] An economic theory is something that 'can be put on a computer and run'.[14] Lucas called structures like these 'analogue economies', because they are, in a sense, complete economic systems. They loosely resemble the world, but a world so pared down that everything about them is either known, or can be made up. Such allegories may provide valuable insights into real worlds but do not describe them — and are certainly not representations of 'the world as it really is'.

The Arrow–Debreu world is a 'small world' of the kind described by Savage. In fact, their economy *is* the small world described by Savage, and to which his probabilistic reasoning applies; in that world, he explained, 'acts and decisions, like events, are timeless. The person decides "now" once for all; there is nothing for him to wait for, because his one decision provides for all contingencies.'[15]

This equivalence between complete markets and the axio-matic basis for probabilistic reasoning is no academic footnote. Many economists today are prepared to accept that markets are incomplete and yet hang on to the view that a complete set of subjective probabilities exists and people can be assumed to behave as if they were maximising their subjective expected utility. But these views are essentially incompatible. Savage's rational decision-maker made a 'grand decision', contemporane-ous with the 'grand auction'. Savage's world was also the world of Arrow and Debreu, and, like Arrow and Debreu, Savage was clear that the proposition that the models closely replicated real worlds was, in his own words, 'utterly ridiculous'.[16]

Making policy in a small world

Many of the followers of Lucas forgot that the purpose of building models is to use imagination so that we can tell plausible stories about the real world. They shared the pleasure chess players derive from living in a world whose rules have been completely defined, and in which there are prizes and promotions for the winners. The fantasy world of *Alice in Wonderland* is better still – as the Dodo explained, 'everybody has won and all must have prizes'.[17] The models such economists designed proved more useful to the playing of an intellectual game rather than describing the world in which companies and people are struggling with the challenge of an unknowable future. Rational expectations models partition the world into the known – the 'communism of models' – and the unknowable – forces and events which, since they are not anticipated by everyone, are not anticipated by anyone. Economic predictions fail when models are disrupted by permanent shifts and temporary shocks. But since the shifts and the shocks are the product of forces which are unknowable, there is, sadly, nothing more that can usefully be said.

Tinbergen had been a pioneer of econometrics – the application of rigorous statistical methods to economic data; and the properties of error terms – the difference between the out-turn and the forecast in economic models – were central to that subject. In macroeconomics the error terms were rebranded as 'shocks'.[18] But if the 'shock' is simply the deviation between the prediction of the model and the reality of the world, we learn nothing by attaching the label 'shock' to these error terms. To go further we have to be able to gain insight into the origins of the shocks, and perhaps be able to formulate some probability distribution or narrative account of their occurrence. The nineteenth-century economist W. S. Jevons propounded a similar thesis.[19] His argument, not then entirely without empirical justification, was that business cycles were the result of fluctuations in nature. In particular, variations in sunspot activity influenced climatic conditions, which in turn affected the prices and volumes of agricultural products, which had consequential effects in other sectors of the economy. Jevons' narrative identified the sources of the shocks, and described the ways in which they gave rise to economic cycles. And even though the determinants of sunspots were not understood, empirical information about their incidence was available.

More recently, economic fluctuations have been attributed to both unexpected changes in demand and supply conditions — 'preference shocks' and 'productivity shocks' — as well as to 'frictions' that slow the adjustment of wages and prices, and also expectations, to their equilibrium values. The underlying growth trend of the economy was interrupted from time to time by these shocks and a return to equilibrium slowed by these frictions. Of course, consumer tastes do change and respond to new products and new fashions. And productivity is affected by disruptive innovation. But there was no explanation of the sources, let alone the size and volatility, of preference shifts or disruptive innovation, nor could their incidence be characterised by any probability distribution. There was only the need for some deus ex machina to reconcile the model with observed data.[20] Productivity has been described as the measure of our ignorance.[21] The distribution of productivity shocks is then the measure of our ignorance of our ignorance.

In a laudable wish to meet the hopes and expectations of policy-makers, business people and television viewers, the economics profession has pursued the holy grail of a macroeconomic model that would make accurate forecasts. The early attempts foundered, as we have seen, on the failure to appreciate that apparently stable empirical relationships could suddenly break down when, for example, the government changes the nature of its policy intervention (the Lucas critique). The intellectual appeal of basing forecasts on a rigorous theoretical foundation describing the behaviour of individuals and the economy is easily understood. But the programme of model-building which searches for a stable underlying set of structural relationships could be made consistent with observations of the economy only by the introduction of the shocks and shifts about which nothing could usefully be said. The result was that phenomena such as the financial crisis or the Great Depression could be explained only in terms of unanticipated developments in technology or a sudden preference for leisure rather than work. Such so-called 'real business cycle' models have generated few persuasive explanations of large movements in the economy.[22] And the presence in such models of 'frictions' – the complexity of the world of millions of individuals learning and adapting to changes in the structure of the economy – meant that forecasts were reasonably accurate only when nothing much was happening, and were wildly inaccurate in the face of any significant event, such as the financial crisis.

The search for a single comprehensive forecasting model of the economy is fruitless. It will come as a surprise to many that the forecasting models used by most central banks had no ability to explain borrowing or lending as the models had no place for banks, ignored most financial assets, and assumed that all people were identical. In short, these models assumed an economy shorn of a financial system, and an economic crisis originating in the financial system was therefore impossible. Such a small-world model might generate insights into the role of central bank independence and inflation targets, but it could not sensibly answer the question 'What is going on here?' in the financial crisis.[23] The pretence that every important macroeconomic issue could be explained in terms of a single model was a major error.

Radical uncertainty and non-stationarity go hand in hand. There is no stable structure of the world about which we could learn from past experience and use to extrapolate future behaviour. We live in a world of incomplete markets in which there are simply no price signals to guide us back to an efficient equilibrium. There are times when expectations have a life of their own.[24] As a result, the models used by central banks perform quite well when nothing very much is happening and fail dramatically when something big occurs – precisely the moment when the model might have something to offer beyond mere extrapolation of the past.

Forecasting without apology

Economic forecasters have a particularly poor track record of forecasting material downturns in the economy. In 2016, *The Economist* examined country forecasts made by the International Monetary Fund (IMF) in its Spring World Economic Outlook. Of the 207 recessions – defined as a fall in output between the year in which the forecast was made and the following year – the World Economic Outlook had predicted precisely none of them.[25] This finding is a stunning indictment of our ability to forecast movements in aggregate economic activity. It seems that we can forecast changes in GDP when there really aren't any but that we cannot forecast large swings in economic activity.

During any major economic crisis, someone will claim to have forecast its occurrence. There are those who specialise in gloomy predictions and, like stopped clocks, are occasionally right. But few economists predicted the financial crisis of 2007–08. And the models used by central banks and private sector forecasters proved better at forecasting output and inflation during the period of economic stability between the early 1990s and the onset of the crisis – when the best forecast was to extrapolate from the recent past – than they were at predicting the onset of the near collapse of the banking system in the industrialised world. But it was obviously more important to be able to forecast the latter than the former.

The demand for forecasts seems as persistent as scepticism about their value.[26] Yet the addiction to economic forecasting, and even claims for its success, continue. In 2010, the European Central Bank published a technical paper reviewing the performance of its model of the European economy which concluded that its forecasting performance had been 'quite impressive'.[27] The paper did not reference the 2007–08 crisis. Jean-Claude Trichet, then president of the institution which built the model and employed the authors of the paper, took a rather different view: 'As a policy-maker during the crisis, I found the available models of limited help. In fact, I would go further: in the face of the crisis, we felt abandoned by conventional tools.'[28] And his experience was reproduced in central banks and finance ministries around the world.

Managing the economy

In models used by international agencies and central banks, beliefs are guided over time towards the correct rational expectation defined by the model. And if we are unsure which is the correct model then statistical learning leads to the right choice. This might make sense in a stationary world. But in a non-stationary world there is no underlying probability distribution or model to discover.

The process of forming expectations is one in which the views of friends and colleagues, the stories in the *Daily Mail* or the *New York Times*, the news and prognostications on Fox News or BBC, play an important role. We are social animals, even in – and perhaps especially in – the trading rooms of investment banks. People talk to each other and learn from each other. They read the same *Daily Mail* and *New York Times*, and Fox News and BBC show the same pictures on every screen. Social media have speeded up this process. Traders imitate each other and may try to outwit each other. It is entirely in accordance with reason and logic to learn from other people's mistakes rather than wait and learn only from one's own.

Beliefs are embodied in a narrative, and the prevailing narrative can change in an abrupt or discontinuous fashion when a sufficiently large number of people see evidence that leads them to change their view. Such evidence might be derived from fresh regression analysis. Or from watching pictures of bewildered former Lehman employees carrying their possessions into the street in cardboard boxes. Or from messages conveyed by social media. The events of September 2008 changed the prevailing narrative and led to discontinuous changes in expectations. No one had imagined that the sophisticated American financial system would find itself on the brink of collapse. Central banks were not prepared to deal with the consequences of such a failure. Compared with the vast array of financial instruments in the world, the simplicity of a single financial asset in the textbook model did not generate insights, and so central banks relied more on a study of financial history than the predictions of econometric models.

When discovering the next big thing, Steve Jobs was not selecting from a menu of existing options, but using his imagination to create something completely new. That is the essence of radical uncertainty. Equally, Nobel Prizes in Economics are not awarded simply for developing the logical implications of a known set of conditions, but for imaginative new ideas which generate flashes of inspiration to stimulate work by other economists. It is strange that radical uncertainty, which captures exactly the world in which economists do their research, is so absent from their formalisation of how the world works.

Engineering versus economics

Edward Prescott, architect of real business cycle theory, makes the claim that 'the methodologies used in aerospace engineering and macroeconomics to make quantitative predictions are remarkably similar'. In support of this assertion, he cites a former colleague at the University of Minnesota, Graham Candler, professor of engineering and consultant to NASA, who describes his approach to aeronautics thus:

> I try to predict what happens when a spacecraft enters the atmosphere of a planet ... We attack the problem from two sides. First, we break the problem into well-defined parts and use theory and experiment to determine specific parameters under controlled conditions ... The second approach to modelling the flow field is to determine what parameters really matter to the design ... Usually with this parametric uncertainty analysis it is possible to isolate several critical parameters that require particular attention ... we fully recognise that representation of the world will never be hundred percent accurate.[29]

The engineer tackles the complex real-world problem by positing a series of small worlds whose behaviour can be understood, and in this way identifies the factors which really matter in understanding the performance of the spacecraft and its behaviour. This is how practical knowledge is advanced.

The reader can judge the validity of the assertion that the methods of aeronautics and economics are 'remarkably similar' by comparing Candler's account with the parallel description Prescott provides of an instance of his own work:

The study that began in late 1999 was motivated by the question of whether the stock market was overvalued and about to crash. At that time people did not know how to use this theory to obtain an accurate answer to this question and relied on historical relations such as price–earnings ratios to answer the question . . . the tax and regulatory system had to be modelled explicitly. For example, we set the model's tax rate on corporate distributions equal to the average marginal tax rates on distributions. This is calibration because in the model world this tax rate is the same for all individuals when in fact it is not . . . we deal with the fact that corporations have large stocks of unmeasured productive assets and that these assets are an important part of the value of corporations, being stocks of knowledge resulting from investment in research and development, organization capital and brand capital. We figure out how to estimate this stock of unmeasured capital using national accounts data and the equilibrium conditions that the after–tax return on measured and unmeasured capital are equal.

A theory is tested through successful use. The theory correctly predicts the great variation in the value of the stock market in relation to GDP, which varied by a factor of 2.5 in the United States and by a factor of three in the United Kingdom in the 1960–2000 period.[30]

The contrast between the humility of Candler's account and the hubris of Prescott's is immediately apparent. But more importantly, even a superficial reading of the two descriptions reveals that there is no equivalence whatever between the methods of the two authors, beyond the fact that both are dealing with systems which are imperfectly understood. The engineer is undertaking empirical research to discover what works; the economist is manipulating data to support a priori assertions.

While Candler recognises that 'representation of the world will never be hundred percent accurate' he rightly believes he can identify the critical uncertainties; the stock market, however, is suffused with radical uncertainty. And, as a result, NASA is successful in executing missions of extraordinary complexity while Prescott, despite the implicit claim, does not have the slightest idea whether the stock market is or is not overvalued at any particular time.

Aeronautical engineers know 'what is going on here' – not completely, but sufficiently to build aircraft which are (with the unfortunate exceptions we have noted) safe to fly and spacecraft which complete their missions. Candler begins by defining the scope of his expertise: 'I try to predict what happens when a spacecraft enters the atmosphere of a planet'. Prescott, too, seeks to predict: 'The study that began in late 1999 was motivated by the question of whether the stock market was overvalued and about to crash. At that time people did not know how to use this theory to obtain an accurate answer to this question . . .' The comparison reveals a fundamental difference between the two tasks. If a theory 'tested through successful use' was available which could determine whether the stock market was overvalued and about to crash – of course there is no such theory – that knowledge would itself change the value of the stock market. That is the essence of the Lucas critique which we described above, and of the efficient market hypothesis. (As a matter of history, the stock market in late 1999 was overvalued and about to crash and a few months later did crash, but the problem of identifying *when* it would crash was altogether different from and harder than the problem of *whether* it would crash.)

Having identified a smaller-world problem within the larger world of space missions, Candler goes on to identify the two critical elements governing his predictions – the level of heat transfer and the aerodynamic performance of the craft. This is the beginning of a more extensive strategy of breaking the whole problem into well-defined parts which can be analysed separately, and is precisely the opposite approach to the macro-economist's demand for a single general equilibrium model with sufficient simplifying assumptions to render it computationally feasible. Candler states that the basic equations of aerodynamic flow are well established, but that a complete model involves over a hundred parameters. However, previous work has shown that only a limited number of these parameters have much impact on the out-turn. Research is undertaken to make the best possible estimates of these parameters in the particular case: 'For example, we might be concerned with how high-temperature oxygen molecules attack a particular heat-shield material. We would commission experiments to address this specific issue at conditions that are as close as possible to the flight conditions.'

The engineer concludes 'there is a calculated risk associated with the uncertainty in our modelling parameters. Of course, we try to reduce this uncertainty, but ultimately we are always forced to live with some level of risk if we want to fly an interesting mission.' Note that Candler's account reproduces the distinction between uncertainty (the product of imperfect knowledge) and risk (the failure to achieve the reference narrative of a successful mission) which we use in this book. The larger question of 'What is going on here?' is one above Candler's pay grade: politicians and the senior staff of NASA have reviewed the future space programme, proposed a mission to Mars, and sought Candler's advice on one critical aspect of implementation of that policy. This delegation is the first step in a general approach of defining a strategic direction in terms of implementable policies. The strategic purpose is specific – it is not an injunction to 'conquer space' or 'be the world's most respected space exploration agency', the type of platitude adopted by too many public sector agencies today.

The next step, given Candler's specific predictive brief, is for him to decompose that relatively large-world problem into small-world problems capable of solution. These small-world problems may be resolved by applying general models (the equations of aerodynamic flow) or ones unique to that particular large world (the heat transfer generated by the arrival of a craft in the atmosphere of Mars). The process of decomposition in turn identifies key issues for research.

The final stage is to reassemble the results of that research and these models into a coherent and consistent narrative which will provide policy-makers, whose grasp of the technical issues may be inferior to that of Candler, with the information they need to make a considered decision as to whether to abort the mission or encourage it to go ahead. That approach is not how economic advice has generally been prepared and presented. But we think it should be. We look forward to a time at which Prescott's claim that 'the methodologies used in aerospace engineering and macroeconomics to make quantitative predictions are remarkably similar' will be well founded, and when macroeconomic models are as practically useful as those of NASA.

The disregard of radical uncertainty by a generation of economists condemned modern macroeconomics to near irrelevance in understanding the global financial crisis. Keynes' critique of 'getting on with the job' without asking 'whether the job is worth getting on with' would prove to be as true of the new macroeconomic theorising as of the older econometric modelling. Some of the most useful contributions to understanding financial and other crises came not from formal modelling but from historical studies of earlier episodes. For example, in 2008 central banks found it difficult to persuade commercial banks to accept emergency loans because of the stigma associated with accepting such assistance – it indicated that the bank concerned might be in difficulty. Most central banks had forgotten that exactly the same problem had occurred after the 1906 US banking crisis; no bank took advantage of the new facilities created by the US Treasury until the outbreak of the First World War when all banks were in need and no stigma attached to any one of them.[31]

As M. Trichet observed, the models that had come to be the embodiment of economic research failed the tests of utility and relevance in the 2007–08 crisis and its aftermath. As Nobel laureate Paul Romer wrote about macroeconomic theorists: 'Their models attribute fluctuations in aggregate variables to imaginary causal forces that are not influenced by the action that any person takes. A parallel with string theory[32] from physics hints at a general failure mode of science that is triggered when respect for highly regarded leaders evolves into a deference to authority that displaces objective fact from its position as the ultimate determinant of scientific truth.'[33]

Over forty years, the authors have watched the bright optimism of a new, rigorous approach to economics – an optimism which they shared – dissolve into the failures of prediction and analysis which were seen in the global financial crisis of 2007–08. And it is the pervasive nature of radical uncertainty which is the source of the problem.

20

———— • ————

THE USE AND MISUSE OF MODELS

Any business craving of the leader, however foolish,
will be quickly supported by detailed rates of return and
strategic studies prepared by his troops.

—WARREN BUFFETT[1]

In the eighteenth century there were country clergymen of exceptional intelligence who had time on their hands. They benefited from a secure reference narrative. Thomas Bayes was one; Thomas Malthus another. In 1798, Malthus set out what might be regarded as the first growth model in economics. He hypothesised that population tended to grow exponentially, as a result of what he coyly termed 'the passions', while food supplies could grow only linearly. The rising population would put pressure on food supplies, and then the resulting destitution would reduce that population. The cycle repeated itself in dismal progression.

As forecaster, Malthus could hardly have been further from

the mark. The two centuries that followed did indeed see an exponential rise in population, but world food production rose by far more. Still, Malthus's original argument would subsequently be reproduced many times. In the widely noted and acclaimed *The Population Bomb* in 1968, the biologist Paul Ehrlich asserted that 'the battle to feed all of humanity is over. In the 1970s hundreds of millions of people will starve to death.'[2] Like many forecasters, Ehrlich responded to the failure of his predictions by deferring the date. He was right, but not yet.[3] For the professional doomster, apocalypse is always postponed but never averted.

With more attention to 'what is going on here', Malthus might have recognised the revolution around him in the English countryside. Crop rotation, new machinery and selective breeding were the precursors of improvements in agricultural productivity which falsified his gloomy expectations. Malthus considered the possibility, canvassed by his contemporary William Godwin, that 'the passions' might be dampened by economic growth, intellectual enlightenment and better education, which would lead men to focus their minds on higher things. But Malthus was sceptical, instead advocating celibacy until late marriage (he himself had three children after marrying at the age of thirty-eight). Yet time would show that as women enjoyed higher incomes and better education, helped by the availability of contraception, they bore fewer children – the 'demographic transition', first described a century ago by Warren Thompson and subsequently observed in many countries.[4] And if Ehrlich had paid more attention to 'what is going on here' he might have observed not only the demographic transition but the 'green revolution' – the hybrid seed varieties which have produced dramatic new gains in agricultural productivity.

The Victorian economist Stanley Jevons published *The Coal Question* in 1865, in which he explained that limitations on coal resources would inevitably constrain Britain's economic growth.[5] In Malthus's model, exponential population growth met linearly expanding food production; in Jevons' book, exponentially growing industrial production met finite resource of coal. Jevons bravely made long-term projections of coal consumption; but he did no more than extrapolate the experience of the prior half century into the foreseeable future. His projections are contrasted with reality in the figure below. Jevons emphasised that these numbers were intended as illustrations, not forecasts; he recognised the impossibility of his projections.

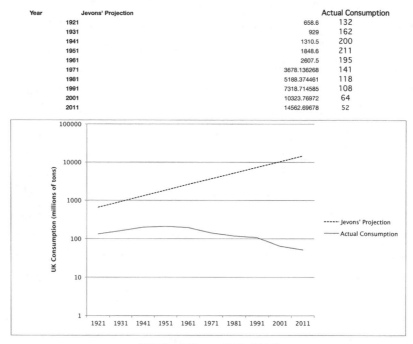

Year	Jevons' Projection	Actual Consumption	
1921		658.6	132
1931		929	162
1941		1310.5	200
1951		1848.6	211
1961		2607.5	195
1971		3678.136268	141
1981		5188.374461	118
1991		7318.714585	108
2001		10323.76972	64
2011		14562.69678	52

UK Coal Usage 1913–2016[6]

Like Malthus, Jevons was succeeded by others who repeated similar analyses, without similar caution. In the later nineteenth century there was concern that the increase in agricultural productivity which had rendered Malthus's fears groundless would be halted by the finite supply of the fertiliser guano, mostly sourced from Peru. The German chemist Fritz Haber discovered a process for the fixation of atmospheric nitrogen and when the First World War led to a blockade of German ports his discovery was rolled out on an industrial scale. Food production no longer depended on the excreta of seabirds.

Marion King Hubbert, an American geologist, popularised the notion of 'peak oil'; in the 1950s he predicted that US oil production would reach an unsustainable peak in 1965 and that the similar peak in global output would occur in around 2000.[7] America did encounter peak oil in 1970 – domestic output subsequently fell; but thanks to shale the peak in US oil production was at the time of writing experienced in 2018 and is expected to be higher in 2019.[8] World petroleum output in 2000 was about twice the level Hubbert anticipated and has continued to grow. Gloomy prognosticators today no longer suggest that the world will run out of oil but that the rejection of fossil fuels will lead to large and once valuable oil and coal reserves remaining forever in the ground – 'stranded assets'. 'The Limits to Growth', a 1972 publication commissioned by the Club of Rome, an international group of environmentally concerned individuals, asserted that economic growth must end within the next century because of constraints on all kinds of mineral resources. Thirty million copies were sold.[9] In fairness, we would have to acknowledge that they have another fifty years to be proved right.

What is going on here? The continued attention paid to these forecasters, and the popularity of their writings – which seems to continue even after it is obvious that they were wrong – reflects the common human predilection for apocalyptic narratives. Lot escaped the wrath of God by fleeing Sodom; Jonah's prophecy enabled Nineveh to avert a similar fate. Today Peter Thiel, billionaire founder of PayPal, has prepared for the armageddon which may arise from the collapse of social organisation through cybertechnologies by building a bunker in a large estate in remote New Zealand. While the failure of all apocalyptic predictions to date[10] justifies considerable scepticism towards new ones, it cannot be concluded that all such narratives are false; human dominance of Earth will end some day, though probably not through shortage of coal, guano or lithium.

Small-world models, such as those of Malthus and Jevons, are valuable in framing arguments but useless as forecasting tools. Ehrlich's predictions were ludicrous but he was right to raise the question of how a growing population would be fed. It is no accident that authors such as Ehrlich, Hubbert and the writers of the Club of Rome report all have backgrounds in natural sciences, and apply an erroneous assumption that demands for resources such as oil, electricity and water are determined by physical relationships among commodities. They ignore the impact on prices of changes in the balance between demand and supply. They also ignore the fact that, although unpredictable, technology is likely to respond to emerging challenges – the essential non-stationarity of the environment. Prices and competition promote not only discovery and innovation, but also changes in preferences and expectations.

Malthus was polemicist as well as economist, but never foolish enough to believe he could predict the crises his model described. And, properly analysed, the framework he sets out invites us to understand what factors influence agricultural productivity and demographic transitions. Jevons – one of the great minds of his time, but also an unpredictable eccentric whose obsession with resource scarcity made him a hoarder of paper – lived long enough after Malthus to understand some of the weaknesses of Malthus's concern about food supplies. He wrote that 'the plains of North America and Russia are our corn fields; Chicago and Odessa our granaries; Canada and the Baltic our timber forests; Australia contains our sheep farms, and in Argentina and on the Western prairies of North America are our herds of oxen ... the Hindus and the Chinese grow our tea for us, and our coffee, sugar and spice plantations are all in the Indies. Spain and France are our vineyards and the Mediterranean our fruit garden.'[11] He seemed not to appreciate that a similar argument might apply to fuels – Saudi Arabia is our coal mine, sun and wind our locomotives. Yet Jevons would never have been able to incorporate as yet unknown resources and resource deposits into a forecasting model, one that would describe 'the world as it really is'.

Transport modelling

In the UK, investment decisions on transport projects are evaluated using a model known as WebTAG. In order to obtain state funding for a transport project, an appraisal must be made in accordance with highly detailed official guidance contained in WebTAG and the Treasury 'Green Book' guidance on project appraisal.[12] In the world of WebTAG, time is given a monetary value depending on which of thirteen modes of transport an individual uses. The time of a taxi passenger is worth £13.57 per hour (as of 2018 and measured in 2002 prices) but the taxi driver's time is less valuable, at £9.94 per hour. Hedge fund managers walking to work and journalists cycling to their offices share a time value of £7.69 per hour, but any delay to the Deliveroo courier on her motorbike is priced, like the taxi passenger's, at £13.57 (less if she uses a pedal bike).[13] The model demands that this level of precision continues into the future. Growth projections yield predictions of how valuable the time of each group will be in 2052, to the penny. If you would also like to know how many people will be travelling in a car on a weekday evening in 2036, the WebTAG spreadsheets will provide an answer. This exercise in fantasy ensures that every cell in the spreadsheet can be filled, and that at the end of the process some numbers will be provided. The reader can make his or her own assessment of how much credence should be attached to them.

Since most of the numbers are invented, they can usually be selected to deliver the desired result. What is the value of a high-speed link from London to Birmingham and beyond? Debate around the WebTAG model centres on these time valuations. Can business people use their time productively on trains with the aid of laptop computers? Or will they fritter their £xx.xx per hour time (readers are invited to make up their own number) on the mindless calls to their office we have too often heard on the existing not-high-speed trains? How could we know? How much would people pay to catch a train which arrives in fifty minutes rather than seventy? Astonishingly – but this is the result of fitting everything into a standard template – the question of the fare structure for the new service is not raised in the course of the modelling exercise. Yet there are already two existing rival routes between London and Birmingham offering journeys at different speeds and different prices. And the bigger question of how a high-speed link would alter the incentive for regional development or expand the opportunity to commute to London cannot sensibly be entered into a spreadsheet.

Edinburgh's tram has since 2014 linked the airport to the city centre. (An established and continuing bus service, run by the same public transport authority, does so more cheaply and generally more quickly, and attracts many more users.) The part-completed tram project cost about £800 million to build, around twice the projected cost, and makes a small operating loss on revenues of around £12 million.[14] It requires only minutes of back-of-the-envelope calculation to demonstrate that this project was absurdly wasteful. However, the expensive modelling exercise of a firm of consultants reached the diametrically opposite conclusion.

The exercise purported to take account of uncertainty by conducting 'Monte Carlo simulations'. Monte Carlo simulation is a technique devised by nuclear physicists to allow the estimation of a joint probability distribution (of two or more variables) when the underlying probability distributions of each variable are known, but the joint probability distribution is too difficult to compute analytically. As we have emphasised, probability distributions can be inferred only when the observations used are the product of some known underlying stationary process and historic data yield evidence on the parameters of that distribution. This Monte Carlo simulation for the tram project involved making up many sets of numbers alternative to those initially chosen, and computing the resulting different outcomes. The modellers claimed that these results represented a probability distribution of possible outcomes. There was no basis for that claim, and it is probably unnecessary to report that the result of the unfinished tram project lay many standard deviations outside the predicted 'confidence interval'.

Lack of knowledge about the future is addressed in these exercises by assuming that the future will be essentially similar to the present, except for mechanical projections of current trends. But we have no idea what modes of transport our successors will be using in 2052. Perhaps the personal flying platforms for which we have waited so long will be available to them, or perhaps our descendants will have reverted to the horse and cart after abandoning the use of fossil fuels. We simply do not know. WebTAG, however, expects that everyone will still be travelling in the same way as now; only their numbers and the value of their time will have changed.

Value at risk

Value at risk models (VaR), used for risk management in banks, were the technique which lay behind Mr Viniar's claim to have observed a '25 standard deviation' event. These models were based on the portfolio theory pioneered by Markowitz and were developed at J. P. Morgan in the late 1980s to help the bank cope with the variety of debt instruments which had appeared in that decade. As in the Markowitz model, the starting point is the variance of daily returns on each security and the covariance of returns between securities. With the aid of all this information[15] you might compute the extreme percentile of the distribution – the amounts you would lose on a truly terrible day, one that would occur say only once in a thousand trials (although such an event would happen on average every four years). That figure represented the 'value at risk' which became a key – the key – risk management tool.

The methodology took the banking world by storm. Quantitative and scientific risk management could supersede the intuitions and judgements of experienced bankers. The tool was too good to be the proprietary system of a single bank, and J. P. Morgan spun off a business, RiskMetrics, to propagate it. Soon almost all major banks were using similar models and value at risk became part of the regulatory apparatus of banking supervision.

Bank portfolios contained literally millions of financial instruments reflecting the spiralling volume of inter-bank trading and the resulting web of interdependencies. But how were the crucial parameters – the means, variances and covariances – of the returns on these portfolios to be determined? The only possible answer was to look to historic data series. Thus an assumption of stationarity was built into the modelling. Of course, these historic data series were of necessity drawn from a period in which the banks that provided the data had not suffered crippling losses. So they were derived in a way which almost inevitably underestimated the variances of the underlying probability distribution.

And also the covariances. In 2007–09, the losses experienced on mortgage loans were far larger than those experienced in a history in which such loans had been made mainly by conservative bankers to respectable borrowers. Defaults on these traditional mortgages were typically the result of individual household misfortunes – relationship breakdown, illness or death. The incidence of such misfortune was fairly low, random and, in aggregate, reasonably predictable. But when loans were made to weak borrowers who depended on rising house prices to refinance unsustainable loans, any setback to a continuing rise in house prices would cause many defaults. So what were believed to be diversified pools of assets turned out to be highly correlated with each other. The models assumed an underlying stationarity of the default process and the modellers did not have the qualitative knowledge of 'what is going on here' which would have enabled them to recognise that this assumption was unjustified.

Although value at risk models may be of some use in enabling banks to monitor their day-to-day risk exposures, they are incapable of dealing with the 'off-model' events which are the typical cause of financial crises – the Viniar problem. Extreme observations such as those encountered in the financial crisis mostly result from events outside the model. Banks do fail, as the experience of 2008 showed, but not usually for the reasons described by value at risk models. Northern Rock failed even though until the day it ran out of money it appeared to be well capitalised according to prescribed risk assessments. Financial institutions fail through fraud or mismanagement, or an amoral carelessness that lies somewhere between the two, or the realisation of a wholly unexpected turn of events in the domestic or world economies.

Fishing with mathematics

In the fifteenth and sixteenth centuries, Spanish and Portuguese explorers ranged the Americas in search of treasures. While the gold and silver of the south received most attention, another treasure was located in the far north: the cod fisheries of the Grand Banks of Newfoundland. Even today, salt cod, or bacalao, is a staple of the Iberian diet. But none of the cod now comes from Canada. For five hundred years, fishermen from Spain, Portugal and other countries exploited the seemingly limitless shoals of the Grand Banks. By the 1960s, the greater effectiveness of modern fishing technology had led to overfishing in many locations. In 1968, an unsustainable catch of 480,000 tonnes of cod was harvested from the shores of Newfoundland, and cod stocks began to decline. Many countries reacted to overfishing by extending their territorial waters to protect their domestic fishermen. In 1977, Canada took control of almost all the waters of the Grand Banks.[16]

The country set out, in organised Canadian fashion, to promote a fishing industry that would revive the flagging economies of Nova Scotia and Newfoundland. The government provided subsidies for trawler construction, and charged the Dominion Fisheries Office with determining the total allowable catch; that catch to be set to ensure not only the survival but the growth of stocks and the gradual expansion of the industry. The Fisheries Office developed complex models on which its recommendations were based. But cod stocks continued to decline. For the year 1992, the total allowable catch was set at 145,000 tonnes. That proved to be the last year of commercial cod fishing on the Grand Banks. The fish are gone, and in the course of that year the industry finally closed. Today only around 5000 tonnes of cod are caught annually on rod and line by recreational and artisanal fishermen.[17]

It would be wrong to hold the modellers solely responsible for the collapse of the Grand Banks fisheries. Greedy fishermen and mendacious politicians should take most of the blame. But the modelling exercises were used to justify the actions and inactions of politicians and the industry. The original impulse to determine catch limits based on insights from modelling and environmental science was effectively inverted; the 'evidence' generated by the models ended up justifying the policy rather than actually protecting fish stocks. The modellers were complicit in an environmental disaster.

Misinformation about migration

In 2004, ten countries, including eight former communist ones, joined the European Union and their citizens gained the right to work in other member states. The European Commission estimated that migration from acceding countries to other members would initially be between 70,000 and 150,000 a year, declining thereafter. The British government anticipated that between 5000 and 13,000 of these would come to the UK.[18] By the time of the Brexit referendum in 2016, no fewer than 1.6 million residents of the UK were immigrants from accession states.[19] Another 450,000 had come to the UK from Romania and Bulgaria, which joined the EU slightly later.[20] In Ireland, some 240,000 people – 5% of the Irish population – were migrants from these new EU members.[21]

We are not concerned here to debate the pros and cons of such migration. But argument should be based on accurate data and careful analysis. The most important study, on which all others partly relied, was commissioned by the European Commission through the European Integration Consortium.[22] That study emphasised that the previous round of accession by poorer countries – Greece, Portugal and Spain in the 1980s – had led to little migration. The highest predictions – still too low – were produced by the German Ifo institute, which explained why this analogy with the earlier round was unreliable.[23] The former communist states had previously made emigration almost impossible. Most importantly, the income difference between the original EU members and the later newcomers was much greater than that for the countries which joined in the 1980s. The European Commission has a history of commissioning academic studies that exaggerate the benefits and downplay the costs of integration.

The British government's admirable emphasis on evidence-based policy too often reduces, as it did in the estimation of migration flows, to policy-based evidence: information is provided to support the conclusions that those who prepare the studies believe policy-makers seek. Our experience, both of developing models ourselves and of observing the use of models in political and business contexts, is that models are rarely used as an input to the decision-making process; their purpose is to help justify an already determined course of action to corporate boards or government ministers or external regulators. Those who run financial institutions want to be reassured that their risks are controlled, and those who sponsor large transport projects want to ensure that such projects will go ahead. The true nature of the exercise is rarely to attempt to resolve uncertainty, but – as in the Canadian fisheries – to provide superficially objective justification for a decision which has been made on other grounds. The economic failure of Edinburgh's tram project did not deter political support for its further extension.

In many of these exercises empirical appraisals are conducted by one of a small number of consulting firms for whom such modelling is a primary business, and who are aware of the answers that those sponsoring the studies would like to hear. Their commercial success depends on delivering what their customers want. Academics who court public attention and official research funding are too easily co-opted into this process.

Abuse of models

The exercises described above have common deficiencies. All display at least some of the following weaknesses, and most illustrate all of them.

First, the modelling exercise applies a common template to disparate situations. There is great variation in the nature and scale of transport projects, in the activities of organisations which describe themselves as 'banks', and in employment and welfare conditions in member states of the European Union. In each of these cases the belief that a common approach achieves either objectivity or comparability has been falsified by events.

Second, the modelling exercises rely on filling in gaps in knowledge by inventing numbers, often in immense quantities. Some of these invented numbers will be prescribed – as in WebTAG – while others are left to the discretion of the modellers who, as a result of the complexity of the models, may be the only people to understand the impact on the answers of the assumptions made. Indeed a superficial advantage of the common template is that most of the modelling can be left to junior analysts, with the result that the connection between assumptions and outcomes may not be understood by anyone at all.

Third, these exercises necessarily assume, almost always without justification, stationarity of the underlying processes. There might have been some reason to assume that the underlying science of fisheries was well understood, although this turned out not to have been the case. But there were not even a priori grounds for believing that historic experience of mortgage defaults would apply in future, that the level of historic returns on investment products was a good guide to future returns, or that models which had been fitted to data from Spain would describe migration from Poland. And none of these things were borne out in practice.

Fourth, in the absence of stationarity, these modelling exercises have no means of accounting for uncertainty and there is no basis for the construction of probability distributions, confidence intervals, or the use of tools of statistical inference. The opinions of different people about the values of a parameter, or the same consultant's different estimates of the value of that parameter, do not constitute either a frequency or a probability distribution. With no defensible basis for describing such assessments of uncertainty, there is no mechanism for valuing the options associated with a project. For example, many transport projects effectively exclude other projects which might achieve similar objectives. Alternatively, they may permit other projects to be undertaken which would not otherwise be viable. Such options, which may be positive or negative in value, are often crucial to an assessment of the project. Major decisions always need to be made in the context of a wider narrative.

Fifth, because of the cost and complexity of the models, their deployment often prevents meaningful public consultation and debate. Those opposing HS2, the proposed high-speed train link from London to Birmingham, felt obliged to commission their own costly assessment of the same project, an exercise which differed little in structure but reached a diametrically opposite conclusion to the official view.

All of these bogus models, as fragile as a balsa-wood structure in a wind tunnel, have a common failing. They begin by considering how you would make a decision if you had complete and perfect knowledge of the world, now and in the future. But very few of the relevant data are known. The solution? Make them all up.

Modelling at NASA and WHO

We have referred often in this book to the impressive achievements of NASA scientists in modelling the solar system and predicting paths of spacecraft. NASA's modelling of the agency's own systems has been altogether another matter. In 1986, the space shuttle *Challenger* exploded on launch, killing all seven astronauts on board. It was the first of two fatal accidents in the Space Shuttle programme; the second happened seventeen years later when *Columbia* disintegrated on re-entry into the Earth's atmosphere, again killing all seven crew members. The brilliant Nobel Prize-winning physicist Richard Feynman was appointed to the inquiry that followed the *Challenger* disaster. Feynman insisted that his note of dissent from the inquiry's bland conclusions be attached to the report. He noted that there had been a wide range of estimates of the probability of a fatal accident arising from a launch – from 1 in 100 from working engineers to 1 in 100,000 from NASA management. Feynman asked, 'What is the cause of management's fantastic faith in the machinery?', ridiculing the notion of any 1 in 100,000 probability, and observing that NASA management professed knowledge and understanding they could not conceivably enjoy. 'For a successful technology, reality must take precedence over public relations, for nature cannot be fooled,' Feynman concluded.

The methods that worked so well in the analysis of the solar system – which required comprehensive knowledge of the underlying system, stationarity of that system, and confidence that the system would be unaffected by the actions of NASA or its agents – comprehensively failed in the conditions of radical uncertainty inevitable at the frontiers of rocket technology. As Obama in a different context would find later in his meeting in the Oval Office, the expressions of probabilities within NASA disguised uncertainty rather than resolved it. Feynman's excoriation of NASA's bureaucracy provides an unmatched account of the misuse of pseudoscience to rationalise administrative decisions made in the face of radical uncertainty. This misuse of models was common to analysing spacecraft in Houston, fish stocks in Newfoundland, trams in Edinburgh and migration in Europe. Sadly, the misuse is widespread and continues.

Thomas Davenport and Brook Manville constructed a series of case studies on how good decisions had been made in large organisations.[24] They begin with an analysis of how in 2009 NASA, chastened by the *Challenger* disaster, first postponed the launch of space shuttle STS-119 and then successfully executed it. They stress features of the agency's revised procedures:

> commitment to tracking small failures, ability to recognise and understand complex issues, real attention to front-line workers, the ability to learn from and rebound from errors, and the ability to improvise effective response to crisis . . . the overarching culture was one of open exchange, honouring of diverse opinions, and the embrace of the right to dissent. Today we admire NASA not just for its successes but for its ability to rebound from the horrible tragedies of *Challenger* and *Columbia*.[25]

NASA had learnt to ask 'What is going on here?' in their own organisation as well as in the solar system and to abandon the pretence of knowledge in favour of solutions that were robust and resilient to unanticipated events. And so should we all.

The first human exposure to HIV is thought to have occurred in the 1920s. But it was not until 1981, when unusual clusters of PCP (a rare lung infection) in five gay men in San Francisco were reported, that the phenomenon we know today was identified. Tasked with creating a model to guide policy-makers as to how the disease would spread and the level of intervention necessary, the World Health Organization designed a complex model informed by the latest country-by-country demographic data. A far simpler model was developed by mathematicians Robert May and Roy Anderson, who came up with more pessimistic projections for the spread of HIV. Unfortunately their projections proved much closer to the eventual out-turns.[26] AIDS infections accelerated across the world, causing particular harm in southern Africa: in 1990 there were estimated to be 120,000 people living with AIDS, a number which had grown to 3.4 million by 2000. The number of new HIV infections had risen ninefold.[27] The world was, it seemed, a much less stable place than the WHO model had assumed.

Why did the (apparently) more sophisticated WHO model fail compared to May and Anderson's simple one? The key factors governing the spread of disease included the probability of an infected person transferring the infection to another person. May and Anderson realised that the probability of infecting another person had two components: the probability that any sexual act would transfer infection; and how many sexual partners infected people had. It was crucial to distinguish between the two. An HIV-positive sex worker who sleeps with ten different people is more likely to spread the disease than someone who sleeps with the same person ten times. But the WHO model did not make this distinction, and that is why its predictions of the spread of AIDS were, tragically, inaccurate. May and Anderson had asked 'What is going on here?'; the WHO model had focused on the detailed demographic data the modellers understood, rather than looking at what really mattered – the different sexual habits of affected groups.

Using models appropriately

We draw a number of lessons for the use of models in business and government.

First, deploy simple models to identify the key factors that influence an assessment. A common response to criticisms of the kind we have described above is an offer to add to the model whatever we think is missing. But this is another reflection of the mistaken belief that such models can describe 'the world as it really is'. The useful purpose of modelling is to find 'small world' problems which illuminate part of the large world of radical uncertainty.

Second, having identified the parameters which are likely to make a significant difference to an assessment, undertake research to obtain evidence on the value of these parameters. For example, what value do rail passengers attach to a faster journey? Quantification can often serve as a reality check even when precise quantification is obviously spurious. The preservation of the beautiful and well-preserved Norman church at Stewkley in England (close to a proposed new high-speed rail line) is worth something, but surely not a billion pounds. Often this kind of calibration is enough to resolve some aspects of a decision.

Third, simple models provide a flexibility which makes it much easier to explore the effects of modifications and alternatives. For example, the WHO demographic model not only diverted attention from the key issue but its complexity made it harder to investigate alternative specifications of the model structure and parameters. Scenarios are always useful in conditions of radical uncertainty. How might this policy decision look in five years' time – or fifty?

Fourth, under radical uncertainty, the options conferred by a policy may be crucial to its evaluation. Faced with a choice as to which of London's two major airports, Gatwick or Heathrow, should be chosen for expansion, recognition that the topography of Gatwick allows piecemeal adaptation of the development of facilities in the light of uncertain future demand, while that of Heathrow does not, should be an important factor in the choice. Options may be positive or negative in value – facilitating policies not directly connected to the initial objectives, or excluding possible attractive alternatives.

In the end, a model is useful only if the person using it understands that it does not represent 'the world as it really is', but is a tool for exploring ways in which a decision might or might not go wrong.

Part V

Living with Uncertainty

21

PRACTICAL KNOWLEDGE

Economics has been increasingly defined in terms not
of subject matter but of methodology. This appears to
be unusual, perhaps unique, among academic and policy
disciplines. Historians study history, chemists study
chemistry, lawyers study law.

—JESSE NORMAN[1]

'Economics is a study of mankind in the ordinary business of
life.' In his magisterial *Principles of Economics*, published in
1890, Alfred Marshall went on to define the scope of that study
more specifically: '[economics] examines that part of individual and social action which is most closely connected with the
attainment and with the use of the material requisites of wellbeing'.[2] As we noted in chapter 7, Gary Becker, who assumed
intellectual leadership of the Chicago School on Milton
Friedman's retirement, took a different view: 'The combined
assumptions of maximizing behavior, market equilibrium, and

stable preferences, used relentlessly and unflinchingly, form the heart of the economic approach.'[3]

The assumptions of optimisation, equilibrium and stationarity are useful as part of small-world approaches to constructing models that throw light on a problem – the method used fruitfully by Smith, Ricardo, Tucker and Akerlof. But such models provide only partial insight into human behaviour in large worlds. Becker, however, had grander ambitions and indeed received a Nobel Prize 'for having extended the domain of microeconomic analysis to a wide range of human behaviour and interaction'. But interdisciplinary cooperation is not the same as economic imperialism. In writing this book, we have consciously drawn from a wide corpus of knowledge and scholarship, and learnt much from doing so. People who know only economics do not know much about economics.

Economics as practical knowledge

Marshall's conception begins from the problem, not the method. It sees economics as a practical subject, like engineering or medicine. The engineer begins with a project, the doctor with a patient, and their success is defined by the completion of the assignment or the improved health of the patient. Similarly, the scope of economics is defined by the issues it seeks to examine – problems of business and public policy. The success of economics should be measured by the help it gives to the minister of finance and the head of the central bank, to David Viniar and Steve Jobs, to people struggling to invest their savings or establish a business, to households buying their homes or their groceries.

When the Queen visited the London School of Economics in 2009, she famously expressed the general view of her subjects when she responded to a presentation on the financial crisis by reportedly asking 'Why did no one see it coming?'[4] The Queen had understood that economics and economists, whatever their prestige, had failed the test of providing useful insight. And her predecessor Charles II recognised that practical knowledge was more important than qualification or status when he urged the admission to the Royal Society of John Graunt (whom we described in chapter 4 trawling the cemeteries of London).

Theory in aviation and aeronautics is valued for its contribution to practical knowledge. Aeronautical engineers are no slouches at mathematics and physics, and their calculations are sophisticated. But they are focused on solving practical problems. So when we say that economics should also focus on solving practical problems we are not saying that mathematical reasoning and knowledge are inappropriate. Practical subjects such as medicine or engineering contrast with mathematics and physics – or for that matter philosophy or literature – where knowledge is sought for its own sake. Of course, fundamental scientific knowledge may often prove of great practical value – the understanding of electricity, for example, may have had greater economic effect than any other scientific discovery: it is no exaggeration to say it made the modern world possible. Yet such application was not the motivation of those who made their discoveries, and as Benjamin Franklin took his kite into a rainstorm to attract lightning he had no appreciation that his work would lead to vacuum cleaners, computers and the splitting of the atom. But it is hard to see any similar pecuniary benefit from our understanding of the causes of the extinction of the dinosaurs, the influence of Jane Austen on later nineteenth-century novelists, or the conduct of Napoleon's Russian campaign. The study of these subjects represents the pursuit of knowledge for its own sake. Through such study humans raise the level of educated discourse, and that knowledge provides the context in which we apprehend 'what is going on here' in a complex situation. And such study enables us to enjoy lives more fulfilling than can be achieved solely through the accumulation of consumer durables and the completion of another eighteen holes of golf. We rightly regard those who ask 'How many degrees in anthropology does Florida need for a healthy economy?' as boorish philistines.

Medicine and engineering are different. We go to the doctor in search of information and advice that will make us well, and are disappointed if we leave the surgery no healthier but better informed. We treat people who design machines which will never be built as cranks, and if a software designer or a NASA engineer tries to explain how he does it, rather than the fascinating topic of what he does, we may be inclined to look for a more interesting companion.

Practical subjects are appropriately promiscuous, drawing on underlying scientific knowledge from many disciplines. They are eclectic in their methods. Respected professionals in practical subjects are generally sceptical of general theories and universal knowledge. Much of their activity uses heuristics which have been shown to work, in their own experience or that of others, an approach derided by many economists as 'ad hoc'. Capable practitioners may have little or no understanding of why their prescriptions work, often because such understanding does not exist.

Models are tools

Imagine that you had a problem in your kitchen, and summoned a plumber. You would hope that he might arrive with a large box of tools, would examine carefully the nature of the problem, and select the appropriate tool to deal with it. Now imagine that when the plumber arrived, he said that he was a professional economist but did plumbing in his spare time.[5] He arrived with just a single tool. And he looked around the kitchen for a problem to which he could apply that one tool. Or perhaps he would explain that the screwdriver he had brought was just what was needed to fix the leak in the drain hose. Or that the multi-purpose tool he carried was relevant to every need (we have both foolishly bought one of these).

You might think the would-be plumber should stick to economics (and perhaps wonder whether and why he had been successful in that profession). Whether you had summoned the plumber to fix a leak or invited an economist to advise on policy issues, you would hope that he or she (though plumbers, like economists, are predominantly male) would begin with a diagnosis. You would then hope that the person had a box of tools from which it was possible to choose the relevant one or ones. A pluralism of 'small world' models illuminating specific issues parallels the plumber's variety of specialist tools. Models should not be judged by the sophistication of the mathematics – in itself neither good nor bad – but by the insights which that model provides into a particular problem that we are trying to solve.

Models are tools like those in the van of the professional plumber, which can be helpful in one context and irrelevant in others. As with the tools in the van, there may be several models which contribute to the solution of a specific problem. And there are times when there is no good model to explain what we see. But we still have to make decisions. So the test of a model is therefore whether it is useful in making the decisions which need to be made in government, business and finance, and in households, in a world of radical uncertainty.

The pursuit of practical knowledge which gives useful advice to policy-makers begins from the question 'What is going on here?' The plumber looks first for the origin of the leak. A doctor conducts a consultation by observing symptoms and taking readings until he or she can begin to formulate a diagnosis and prescribe a treatment. An engineer or architect begins by scoping the project, and a dentist makes an examination and assessment before recommending a course of action. All these approaches are distinct from the search for abstract knowledge of 'the world as it really is' which characterises the work of physicists and philosophers. But the crucial contribution of economics to the world is defined by its role as practical knowledge, not as scientific theory. Keynes reported:

> Professor Planck, of Berlin, the famous originator of the Quantum Theory, once remarked to me that in early life he had thought of studying economics, but had found it too difficult! Professor Planck could easily master the whole corpus of mathematical economics in a few days. He did not mean that! But the amalgam of logic and intuition and the wide knowledge of facts, most of which are not precise, which is required for economic interpretation in its highest form is, quite truly, overwhelmingly difficult for those whose gift mainly consists in the power to imagine and pursue to their furthest points the implications and prior conditions of comparatively simple facts which are known with a high degree of precision.[6]

If we were to delete the word 'imagine', we would describe the skill of a powerful computer. Of course, deleting the word 'imagine' makes a big difference, which is why no computer has won the Nobel Prize in Physics, nor is likely to in the foreseeable future.

Modern economics has lost a great deal in seeking to imitate Planck rather than Keynes. Axiomatic rationality is not evolutionary rationality, and critiques of the kind launched by behavioural economists fail to acknowledge the importance of the human ability to interpret problems in context, a skill which computers are still very far from achieving. Solving the CAPTCHA – the slightly distorted text which is set to distinguish humans from robots – is trivially easy for humans and difficult for a computer. And Google's research in this area is, fortunately, devoted not to training robots to be more like humans, but to accumulating the knowledge from solved CAPTCHAs to enable computers to distinguish artificial intelligence from human intelligence even more effectively. So effectively, in fact, that your keystrokes give you away and it is now often enough to tick a box to confirm that 'I am not a robot'.

Keynes would later write: 'If economists could manage to get themselves thought of as humble, competent people, on a level with dentists, that would be splendid!'[7] It is understandable that economists would prefer to be more like physicists than dentists. Few dentists have achieved the status and profile of Max Planck.[8] Planck received the Nobel Prize in Physics but dentists play a crucial, if unexciting, role in our daily lives. Pierre Fauchard, a French physician, is to dentistry what Adam Smith is to economics, and their work was broadly contemporaneous, reflecting the breadth of influence of the eighteenth-century Enlightenment. Fauchard's assembly and extension of practical knowledge in dentistry began the shift in dental practice from the extraction of teeth to their repair. Most subsequent fundamental innovations in dentistry have resulted from the application to dentistry of advances in general science, such as the discovery of anaesthesia and the germ theory of disease. The modern dental implant is the product of research by a Swedish anatomist, Per-Ingvar Brånemark, who discovered the properties of titanium in bonding to bone.[9]

A good dentist is someone who can improve the health of

the patient while avoiding unnecessary pain, not someone who produces a new theory or model of dentistry. There is no such thing as a general theory of dentistry, but there is a large store of practical knowledge to which dentists have access. An accomplished dentist is one who identifies the source of the patient's problem – 'What is going on here?' – and draws effectively on old and new techniques from that store of knowledge to relieve that problem. A great contributor to dentistry, like Brånemark, develops a new technique of wide practical application.

Economics demands data

The American historian of economic thought Philip Mirowski popularised the term 'physics envy' to describe the longing of many economists to emulate Max Planck rather than Keynes' dentist. And while Keynes' description of Planck's deductive reasoning is accurate, the knowledge of the solar system which lies behind NASA's success originates not in axiomatic reasoning but in the careful and extensive observation of the planets undertaken in the sixteenth century by the Danish nobleman Tycho Brahe. His data collection was subsequently analysed by the German mathematician Johannes Kepler, with whom Brahe collaborated at the end of his life. Physics is inductive as well as deductive. But the underlying stationarity of physical processes reduces the need for abductive reasoning. Economists, however, face unique situations, such as the one encountered in the last months of 2008, and must make 'inference to best explanation'.

Like physics, economics demands data, and the world of business and finance provides plentiful data. But such data, we have emphasised, can be interpreted only in the light of some economic theory – and, as we explained in chapter 6, are generally collected only on the basis, usually unstated, of some underlying theory. The motivating theory need not be correct – Tycho

Brahe believed until the day he died that the Earth was the centre of the universe, and elaborated fanciful explanations to reconcile his observations with his beliefs, in a manner all too familiar today. The mark of science is not insistence on deductive reasoning but insistence that observation trumps theory, whatever the purported authority supporting the theory – the insistence which led Galileo to face the Inquisition before the truth of planetary motion won general acceptance.

The meticulous recording by Brahe of observations, regardless of their implications, remains an example to all social science. We have listened far too often to people pontificating about politics and economics in ignorance of readily available data. A survey in 2016 across twenty-six countries showed that 84% of respondents believed that extreme poverty in the world had risen or remained the same.[10] But extreme poverty has fallen by more than half in the last two decades, benefiting more than a billion people.[11] This may be the single most important fact about the global economy over the period. In his bestselling *Factfulness*, Hans Rosling has reported that such ignorance was even widespread in India and China, whose rapid economic growth has been responsible for much of the improvement.[12] College students did a little better than the population as a whole. But we are concerned that modern economics teaching puts emphasis on quantitative methods without giving students the opportunity to learn much either about data sources or about the principles by which data are compiled.

Decisions about politics, finance and business should be made in the light of the best and most extensive data. But while data are essential, it is necessary to be careful in making inferences, and especially causal inferences, about the world based on data alone. The availability of what are now called 'big data' – the very large databases permitted by the power of modern computers – increases these dangers. The existence of a historic data set does not yield a basis for calculating a future probability distribution. Predictions of the scale of mortgage losses and the correlations between the incidence of defaults by different groups of borrowers were based not only on information from a different time period but on the experience of borrowers with very different characteristics from those who defaulted in large numbers in the subprime crisis. The student of business, economics and finance who relies on observed relationships must seek, and will rarely find, compelling reasons for believing that the process generating that data is stationary.

Never rely on data without asking 'What is the source of this information?' The information on extreme poverty described above is derived from the World Bank, a careful and reliable source, and refers to the number of people who have incomes of less than $1.90 per day. The United Nations uses a rather lower figure, $1.25 per day, in its Millennium Development Goals, and reports that its target of a 50% reduction in extreme poverty by 2030 has already been reached.[13] These income levels are based on an assessment of minimal levels of housing and nutrition, and seem incredibly low to anyone who lives in Europe and North America. Here, as elsewhere, useful measurement generally requires some underlying theory or model – in an advanced country, poverty is measured in a very different way. And having asked where data come from, it is also important to ask what model is being used to interpret it. Remember the fate of the *Literary Digest* which predicted a landslide victory for Landon, not Roosevelt. Even now pollsters disagree about how to translate the raw data they collect into predictions of results.

The map is not the territory

Models can also be used to reproduce large – real – worlds. Engineers   must   have   comprehensive   and   quantitative understanding of how aircraft and bridges will respond to changes in wind speed and shear. Bridges can literally be modelled by the construction of small-scale replicas, although the degree to which the properties of the model carry over to the bridge itself requires experience and judgement. In 2018, the engineers of the McLaren racing team struggled to explain the disappointing aerodynamic performance of their car. Even though they could put the complete vehicle in a wind tunnel, performance on the track differed from performance in the tunnel – and the company's head of engineering lost his job.[14]

The only fully reliable model is one which replicates the bridge (or car) at full scale and in which the wind tunnel replicates the conditions in which the bridge will be installed or the car driven. But a replica is not a model. The paradox is demonstrated in the oft-told story, perhaps most eloquently described by the Argentinian writer Jorge Luis Borges, of the quest to create a perfect map of the world.[15] The search ends with a map which itself completely reproduces the world, and is therefore useless. A map, or a model, is necessarily a simplification, and the appropriate simplification is matched to a purpose – a walking map differs from a subway map or road atlas, even of the same area. 'The map is not the territory', in the famous words of the Polish philosopher Alfred Korzybski, and the same is true of models.[16] Nevertheless, some models successfully represent the essential features of the system which are needed for accurate prediction. And these representations are the basis of the scientific advance which followed the formulation of Newtonian mechanics.

The models that NASA has developed – based on the long-established and empirically verified equations of planetary motion, and the agency's knowledge of the capabilities of its own rockets – represent the limits of human achievement in model building. Their map is not the territory, but it represents the relevant features of the territory sufficiently well that computer simulations reproduce more or less exactly the experience of the rocket in outer space. Such modelling is possible because of NASA's knowledge of the solar system (it can be represented precisely by a relatively simple set of equations), because the agency is confident of the stationarity of that system, and because it is not necessary to anticipate how that system will respond to the agency's actions. There is no radical uncertainty in the part of the solar system which NASA models. But sadly, in almost all economic problems there is such uncertainty, especially in finance and macroeconomics, where the misperception that 'small world' models can be deployed as if they were 'wind tunnel' models has proved so costly.

'Wind tunnel' models have little role to play in economics despite the widespread attempt to develop similar models for macroeconomic forecasting. As Savage had recognised, 'judgment and experience about which it is impossible to enunciate complete and sharply defined general principles' are crucial to the choice of an appropriate 'small world' model.[17] Microeconomic research in the last two decades has increasingly focused in this way on simple models of small worlds which yield propositions capable of being empirically tested. In modern macroeconomics and in finance theory the quest for a model which is a comprehensive description of a large world, a model which like NASA's model of the solar system approximates to 'the world as it really is', continues. But the notion that economists can construct 'wind tunnel' models in these domains is no longer worth pursuing when that world is unavoidably characterised by radical uncertainty.

Many economists in these fields respond to criticism by saying that 'all models are wrong'. They do not mean that models are mathematically incorrect. They mean that models are 'wrong' in the sense that Tucker's description of criminal justice and

Shakespeare's account of Scottish history are 'wrong'. But the observation that 'all models are wrong' requires qualification by the second part of George Box's famous aphorism – 'but some are useful'. The Prisoner's Dilemma describes an idea with wide application, and *Macbeth* is an insightful depiction of a common human folly. The relevant criticism of models in macroeconomics and finance is not that they are 'wrong' but that they have not proved useful in macroeconomics and have proved misleading in finance.

When we provide such a critique, we often hear another mantra to which many economists subscribe: 'It takes a model to beat a model'.[18] On the contrary, we believe that it takes facts and observations to beat a model. And the reaction of the Queen reminds us that if a model manifestly fails to answer the problem to which it is addressed, it should be put back in the toolbox. And if it fails to answer *any* economic problem, it should not be in the toolbox in the first place. People with access to the best possible advice found in the financial crisis that economic models did not help them understand 'what is going on here'. No one in their senses would ask the Queen 'So what is your model?' and the wise sovereign would sensibly seek not another economic model, but another adviser on economic issues. It is not necessary to have an alternative tool available to know that the plumber who arrives armed only with a screwdriver is not the tradesman we need.

In Michael Lewis's book *The Undoing Project*, a revealing passage describes the transformation of Amos Tversky's thinking after he gave a seminar in the course run by Daniel Kahneman.[19] Before that, Lewis describes Tversky's thinking as 'Until you could replace a theory with a better theory – a theory that better predicted what actually happened – you didn't chuck a theory out.' After the seminar, 'he treated theories that he had more or less accepted as sound and plausible as objects of suspicion'.

He embraced 'a state of mind unusual for him: doubt'. After the financial crisis, it would be reasonable to treat most formal macroeconomic models with a degree of doubt. Just as we would be sceptical of the competence of the plumber when water continued to flood the kitchen floor.

Astrologers have a loyal following of people who believe in the effect of the stars on human behaviour. We do not subscribe to the value of such forecasts and we do not believe we need to have a better model of the influence of the stars on business or romantic life to know that the predictions of astrologers are bunkum. Nor, to use an example cited by Paul Romer, is it necessary to have an alternative theory of the causes of autism – which are almost certainly multiple and complex – to know that the claim that the condition was induced by the MMR triple vaccine was not only wrong, but dangerously misleading, and that the falsehood has caused the deaths of many children.[20]

Economics as Waze

The dentist can if necessary address the problem of reflexivity by anaesthetising the patient. The economist has no similar option; the economy never remains still. The behaviour of the stock market is the product not of unchanging physical laws, but of constantly mutating economic and social conditions and the fickle nature of investors' expectations. Non-stationarity and the dependence of systems on our behaviour and beliefs make a lot of difference. Although they could forecast the path of MESSENGER for six and a half years and 4.9 billion miles ahead, engineers cannot forecast with similar, or even very much, accuracy the position of your car twenty minutes from now even if informed of your intended direction. And they cannot do so because underlying traffic conditions are constantly changing – they are non-stationary in almost every sense, though sometimes not the one that matters – and because your arrival time depends on what you, and other motorists, will choose to do in future.

Waze, a sat nav system provided by Google, has available to it any scientific or engineering knowledge the company might want. Even central banks do not have the intellectual resources or data to which Google has access. Waze has smart programmers, and millions of customers contributing data in real time. With the aid of sophisticated software, Waze can predict your arrival time with greater accuracy than was possible a decade ago. But the forecast is still not very good. And never will be. The length of time it took you to drive home yesterday is still almost as good a predictor of the length of time it will take you to drive home today as the best estimate modern technology can provide.

Waze is not, primarily, a forecasting tool, but a source of practical knowledge of value to decision-makers. A program like Waze will within seconds give you directions and a typical travel time to an unfamiliar destination. The analysis of that problem treats the system as stationary – the skill of map reading has been taken over from slow humans by smart and fast computers. Waze will give you an estimate of arrival time for your routine journey home based on analysis of past frequencies. But the greatest value of the application to users lies in its ability to give you advance notice of disruptive events such as unexpected traffic jams, roadworks, accidents. By accumulating 'big data', problem-specific information derived from many sources, the program can provide indications of the consequences and suggestions for alternative courses of action.

What Google programmers are *not* trying to do is to construct a general theory of traffic from which all motorists could anticipate the trajectories of all other motorists for the next several years and make their own decisions accordingly, iterating towards an equilibrium in which every journey plan is optimal given the optimal journey plans of all other motorists. And – significantly – they are not trying to do this even when they plan for a future of autonomous vehicles from which much, though not all, of the human element in decision-making has been removed. The construction of an optimal traffic plan for all vehicles for the foreseeable future is beyond the capacity even of Google's programmers and the most powerful computer available. Even if Waze had built such a model, it would have to be nearly perfect before it could be even slightly useful in providing information relevant to our particular journey.

Many economic models have been constructed by assuming the existence of a 'representative' household. But a good model of traffic flow could not be based on a representative vehicle – congestion arises in large part because traffic is heterogeneous. Treating 'London' as a single entity would not give useful advice to the travelling motorist; it is because London is not a single entity that we need directions to our specific destination. The simplifications needed to represent the aggregate by a small-world model would render that model useless. Modelling divergent expectations and human interactions requires far more granularity.

If the exercise of building a universal theory of traffic sounds ludicrous, it more or less exactly parallels the exercise in which many macroeconomists have been engaged for the past forty years and in which many of them are still engaged. Waze is useful precisely because it uses data not to build general models but to provide rapid access to information suggesting the location of problems and possible solutions. And we think economists should do the same. If Keynes were writing today, we think he might suggest that if economists should aspire to be like dentists, economics should aspire to be like Waze.

Economists and radical uncertainty

The public role of the social scientist is to provide the necessary information to enable politicians, public servants, business people and ordinary families, who are required to *act* under conditions of radical uncertainty, to make decisions. To fulfil that mission, the social scientist can help by explaining 'what is going on here' – providing a narrative which is coherent and credible and which establishes the context within which decisions are to be taken. These narratives may include stories – literary fictions. Or numbers – constructs from big or small data sets, such as statistics on the economy or the results of social surveys. Or models – those small-world accounts which have the appearance of exact solutions. In economics, business and finance, all these types of reasoning will frequently be relevant.

Economists cannot tell policy-makers what decisions to make. But they can help them think about their problems and provide relevant information. The social scientist's narrative is akin to that of the professional practitioner – the diagnosis of the doctor, the project specification of the engineer, the lawyer's statement of case. The selection of relevant narratives is problem- and context-specific, so that the choice of fictions, numbers and models requires the exercise of judgement in relation to both problem and context. The narratives we seek to construct are neither true nor false, but helpful or unhelpful.[21] The exercise of judgement in the selection of narratives is eclectic and pragmatic. As economists, we are not neoclassical or neo-Keynesian, or Austrian or socialist or behavioural. But we are willing to draw on any or all of these schools of thought if they offer relevant insight in the context of a particular problem. We are suspicious of all 'schools' which claim to provide a wide range of answers to problems based on a priori assertions of a general kind about the world.

A mystery cannot be solved as a puzzle can. Reasoning through mysteries requires us to acknowledge ambiguities and to resolve them sufficiently to clarify our thinking. But even to frame a problem requires skill and judgement. That is one of the most important contributions that economists can make. A mystery must first be framed, well or badly, to aid people in reaching the decisions they have to make in conditions of radical uncertainty. Framing begins by identifying critical factors and assembling relevant data. It involves applying experience of how these factors have interacted in the past, and making an assessment of how they might interact in the future. The process of decision-making requires an understanding of the broader context within which a specific problem must be tackled, and most judgements will need to be communicated to others and will require the assistance of others in their implementation.

The role of the economist, like that of other social scientists, is to frame the economic and social issues that political and business leaders face when confronted by radical uncertainty.

The role of the practical economist, like that of the fire-fighter, the doctor, the dentist and the engineer, is to be a problem-solver. These other competent professionals – foxes, not hedgehogs – do not begin from a set of axioms or an over-arching theory. A major part of the reason medicine was of little practical use before the twentieth century is that its practitioners *did* begin from theories which dominated medical thinking but contributed little to real understanding – most notoriously, the Greek physician Galen's notion, from the second century AD, that illness was caused by imbalances between the humours. Modern scientific medicine has been built through the piece-meal accretion of knowledge about details, making full use of inductive, deductive and abductive reasoning, a process which is still contributing to an understanding of human anatomy and physiology.

The good doctor begins by listening to the patient, asking pertinent questions, and gradually forming a provisional diagnosis; then reaching for specific tools relevant to a solution in that particular case. Graham Candler's description of the engineering approach in chapter 19 describes a similar mode of thinking – framing the problem, decomposing it into smaller problems for which solutions are known or can be calculated, and arriving through trial and error at possible answers to the larger question. To put a man on the moon, you begin with a grand objective but find the method of achieving it through the implementation of a mass of detail.

If economics is a practical subject, a problem-solving science, the relevant test of economics and economists is their problem-solving capabilities. When the financial crisis struck in 2008, as we saw in chapter 19, Jean-Claude Trichet observed that he found little help from the macroeconomic models which, following best academic practice, central banks and finance ministries had developed and implemented. Policy-makers found themselves instead in the position of Gary Klein's fire-fighters confronting a unique situation. Like those firefighters, policy-makers were not seeking to optimise but were drawing on their experience in the manner which Klein described as 'primed recognition decision-making' – searching for the best explanation and finding a workable solution.[22]

Perhaps the solution which these policy-makers found was the optimal solution, but it seems unlikely. In any event we will never know. Neither then nor now does anyone have the information needed to determine what would have been the optimal policy. Optimal policies and the concept of optimisation itself are artefacts of small worlds. And small-world models can give us insights into the large economic world but only if we do not make the mistake of believing that they describe 'the world as it really is'. We cannot treat people facing radical uncertainty 'as if they attach probabilities to every conceivable event', as Milton Friedman claimed. It is impossible to compile listings of every conceivable event. Or to acquire the information needed to speculate intelligently about more than a handful of these events.

Rational people answer most questions about the future – whether the question is 'Which horse will win the Kentucky Derby?', 'What will be the level of the stock market at the end of 2025?' or 'How will artificial intelligence develop?' – by saying 'I do not know'. The claim that we can and should attach subjective probabilities to every event, far from enhancing understanding of the future, impedes that understanding. And since there is no compelling reason to accept axiomatic rationality as definitive of rational behaviour in large worlds, such reasoning fails to provide either guidance as to how individuals *should* behave or insight as to how they *do* behave in large worlds. In his seminal work published in 1954, Jimmie Savage explained the limits of a concept of rationality represented by the ability to find correct solutions to small-world problems. That understanding has been largely forgotten in the decades that have followed his work.

If we do not act in accordance with axiomatic rationality and maximise our subjective expected utility, it is not because we are stupid but because we are smart. And it is because we are smart that humans have become the dominant species on Earth. Our intelligence is designed for large worlds, not small. Human intelligence is effective at understanding complex problems within an imperfectly defined context, and at finding courses of action which are good enough to get us through the remains of the day and the rest of our lives. The idea that our intelligence is defective because we are inferior to computers in solving certain kinds of routine mathematical puzzles fails to recognise that few real problems have the character of mathematical puzzles. The assertion that our cognition is defective by virtue of systematic 'biases' or 'natural stupidity' is implausible in the light of the evolutionary origins of that cognitive ability. If it were adaptive to be like computers we would have evolved to be more like computers than we are. What is correct, however, is that humans do now face problems – like trying to put a value on extremely complex financial assets – which are very different from the problems encountered in the historical periods when human genes mutated and were selected and in which human cultures evolved. There were no derivative contracts on the savannahs. Perhaps it is reassuring that computers proved no better than humans at managing the risks such contracts involved.

Our knowledge of context and our ability to interpret it has been acquired over thousands of years. These capabilities are encoded in our genes, taught to us by our parents and teachers, enshrined in the social norms of our culture. It is probably for historical reasons, the legacy of those nineteenth-century utilitarian social reformers, that economists are focused more on equilibrium and optimisation than on evolution and adaptation. Indeed, economists have often assumed that these processes are essentially the same – that the maximisers would drive out the non-maximisers. And the underlying mathematics of adaptation and optimisation do have some similarities. But adaptation is not the same as optimisation. Adaptation is above all about survival. Survival involves finding not the best solution, but one that is good enough. And for survival the tails of distributions matter a lot. Especially, we think, in understanding financial crises.

22

ADAPTING TO RADICAL
UNCERTAINTY

For now we see through a glass, darkly; but then face to
face: now I know in part; but then shall I know even as
also I am known.

—1 Corinthians 13:12

We considered using 'Through a Glass, Darkly' as the
title of this book, but in the end concluded that it was
too – well, opaque. But the metaphor is apt. The world cannot
be partitioned into the known and the unknowable. The asteroid which wiped out the dinosaurs when it landed at Yucatán
was, at least for the dinosaurs, an unpredictable and unavoidable event. The boom and bust of the internet and technology
mania at the end of the last century, and the growth of fissures
in the financial system before the 2007–08 crisis, were not
unpredictable or unavoidable events. Nor could these economic

developments be described as outcomes of stationary processes which remain unchanged over long periods of time, capable of being characterised by probability distributions. No one could predict exactly how these financial excesses would work themselves out, but that does not mean we knew nothing about them at all.

Acknowledging radical uncertainty does not mean that anything goes. Look to the future and contemplate the ways in which information technology will be deployed in the coming decades, or consider the ways in which the growth of prosperity and political influence in Asia will affect the geopolitical balance. They are all things about which we know something, but not enough; things we see through a glass, darkly. We can construct narratives and scenarios to describe the ways in which technology and global politics might develop in the next twenty years; but there is no sensible way in which we can refine such dialogue by attaching probabilities to a comprehensive list of contingencies. We might, however, talk coherently about the confidence we place in scenarios and the likelihood that they will arise. As we have emphasised, the words 'confidence', 'likelihood' and 'probability' are often used interchangeably, but they have different meanings.

We do not enhance our understanding of the future by inventing facts and figures to fill in the inescapable gaps in our knowledge. We cannot rely on forecasts in planning for the future. But the demand for economic forecasts is insatiable and many people think that economics is mainly about forecasting. As economists we are routinely asked to predict what the level of growth will be or to make projections of the movement of the stock market or the level of interest rates. We are not afraid to answer these questions with 'we do not know'. Moreover, we find that the questioners mostly don't take economic forecasts very seriously, and rightly so given the track record of forecasting. Our interlocutors often seek this information not because they attach credence to the numbers, but because they wish for reassurance, or they need to fill in another cell in their own spreadsheets, or because having asked the question offers an excuse when their plans go wrong.

Policy-makers and campaigners routinely invent numbers to support their assertions. Before the Brexit referendum in 2016, the Leave campaign drove a bus around the country bearing the message 'We send the EU £350 million a week. Let's fund our NHS instead'. George Osborne, Chancellor of the Exchequer, leading the Remain campaign, stood in front of a poster saying that leaving the EU would cost each UK household £4300 per year.[1] The precision of both figures is an indicator of their preposterous nature. Neither side presented any contingent and coherent narrative description – the only one realistically possible – of what the likely consequences of the vote would be.

Not all relevant knowledge is quantitative. While the £350 million per week figure was based on a misleading interpretation of published data, the £4300 per year was derived from a complex model based on an extensive series of flimsy assumptions. Elaborate models such as WebTAG and actuarial 'technical valuations', which rely on a cornucopia of invented numbers to fill in inescapable gaps in knowledge arising from radical uncertainty, are widely employed. We observe an obsession with cost-benefit analysis, or 'impact assessment' or even the 'business case' for major government decisions. Enthusiasm for 'evidence-based policy' is seen as the hallmark of sophisticated decision-making. The problem is not so much that these models give rise to bad decisions but that they provide supposedly objective cover for bad decisions which have been made on quite different grounds.

We should not give up modelling or the use of mathematics

in making decisions; rather we should recognise what models can and cannot do to illuminate a problem, and accept that there is no standardised spreadsheet framework which can answer the question 'What is going on here?' Evidence-based policy has become policy-based evidence, eroding the confidence of the public in 'evidence'. Political debates increasingly reflect an unseemly media battle between unsubstantiated assertions rather than a dispassionate argument of pros and cons, or a genuine attempt to find out 'what is going on here'. Too many economists have been willing to join the fray, and the reputation of the profession has understandably suffered.

We have described value at risk modelling undertaken in banks, and the actuarial appraisal of pension schemes, both encouraged by regulatory agencies. These exercises were at best useless and in some cases considerably worse than useless. But the use of irrelevant and incomprehensible black-box models continues. And these exercises are not confined to government; many large firms use similar procedures internally for planning or investment appraisal. Today there are many modellers in consulting firms, big and small, who experience no difficulty in filling in every cell in a spreadsheet, however large. The appropriate use of models in all these instances involves simple structures which identify the key parameters, and therefore provide a basis for research which will compute, or at least identify the bounds of, these critical parameters.

Many different models form part of the economist's repertoire, and skill and judgement are required to identify which models may be, or are not, illuminating in the context of particular problems. We value Frank Knight's insight that people who challenge conventional approaches are the drivers of entrepreneurship, a source of profit opportunities, and a key dynamic of the market economy – and are in economics, as in other subjects, the source of practical knowledge.

Non-stationarity

Neither humans nor computers were successful in controlling the risks bubbling up in the financial system before 2008. The 'training base' – the historical data series from which the experience of risk managers and the algorithms of machines were deduced – was largely irrelevant, drawn from a past which was very different from the present and the future. The worlds of business and finance are not 'stationary'.

Some economists have responded to this criticism with the claim that the relevant data *were* in fact generated by a process – axiomatically 'rational' choices by optimising individuals – which remained unchanged over long periods of time; but one which was disrupted by 'shocks', changes in technology or preferences – originating outside the process itself. But this claim takes us no further, relegating almost everything of interest to these 'shocks'. And so we end up with forecasting models which work well so long as nothing much changes, and give us no insight into when things might change, or why. The meteorologist who tells us that in the absence of any other information the best predictor of tomorrow's weather is that it will be like today's makes an accurate statement, but we are justified in expecting that a professional weather forecaster will either do better or refrain from forecasting at all.

If not shocks, then shifts? We might seek to build models that are valid for a period of years, in which a degree of stationarity can be observed, but recognise that there are shifts from time to time to a new economic trajectory (a 'regime shift'). This structure of thought is not as thin a source of explanation as the reliance on shocks originating outside the system, but suffers from similar weaknesses. Unless we have a good understanding of the origins and effects of these shifts, we have not increased our knowledge by much. What is missing from the discourse of shocks and shifts is the narrative reasoning which enables us to understand how technology and preferences and other factors relevant to economic outcomes happen. And both shocks and shifts hypotheses suppose a degree of discontinuity in the world which surely exists, but not as frequently as these approaches would require. There is an obvious analogy with the biological evolutionary debate which has mostly rejected theories of 'punctuated equilibria' in favour of the belief in evolution as an essentially continuous process.[2] And understanding of such evolution is enhanced by the study of complex systems which demonstrates how continuous changes in initial conditions can give rise to discontinuous changes in outcomes. In this way we can build up an account of economic and financial crises which is richer and more insightful than characterising them as 'shocks'.

We have been impressed by the power of the simple question 'What is going on here?' Perhaps the most telling illustration of this power is the range of mistakes made by those who failed to ask it. The Johnson and Bush administrations did not ask, far less know, what was going on in Vietnam and Iraq – they acted on the basis of a general predisposition to certain kinds of action and an erroneous assumption that institutions they recognised in their own societies could be transposed successfully to alien environments. The participants in those business strategy weekends were bombarded with numbers, seized by visions, or blinded by inspirational messages. Bankers and regulators ahead of the 2007–08 crisis, with misplaced faith in their risk models, failed to see the wood for the trees. Users of the transport analysis program WebTAG, or actuarial models, place faith in models which obscure rather than illuminate 'what is going on here'. The attendees at the strategy weekends could more usefully have stayed at home and read Dick Rumelt's book on business strategy.

Humans are social animals

Still, the participants at the weekend retreats perceived a need for an opportunity to discuss the affairs of the company collectively. Humans are successful because, to a far greater extent than any other species, they communicate with each other. That makes it odd that economics should have put so much emphasis on optimising behaviour by independent individuals. This approach seems to omit not just an important part of what makes us human, but a central cause of our economic achievements. We have commented on the fact – which would have seemed extraordinary even two centuries ago – that tens of thousands of people can now participate in the production of a single complex artefact such as an Airbus without knowing each other, but exploiting a whole variety of connections and mechanisms of communication. We are only at the edges of understanding the mixture of markets and hierarchies, of competition and cooperation, which makes these achievements possible, and these capabilities emerged more as a product of evolution than design. The large corporation is the most important actor in the modern economy, and it is surprising how little attention has been given to the economics of organisation.

In business, in finance, and in public policy, judgements are reached and decisions made in organisations – companies, banks, departments and agencies. All these institutions have multiple goals and the individuals and groups within them will typically have multiple goals of their own. Economists emphasise the role of incentives, and construct models to describe the problem of decentralising the objectives of an organisation to the individuals who will have to carry them out. But these models do not describe 'the world as it really is'. The presumption that financial incentives are everywhere primary, and that the complex issues involved in delivering public services efficiently and fairly can be dealt with by the sticks of targets and the carrots of bonuses, has created as many problems as it has solved. We see the distortion of educational processes and health services by the pursuit of targets. What is meant by a good or bad hospital or school is multi-dimensional and hard to define precisely; and yet we would encounter very wide agreement on which hospitals and schools were good and which were bad.

Piece rates on automobile assembly lines were abandoned because they led workers to pursue quantity at the expense of quality – Toyota showed that superior products could be manufactured by encouraging groups of workers to take pride in the reliability of their output and to 'stop the line' if they believed that goal was in jeopardy.[3] Financial economics must take much of the responsibility for spreading the idea that senior executives could be treated as actors whose role was to respond to the incentives they were given tailored to maximise shareholder value. The results have seriously distorted corporate behaviour and led to an explosion of executive remuneration which has exacerbated social divisions. The introduction of 'eat what you kill' policies in law and accountancy – the primary driver of personal remuneration is your own revenue generation rather than the profitability of the firm – has eroded the professional ethos which historically characterised these activities. In the years before 2008, banks represented the closest approximation in the business world to organisations which treated both senior management and lowly employees as people whose interests were to be aligned with those of the company solely through incentive schemes. The outcomes – the destruction of corporate reputations built up over decades and the collapse of organisations torn apart by the greed of their own employees – are all too well known.

The importance of narrative

We live in a world of radical uncertainty in which our under-standing of the present is imperfect, our understanding of the future even more limited, and in which no one person or organisation can hold the range of information required to arrive at the 'best explanation'. Narrative reasoning is the most powerful mechanism available for organising our imperfect knowledge. Understanding the complex world is a matter of constructing the best explanation – a narrative account – from a myriad of little details and the knowledge of context derived from personal experience and the experience of others.

Another of the few business strategy writers worth reading, Henry Mintzberg, describes the problem created by the approaches to business caricatured by the weekend strategy retreats as follows: 'We are often, in the business world, over-led and undermanaged ... Senior management is supposedly seeing the big picture but, in dysfunctional cases, is not in touch with the details.'[4] Mintzberg continues with a quotation from Konosuke Matsushita, founder of Panasonic Corp., asserting that 'Big things and little things are my job. Middle level arrangements can be delegated.' So, Mintzberg summarises, 'In other words, you construct the big picture out of the little details. It's like painting a painting; you paint it one brush stroke at a time.' We have ourselves learnt that you come to understand an organisation much better when you make contact with the people who are actually delivering products as well as, or even instead of, the people who occupy the C-suite.

Narrative processes are at the centre of legal decision-making, one of the oldest forms of structured reasoning we have. It is through shared narratives that we persuade other people to cooperate in the complex processes of manufacturing an Airbus or contributing to the success of an organisation. The financial institutions which failed in 2008, such as Lehman Brothers, combined pernicious narrative with misconceived incentive structures.

Computers don't do narratives. They don't do emotions, and yet we have learnt that lack of emotional depth makes it impossible or difficult to make decisions even on trivial matters in a large world. Computers don't do empathy, and we have learnt from studies of high-functioning autistics that people who lack insight into the feelings of others can do very well the sorts of things that computers, or Max Planck (who was not at all autistic), can do very well, but that they struggle with activities which are part of most people's everyday lives and the working lives of almost everyone who is successful in organisations.[5]

Shortly before Barings Bank went bust in 1995, chairman Peter Baring congratulated himself and his colleagues on the extraordinary profits that rogue trader Nick Leeson falsely claimed to be making in Singapore, asserting that 'it is not actually terribly difficult to make money in the securities business'.[6] As a result of Leeson's trades, the bank was actually haemorrhaging cash while reporting large profits. There is no more salutary example of the need to ask 'What is going on here?', or of the wilful blindness which fails to look behind reported numbers. If it seems too good to be true, it generally is.

Challenging narratives

Decision-making under radical uncertainty requires a multiplicity of skills, and rarely will all these skills be found in a single individual. Successful leaders have benefited from advisers who could assist in problem framing. Louis XIV had the support of his minister of state Jean-Baptiste Colbert, Franklin Roosevelt was so dependent on the ailing Harry Hopkins that the foreign policy adviser took up residence in a bedroom of the White

House, and such modest reputation as Richard Nixon retained was largely attributable to the support of Henry Kissinger. Even the self-confident Margaret Thatcher would observe of William Whitelaw, her aide and deputy, that 'every Prime Minister needs a Willie'.[7]

Successful decision-making under uncertainty is a collaborative process. Having arrived at the best explanation, it is important to open that explanation to challenge and be ready to change the guiding narrative when new information emerges. The mistakes made by people who enjoyed the flattery of supportive sycophants – George W. Bush planning the Iraq war, or Dick Fuld leading Lehman to self-destruction – contrast with the achievements of those who were not afraid of honest critique: Alfred Sloan building the world's most successful corporation, the chastened John F. Kennedy responding to the challenge of the Cuban Missile Crisis. A narrative was in the minds of the Republican ideologues in the George W. Bush administration who believed that the rapid establishment of a stock exchange in Iraq was a central building block of stability and democracy, but it was a narrative constructed from a priori assertions rather than from specific – or any – knowledge of Iraqi politics and culture. Beware the narrative of the hedgehog derived from 'universal' explanations, ideologies and grand theories, or from formal axioms based on abstract reasoning. In the ordinary business of life, where we are constantly confronted with unique situations, we need a pluralism of approaches and models.

Experts could have explained the nuances of recent Vietnamese history, the tactics of guerrilla warfare, and provided an assessment to US policy-makers of the reality of what was happening on the battlefields of Indochina in the 1960s. But little attempt was made to consult such experts, and when they did attempt to offer advice they were ignored. As a result, the decision-makers heard only what they wanted to hear. And soon they did not want to hear anything at all. The history of the invasion of Iraq tells a similar story, but also demonstrates an extreme contrast: on the one hand, meticulous assessment of military strengths, weaknesses and options, accompanied by genuinely challenging grilling from Rumsfeld and others, which preceded the skilfully planned and executed military operation; on the other hand, a complete absence of similar understanding of or planning for the politics of post-Saddam Iraq.

Collective intelligence and communicative rationality

If our knowledge was confined to what we have ourselves been able to ascertain, by observation or calculation, it would be limited indeed; and so would be our capacity to deal with radical uncertainty. If our knowledge derives only from our personal experience, our capacity to make good decisions is also limited. And that applies to most non-human species; ask anyone who has tried to administer a healing medicine to a pet. Even other primates, whose intelligence most closely parallels our own, are typically bemused by non-routine questions. They can sometimes solve simple puzzles, but demonstrate little capacity to deal with mysteries.

Our ability as humans to deal with radical uncertainty is the product of our much greater capacity for social learning and greater ability to communicate relative to other species. We are social animals; we manage radical uncertainty in a context determined by the knowledge we have acquired through education and experience, and we make important decisions in conjunction with others – friends, family, colleagues and advisers.

Reference to the 'wisdom of crowds' makes an important point while missing another. The crowd always knows more than any individual, but what is valuable is the *aggregate* of its knowledge, not the *average* of its knowledge. Given the overwhelmingly large body of knowledge and experience which makes up our collective intelligence, and the obvious necessity for specialisation, the rational person following the requirements of logic and reason answers most questions about what will happen in the future or what will be the consequence of particular actions by saying 'I do not know – if it matters I will try to find out'.

Recall the example of a commercial aircraft with two pilots, a flight crew and five hundred passengers, and the assistance of maintenance staff and air traffic controllers on the ground, and in the event of problems access to expert advice. The aircraft is flown not by constantly polling the opinions of hundreds of people, but by the disciplined process of making the best use of the specialist knowledge and experience of many people, few of whom are on the plane. And the reason representative democracy has proved to be the best form of government is that, properly conducted, it draws on the whole collective intelligence of the community.

We trust the pilot's competence and experience, but if we ask him to explain the workings of the aircraft we will probably be disappointed, as we would be if we quizzed David Beckham about those differential equations. Good judgement and good explanation are not the same. The reasons people give for their judgements and decisions do not necessarily describe how those decisions were reached, nor do those people always know how they were made. But we learn from the process of effective decision-making by people engaged in difficult practical activities – those who save lives in fires or on the battlefield or at the roadside, or who rise to heights of sporting achievement, or who can detect at a glance the real image from the fake – that people may be very good at what they do without being good at explaining what it is they do. One of Klein's most inspiring stories is of the fire chief who abruptly pulled his crew out of a burning building minutes before the floor collapsed, having sensed that there was something wrong with what he and his colleagues regarded as the best explanation while remaining uncertain what it was that was wrong. Administered by someone with a proven record of success in decision-making, the question 'Does this feel right?' is valuable. To admire this expertise is not the same as applauding people who make decisions 'from the gut', relying only on their bombast or seniority to attest to the quality of their judgement.

In large organisations today, it is often the case that decisions are made on the basis of what is easiest to justify rather than what is the right thing to do. 'No one ever got fired for buying IBM' was for long a mantra among mid-ranking executives, and a crucial factor in the success of that company's technically unremarkable PC. The meaning of risk to the executives who hired IBM was not the same as the meaning of risk to the organisation that employed them. The false assumption that good process leads to good outcome is pervasive in public sector organisations, where good often means lengthy, involves many people with little responsibility for the result, and is imbued with ill-defined concepts of fairness centred around issues of representativeness and statistical discrimination. Process has become the policy, with deleterious effects on outcomes.

In the courtroom, of course, the judge must provide reasoned argument for what has been decided. But even there the decision of the creative judge reflects as far as possible what he or she believes to be right, and then expresses the argument in the terms required by statute and precedent. The phrase 'communicative rationality' as employed by Mercier and Sperber describes the terms in which people express their views and judgements to others, and particularly to others with whom they plan to debate these views and judgements, or who will be required to implement the resulting decisions.[8] We should not assume that such expressions describe 'the real reason' for the views, judgements or decisions they express, or even that there is such a thing as 'the real reason' for them. And the terms of communicative rationality are culturally specific. The judge expresses the finding of the court in one way, the arresting policeman frames his request in a different way; the chief executive uses one style of speech to announce a decision, the tribal chief another.

Often it is more important to make a decision than what that decision is. We learn from Gary Klein how people who must make life and death decisions do not take time to assess a menu of options. They quickly find one that is good enough. It usually *is* good enough, and if it is not they move on to something else. By contrast we both have ample experience of the committee whose deliberations extend indefinitely because there are so many different views of the best course of action.

Nevertheless, we make better decisions in groups, because in a radically uncertain world the group holds more information than any individual member. The committee is wasting time when its members bring their opinions rather than their distinctive knowledge, and when it becomes a mechanism for diffusing rather than acknowledging responsibility for the outcomes. The effective leader is one who recognises that his membership of the group is marked by his superior responsibility rather than his superior wisdom.

Philosophers have speculated about the nature of human reasoning over thousands of years. But it is only very recently that neurophysiology has begun to elucidate the physical and chemical processes by which our brains work, and through which we interpret the things we see, and decide to act. And that evolutionary psychology has described how these processes have developed over thousands of years to aid us in making choices and decisions in a world of radical uncertainty. We find it humbling to realise how little we know about how humans really think, humbling to see how much scientists outside economics are beginning to know, and perhaps most humbling of all to see how little impact this work has so far made on economic science.

23

EMBRACING UNCERTAINTY

Knowledge would be fatal, it is the uncertainty that charms one. A mist makes things beautiful.

—Oscar Wilde, *The Picture of Dorian Gray*[1]

Nobody thinks in terms of human beings . . . they have their five-year plans.

—Harry Lime in *The Third Man*

Harry Lime, played by Orson Welles in the film *The Third Man*, famously observed that 'in Italy, for thirty years under the Borgias, they had warfare, terror, murder and bloodshed, but they produced Michelangelo, Leonardo da Vinci and the Renaissance. In Switzerland, they had brotherly love, they had five hundred years of democracy and peace – and what did that produce? The cuckoo clock.' Like so many people, Lime is unfairly maligning the Swiss; theirs is the country that produced Albert Einstein, Carl Jung, Le Corbusier, Paul Klee and Hermann Hesse, not to mention Ursula Andress and Roger Federer, and more Nobel Prize winners per head of population than any other nation in the world.[2] The cuckoo clock caricatures the country's genuine strengths in precision engineering. These industries, along with speciality chemicals, have made Switzerland one of the richest countries in the world. Still, Lime's point that the political volatility which was characteristic of Renaissance Italy was compatible with one of the great eras of extraordinary creativity is well made.

In *Groundhog Day*, a very different movie starring a very different character, Bill Murray is condemned to live in a stationary world which repeats itself every day. Experience leads him not to bask in the certainty of knowing what is to come next, to which every risk-averse person supposedly aspires, but to attempt suicide in despair, only to discover that there is no such thing as death in a stationary world. The film has a happy ending, perhaps because Hollywood comedies must, but also because Murray's character has learnt enough from repeated experience to escape from the loop of stationarity.

More than fifty years before Columbus crossed the Atlantic, Chinese vessels embarked on expeditions no less ambitious. But then the Ming emperors turned inwards, rejecting outside influence. They aspired to stationarity. Two centuries later, the Japanese shogunate adopted a similar policy. When Lord Macartney led a British delegation to China in 1792–3, his gifts and proposals were rebuffed. 'Our Celestial Empire possesses all things in prolific abundance and lacks no product within its borders. There is therefore no need to import the manufactures of outside barbarians in exchange for our own produce,' said the Qianlong Emperor.[3]

And so began the Great Divergence; the Industrial Revolution took place in Western Europe, not in the equally well-resourced south-east of China. Chinese stationarity began to change only when the power of the Royal Navy imposed British will on China in the discreditable Opium Wars of the nineteenth century. Even then internal dysfunction inhibited substantive economic development until the events which followed Nixon's visit to China in 1972. After the arrival of Captain Perry in 1853, Japan began to open its economy to the rest of the world. But it was the forcible landing of General MacArthur in 1945 which brought that country – and over the next half century most of South-east Asia – into the modern world. Stationarity is not a happy choice in human affairs, nor in the long run is it a sustainable one.

Risk and uncertainty

The distinction between problems such as the unpredictable outcome of games of chance, which could be represented probabilistically, and radical uncertainty, which could not, was understood by both Keynes and Knight. After the Second World War Friedman denied the existence of such a distinction and the two concepts were elided not just in the field of economics, but in a much wider arena in which decision theory and Bayesian reasoning held sway.

We could attach probabilities to every conceivable event. Whatever might happen in the future could be spelt out as a set of mutually exclusive alternatives, and probabilities could be attached to each of those events. The implication was that risk was something that could be priced. Once it had been priced, risk was tamed. In effect, uncertainty was suppressed by markets.

In finance theory, risk is defined as a spread around a known average return. The lower the spread the less the risk. Since people are assumed to be 'risk-averse', they must be offered an incentive to hold assets that are risky in this sense. And so there is a trade-off between risk and return. Risk-averse individuals will be content to assume risk provided there is adequate compensation. Risk is no longer feared because it is priced and has been accepted in return for its price. And risky assets are simply commodities to be bought and sold just like soap powder and motor cars, and like these commodities risks will end up in the hands of those most willing and able to buy them. Radical uncertainty must be erased from the picture because it cannot be measured and cannot be priced.

But this small world is not ours or yours. In everyday language, the words 'risk' and 'uncertainty' are used in different senses and much confusion has been generated both by the multiplicity of interpretations and by the attribution of technical meanings which do not correspond to the ordinary usage of these terms. We have defined risk as the failure of a reference narrative to be realised. Leonardo, whose talents were avidly sought by rich patrons such as Ludovico Sforza and Cesare Borgia, was secure in a reference narrative which left him free to paint and think. Such patronage was an opportunity which enabled an illegitimate child from a small village to realise his genius even as the Borgias were murdering each other. For Leonardo and Michelangelo, the intellectual vibrancy of these tumultuous times was an opportunity, not a threat. While Sforza died in a French prison and Borgia was stripped naked and killed in battle in Navarre, Leonardo died at home of a stroke and Michelangelo lived to the age of eighty-eight.

The absence of observed volatility should never be confused with the absence of risk. Hume's formulation of the problem of induction assured us that we are not justified in believing that the sun will rise tomorrow on the basis of the information that it has always risen in the past. The modern formulation, often attributed to Bertrand Russell, describes the experience of the turkey which is fed reliably every morning until 24 December. Nassim Nicholas Taleb reframes this narrative in contrasting the banker who receives a regular salary at the end of each month but always runs the risk of abrupt termination with the cab driver whose earnings vary constantly but are secure because they are derived on a continuing basis from multiple sources.[4] The erroneous belief that the absence of current volatility demonstrates the absence of risk was at the heart of the financial crisis. Like the Christmas turkey, many financial institutions reported the steadily growing quarterly earnings per share that Wall Street required until they suddenly faced insolvency in 2008. The earnings stability they, and many other businesses, reported was properly a cause for concern, not congratulation; greater variability would have demonstrated a sounder basis for these earnings. The world is inherently uncertain and to pretend otherwise is to create risk, not to minimise it.

Taleb describes 'anti-fragility' – positioning oneself to benefit from radical uncertainty and the unknowable future. The value of an option is *increased* by volatility. The details of Thales of Miletus's transaction with the olive presses remain obscure – if indeed any such transaction actually occurred. Perhaps he made a futures contract with the owners of the olive presses, perhaps he bought what we would now describe as a call option: the right, but not the obligation, to rent the presses at a price agreed in advance – a price which would seem low if the harvest was as good as Thales anticipated. In either case, he engaged in the first reported transaction in financial derivatives. Derivative markets exist because of volatility in securities prices. And the greater the volatility, the greater the value of an option – whether that option is a call option (the right to buy) or a put option (the right to sell). Most option transactions – such as the Big Short, the notorious bets against the US subprime mortgage market by hedge fund manager John Paulson and others – are simply wagers, in which two people have different views of the future and the one whose opinion is more nearly right gains at the expense of the other. Option transactions, however, can benefit both sides. The Chicago Mercantile Exchange, today a global centre for financial speculation, came into being to enable farmers and food processors to protect their reference narrative by fixing in advance the price of crops which had not yet been harvested.[5] Although the term 'option' is nowadays most often used in financial markets, options in the real economy are of far more practical importance. A strategic decision may open up new possibilities, or close off alternatives.

Robustness and resilience

Good strategies for a radically uncertain world avoid the pretence of knowledge – the models and bogus quantification which require users to make up things they do not know and could not know. In chapter 19 we described how pension planning in Britain, under regulatory pressure, had demanded a certainty which is unattainable, represented it with a spreadsheet of imagined numbers, and far from achieving certainty created a structure so fragile that the outcome was the destruction of the schemes whose security it was designed to protect. This narrative of decision-making misled by unfounded confidence in understanding and prediction has been repeated many times in recent decades. On the Canadian fishing grounds, where sophisticated modelling led in less than twenty years to the loss of the stocks which had been successfully protected for centuries. In the banks which believed, or found it convenient to believe, that their risk management processes, based on a common view of good industry practice negotiated with international regulatory agencies, protected them against the greed and malfeasance of their traders.

Good strategies for a radically uncertain world acknowledge that we do not know what the future will hold. Such strategies identify reference narratives, visualise alternative future scenarios, and ensure that plans are robust and resilient to a range of plausible alternatives. The relevant reference narrative for the Grand Banks of Canada would have estimated a sustainable catch but acknowledged the imperfections of the regulators' understanding and would have been associated with a strategy for fisheries management which incorporated triggers warning of impending problems and activated buffers and recovery plans. The similar reference narrative for a pension plan is one in which it meets its obligations for the foreseeable future and has reasonable grounds for believing it can continue to do so at the end of that foreseeable future. The immensely long-time horizons of pension funds allow much time for adjustment when scenarios emerge at the low – or high – end of expectations. And the relevant reference narrative for a bank is – fundamentally – that it can continue to operate as a bank, meeting its obligations as they fall due. The banks of 2008 were not within miles of being either robust or resilient, whatever their elaborate calculations of value at risk and risk weighted capital told them and their supervisors.

Robust and resilient plans confer positive options – opportunities to take advantage of developments which are not currently foreseen with any specificity or perhaps at all – and avoid negative ones, which close off alternatives and limit future developments to those which can currently be envisaged. Planners in modern cities benefit enormously from the foresight of their predecessors who created positive options. The Manhattan grid plan and the embankments along London's River Thames, the corridors along which transport serves the centre of those cities, are assets which have been valuable for almost two centuries and will continue to be, even though the visionaries who built them had no idea, and could have had no idea, of the ways in which they would be used today. But they made plans which have proved to be robust and resilient to a wide variety of subsequent developments. We need to accept that we do not know and cannot know what is going to happen, and make plans accordingly; to practise resilience and acquire and retain as many options as possible.

But some decisions reduce future options, and these can be costly. Many visitors to New York must have wondered why it is so difficult to travel between the city's two principal airports and Manhattan. Perhaps you have fumed in frustration on the Van Wyck expressway, like millions of travellers before you, and like thousands of airport and airline employees every day. When that road was planned in 1945, Dodd McHugh, chief of the Office of Master Planning in the City Planning Commission, proposed simple and relatively inexpensive modifications which would have added a rapid transit link to the corridor the city razed to build the expressway. That would have taken travellers to midtown or the financial district in twenty minutes. The plan was rejected out of hand by the brilliant but autocratic Robert Moses, who – holding multiple offices – dominated New York's built environment from 1924 to 1968.[6]

Moses not only dismissed McHugh's plan but ensured that the width of the corridors and, most importantly, the bridge clearances on his expressways made it impossible to implement such a scheme in future. His clientele consisted of the kind of people who owned automobiles in 1945 and the city he envisaged was one in which poor people and African-Americans did not venture far from home. Many more people now do own automobiles, or hire them from Uber, and each morning and evening they are stuck in traffic jams. Negative options limit future decisions, positive options offer new possibilities. Creatively used, options exploit uncertainty. Inappropriately used, they increase the costs of uncertainty.

Denmark as top nation

At a conference in an English country house on the topic of future geopolitics, pundits emphasised the significance of the coming competition between China and the United States to be 'top nation', as Sellar and Yeatman put it in their classic satire on British history *1066 And All That*.[7] Provocatively, one of the authors observed that for many modern Europeans, Denmark was 'number one' – rich, socially cohesive, with enviable infrastructure and environmental standards – and it regularly features near the top in surveys of the world's happiest populations. 'Hygge', sometimes defined as 'cosy contentment and well-being through enjoying the simple things in life', has recently become one of the few Danish words to enter the English language.

But Denmark is so boring, responded a former ambassador to Denmark. Following Harry Lime, he might have said the same of Switzerland. And, for an ambassador, Denmark, like Switzerland, *is* boring. Its politics are of no global significance, its economy is stable, there is no need for embassies to respond to urgent cables or consultations. The life of the ambassador was a round of receptions at which congenial guests spoke excellent English. By contrast, Zimbabwe is not boring either for ambassadors or the general population, but the general population wishes it were. Denmark provides its inhabitants with a secure reference narrative – they do not feel threatened by loss of income, or crippling medical bills, or terrorist threats, or insecure retirement. Natural disasters are rare, and when they occur efficient emergency services are there to help. What was profoundly shocking about the devastation in New Orleans caused by Hurricane Katrina in 2005 was that the resources of the nation with the world's largest GDP were not organised to protect the fundamental needs, far less the reference narrative, of its citizens in time of crisis. And that is why almost all Europeans are puzzled by the American idea that the provision of universal health care should be controversial.

There is a strand of thought which associates the extraordinary innovative capacity of the US economy with this reluctance of its governments to provide the social insurance against risk – in the broadest sense – which is taken for granted in Denmark, and most European countries. But we need to probe deeper. Bill Gates did not drop out of Harvard to set up Microsoft because the alternative was unemployment, or because he feared an illness that would threaten his bank balance as well as his life; rather the opposite. He was able to follow his dream because he had little fear of these things; he was the son of a prosperous attorney and already marked for success by his education. Leland Stanford had qualified as an attorney before moving to California. Peter Thiel, the putative refugee in a New Zealand bunker, and perhaps the most outspoken representative of Silicon Valley libertarians, also began his career as a lawyer (he graduated from Stanford University), clerking for a federal circuit judge, and practising with a premier securities law firm before founding PayPal.

In the nineteenth century, when poor but adventurous European immigrants flooded into the United States, there was some foundation to the narrative of the boy who risks all, but whose grit and enterprise creates a great business and makes him rich. Johann Suter tried – and failed; Andrew Carnegie succeeded. But as with the myth of log cabin to White House, real examples are few. If PayPal had failed, and it might have (many attempts were made to develop new payments systems for the digital age and few succeeded), Thiel might not have been a billionaire but would still have enjoyed a much more comfortable lifestyle than most of his fellow Americans.

America's innovative hegemony is in technology. You will

find more adventurous food in Copenhagen than in Chicago or even New York (except in that city's Scandinavian restaurants), and in the Danish capital today there is a cultural milieu unmatched in any US city of comparable size. Denmark – and Italy – stand out for creative design. If we look for innovation in art, or literature, or music, our search extends across the developed world. But not to Zimbabwe, or Syria. While Borgia and Sforza had reason for constant fear for their lives, Leonardo and Michelangelo did not; and neither had to worry about ZANU-PF goons or chemical bombs.

The people of Denmark or Switzerland can enjoy uncertainty because they experience little risk and are secure in their reference narratives. Far from representing a threat, uncertainty can be the source of all that makes life worth living. Delight in discovering a previously unknown place while on holiday. Or a new book, or piece of music, or friend. In places such as Zimbabwe or Syria, risk dominates. The collapse of the Zimbabwean economy and the civil war in Syria deprived much of the population of any secure reference narrative; many are refugees in South Africa or Europe, and those who remain in their own countries are fearful of what tomorrow will bring. In the absence of a secure reference narrative, uncertainty is scary. Within the context of such a narrative, uncertainty – the prospect of new experiences – can be a source of joy rather than despair.

Uncertainty and evolution

Without uncertainty, there could be no evolution. Sexual reproduction is a mechanism which ensures that every child inherits genes from two parents, so that no two individuals are ever the same. Even viruses and bacteria mutate, since cloning is imperfect. And most mutations are for the worse. The mutated gene is less likely than its colleagues to be passed on in subsequent generations. But the occasional mutation which adds to fitness spreads through the population.

If the world was stationary, and if it was also linear – so that every small change could be scaled up in proportion to a similar large change – then the results of this process of mutation would look very like the economic concept of 'optimising behaviour'. One reason why evolution is not optimisation is that the external world is constantly changing. At its simplest, humans are engaged in a constant battle with parasites, which themselves mutate to take greater advantage of us. They are evolving to resist our antibiotics, and we are evolving new antibiotics to keep them at bay.[8] A cloned population runs extreme risk, as the Irish potato famine illustrated. Without uncertainty there would be little need for evolution, but without uncertainty there would be little possibility of evolution.

But as the example of antibiotics illustrates, genetic evolution is only one form of evolution. The co-evolution of culture and technology with biology has been the source of social and economic progress. Stationarity is boring. Pity the young student who is told his subject is 'a highly developed, nearly fully matured science, that through the crowning achievement of the discovery of the principle of conservation of energy will soon take its final stable form'.[9] That student was Max Planck, who received this advice in 1874 from his distinguished mentor, the German physicist Philipp von Jolly. Fortunately, Planck ignored the recommendation to seek new frontiers elsewhere – perhaps that was when he contemplated the study of economics. If so, he might have learnt that young economists were receiving a similar warning from that towering figure of mid-nineteenth-century thought John Stuart Mill, who told them: 'Happily, there is nothing in the laws of Value which remains for the present or any future writer to clear up; the theory of the subject is complete.'[10] A quarter century after Jolly, his verdict on his subject was reiterated by the irrepressible Lord Kelvin, who assured the British Academy for the Advancement of Science that, at least as far as physics was concerned, little advancement was possible or necessary; Albert Michelson, the first American scientist to be awarded a Nobel Prize, pronounced, 'It seems probable that most of the grand underlying principles have been firmly established ... An eminent physicist remarked that the future truths of physical science are to be looked for in the sixth place of decimals.'[11] Perhaps the older Planck had Jolly's advice in his mind when he suggested that science progressed only through the funerals of the previous generation. That observation may perhaps be even more pertinent today, when the young scholar who resists the advice of his or her sage elders is at risk of losing patronage and postdoctoral positions.

And yet the stable reference narrative provided by tenure remains important in enabling academics to navigate the radical uncertainty which surrounds advancement of knowledge. But in the academy as elsewhere the stable reference narrative can degenerate into the stationarity which led China and Japan to turn their backs on the rest of the world; 'hygge' becomes what the Danish writer Aksel Sandemose identified as Jante's Law – 'you are not to think *you* are anything special'.[12]

Evolution is at work in scholarship, where people compete to write fresh articles and books, most of which attract few readers or citations. Evolution is at work in entrepreneurship; people try new business ideas, most of which fail. Evolution is at work in competitive markets in which corporations compete, often unsuccessfully, to develop alternative strategies. Evolution is at work in technology, where constant tinkering leads to incremental development. 'Darwin's dangerous idea' is key, not just to explaining the origin of species, but to understanding the development of our economy and society.

Those kinds of evolution in human institutions – universities, markets, corporations and workshops – are differentiated from biological evolution by the contribution of intentionality. The gene mutates randomly. But scholars believe they have some contribution to make to knowledge. Entrepreneurs select the ventures they hope will succeed. Corporate leaders adopt strategies which they think will be more effective than their existing courses of action. Engineers and software compilers think they are making improvements. These judgements are often wrong, and we are often inclined to exaggerate the role of skill relative to luck in favourable outcomes – the error of analysing to the result. But it would be an error to describe – or model – these processes as if they were simply random.

Entrepreneurship and radical uncertainty

Knight's insight – that it is radical uncertainty which gives opportunity for entrepreneurship – is fundamental to an understanding of social, technological and economic progress. Through evolutionary processes – biological, institutional, political, market-driven – entrepreneurship drives us forward. Not just in business but in scholarship, practical knowledge, the arts, and many other areas of life.

The model of the lone entrepreneur – the poor boy with a brilliant business idea who rises single-handedly from poverty; the isolated scholar scribbling brilliant ideas in a garret or country vicarage – is largely mythological. There are contrary examples. Thomas Edison was fired from the only two jobs he held, the first as telegraph boy for Western Electric and the other as CEO of the corporation which is now General Electric. The Reverend Thomas Bayes died unknown. But such examples are few, and to find them we have to go some way back in history. The most common profile of the successful entrepreneur today is the individual who draws on his or her past experience in a larger organisation, and works from inception with a team of like-minded individuals. And such individuals can contribute to society only in a supportive social context. There is no shortage of entrepreneurial talent in Nigeria, but too much of it is directed to opportunistic scams and rent seeking. Barack Obama was widely criticised for his Roanoke campaign speech of 2012 in which he said 'if you've been successful, you didn't get there on your own'.[13] But if you look further at what he said you see that he got it exactly right: 'when we succeed, we succeed because of our individual initiative, but also because we do things together'.[14] Perhaps the most remarkable of all lone geniuses was Srinivasa Ramanujan, the destitute Indian mathematician who failed his college exams, learnt mathematics from a public library book, impressed an Indian revenue official enough to be offered a job, and whose letter to G. H. Hardy took him to England and to a Fellowship at Trinity College, Cambridge. But without Hardy he would never have gained acceptance for his ideas among the community of mathematicians.

Humans thrive in conditions of radical uncertainty when creative individuals can draw on collective intelligence, hone their ideas in communication with others, and operate in an environment which permits a stable reference narrative. Within the context of a secure reference narrative, uncertainty is to be welcomed rather than feared. In personal matters – friends, holidays, leisure – stationarity is boring. In politics and business, uncertainty is a source of opportunity for the enterprising, though also associated with paralysis of decision-making in bureaucracies staffed by risk-averse individuals determined to protect their personal reference narratives. In the arts, uncertainty and creativity are inseparable. Embrace uncertainty; avoid risk.

Borodino

We end where we began – at the battle of Borodino. Fighting with the Russians against Napoleon was a young Prussian officer, Carl von Clausewitz, who would become a military strategist whose works are still widely read today. Clausewitz had learnt the importance of radical uncertainty on the battlefield, and argued forcefully that good judgement was the distinguishing mark of a successful general. In *On War*, he describes attempts by some to reduce war to mathematical terms: 'They wanted to reach a set of sure and positive conclusions, and for that reason considered only factors that could be mathematically calculated.'[15] But Clausewitz knew that war does not work in this way because it is radically uncertain, reflexive, and by its nature a collective activity.

> It is only analytically that these attempts at theory can be called advances in the realm of truth; synthetically, in the rules and regulations they offer, they are absolutely useless. They aim at fixed values; but in war everything is uncertain, and calculations have to be made with variable quantities. They direct the inquiry exclusively towards physical quantities, whereas all military action is intertwined with psychological forces and effects. They consider only unilateral actions, whereas war consists of a continuous interaction of opposites.

To think otherwise was 'to do violence to the facts'.[16]

Tolstoy described that battle in twenty chapters of one of the great narratives of literature, in which fact and fiction are intertwined. He understood radical uncertainty. We see through a glass, darkly. And we communicate with each other through narratives, not probabilities, to describe our endlessly fascinating world.

APPENDIX:

Axioms of Choice under Uncertainty

In chapters 1–7 we explained why radical uncertainty precluded the formation of subjective probabilities for all possible states of the world, a prerequisite for the theory that people make decisions in a world of uncertainty by maximising their expected utility. That 'optimising' view of human behaviour rested on a set of assumptions, or 'axioms', about behaviour that drew heavily on an analogy with choices in a world of certainty. In the latter case, the assumptions of well-defined and consistent choices from a known set of possibilities seemed relatively innocuous. Applied to uncertainty they are far from innocuous. In this appendix we provide a brief explanation of why the economics profession was wrong to accept too readily the axioms of choice under uncertainty in order to justify the assumption of expected utility maximisation.[1]

There are evident similarities between the Hicks–Samuelson axioms of consumer choice under certainty and the von Neumann–Morgenstern axioms (as modified by Savage) of behaviour under uncertainty. The description of these approaches as 'utility maximisation' and 'expected utility maximisation' further emphasise the resemblance. But the analysis of consumer behaviour is distinct from the analysis of decision-making under uncertainty, and the apparent equivalence is the product of the long tradition in economics of using the word 'utility' and the modern emphasis on the term 'rational' not only to refer to a number of different things but also in ways which may not necessarily reflect ordinary usage. It is entirely possible to be 'rational' (in the Hicks–Samuelson sense) in consumer choice and not 'rational' (in the von Neumann–Morgenstern sense) in making decisions under uncertainty.

The von Neumann–Morgenstern approach is based on a priori assumptions about how such choices are made, and not on any study of how such decisions are made, still less on any evidence of which decision-making procedures led to good outcomes. 'Rational' decision-makers supposedly can translate their preferences over risky outcomes into a ranking – a preference ordering over different alternative probability distributions. Von Neumann and Morgenstern assumed that these preferences over alternative probability distributions are:

(i)   complete – the decision-maker is able to choose between all possible probability distributions;

(ii) transitive – if I prefer A to B and B to C then I prefer A to C;

(iii) continuous – if A is preferred to B, and B to C, there is always some gamble involving A and C which will be preferred to B, and this is true whether A, B and C are fixed outcomes or probability distributions;

(iv) independent – if A is preferred to B, that preference of A over B is maintained regardless of other gambling options available.

But why should we suppose that rational individuals must observe these axioms? The axioms appear abstract, and are probably meaningless to many, and so may appear to be little more than technical details. But in fact they represent strong assumptions about human behaviour that are difficult to reconcile with how real people behave. The assumption of completeness is satisfied for well-defined games of chance but is fundamentally incompatible with radical uncertainty. The assumption of transitivity is probably relatively innocuous, and we do not discuss it further. Moreover, neither continuity nor independence are compelling, and are contradicted by observation of what most ordinary people would regard as rational behaviour. Take the axioms in turn.

Completeness

In his famous treatise, Savage showed that, provided people conformed to certain axioms which he described as constituting 'rational behaviour' under uncertainty, there existed numbers that could be interpreted as subjective probabilities, and that 'rational behaviour' was equivalent to maximising expected utility calculated using those subjective probabilities.[2] Savage's axioms are similar to those of von Neumann and Morgenstern, although there are a number of technical changes and additions. But the most significant difference between the von Neumann–Morgenstern approach and that of Friedman and Savage lies not in the axioms themselves, but in their extension to the case where there are no objective probabilities. Von Neumann and Morgenstern were working with well-defined problems for which frequencies could be deduced or – as at a casino, in the Monty Hall game, or at dinner with Professor Allais – in which the probabilities were set by the designers of the game. The completeness axiom is formally the same when applied to choices between goods and services, choices among lotteries with objective probabilities, and choices with subjective probabilities. But its significance and implications are very different.

The extension of the completeness axiom to lotteries with objective probabilities is itself problematic. Faced with the choice between a large gamble on the National Lottery and a smaller one on the spin of the wheel at Atlantic City, our answer is that we do not have the slightest interest in either proposition. As we observed in the discussion of pignistic probabilities in chapter 5, most people do not bet on most things. And where there are objective probabilities – as there are in the National Lottery or in the roulette game of an honest casino – the odds are usually unfavourable.

But if there are reasons for reservations in extending the axiom of completeness to lotteries characterised by objectively defined and quantifiable risks, they are multiplied many times when the axiom is applied to situations characterised by subjective probabilities. If there are possibilities of which we cannot conceive then we cannot attach probabilities to them and completeness is simply inconsistent with radical uncertainty.

Continuity

The problems with the assumption of continuity are also readily understood. Recall that the axiom implied that if A is better than B and B better than C, some combination of A and C is preferable to B. In Russian roulette you fire a gun at your own head; one, but only one of the six chambers is loaded. This spectacularly foolish game was played, evidently without disaster, by the novelist Graham Greene and by William Shockley, the inventor of the transistor, when young (and fatally in the film *The Deer Hunter*).[3] Nassim Nicholas Taleb uses the example of someone invited to play the game for a $10 million pay-off; you would be foolish to accept but would probably survive, and if Taleb had successfully dissuaded you from playing you might then justifiably complain that he had deprived you of $10 million. Now suppose A is receiving $1, B is receiving nothing, and C is being shot in the head. Obviously A is better than B and B is better than C. I warn you that there is a lone gunman in the park who randomly shoots people in the head. But, with the confidence in models that enabled bankers to believe that they had brought risk under control, I assure you that the probability that the gunman will successfully fire at you is very low. Moreover, if you complete the traverse of the park successfully you will receive $1. We know of no one who would take the slightest interest in such a gamble, or would enter a discussion of 'how low does the probability have to be to persuade you to cross the park?' And we say that in the knowledge that many people, including us, take extremely small risks of catastrophic loss in return for extremely small gains every day, when we cross the road or overtake another vehicle.

What is going on here? It is simply not worth contemplating any risk of being shot in the head in return for an emolument of $1. If C is being shot in the head, no combination of A and C is preferable to B, violating the assumption of continuity. In an uncertain world, our choices are influenced by hopes and fears to a degree that is not necessarily determined by the probability that the events we dream of or dread in fact materialise. And, like most people, we take more care on the roads after we have seen an accident, or heard a report from an accident victim, even though our reflective selves know that the fact that someone else has suffered an accident does not increase our vulnerability to an accident. Such behaviour is the converse of those who hold to the dream when they buy a lottery ticket; the utility they gain from contemplating the outcome is little affected by their

knowledge of the probability that it will occur. We attach significance to such salient outcomes independently of, and often
in ignorance of, their probability.

Independence

The axiom of independence is perhaps the most interesting
because it gave rise to controversy almost from the outset. It
may be stated precisely as follows. Suppose you prefer A to B,
where A and B may be either determinate outcomes or probability distributions. You are then offered the choice between
the alternatives AC and BC. AC is A with probability p and C
with probability (1-p), and BC is B with probability p and C
with probability (1-p). Independence requires that you prefer
AC to BC. The possibility of C does not affect your preference
between A and B. Or at least that is one way of interpreting
the axiom.

This somewhat strange axiom is modelled on an axiom of
consumer and political choice which has become known as
the 'independence of irrelevant alternatives'. If you have the
option of A or B, and you prefer A to B, you will still prefer A
to B if you are choosing from a set that contains A, B and C. A
restaurant offers a choice of meat or fish, and you choose meat.
The waiter then tells you that there is a vegetarian option. If
you said 'in that case I will have the fish' you would violate
the independence of irrelevant alternatives axiom (although
with a little ingenuity you may be able to think up reasons for
such a decision). Independence of irrelevant alternatives gained
significance and prominence because the American economist
Kenneth Arrow showed that most social and political decision
rules, such as majority voting, produce preferences for the group
that violate that requirement.[4]

The Allais paradox noted in chapter 8 reflected violation of the independence axiom. Maurice Allais initially posed the following question: would you prefer an 11% probability of winning 100 million FF (otherwise nothing), or a 10% probability of winning 500 million FF and otherwise nothing? A majority preferred the latter, hoping for the larger prize and untroubled by the slight reduction in the probability of success.

Allais then proposed a rather generous modification of the problem. Would you take 100m FF for sure? Or would you prefer an 89% probability of 100m FF, a 10% probability of 500m FF, and 1% probability of nothing at all? Most agreed that offered such a choice, they would take the certainty of 100m FF.

Allais then reminded the participants of the expected value of the various options. The first choice was between an expected value of 11m FF (11% of 100m FF), and an expected value of 50m FF (10% of 500m FF). The second choice compares 100m FF for sure with an expected value easily calculated but generally rejected of 139m FF. And if you look carefully at the two propositions, you will see that the issue in both cases is whether raising the expected winnings by 39m FF compensates for a 1% increase in the probability of winning nothing at all.[5]

Whatever was going on here, it was not that the diners were incapable of doing the simple arithmetic required to compute expected value. All the prizes represented life-changing amounts of money, even for Samuelson, already the author of a bestselling textbook and a future winner of a Nobel Prize. But we suspect many readers will already have made the same choice as the diners without focusing on the values of the prizes on offer. Perhaps the participants were moved by fear of regret at leaving empty-handed, even if there was only a 1% chance of doing so.

Allais then pointed out that the choices violated the assumption of expected utility maximisation. Under that assumption, the first choice implied that

$$0.1 \times u(500) + 0.9 \times u(0) > 0.11 \times u(100) + 0.89 \times u(0)$$

and the second choice implied that

$$u(100) > 0.89 \times u(100) + 0.1 \times u(500) + 0.01 \times u(0).$$

Simple rearrangement shows that the first choice implied that

$$0.11 \times u(100) < 0.1 \times u(500) + 0.01 \times u(0)$$

and the second choice implied that

$$0.11 \times u(100) > 0.1 \times u(500) + 0.01 \times u(0).$$

But both cannot be true, and so, to some consternation, Allais had demonstrated that the preferences of most of the participants were not compatible with the assumption that they maximised expected utility.

Allais was heard to remark – and subsequently wrote – 'the experimental observation of the behaviour of men who are considered rational by public opinion invalidates Bernoulli's principle'.[6] With appropriate French courtesy, Allais refrained from emphasising that what he described as Bernoulli's principle was in fact the theory of rational choice under uncertainty which had been developed by his fellow diners. But Allais' presentation of his paradox was the forerunner of studies of behaviour that deviates from the economists' definition of rational behaviour – expected utility maximisation. In effect, he had founded what would become known as behavioural economics – a subject for which Daniel Kahneman would be awarded the Nobel Prize almost fifty years later.[7]

Savage had been unable to set aside the implications of that agreeable occasion in Paris. When he returned to Chicago from Paris, he thought long and hard about the embarrassing fact that his stated preferences had violated his own principles of rational behaviour. He came to the conclusion that he had made a mistake – not in the formulation of the axioms but in his preferences. As he wrote: 'there is, of course, an important sense in which preferences, being entirely subjective, cannot be in error; but in a different, more subtle sense they can be'.[8] This appears to be sophistry. But, reassured that he understood properly his own preferences now that he was firmly on American soil, Savage published his magisterial *Foundations of Statistics* in 1954, and in so doing he created the basis for modern decision theory.

Some theorists have tried to rescue probabilistic reasoning by asserting that just as we define a probability distribution of outcomes when we do not know the outcome, then if we do not know the probabilities, we need to look at a distribution of probabilities.[9] Such a distinction misses the true difference between the small world of probabilities and the ubiquity of radical uncertainty. And it leads down a treacherous path, long known to statisticians wary of the implied infinite regress in the argument. If there can be probabilities over probabilities, then why not probabilities of probabilities over probabilities, and so on. This attempt to sustain probabilistic reasoning leads to the infinite regress described by Savage himself:

> There is some temptation to introduce probabilities of a second order so that the person would find himself saying such things as 'the probability that B is more probable than C is greater than the probability that F is more probable than G.' But such a program seems to meet insurmountable

difficulties ... once second order probabilities are introduced, the introduction of an endless hierarchy seems inescapable. Such a hierarchy seems very difficult to interpret, and it seems at best to make the theory less realistic, not more.[10]

What is so striking about the development of expected utility theory is how the leading protagonists saw the theory exclusively in terms of how it explained choices among well-defined lotteries. The richness of uncertainty in real-life decisions – radical uncertainty – was simply ignored.

NOTES

1. THE UNKNOWABLE FUTURE

1   Tolstoy (1978) p. 408.
2   The numbers are uncertain, but Christopher Duffy estimates that 450,000 troops set out, and only a few thousand, most unfit for combat, made it back (Duffy 1972 p. 162).
3   Mearsheimer (2001) p. 285 reports that the Grand Armée reached a peak of 1 million in 1812. Similar numbers have been reported for the Mongol army, but these are likely to be overestimates given the Mongol practice of assigning each warrior multiple horses.
4   Larsen (2007).
5   Dowd et al. (2008).
6   US DoD (2002).
7   We do not, however, attribute the subsequent failures in Iraq to 'unknown unknowns' but to a failure to allow sufficient challenge to a prevailing narrative – see chapter 16.
8   US DoD (2002).
9   Bowden (2012) p. 160.
10 Ibid. p. 163.
11 Friedman and Zeckhauser (2014, p. 2) argue that Obama concluded 'that the odds that bin Laden was living in Abbottabad were about 50/50'. We think it is clear from Obama's further comment that this is not what he meant.
12 Bowden (2012) p. 160.
13 Rumelt (2011) p. 79.
14 For example, more than 90% of members in the UK National Employment Savings Trust (NEST) occupational pension scheme backed by the government remain in the default fund (NEST 2019).
15 Such as Fidelity.

16   Larry Kotlikoff of Boston University is the architect of a suite of calculators
     called ESPlanner.
17   Knight (1921) p. 20.
18   Keynes (1937) pp. 213–14.
19   Taleb (2008).
20   Keynes (1936) p. 162.

2. PUZZLES AND MYSTERIES

1   Stevenson (1887) p. 472.
2   On average, Mercury is 57 million miles from Earth but the distance varies
    between 45 and 140 million miles.
3   NASA (2011).
4   The equations of planetary motion are not only stationary but *deterministic*;
    the distance from Earth varies according to a known formula, and this
    distance at any specified time is completely predictable.
5   By virtue of Newton's third law (action and reaction) there is
    some – imperceptible – effect.
6   Letter to Max Born (1926). Einstein himself used variants of this quote at
    other times. For example, in a 1943 conversation with William Hermanns
    recorded in Hermanns' book *Einstein and the Poet* (p. 58), Einstein said: 'As I
    have said so many times, God doesn't play dice with the world.'
7   The low-key headquarters building of Goldman Sachs.
8   Treverton (2007).
9   The term 'mystery' is also used for the puzzles set by novels such as those of
    Conan Doyle or Agatha Christie, which have a solution revealed at the end
    of the book. In this book we use the word in Treverton's sense.
10 Tetlock (2005) and Tetlock and Gardner (2016).
11 Tetlock and Gardner (2016) pp. 92–3. Serbia wasn't and Italy didn't.
12 Rittel and Webber (1973).
13 Stuart, '1952 Now Looms', 4 May, 1; Dempster, *Tale of the Comet*, 20–21,
    quoted in Engel (2007) p. 136.
14 Federal Aviation Administration (2018), from which this history is derived.
15 Newhouse (1982) p. 65.
16 Self (2006) p. 415.
17 Reportedly in a talk at a 1977 meeting of the World Future Society, quoted
    in Bolton and Thompson (2015) p. 142.
18 Wozniak suffered serious injuries in a plane crash in 1981 and finally left
    the company in 1985. Jobs hired a PepsiCo executive, John Sculley, as
    CEO.
19 Lovallo and Mendonca (2007).
20 Ballmer (2007).
21 Schulte et al. (2010).

22 'The Tay Bridge Disaster' is the best-known work of the notoriously bad poet William McGonagall (McGonagall, 1980).
23 According to McGonagall; more reliable commentators put the number lower.
24 Doyle (1884).
25 The latest (at the time of writing) 'solution' was published in *The Ghost of the Mary Celeste* by Valerie Martin in 2014.

3. RADICAL UNCERTAINTY IS EVERYWHERE

1 Merton (1960).
2 Soros (2009).
3 'Any observed statistical regularity will tend to collapse once pressure is placed upon it for control purposes': Goodhart (1984) p. 96.
4 Oxford Dictionary (2019). We have chosen to quote definitions from the ODO because 'The dictionary content in ODO focuses on current English and includes modern meanings and uses of words. The *OED*, on the other hand, is a historical dictionary'. See <https://www.oed.com/page/oedodo/The+OED+and+Oxford+Dictionaries>.
5 Section 17 of the Gaming Act 1845 stated that 'every person who shall, by any fraud or unlawful device or ill practice in playing at or with cards, dice, tables, or other game, or in bearing a part in the stakes, wages, or adventures, or in betting on the sides or hands of them that do play, or in wagering on the event of any game, sport, pastime, or exercise, win from any other person to himself, or any other or others, any sum of money or valuable thing, shall on conviction on indictment be liable to imprisonment for a term not exceeding two years'. The Act was repealed in 2007. See also Morris (2004), Laville (2004).
6 Thorp (2017).
7 Alasdair MacIntyre attributes the illustration to Karl Popper, who describes the impossibility of predicting the invention of the wheel (MacIntyre 2003, p. 93).
8 Thomson (1896). There is no evidence for many of the most hubristic quotes attributed to Lord Kelvin, such as 'X-rays will prove to be a hoax', but inventions appear to have been a weak spot: when he heard about wireless he snorted, 'Wireless is all very well but I'd rather send a message by a boy on a pony' (Marconi 2001 p. 40).
9 Samuelson (2009).
10 Department for Transport (2015) p. 2.
11 Private information.
12 King et al. (1999), Question 46.
13 Galton (1907), Surowiecki (2004). To be clear, neither Galton nor Surowiecki claims to disagree!
14 Gigerenzer (2008) p. 1.
15 *The Economist* (8 January 1853).

4. THINKING WITH PROBABILITIES

1   Jowett translation (1892).

2   Hacking (1975), David (1962), Devlin (2010).

3   Cited by Hacking (1975) p. 19. The reference is found in footnote 116 of
    chapter 24, Gibbon (1784).

4   Drake (1978).

5   In 1662, King Charles II successfully appealed to the Royal Society, whose
    establishment he had graciously favoured two years earlier, to elect Graunt
    a Fellow. The King considered that Graunt should be recognised in view
    of the public importance of his contributions to knowledge, despite his
    humble origins (Sprat 1734, p. 67).

6   Halley calculated that the comet which he saw in 1682 had the same
    orbit as one which had appeared in 1607 and 1531. He was proved right
    when the comet reappeared in 1757, fifteen years after his death. Recent
    improvements in life expectancy mean that anyone born in the early 1980s
    may be among the very few people to have the opportunity to see the
    comet twice in their lifetime. Halley, who died in 1742 aged eighty-five,
    did not see his prediction validated.

7   The Society closed to new business in December 2000. It was unable to
    meet payments that had been, in the view of the Law Lords, promised to
    policy-holders.

8   GBD 2013 Mortality and Cause of Death Contributors (2013).

9   Case and Deaton (2015), Hiam et al. (2018), Eurostat (2017).

10 The film version of Michael Lewis's *The Big Short* opens with the quote 'It
    ain't what you don't know that gets you into trouble, it's what you know for
    sure that just ain't so', attributed to Mark Twain, but we have failed to find
    any other evidence that Twain actually wrote that. This does not make the
    observation less true.

11 But even here climate change threatens the stationarity of weather-related
    phenomena.

12 Katz (1993), chapter 11.3.1.

13 Bayes is buried in Bunhill Fields Cemetery in the City of London.

14 An excellent discussion of the development of probability theory may be
    found in Daston (1995).

15 The original problem is from Selvin et al. (1975) p. 67 who named the host
    Monte (*sic*) Hall. But the real Monty participated enthusiastically in the
    subsequent correspondence and ever since the game has been known as the
    Monty Hall problem. It was popularised in an article in *Parade* magazine
    in 1990 by the American columnist calling herself Marilyn vos Savant and
    claiming to have the world's highest IQ.

16 For example, <https://www.mathwarehouse.com/
    monty-hall-simulation-online/>.

17 The claim that if we do not know the relative probabilities, then all possible outcomes are equally likely, can be traced back to the eighteenth century and the writings of Bayes and Laplace. Laplace used the term Principle of Insufficient Reason – Laplace (1951) p. 6.

18 Keynes (1921) p. 44.

19 Ibid. p. 82.

20 Pascal (1958) pp. 66–7.

21 Ohuchi et al. (2016).

22 Bayes' theorem gives a general formula for such calculations. The probability that someone has cancer, given a positive test, P(C|Pos), is the probability that someone has cancer *and* a positive test, P(C and Pos) divided by the probability that someone has a positive test, P(Pos). Simple arithmetic gives P(C and Pos) as 0.009 (0.01 × 0.9) and P(Pos) as (0.99 × 0.1) + (0.01 × 0.9) = 0.108. The probability that someone with a positive test has cancer is, therefore, 0.009 divided by 0.108, which is 1/12. As Gigerenzer observes, the frequentist reasoning in the text is much easier to understand.

23 Gigerenzer (2015) pp. 207–12.

24 Mr Viniar retired as CFO of Goldman Sachs in 2013, and at the time of writing was serving as a non-executive on its board of directors, as well as on the boards of several charitable foundations.

5. A FORGOTTEN DISPUTE

1 Pascal (1670) pp. 64, 66.

2 Mill (1843) p. 75. However, he changed his mind in subsequent editions.

3 Bertrand was also the author of the eponymous model of small-group competition familiar to economists.

4 Bertrand, *Calcul des Probabilités* (1889) p. 174 (quoted in Daston 1995, p. 375).

5 Hume (2000) p. 24.

6 Zabell (1989).

7 Knight was scathing about Keynes' General Theory. Keynes' opinion of Knight is unreported (Nahl 1936).

8 Ramsey's brother became Archbishop of Canterbury and his sister, who was a member of the economics faculty at Oxford, wrote a moving memoir which gave special emphasis to his contributions to probability theory (Paul 2012).

9 Ramsey (1926).

10 de Finetti (1989) p. 219 – although do not expect to understand his reasoning!

11 A few economists continued to argue for the importance of a distinct conception of uncertainty, notably G. L. S. Shackle in Britain (see chapter 7).

12 Friedman (2007) p. 282.

13 LeRoy and Singell (1987) p. 394.

14 Ibid. p. 395.

15 Silver (2012) p. 247.

16 This calculation might be appropriate if incidents such as the Twin Towers catastrophe were the outcome of an ergodic process in which a population of aircraft was randomly flying around Manhattan, occasionally colliding with tall buildings. But this is not the case.

17 Falk (2011). The two-child problem is in fact a variant on the two packs of cards problem described by Keynes in chapter IV of Keynes (1921) and attributed by him to von Kries in *Die Principien der Wahrscheinlichkeit*, published in 1886. Keynes paid fulsome tribute to von Kries as the inspiration for his critique of the Indifference Principle.

18 Kennes and Smets (1994).

19 Nassim Nicholas Taleb describes the incredulity of many of his colleagues when told he was betting against an event he did not expect to happen (Taleb 2007, pp. 26–7). One of the authors recalls a similar experience in discussion with a senior executive of a financial institution selling 'precipice bonds', which offered a high rate of return but loss of capital if some unlikely event occurred. 'Do you think the stock market will halve in value over the next five years?' he asked. On receiving the answer 'no', he went on, 'So why would you not buy these bonds?' and disclosed that he had purchased some for himself.

20 At odds of 20 to 1, you bet one to win 21 (20 and your stake) if Dobbin wins, and 0.047 is 1/21.

21 In other words, they were vulnerable to what is known as a 'Dutch book'. A Dutch book is a series of gambles, each of which at first sight seems attractive but which would necessarily leave anyone who accepted all of them worse off.

22 <http://www.tcm.com/mediaroom/video/415267/Guys-And-Dolls-Movie-Clip-Have-We-Got-A-Bet-.html>.

23 Graham and Zweig (2005) pp. 512–24.

24 *Forbes* (2008).

25 Buffett (2017) p. 30.

26 Rhodes (1988) p. 664. We do not know what the odds were, or whether there were many takers.

6. AMBIGUITY AND VAGUENESS

1 Carroll and Gardner (2000) p. 224.

2 R&A (2019). The rulebook was agreed by the UK R&A and the US Golf Association. The R&A is the rule-making spin-off from the Royal and Ancient Golf Club of St Andrews, which maintains the world-famous links of that town.

3 Carter (2019).

4 Kelvin was the great physicist whom we met in chapter 3 dismissing the possibility of manned flight.

5 Knight (1940) fn. 10.

6 McCoy, Prelec and Seung (2017).

7 Goldstein and Gigerenzer (2002) p. 76.

8 Lenin (1909) p. 397.

9 Kahneman (2011) pp. 156–8.

10 Ibid. p. 158.

11 Carroll and Gardner (2000) p. 155.

12 Carroll and Gardner (2000) pp. 157–64.

13 We take comfort from the knowledge that one of the doyens of classical statistics, Maurice Kendall, used the same analogy with Carroll sixty years ago and added, 'if you think all this is ridiculous and beneath the notice of grave and serious-minded adults, you may care to know that the students of the theory of probability are still discussing the question whether one can take an even chance on the truth of any proposition whose meaning is not known' (quoted in Shackle 1968, p. 35).

14 Lucas (1988), published (2011) p. 4.

15 Cochrane (2009).

16 Romer (2015).

17 Carroll and Gardner (2000) pp. 225–6.

18 GDP is a construct, created by national statistical agencies, and derived from many thousands of data points drawn from a multiplicity of sources. The principles of the estimation of GDP were established in the late 1930s and early 1940s, by the American Simon Kuznets and the British economists Richard Stone and James Meade. These principles have subsequently been greatly elaborated by statisticians around the world, and today there is a United Nations System of Standardised National Accounts, a weighty document which is subject to regular revision and whose procedures are followed in statistical agencies in all major countries. However, there remains considerable scope for discretion in the application of the principles, and cross-country variation in the data which are available to the compilers, and in all major countries there are further lengthy volumes that describe the particular practices of their national agencies.

19 Although, as Nick Chater observes, the differences between heat and temperature or momentum and velocity are not intuitive – measurement is in the context of an underlying physical theory (Chater 2018 p. 25).

20 Haldane, Brennan and Madouros (2010) p. 88.

21 See Coyle (2014) pp. 93–104 for more.

22 See Adams and Levell (2014) for more.

23 An excellent account of the Tonkin incident can be found in Hastings (2018), chapter 9.

24 See World Bank (2019) for more details on this.

25 Leamer (1983) p. 37. See also Leamer (1978).
26 This interpretation of the use of probabilities in assessing the accuracy of multiple forecasts was used by Nate Silver in 2019: 'out of the 5,589 events (between sports and politics combined) that we said had a 70 percent chance of happening (rounded to the nearest 5 percent), they in fact occurred 71 percent of the time'.
27 Met Office (2014).
28 Bank of England (2013) p. 6.
29 Keynes (1921) p. 51.

7. PROBABILITY AND OPTIMISATION

1 Keynes (1921) p. 56.
2 Samuelson does acknowledge that it would be rational to reject the single wager of a 50% chance of winning $200 and a 50% chance of losing $100 and accept a sequence of 100 wagers in which the prize was $2 and the potential loss $1.
3 Shackle (1949).
4 Savage had a troubled youth and he died early, aged only fifty-three. Born Leonard Ogashevitz, he suffered from poor eyesight during his school and college career. In consequence he could see little written on the blackboard; in frustration he started a fire in the chemistry laboratory at the University of Michigan, for which he was expelled.
5 These axioms are described in the appendix, and it can be seen that they are formally very similar to the standard economic axioms of consumer choice, although the implications are very different.
6 Friedman and Savage (1948).
7 Savage (1954) p. 16.
8 Ibid.
9 Friedman (2007) p. 82.
10 Kruskal (1971) in Brooks (2004).
11 Becker (1978) p. 14.
12 Daniel was just one of several members of the Swiss Bernoulli family to make important contributions to pure and applied mathematics.
13 Bernoulli (1954).
14 The founder of Amazon and, at the time of writing, the world's richest man with a net worth of over $100 billion, even after his divorce settlement reached in 2019.
15 Khaw et al. (2016).
16 The eleven subjects were paid $10 for each session, and up to $0.02 for each successful estimate: a potential total of $30 per trial.
17 Khaw et al. (2016) p. 1.
18 Thaler (2016) p. 4.

19 Nor was it very useful here, since the maximum gain from a correct calculation was two cents.
20 By the Indifference Principle discussed in chapter 4.
21 Oxford Dictionary (2019).
22 Within the Friedman–Savage framework, this transaction can make sense only if the utility of wealth function is appropriately convex – the marginal utility of wealth is actually increasing. And so Friedman and Savage concluded that the utility of wealth function must have a bizarre shape, being alternately convex and concave.
23 Consumer Rights Act (2015) Section 19.

8. RATIONALITY IN A LARGE WORLD

1 Mandeville (1732) p. 25.
2 Allais (1953).
3 The Prize in Economic Sciences in Memory of Alfred Nobel, commonly referred to as the Nobel Prize in Economics, was created to commemorate the tercentenary of the Swedish central bank, the Riksbank.
4 Allais (1953), in the first footnote.
5 Ellsberg (1961). The events were recounted in *The Post*; no one, to the best of our knowledge, has made a film about his thought experiment with urns, though many such experiments have been performed. And any reader who still doubts the prevalence of radical uncertainty will learn much from his memoir (Ellsberg 2003).
6 Schoemaker (2011) p. 19.
7 See *Nicomachean Ethics*, Book VI.
8 Gilboa (2015) p. 316.
9 Simons and Chabris (1999).
10 Available at youtu.be/vJG698U2Mvo.
11 Kahneman (2011) p. 24.
12 Csikszentmihalyi (1991).
13 Brearley (2017) p. 39.
14 Kahneman (2011) p. 100.
15 Tversky and Kahneman (1973) pp. 211–12.
16 Mayzner and Tresselt (1965). The paper is based on just twenty thousand English words between three and seven letters in length.
17 English spelling and pronunciation are bewildering even to native speakers. 'Cake' has K as its third letter but not its first; 'see' does not contain the letter C; we say 'pace' but also 'case'; and 'acknowledge' is not spelt either as 'aknowledge' or 'acnowledge'. BestWordList contains many words borrowed from other languages, such as 'kaama', and 'koala' and 'karma', in which the hard C of the original is rendered as K.
18 Kahneman (2011) pp. 3–4.

19   Ibid. p. 277.
20   The Committee for the Prize in Economic Sciences (2017).
21   Thaler and Benartzi (2004); see Cribb and Emmerson (2016) for an analysis of the impact of implementing automatic enrolment in the UK.
22   Simon (1957).
23   Quotation from Simon's endorsement of the book by Gerd Gigerenzer, *Simple Heuristics That Make Us Smart* (2001).
24   Gigerenzer (2004).
25   Klein (1998) p. 30.
26   Kahneman and Tversky responded to the work of Gigerenzer and colleagues with extreme hostility – see, for example, Kahneman and Tversky (1996). Michael Lewis (2017, p. 335) states that Tversky 'did not merely want to counter Gigerenzer; he wanted to destroy him'.

9. EVOLUTION AND DECISION-MAKING

1   Sterling et al. (2015).
2   And is a metaphor, or story, rather than an empirical claim about the world.
3   Hamilton (1964) p. 16.
4   See Evans-Pritchard (1940) p. 140 for an example of a tribe which explained that they would – and in his case did – offer wilfully misleading directions to someone not well known to them. The anecdote is striking because our expectations are so different.
5   Alchian (1950).
6   He calls this 'consilience' (Wilson 1999).
7   Maynard Smith (1964).
8   Bear Stearns refused to join the syndicate which bailed out Long Term Capital Management. When Bear Stearns itself ran into trouble ten years later, no one was willing to help them – see Taft (2012).
9   Gilman (1996).
10   Aktipis et al. (2011) p. 132.
11   Maddison Project Database, version 2018; Office for National Statistics (2015).
12   Wrangham (2019).
13   This is the cooperative principle of linguistics, which recognises that statements are part of conversations and derive their meaning from the background to those conversations.
14   Mercier and Sperber (2017), from the book description.
15   In the words of the Harvard evolutionary biologist Joseph Henrich (Henrich 2017).
16   Ortiz-Ospina and Roser (2019).
17   Ferguson (1782) p. 205.
18   Smith (1776b) p. 35.
19   Upton and George (2010).

20 Sometimes ascribed to Aesop, but first sourced to Orson Welles' *Mr Arkadin* (1955); see also *The Crying Game*.

21 The two points of view are represented by Plomin (2018) and Pinker (2003), respectively.

22 The quotation is attributed to the American comedian George Burns.

23 Whately (1854) p. 127.

24 For example Cosmides and Tooby (1989) and Cosmides (1989); for a summary of criticisms, in particular those of Sperber, see Atran (2001).

25 Taleb (2018), chapter 19.

26 There is a wide range of estimates of the extent of mortality in the Black Death but there were certainly many locations in which a majority of the population died.

27 The MIT economist Andrew Lo has developed an extended example to reinforce the point (Lo 2017, chapter 6).

28 Scott (1998), Part I.

29 Gráda and Mokyr (1984).

30 And later vice presidential candidate in Ross Perot's quixotic bid for the US presidency in 1992.

31 Collins (2001) p. 85.

32 HC Deb (4 June 1940), Vol. 361, cc. 787–98.

33 Isaacson (2011) pp. 107–8.

34 Lohr (2011).

35 Bower's characteristically unsympathetic biographies are controversial.

36 Bower (2001) p. 25.

37 See for example Keren and Schul (2009), Keren (2013), Kruglanski and Gigerenzer (2011), and Mercier and Sperber (2017).

38 Libet et al. (1983).

39 Damasio (1995), chapter 3.

40 See Henrich (2017) for further analysis of this point.

41 Of course, at most one player can win. Many people think the perfect game would result in a draw, but no compelling argument to that effect can be found. See <https://www.quora.com/Is-chess-a-draw-with-perfect-play-by-both-players>.

42 Kahneman (2017).

43 Ibid.

44 For more analysis see Hofstadter (2018).

10. THE NARRATIVE PARADIGM

1 Hobbes (1843) p. xxii.

2 Odurinde (2015) and Defra (2012).

3 Churchill (1949) p. 157.

4 Iggers in von Ranke (2010) p. xiii.

5   Anderson (2011).

6   Coase (1937).

7   Marwell and Ames (1981).

8   Ibid. p. 309.

9   Smith (1776a) p. 16.

10   Mauss (1990) p. 3.

11   Ibid. p. 33. See also Kolm and Ythier (2006).

12   Waldfogel (1993) and (2009).

13   Smith (1776a) p. 6.

14   Wolfe (1988) p. 384.

15   HoC Treasury Committee (2012) 32.

16   Boas (1888) p. 636.

17   For example Vandevelde (2010).

11. UNCERTAINTY, PROBABILITY AND THE LAW

1   Lipshaw (2013) p. 283.

2   Meadow (1997) p. 29.

3   Royal Statistical Society (2001).

4   General Medical Council v. Meadow [2006] EWCA Civ 1390.

5   Wansell (2007).

6   Daston (1995).

7   Bernoulli (1709).

8   Condorcet (1785), Laplace (1812), Poisson (1837).

9   Condorcet (1785) pp. 285–7.

10   Fleming et al. (2000).

11   Although Simpson was acquitted, Nicole's family launched a civil suit against him, which was successful, and he was ordered to pay substantial damages. A few years later, Simpson was convicted of armed robbery and went to prison. He was released on parole in October 2017.

12   Himmelreich (2009).

13   The distinguished statistician Sir David Cox explained this to the court in later proceedings in the Clark case.

14   This observation is described as 'the crumpled paper fallacy' by the authors of the SAS data analytics software and attributed to David Thouless, a topologist who received the Nobel Prize in Physics in 2016.

15   The RSS produced four guides, available at <http://www.rss.org.uk/RSS/ Influencing_Change/Statistics_and_the_law/Practitioner_guides/RSS/ Influencing_Change/Current_projects_sub/Statistics_and_the_law_sub/ Practitioner_guides.aspx?hkey=2cfdf562-361e-432e-851b-ef6ff5254145>.

16   The number of recorded sudden infant deaths in England and Wales exceeded the number of infant homicides in the official data by a multiple of four in 2015 (Office for National Statistics 2015a and 2015b; and 2018, Appendix Table 3).

17 Eco (2004) p. 254.

18 Simon and Mahan (1971) pp. 325–8.

19 See Hannibal and Mountford (2002) pp. 226–7 for a discussion for the UK; see 'Reasonable Doubt: An Argument Against Definition' (1995) for an overview for the US.

20 Cohen (1977) pp. 74–81 and Tribe (1971).

21 For a survey of the response of legal scholars to the rodeo problem, see Nunn (2015).

22 Cohen (1977) p. 120.

23 Tribe (1971) p. 1374, footnote 143.

24 Captain Renault in *Casablanca* (1942).

25 There is a large and growing literature on statistical discrimination as applied to legal issues – for example, Harcourt (2007) and Monahan (2006).

26 The use of statistical discrimination to infer the likelihood of a convicted person committing another crime – both to incarcerate high-risk and release low-risk persons – has expanded significantly, especially in the United States where risk assessment is used in sentencing and parole decisions. See Monahan (2006), Monahan and Skeem (2016), and the tools produced by the Laura and John Arnold Foundation (2016).

27 See, for example, O'Neil (2016) and Noble (2018).

28 See also Pardo and Allen (2008). A flawed attempt to reconcile probabilistic reasoning and inference to the best explanation can be found in Cheng (2013) pp. 1269–71.

29 Holmes (1881) p. 1. For a fascinating account of the development of Holmes's thinking and his relationship with the pragmatic school of philosophy of Charles Pierce, see Menand (2011).

30 The fact-finding duty of judge or jury is to explore the various alternative accounts put forward, and establish the best explanation of the facts adduced in evidence. Questions of law concern legal rules and principles, which are determined by the judge or judges, and if the trial does not involve a jury the presiding officer decides the case in the light of the best explanation of the facts. In a jury trial the judge sets out the law for the jury which determines the outcome of the case by applying the relevant legal rules to the facts, as disclosed by the best explanation.

31 Doyle (1927) p. 72.

32 Ibid. p. 74.

33 Blackstone, *Commentaries*, Book III, chapter XXIII.

34 Slaughter (2002).

12. GOOD AND BAD NARRATIVES

1 Lewis (2017) p. 250.

2 Ibid. p. 194.

3   Wiessner (2014) p. 14029.
4   Ibid.
5   Wood (1960).
6   Smolin (2006).
7   Eliot (1871–2).
8   Lakoff and Johnson (1980).
9   Fisher (1989), chapter 8.
10 Tetlock and Gardner (2016) p. 167.
11 Ibid. p. 68.
12 Derrida (1967) p. 233.
13 Doyle (2004) p. 15.
14 Colyvan (2008) p. 646.
15 Knights (1933).
16 Bradley (1886) p. 106.
17 Donoghue (1992) pp. xxxii–xxxiii. He goes on to contrast this approach
    with theorists who do the opposite, interpreting everything through one
    lens: cf. Donoghue (1983).
18 Márquez and Stone (1981).
19 Tuckett and Nikolic (2017) p. 502.
20 Ibid. p. 501.
21 Walton and Huey (1993) p. 298.
22 Serling (1992) p. 68.
23 Ibid. p. 285.
24 Kay (2011) pp. 21–2.
25 Shubber (2018).
26 Wolfe (1988) p. 57.
27 Shiller (2017) and Chong and Tuckett (2015).

13. TELLING STORIES THROUGH NUMBERS

1   That distribution was subsequently, and seemingly independently,
    discovered by another Frenchman, Pierre-Simon Laplace, and by the
    German Carl Gauss, and is still often called the Gaussian distribution.
2   Quetelet (1835).
3   We owe these discoveries to distinguished professors of applied mathematics
    in the early twentieth century, scholars such as Francis Galton, Karl Pearson
    and Jerzy Neyman – and to 'Student', who published anonymously. We
    now know 'Student' to have been W. J. Gossett, an employee of the
    Guinness Brewery in Dublin. The Guinness family imaginatively recruited
    outstanding graduates from Oxford and Cambridge and Gossett would in
    due course be managing director of Guinness's English operations at Park
    Royal in London. But it was Keynes' philosophically based scepticism of the
    extended application of their ideas which prompted his *Treatise on Probability*.

4 A lognormal distribution is one in which the logarithm of the variable is described by a normal distribution. If the variable is the *product* of many such independent factors, the resulting frequency distribution will be *lognormal*.

5 Table 205, *Statistical Abstract of the United States: 2011*, p. 135.

6 The distribution was first published by Poisson, together with his probability theory, in 1837 in his work *Recherches sur la Probabilité des Jugements en Matière Criminelle et en Matière Civile*.

7 Zipf (1935 and 1949).

8 Technically, the expectation will be infinite if the exponent is less than 2 (and the second and higher moments are always infinite).

9 Mandelbrot (1963).

10 An exception is the excellent survey of power laws by Gabaix (2009).

11 Midanik (1982).

12 For further analysis, see Nate Silver's discussion of how polls performed in the 2016 presidential election (2016).

13 Lowe et al. (2017).

14 Barns (2015).

15 Bohannon (2015).

16 Cartwright and Hardie (2012) emphasises the importance of differentiating between efficacy – 'it worked there' – and effectiveness – 'it will work here'.

17 Ioannidis (2005).

18 Chang and Li (2015).

19 Camerer et al. (2016).

20 Nelson, Simmons and Simonsohn (2011).

14. TELLING STORIES THROUGH MODELS

1 Box (1979) p. 202.

2 Tucker (1983).

3 Of course, third parties may – and generally will – be adversely affected.

4 Ricardo (1817) pp. 158–60.

5 Akerlof (1970).

6 The term appears to originate in a Volkswagen advertising campaign of the 1960s. Importers were emphasising the superior quality of their product at a time when US consumers talked of 'Friday' or 'Monday morning' cars (see Coleman 2009).

7 Clapham (1913) p. 401.

8 Burns (1787).

9 Arrow and Debreu (1954).

10 We have reservations: Smith's text does not sustain the market fundamentalism which some modern admirers, not necessarily his readers,

attribute to him. And Arrow and Debreu were no market fundamentalists either.

11   Spence (1973).
12   Grossman and Stiglitz (1980).
13   That he made a fortune is certain; that part of it came from the incident outlined above is not. See Samuelson (2011) p. 251 but also Skousen (2001) p. 97.
14   Plender and Persaud (2006).
15   Vickrey (1961).
16   Capen et al. (1971).
17   In 2008, the UK government recapitalised RBS and at the time of writing the bank is still largely owned by the state.
18   Klemperer (2002) pp. 169–70.
19   Friedman (1953) pp. 21–2.
20   Ibid. p. 15.
21   Hausman (1984) pp. 231–49, 235.
22   Albeit not for the theory of relativity but for his discovery of the photoelectric effect which envisaged light as a particle and was the forerunner of the quantum theory of particles.
23   Duhem (1906) and Quine (1951).
24   Committee on Oversight and Government Reform (2008) p. 37.
25   It used a dynamic stochastic general equilibrium model to derive an efficient forward path for interest rates.

15. RATIONALITY AND COMMUNICATION

1   Vaihinger (1924) p. 15.
2   Potter van Loon et al. (2015).
3   Duke (2018) p. 7.
4   Smith (2013) pp. 41–5.
5   Ibid.
6   Brearley (2017), Csikszentmihalyi (1991).
7   Kasparov (2018) p. 172.
8   Moore (2008).
9   Carré et al. (2002a and b).
10   Leamon (2018) p. 215.
11   Keynes (1925) in Keynes (1978) p. 212.
12   Keynes (1933) quoted in Harrod (1951) p. 445. The quote is from the headline of his article in the *Daily Mail*.
13   Gladwell (2006) and Kaplan (2018).
14   Klein (1998) pp. 35–9.
15   Quoted in Haidt (2013) p. 237.
16   Gao et al. (2018).

17   Herbranson and Schroeder (2010).
18   See Coase (1937) and Williamson (1975).
19   For an example of the effects of limited social organisation in Nigeria, see Nwauwa (2017).
20   Both of these are groupings of different but closely associated firms around a master firm such as Toyota or Samsung.
21   Kay (2019).
22   Paraphrase of Marshall (1890) p. 332.
23   Collier (2018) pp. 147–53.

16. CHALLENGING NARRATIVES

1   Sloan, quoted in *The Economist* (2009).
2   Janis (1972).
3   Ambrose (1984) p. 638.
4   An excellent first-hand account of the debate within the White House is contained in Kennedy (1999).
5   Schlesinger in ibid. p. 12.
6   Kennedy (1999) pp. 26–7 and 35–6.
7   Ibid. pp. 85–6.
8   Schelling (2008) p. 94.
9   Kennedy (1999) p. 8.
10   Hastings (2018).
11   World Health Organization (2009) I.4.
12   Marshall and Adams (2008).
13   Although Marshall was cured following his taking an antibiotic, tests from an earlier endoscopy revealed that he had somehow fought off the infection himself (Marshall 2005).
14   Fitzgerald (2017).
15   Samuelson (1975) p. 72.
16   In fact Planck said 'A new scientific truth does not triumph by convincing its opponents and making them see the light, but rather because its opponents eventually die, and a new generation grows up that is familiar with it' (Planck 1968, pp. 33–4).
17   Letter (December 1851) quoted in Barry (2004).
18   Sloan quoted in Farber (2002) p. 90.
19   Drucker (1946) p. 61.
20   Lampert (2010).
21   Quoted in Cohan (2018).
22   Kimes (2013).
23   Lampert (2016).
24   Bezos (2018) p. 2.
25   Quoted in Gapper (2018).

26 For more, see Goodwin (2005).

27 Fowler (2013).

28 Howe in *Hansard*, 6th Series, Vol. 180, Col. 464.

29 Howe (1994) p. 691.

30 It is an interesting comment on the transformation in US politics that in 2016 all the states won by Eisenhower's opponent Adlai Stevenson were won by Donald Trump and that every state Hillary Clinton carried had backed Eisenhower.

31 Truman claimed he relieved MacArthur for not respecting the authority of the President (see Brands 2016).

32 Truman (1945).

33 Possibly apocryphal; quoted in Gavin (1958) p. 64.

34 Orange (2012) p. 311.

35 Greenstein (1994).

36 Patton quoted in Torricelli and Carroll (2000) p. 142.

37 Eisenhower (1944).

38 Tetlock and Gardner (2016) p. 245.

39 Eland (2001), Lawrence (2012).

40 Mintzberg et al. (2005) p. 373.

41 Bowden (2012) pp. 169–73.

42 Hastings (2018) p. 146.

43 McNamara (1995) pp. 270–1.

44 Hastings (2018) p. 378.

45 Ibid. p. 147.

46 McNamara (1995) p. 311.

47 Ibid. p. 332.

17. THE WORLD OF FINANCE

1 Mackin (1963) p. 29.

2 Quoted in Mandel (1990).

3 Aristotle's *Politics*, Book I, Part XI.

4 Shakespeare (1912) p. 9.

5 Ibid.

6 Markowitz (1952).

7 Markowitz (1990).

8 Nevertheless, the internationally agreed method for bank regulation, as embodied in the Basel rules, continues to rely on the aggregation of 'risk weighted' individual assets to determine the required equity capital which a bank must create, either by accumulating retained profits or by issuing new shares.

9 Quoted in Zweig (2007) p. 4.

10 House of Commons Treasury Committee (2008) p. 25.

11 Shiller (2019), Shiller (2017).
12 Shiller (2017) p. 969.
13 Shiller (2019), p.100.
14 Rajan (2005).
15 Greenspan (2002).
16 Ibid.
17 Greenspan (2005).
18 Lux (2000).

18. RADICAL UNCERTAINTY, INSURANCE AND INVESTMENT

1 Frydman and Goldberg in Frydman and Phelps (2013) p. 148.
2 It has been claimed that the origin of insurance is found in the Code of Hammurabi §103 (see also Trenerry 1911, pp. 53–60); however, what the code actually says is that if a merchant, who is carrying goods for sale on behalf of someone else, is robbed by an enemy while they are travelling abroad then they do not need to make restitution for the stolen goods. This is not insurance but an example of equity financing with mezzanine debt: equity financing because the owner of the goods – the merchant – has a right to a portion of any return; mezzanine debt because the owner's claim is unsecured.
3 Scottish Widows (2018).
4 Borch (1976).
5 Technically you cannot insure against this (yet) but you can bet on it – which demonstrates that, in such cases, the distinction between insurance and gambling becomes very unclear. See Kay (2017) for a discussion of that issue.
6 J. G. W. (1954) p. 441.
7 Baur and Breutel-O'Donoghue (2004) p. 10.
8 Though catastrophic losses will be a different matter. In 2001 Mr Gary Hart drove his Land Rover off a bridge and into the path of a high-speed train. Hart survived but the train driver was killed. Insured losses exceeded £22 million. [2003] EWHC 2450 (QB).
9 Nelson and Nikolov (2002) p. 29.
10 Department for Work and Pensions (2010).
11 FT Ordinary Share (2018).
12 Smyth (2018).
13 *Forbes* (2008).
14 Buffett (2015) p. 18.
15 Buffett (1988).

19. (MIS)UNDERSTANDING MACROECONOMICS

1   Ignatieff (2017).
2   Lucas (2003) p. 1.
3   Phillips (1958).
4   Keynes (1939).
5   Ibid. p. 566.
6   Ibid. p. 559.
7   Coase (1999).
8   Sargent (1979).
9   Sargent (2005) p. 566.
10 Walras (1874).
11 Arrow and Debreu (1954).
12 Arrow and Hahn (1983) pp. vi–vii.
13 Lucas (2002) p. 21.
14 Ibid.
15 Savage (1954) p. 17.
16 Ibid. p. 16.
17 For instructions on how to hold a Mad Hatter's tea party, see <http://www.alice-in-wonderland.net/fun/mad-tea-party-ideas/>.
18 Kydland and Prescott (1982).
19 Jevons (1878).
20 The idea of incorporating frictions directly into the model of economic behaviour, and not relying on shocks or shifts to reconcile theory and data, reached its culmination in the family of models known as Dynamic Stochastic General Equilibrium (DSGE) models. Most central bank forecasting models derive from this family.
21 Abramovitz (1956) p. 11.
22 Contributions to real business cycle modelling are associated with the names of Finn Kydland and Edward Prescott.
23 See the critique by Friedman (2017).
24 As Hendry and Mizon (2014) explain, the importance of non-stationarity is that it undermines the inferential basis of empirically estimated models.
25 The Economist (2016).
26 The fact that forecasts are useless at providing accurate projections of the future, combined with the fact that there remains such large demand for them, raises the obvious question: 'What is going on here?' We believe that the jury is still out on this question, but Beckert (2016) provides an interesting perspective.
27 Christoffel et al. (2010) p. 6.
28 Trichet (2010).
29 Candler and Prescott (2016).
30 Ibid.

31 For this and other examples see King (2016).
32 Lee Smolin's critique of modern theoretical physics observes that the string theory community has several unusual aspects: 'Tremendous self-confidence . . . unusually monolithic community, with a strong sense of consensus, whether driven by the evidence or not, and an unusual uniformity of views on open questions . . . a sense of identification with the group, akin to identification with a religious faith or political platform. A strong sense of the boundary between the group and other experts. A disregard for and disinterest in the ideas, opinions, and work of experts who are not part of the group . . . a tendency to interpret evidence optimistically . . . coupled with a tendency to believe results are true because they are "widely believed," even if one has not checked (or even seen) the proof oneself. A lack of appreciation for the extent to which a research program ought to involve risk' (Smolin 2006, p. 284). We (with Romer) recognise the similarities. We sense that the same phenomenon may be observed in other parts of the academic community.
33 Romer (2016a) p. 1.

20. THE USE AND MISUSE OF MODELS

1   Buffett (1989).
2   Ehrlich (1970) p. 11.
3   Ehrlich (2004).
4   Thompson (1929). For more, see Caldwell (2006) Part II.
5   Jevons (1865).
6   Ibid. p. 213 and Department for Business, Energy & Industrial Strategy (2017).
7   Hubbert (1956) pp. 22, 24.
8   US Energy Information Administration (2019).
9   Meadows et al. (1972).
10 Modern scholarship suggests, however, that the destruction of Sodom describes a volcanic eruption in the middle Bronze Age (Collins 2013).
11 Keynes (1936) p. 523, Jevons (1865) p. 331.
12 HM Treasury (2018b).
13 HM Treasury (2018a) Table A 1.3.1.
14 Swanson (2017).
15 And a formula known as the 'Gaussian copula' – later to be described as 'the formula that killed Wall Street' – which provided a partial answer to the problem of computing joint probability distributions which had concerned von Neumann and his Manhattan Project colleagues.
16 Hamilton et al. (2004) pp. 199–200.
17 Pilkey and Pilkey-Jarvis (2007) p. 9.
18 Dustmann et al. (2003) p. 57.

19 Office for National Statistics (2017) Table 2.1.
20 Ibid.
21 Central Statistics Office (2016) Table 9.
22 Boeri and Brücker (2001).
23 Sinn (2003).
24 Davenport and Manville (2012).
25 Ibid. p. 38.
26 May (2004) p. 792.
27 UNAIDS (2018).

21. PRACTICAL KNOWLEDGE

1   Norman (2018) p. 185.
2   Marshall (1890) p. 1.
3   Becker (1978) p. 4.
4   Professor Luis Garicano, director of research at the London School of Economics' Management Department, explained the origins and effects of the credit crisis when the Queen opened the £71 million New Academic Building. Professor Garicano said, 'She was asking me if these things were so large how come everyone missed it' (Pierce 2008).
5   We are not referring to the economist as a plumber in the same sense as Esther Duflo (2017), who focused on the important issue of the details, 'the plumbing', of how policies are implemented, although that is also an important consideration.
6   'Alfred Marshall: 1842–1924' (1924), in Keynes and Keynes (1933) pp. 191–2.
7   Keynes (1930).
8   However until 2018, the annual rankings by US News regularly reported dentist as 'best job in America'. Dentists have now been overtaken by software developers.
9   Shulman and Driskell (1997).
10 Ipsos MORI (2017).
11 World Bank (2019).
12 Rosling et al. (2018) p. 7.
13 United Nations (2015) p. 15.
14 Benson (2018).
15 'On Exactitude in Science' in Borges (2018) p. 35.
16 'A map is not the territory it represents, but, if correct, it has a similar structure to the territory, which accounts for its usefulness' (Korzybski 1933, p. 58). See also Greenspan (2013).
17 Savage (1954) p. 16.
18 The origin of the phrase is difficult to source; the earliest published example we have found was in Gibbons (1982), a paper critiquing the CAPM model. The author stresses that he is not providing an alternative model.

19 Lewis (2017) p. 151.
20 Romer (2016b).
21 Although we find assistance here in the American pragmatist school, most recently represented by Richard Rorty. In Rorty's language, truth is justified belief: 'Pragmatists think that if something makes no difference to practice, it should make no difference to philosophy. This conviction makes them suspicious of the philosophers' emphasis on the difference between justification and truth' (Rorty 1995, p. 281).
22 Klein (1998) pp. 15–30.

22. ADAPTING TO RADICAL UNCERTAINTY

1 Viña et al. (2016).
2 See for example Dennett (1995) pp. 282–99 and Gould (1997a and b).
3 Ohno (1988).
4 Mintzberg and Mangelsdorf (2009).
5 The claim that robots have greater emotional intelligence than humans because, for example, they recognise facial expressions and are always nice is in fact an illustration of emotional programming rather than emotional intelligence.
6 Leeson (1996) p. 56.
7 Quoted in Aitken (1999).
8 Mercier and Sperber (2017).

23. EMBRACING UNCERTAINTY

1 Wilde (1891) p. 306.
2 Strictly speaking this accolade goes to the Faroe Islands, with 50,000 inhabitants: Niels Finsen won the 1903 prize in medicine. Of countries with populations above a million, Switzerland is top and Sweden, Denmark and Norway follow.
3 Quoted in Backhouse and Bland (1914) pp. 322–3.
4 Taleb (2013) pp. 83–5.
5 Although Buffett has described derivatives as 'weapons of mass destruction', his Berkshire Hathaway has written large put options which run for as long as fifteen and twenty years against the world's major stock market indices. These transactions protect the reference narrative of pension funds or the counterparties – unidentified but presumed to be institutions with equity portfolios and fixed long-term obligations – against a failure of their reference narrative, without jeopardising Berkshire Hathaway's reference narrative, which gives its stockholders a share in the prosperity of well-managed (principally US) companies.

6   This account is based on Caro (1974).
7   Sellar and Yeatman (1930).
8   See Ventola (2015).
9   Translation by Wells (2016).
10 Mill (1909) p. 436.
11 Michelson quoted in University of Chicago (1896) p. 159.
12 Jante is the fictional setting for Sandemose's novel *A Fugitive Crosses his Tracks* (1933). Jante's law in full runs:

    1. You're not to think *you* are as good as *we* are.
    2. You're not to think *you* are smarter than *we* are.
    3. You're not to imagine yourself better than *we* are.
    4. You're not to think *you* know more than *we* do.
    5. You're not to think *you* are more important than *we* are.
    6. You're not to think *you* are good at anything.
    7. You're not to laugh at *us*.
    8. You're not to think anyone cares about *you*.
    9. You're not to think *you* can teach *us* anything.

13 Obama (2012).
14 Ibid.
15 Clausewitz (1976) p. 134.
16 Ibid. p. 135.

APPENDIX: AXIOMS OF CHOICE UNDER UNCERTAINTY

1   An exposition of the historical development of expected utility theory, and in particular of the independence axiom, is provided by Moscati (2016).
2   Savage (1954).
3   Taleb (2018) p. 225.
4   Arrow (1950).
5   As a result, the axiom of *independence* is violated. This axiom remained controversial and so to some extent did the axiom of *continuity*. Our principal criticism, however, will be of the axiom of *completeness*. The other principal assumption – *transitivity* – seems innocuous.
6   Allais (1953) p. 505.
7   Allais had himself been awarded the Nobel Prize in 1988 for his earlier 'pioneering contributions to the theory of markets and efficient utilization of resources' in his books *Traité d'économie pure* and *Économie et Intérêt*.
8   Savage (1954) p. 103.
9   For example Izhakian et al. (2017).
10 Savage (1954) p. 58.

BIBLIOGRAPHY

Abramovitz, M., 'Resource and Output Trends in the U.S. Since 1870', *American Economic Review*, Vol. 46, No. 2 (1956), 5–23

Adams, A. and Levell, P., 'Measuring Poverty When Inflation Varies Across Households', Joseph Rowntree Foundation (2014)

Aikman, D. et al., 'Taking Uncertainty Seriously: Simplicity Versus Complexity in Financial Regulation', Bank of England Financial Stability Paper Number 28 (2014)

Aitken, I., 'Obituary: Viscount Whitelaw of Penrith', *Guardian* (2 July 1999)

Akerlof, G. A., 'The Market for "Lemons": Quality Uncertainty and the Market Mechanism', *Quarterly Journal of Economics*, Vol. 84, No. 3 (1970), 488–500

Aktipis, C. A., Cronk, L. and de Aguiar, R., 'Risk-Pooling and Herd Survival: An Agent-Based Model of a Maasai Gift-Giving System', *Human Ecology*, Vol. 39, No. 2 (2011), 131–40

Alchian, A. A., 'Uncertainty, Evolution, and Economic Theory', *Journal of Political Economy*, Vol. 58, No. 3 (1950), 211–21

Allais, M., 'Le Comportement de l'Homme Rationnel devant le Risque: Critique des Postulats et Axiomes de l'Ecole Américaine', *Econometrica*, Vol. 21, No. 4 (1953), 503–46

Ambrose, S. E., *Eisenhower: The President: Volume Two, 1952–1969* (London: George Allen and Unwin, 1984)

Anderson, Z., 'Rick Scott Wants to Shift University Funding Away From Some Degrees', *Herald-Tribune* (10 Oct 2011) <http://politics.heraldtribune.com/2011/10/10/rick-scott-wants-to-shift-university-funding-away-from-some-majors/> (accessed 12 Oct 2018)

Appiah, K. A., *As If: Idealization and Ideals* (Cambridge, Massachusetts: HUP, 2017)

Aristotle, *Complete Works of Aristotle, Volume 2: The Revised Oxford Translation* (Princeton: PUP, 2014)

Aristotle (trans. Ross, W. D.), *Nicomachean Ethics, Book VI*, available at <http://classics.mit.edu/Aristotle/nicomachaen.6.vi.html>

Aristotle (trans. Jowett, B.), *Politics* (1885)

Arkansas Teachers Retirement System v. Goldman Sachs Group, Inc., No. 16–250 (2d. Cir. 2018)

Arrow, K. J., 'A Difficulty in the Concept of Social Welfare', *Journal of Political Economy*, Vol. 58, No. 4 (1950), 328–46

Arrow, K. J. and Debreu, G., 'Existence of an Equilibrium for a Competitive Economy', *Econometrica*, Vol. 22, No. 3 (1954), 265–90

Arrow, K. J. and Hahn, F., *General Competitive Analysis* (Amsterdam: North Holland Publishing, 1983)

Atran, S., 'A Cheater-Detection Module? Dubious Interpretations of the Wason Selection Task and Logic', *Evolution and Cognition*, Vol. 7, No. 2 (2001), 187–92

Backhouse, E. and Bland, J. O. P., *Annals and Memoirs of the Court of Peking* (New York: Houghton Mifflin, 1914)

Ballmer, S., 'Ballmer Laughs at iPhone' (18 Sept 2007) <https://www.youtube.com/watch?v=eywi0h_Y5_U> (accessed 21 June 2018)

Bank of England, 'Inflation Report' (May 2013)

Barns, S., 'Chocolate Accelerates Weight Loss: Research Claims It Lowers Cholesterol and Aids Sleep', *Daily Express* (30 Mar 2015)

Barry, J. M., *The Great Influenza: The Epic Story of the Deadliest Plague in History* (New York: Viking, 2004)

Baur, P. and Breutel-O'Donoghue, A., 'Understanding Reinsurance: How Reinsurers Create Value and Manage Risk', Swiss Re (2004)

Becker, G. S., *The Economic Approach to Human Behavior* (Chicago: University of Chicago Press, 1978)

Beckert, J., *Imagined Futures* (Cambridge, Massachusetts: HUP, 2016)

Benson, A., 'French Grand Prix: Lewis Hamilton Says: "I Need Win"', BBC Sport (24 June 2018) <https://www.bbc.co.uk/sport/formula1/44590425> (accessed 9 Oct 2018)

Bernanke, B. and Hutchins, G., 'Central Banking After the Great Recession: Lessons Learned and Challenges Ahead', The Brookings Institution (16 Jan 2014)

Bernoulli, D., 'Exposition of a New Theory on the Measurement of Risk', *Econometrica*, Vol. 22, No. 1 (1954), 23–36

Bernoulli, N., *De usu Artis Conjectandi in Jure* (1709)

Bezos, J., '2017 Letter to Shareholders', Amazon (18 Apr 2018)

Blackstone, W., *Commentaries on the Laws of England (1765–9)*, accessed via <http://avalon.law.yale.edu/subject_menus/blackstone.asp>

Boas, F., 'The Indians of British Columbia', *Popular Science Monthly*, Vol. 32 (Mar 1888)

Boeri, T. and Brücker, H., 'The Impact of Eastern European Enlargement on Employment and Labour Markets in the EU Member States', European Integration Consortium (2001)

Bohannon, J., 'I Fooled Millions Into Thinking Chocolate Helps Weight Loss. Here's How', Io9 <Io9.gizmodo.com> (27 May 2015)

Bolton, B. and Thompson, J., *The Entirepreneur: The All-In-One Entrepreneur-Leader-Manager* (London: Routledge, 2015)

Borch, K., 'The Monster in Loch Ness', *Journal of Risk and Insurance*, Vol. 43, No. 3 (1976), 521–5

Borges, J. L., Yates, D. A., Hurley, A. and Irby, J. E. (trans.), *The Garden of Forking Paths* (London: Penguin, 2018)

Bowden, M., *The Finish: The Killing of Osama bin Laden* (New York: Atlantic Monthly Press, 2012)

Bower, T., *Branson* (London: Fourth Estate, 2001)

Box, G. E. P., 'Robustness in the Strategy of Scientific Model Building' (1979) in Launer, R. L. and Wilkinson, G. N. (eds), *Robustness in Statistics* (Cambridge, Massachusetts: Academic Press, 1979), 201–36

Bradley, H. in Stephen, L. (ed.), 'Jedediah Buxton', *Dictionary of National Biography* Vol. VIII (1886), 106

Brands, H. W., *The General vs. The President* (New York: Doubleday, 2016)

Brearley, M., *On Form* (London: Little Brown, 2017)

Brooks, B. E., 'Jimmie Savage: 20 Nov 1917–1 Nov 1971', *Tales of Statisticians* (4 Sept 2004) <https://www.umass.edu/wsp/resources/tales.html>

Buffett, W. E., *Berkshire Hathaway 2016 Annual Report* (2017)

Buffett, W. E., 'Chairman's Letter to Shareholders' (1988)

Buffett, W. E., 'Chairman's Letter to Shareholders' (1989)

Buffett, W. E., 'Chairman's Letter to Shareholders 2014' (2015)

Burns, R., 'Impromptu on Carron Iron Works' (1787) <http://www.robertburns.org/works/176.shtml> (accessed 9 Oct 2018)

Caldwell, J. C., *Demographic Transition Theory* (Dordrecht: Springer, 2006)

Camerer, C. F. et al., 'Evaluating Replicability of Laboratory Experiments in Economics', *Science*, Vol. 351 (2016), 1433–6

Candler, G. V. and Prescott, E. C., 'Calibration', *The New Palgrave Dictionary of Economics* (10 Dec 2016), accessed 17 May 2018

Capen, E. C., Clapp, R. V. and Campbell, W. M., 'Competitive Bidding in High-Risk Situations', *Journal of Petroleum Technology*, Vol. 23, No. 6 (1971), 641–53

Caro, R. A., *The Power Broker: Robert Moses and the Fall of New York* (New York: Knopf, 1974)

Carré, M. J. et al., 'The Curve Kick of a Football I: Impact with the Foot', *Sports Engineering*, Vol. 5, No. 4 (2002a)

Carré, M. J. et al., 'The Curve Kick of a Football II: Flight Through the Air', *Sports Engineering*, Vol. 5, No. 4 (2002b)

Carroll, L. and Gardner, M., *The Annotated Alice: The Definitive Edition* (New York: Norton, 2000)

Carter, I., 'Rulebook Overhaul is Welcome – But Some Changes Will Need Precise Policing', BBC Sport (1 Jan 2019) <https://www.bbc.co.uk/sport/golf/46728272> (accessed 11 Jan 2019)

Cartwright, N. and Hardie, J., *Evidence-Based Policy: A Practical Guide to Doing It Better* (Oxford: OUP, 2012)

Case, A. and Deaton, A., 'Rising Morbidity and Mortality in Midlife Among White Non-Hispanic Americans in the 21st Century', *Proceedings of the National Academy of Sciences*, Vol. 112, No. 49 (2015), 15078–83

Central Statistics Office, 'Population and Migration Estimates' (2016)

Chandler, A. D., *Strategy and Structure* (Cambridge, Massachusetts: MIT Press, 1962)

Chang, A. C. and Li, P., 'Is Economics Research Replicable? Sixty Published Papers from Thirteen Journals Say

"Usually Not"', *Finance and Economics Discussion Series 2015–083* (2015)

Chater, N., *The Mind is Flat* (London: Allen Lane, 2018)

Cheng, E. K., 'Reconceptualizing the Burden of Proof', *Yale Law Journal*, Vol. 122, No. 5 (2013), 1254–79

Chong, K. and Tuckett, D., 'Constructing Conviction Through Action and Narrative: How Money Managers Manage Uncertainty and the Consequences for Financial Market Functioning', *Socio-Economic Review*, Vol. 13, No. 2 (2015), 1–26

Christoffel, K., Coenen, G. and Warne, A., 'Forecasting with DSGE Models', *ECB Working Paper Series*, No. 1185 (2010)

Churchill, W., *The Second World War, Volume II* (London: The Reprint Society, 1949)

Clapham, J. H., *Bibliography of English Economic History* (London: Historical Association, 1913)

Clausewitz, K., Howard, M. and Paret, P. (trans.), *On War* (Princeton: PUP, 1976)

Coase, R., 'The Nature of the Firm', *Economica*, Vol. 4, No. 16 (1937), 386–405

Coase, R., 'Opening Address to the Annual Conference', *International Society of New Institutional Economics, Washington DC* (17 Sept 1999) <http://www.coase.org/coasespeech. htm> (accessed 16 May 2018)

Cochrane, J. H., 'How did Paul Krugman Get it so Wrong?' (16 Sept 2009) <https://faculty.chicagobooth.edu/john. cochrane/research/papers/krugman_response.htm> (accessed 23 Apr 2019)

Cohan, W. D., 'Inside the Strange Odyssey of Hedge-Fund King Eddie Lampert', *Vanity Fair* (2018)

Cohen, L. J., *The Probable and the Provable* (Oxford: OUP, 1977)

Coleman, R. 'Lemon', *Writing for Designers* (26 Feb 2009) <http://www.writingfordesigners.com/?p=1731> (accessed 24 Jan 2019)

Collier, P., *The Future of Capitalism: Facing the New Anxieties* (London: Allen Lane, 2018)

Collins, J. C., *Good to Great: Why Some Companies Make the Leap . . . and Others Don't* (Chatham: Mackays of Chatham, 2001)

Collins, S., 'Where is Sodom? The Case for Tall el-Hammam', *Biblical Archaeology Review*, Vol. 39, No. 2 (2013)

Colyvan, M., 'Is Probability the Only Coherent Approach to Uncertainty?', *Risk Analysis*, Vol. 28, No. 3 (2008), 645–52

Committee on Oversight and Government Reform, 'The Financial Crisis and the Role of Federal Regulators', House of Representatives (23 Oct 2008)

Committee for the Prize in Economic Sciences in Memory of Alfred Nobel, 'Scientific Background on the Sveriges Riksbank Prize in Economic Sciences in Memory of Alfred Nobel 2017' (2017)

Condorcet, M. J. A. N. de C., *Essai sur l'application de l'analyse à la Probabilité des Décisions Rendues à la Pluralité des Voix* (1785)

Cosmides, L., 'The Logic of Social Exchange: Has Natural Selection Shaped how Humans Reason? Studies with the Wason Selection Task', *Cognition*, Vol. 31 (1989), 187–276

Cosmides, L. and Tooby, J., 'Evolutionary Psychology and the Generation of Culture, Part II. Case Study: A Computational Theory of Social Exchange', *Ethology and Sociobiology*, Vol. 10, No. 1–3 (1989), 51–97

Coyle, D., *GDP* (Princeton: PUP, 2014)

Cribb, J. and Emmerson, C., 'What Happens When Employers Are Obliged to Nudge? Automatic Enrolment and Pension Saving in the UK', *IFS Working Paper W16/19* (2016)

Csikszentmihalyi, M., *Flow: The Psychology of Optimal Experience* (London: HarperCollins, 1991)

Curtiz, M. (director), *Casablanca*, Warner Bros. (1942)

Damasio, A. R., *Descartes' Error: Emotion, Reason and the Human Brain* (London: Picador, 1995)

Daston, L., *Classical Probability in the Enlightenment* (USA: PUP, 1995)

Davenport, T. H. and Manville, B., *Judgement Calls: Twelve Stories of Big Decisions and the Teams That Got Them Right* (Cambridge, Massachusetts: Harvard Business School Publishing, 2012)

David, F. N., *Games, Gods, and Gambling: A History of Probability and Statistical Ideas* (London: Griffin, 1962)

Davidson, D., *Truth, Language, and History* (Oxford: Clarendon, 2005)

Dawkins, R., *The Selfish Gene* (Oxford: OUP, 1976)

de Finetti, B., 'Probabilism: A Critical Essay on the Theory of Probability and the Value of Science', *Erkenntnis*, Vol. 31, No. 2/3 (1989), 169–223

Debt Management Office, 'Gilt Reference Prices' (25 Oct 2018)

Defra, 'Water Use by Industry', National Archives (2012) <http://webarchive.nationalarchives.gov.uk/20130124043757/http://www.defra.gov.uk/statistics/environment/green-economy/scptb10-wateruse/> (accessed 25 Oct 2018)

Dennett, D., *Darwin's Dangerous Idea* (New York: Simon and Schuster, 1995)

Department for Business, Energy & Industrial Strategy, *Historical Coal Data: Coal Production, Availability and Consumption 1853 to 2016* (2017)

Department for Transport, 'Facts on Pedestrian Casualties' (2015)

Department for Work and Pensions, 'Statement on Moving to CPI as the Measure of Price Inflation' (12 July 2010) <https://www.gov.uk/government/news/statement-on-moving-to-cpi-as-the-measure-of-price-inflation> (accessed 10 Oct 2018)

Derrida, J., *De La Grammatologie* (Paris: Minuet, 1967)

Devlin, K., *The Unfinished Game: Pascal, Fermat and the Seventeenth-Century Letter that Made the World Modern* (New York: Basic Books, 2010)

Dirac, P. A. M., 'Nobel Banquet Speech' (10 Dec 1933) <https://www.nobelprize.org/prizes/physics/1933/dirac/speech/> (accessed 9 Oct 2018)

Donoghue, D., 'A Guide to the Revolution', *New York Review of Books* (8 Dec 1983)

Donoghue, D., 'The Use and Abuse of Theory', *Modern Language Review*, Vol. 87, No. 4 (1992), xxix–xxxviii

Dowd, K., Cotter, J., Humphrey, C. and Woods, M., 'How Unlucky Is 25-Sigma?', *Journal of Portfolio Management*, Vol. 34, No. 4 (2008), 76–80

Doyle, A. C., 'The Adventure of the Blanched Soldier' in *The Case-Book of Sherlock Holmes* (London: John Murray, 1927), 47–74

Doyle, A. C., *The Adventures and the Memoirs of Sherlock Holmes* (New York: Sterling, 2004)

Doyle, A. C., 'J. Habakuk Jephson's Statement', *Cornhill Magazine* (Jan 1884), 1–32

Drake, S., *Galileo at Work: His Scientific Biography* (Chicago: University of Chicago Press, 1978)

Drucker, P. F., *Concept of the Corporation* (New York: The John Day Company, 1946)

Duffy, C., *Borodino and the War of 1812* (London: Seeley, Service and Co., 1972)

Duflo, E., 'Richard T. Ely Lecture: The Economist As Plumber',

American Economic Review, Vol. 107, No. 5 (2017), 1–26

Duhem, P., *La Théorie Physique: Son Objet et sa Structure* (Paris: Chevalier and Rivière, 1906)

Duke, A., *Thinking in Bets: Making Smarter Decisions When You Don't Have All the Facts* (New York: Penguin, 2018)

Dustmann, C. et al., 'The Impact of EU Enlargement on Migration Flows', Home Office Online Report (25 Mar 2003)

Eco, U., *The Name of the Rose* (London: Vintage, 2004)

The Economist, 'Alfred Sloan' (30 Jan 2009)

The Economist, 'Business in 1852' (8 Jan 1853)

The Economist, 'A Mean Feat' (9 Jan 2016)

Ehrlich, P. R., *The Population Bomb* (San Francisco: Sierra Club, 1970)

Ehrlich, P. R., 'When Paul's Said and Done', *Grist Magazine* (13 Aug 2004) <https://web.archive.org/web/20041115081108/http://www.grist.org/comments/interactivist/2004/08/09/ehrlich/index1.html> (accessed 29 Apr 2019)

Einstein, A., 'Letter to Max Born' (1926) in Born, I. (trans.), *The Born-Einstein Letters* (London: Macmillan, 1971)

Eisenhower, D. D., 'In Case of Failure', Eisenhower's Pre-Presidential Papers, Principal File, Box 168, Butcher Diary June 28-July 14 (1944); NAID #186470

Eland, I., 'Rumsfeld vs. The Pentagon', Cato Institute (11 Apr 2001) <https://www.cato.org/publications/commentary/rumsfeld-vs-pentagon> (accessed 15 Oct 2018)

Eliot, G., *Middlemarch* (1871–2)

Ellsberg, D., 'Risk, Ambiguity, and the Savage Axioms', *Quarterly Journal of Economics*, Vol. 75, No. 4 (1961), 643–69

Ellsberg, D., *Secrets: A Memoir of Vietnam and the Pentagon Papers* (London: Penguin, 2003)

Engel, J. A., *Cold War at 30,000 Feet: The Anglo-American Fight for Aviation Supremacy* (Cambridge, Massachusetts: HUP, 2007)

European Commission, 'Annexes to the Commission Delegated Regulation Supplementing Key Information Documents for PRIIPS' (8 Mar 2017) <http://ec.europa.eu/finance/docs/level-2-measures/priips-delegated-regulation-2017-1473-annex_en.pdf> (accessed 28 Aug 2019)

Eurostat, *Mortality and Life Expectancy Statistics* (2017)

Evans-Pritchard, E. E., *The Nuer: A Description of the Modes of Livelihood and Political Institutions of a Nilotic People* (Oxford: Clarendon, 1940)

Falk, R., 'When Truisms Clash: Coping with a Counterintuitive Problem Concerning the Notorious Two-child Family', *Thinking & Reasoning*, Vol. 17, No. 4 (2011), 353–66

Farber, D., *Sloan Rules: Alfred P. Sloan and the Triumph of General Motors* (Chicago: University of Chicago Press, 2002)

Federal Aviation Administration, 'Lessons Learned: de Havilland DH-106 Comet 1' <lessonslearned.faa.gov> (accessed 19 Mar 2018)

Felin, T., 'The Fallacy of Obviousness' (2018) <https://aeon.co/essays/are-humans-really-blind-to-the-gorilla-on-the-basketball-court> (accessed 5 Oct 2018)

Ferguson, A., *An Essay on the History of Civil Society* (1782)

Feynman, R. P., *Rogers Commission Report, Appendix F* (1986)

Financial Conduct Authority, 'Statement on Communications in Relation to PRIIPs' (24 Jan 2018) <https://www.fca.org.uk/news/statements/statement-communications-relation-priips> (accessed 9 Oct 2018)

Fisher, W. R., *Human Communication as Narration: Toward a Philosophy of Reason, Value, and Action* (Columbia, South Carolina: University of South Carolina Press, 1989)

Fitzgerald, F. S., 'The Crack-Up', *Esquire* (2017)

Fitzgerald, F. S., *The Great Gatsby* (New York: Charles Scribner's Sons, 1925)

Fleming, P. J. et al., *The CESDI SUDI Studies 1993–1996* (2000)

'Fondements et Applications de la Théorie du Risque en Econométrie' (1952) in *Econométrie*, Collection des Colloques Internationaux du Centre National de la Recherche Scientifique, Vol. 40 (1953), 127–40

Forbes, 'Warren Buffett – In 1974' (30 Apr 2008)

Fowler, N., 'Margaret Thatcher's Cabinet was a Battle of Wills', *Telegraph* (12 Apr 2013)

Friedman, B., 'The Search for New Assumptions', *Democracy*, No. 45 (2017)

Friedman, J. A. and Zeckhauser, R., 'Handling and Mishandling Estimative Probability: Likelihood, Confidence, and the Search for bin Laden', *Intelligence and National Security*, Vol. 30, No. 1 (2014), 77–99

Friedman, M., *Essays in Positive Economics* (Chicago: University of Chicago Press, 1953)

Friedman, M., *Price Theory* (New Brunswick, NJ: Transaction Publishers, 2007)

Friedman, M., *There's No Such Thing as a Free Lunch* (Illinois: Open Court Publishers, 1975)

Friedman, M. and Savage, L. J., 'The Utility Analysis of Choices Involving Risk', *Journal of Political Economy*, Vol. 56, No. 4 (1948), 279–304

Frydman, R. and Phelps, R. (eds), *Rethinking Expectations: The Way Forward for Macroeconomics* (Princeton: PUP, 2013)

FT Ordinary Share <https://uk.investing.com/indices/ft30-chart> (accessed 25 Oct 2018)

Gabaix, X., 'Power Laws in Economics and Finance', *Annual Review of Economics*, Vol. 1 (2009), 255–93

Galton, F., 'Vox Populi', *Nature*, Vol. 75 (1907), 450–1

GAO, 'Key Issues: Disposal of High-Level Nuclear Waste', U.S. Government Accountability Office <https://www.gao. gov/key_issues/disposal_of_highlevel_nuclear_waste/issue_ summary#t=0> (accessed 5 Dec 2018)

Gao, J. et al., 'Learning the Rules of the Rock-Paper-Scissors Game: Chimpanzees Versus Children', *Primates*, Vol. 59, No. 1 (2018), 7–17

Gapper, J., 'Memo From Amazon: Tell a Good Story', *Financial Times* (9 May 2018)

Gavin, J. M., *War and Peace in the Space Age* (New York: Harper, 1958)

GBD 2013 Mortality and Cause of Death Contributors, 'Global, Regional, and National Age–Sex Specific All-Cause and Cause-Specific Mortality for 240 Causes of Death, 1990–2013: A Systematic Analysis for the Global Burden of Disease Study 2013', *The Lancet*, Vol. 385, No. 9963, 117–71

Geertz, C., 'Thick Description: Towards an Interpretive Theory of Culture' in *The Interpretation of Cultures: Selected Essays* (New York: Basic Books, 1973), 3–30

General Medical Council v. Meadow [2006] EWCA Civ 1390 (26 Oct 2006)

Gibbon, E., *The History of the Decline and Fall of the Roman Empire*, Volume IV (1784)

Gibbons, M. R., 'Multivariate Tests of Financial Models: A New Approach', *Journal of Financial Economics*, Vol. 10, No. 1 (1982), 3–27

Gigerenzer, G., *Gut Feelings* (London: Penguin, 2008)

Gigerenzer, G., *Risk Savvy: How to Make Good Decisions* (London: Penguin, 2015)

Gigerenzer, G., *Simple Heuristics that Make Us Smart* (Oxford: OUP, 2001)

Gigerenzer, G., 'Striking a Blow for Sanity in Theories of Rationality' in Augier, M. and March, J. G. (eds), *Models of a Man: Essays in Memory of Herbert A. Simon* (Cambridge, Massachusetts: MIT Press, 2004)

Gilboa, I., 'Rationality and the Bayesian Paradigm', *Journal of Economic Methodology*, Vol. 22, No. 3 (2015), 312–34

Gilbert, W. S. and Sullivan, A., *HMS Pinafore* (1878)

Gilman, A., 'Explaining the Upper Paleolithic Revolution' in Preucel, R. W. and Hodder, I., *Contemporary Archaeology in Theory: A Reader* (New York: Wiley and Sons, 1996)

Gladwell, M., *Blink: The Power of Thinking Without Thinking* (London: Penguin, 2006)

Goldman Sachs, 'Goldman Sachs Business Principles' <http://www.goldmansachs.com/who-we-are/business-standards/business-principles/> (accessed 10 Oct 2018)

Goldstein, D. G. and Gigerenzer, G., 'Models of Ecological Rationality: The Recognition Heuristic', *Psychological Review*, Vol. 109, No. 1 (2002), 75–90

Goodhart, C. A. E., 'Problems of Monetary Management: The UK Experience' (1984) in *Monetary Theory and Practice* (London: Macmillan, 1987), 91–121

Goodwin, D. K., *Team of Rivals: The Political Genius of Abraham Lincoln* (New York: Simon and Schuster, 2005)

Gould, S. J., 'Darwinian Fundamentalism', *New York Review of Books* (12 June 1997a)

Gould, S. J., 'Evolution: The Pleasures of Pluralism', *New York Review of Books* (26 June 1997b)

Gráda, C. Ó and Mokyr, J., 'New Developments in Irish Population History 1700–1850', *Economic History Review*, Vol. 37, No. 4 (1984), 473–88

Graham, B. and Zweig, J., *The Intelligent Investor* (New York: HarperCollins, 2005)

Greenspan, A., *The Map and the Territory 2.0: Risk, Human Nature, and the Future of Forecasting* (London: Allen Lane, 2013)

Greenspan, A., 'Reflections on Central Banking', *Financial*

Markets, Financial Fragility, and Central Banking: A Symposium Sponsored by the Federal Reserve Bank of Kansas City at Jackson Hole (26 Aug 2005) <https://www.federalreserve.gov/boarddocs/speeches/2005/20050826/default.htm> (accessed 16 May 2018)

Greenspan, A., 'World Finance and Risk Management', speech at Lancaster House, London (25 Sept 2002) <https://www.federalreserve.gov/boarddocs/speeches/2002/200209253/default.htm> (accessed 16 May 2018)

Greenstein, F. I., *The Hidden-Hand Presidency: Eisenhower As Leader* (Baltimore: Johns Hopkins University Press, 1994)

Groopman, J., *How Doctors Think* (New York: Houghton Mifflin, 2008)

Grossman, S. J. and Stiglitz, J. E., 'On the Impossibility of Informationally Efficient Markets', *American Economic Review*, Vol. 70, No. 3 (1980), 393–408

Hacking, I., *The Emergence of Probability* (Cambridge: CUP, 1975)

Hacking, I., *The Social Construction of What?* (Cambridge, Massachusetts: HUP, 1999)

Haidt, J., *The Righteous Mind: Why Good People Are Divided by Politics and Religion* (London: Penguin, 2013)

Haldane, A., Brennan, S. and Madouros, V., 'What is the Contribution of the Financial Sector: Miracle or Mirage?' in Turner, A. et al., *The Future of Finance* (London: LSE, 2010)

Hamilton, L. C., Haedrich, R. L. and Duncan, C. M., 'Above and Below the Water: Social/Ecological Transformation in Northwest Newfoundland', *Population and Environment*, Vol. 25, No. 6 (2004), 195–215

Hamilton, W. D., 'The Genetical Evolution of Social Behaviour I', *Journal of Theoretical Biology*, Vol. 7, No. 1 (1964), 1–16

Hammurabi (trans. King, L. W.), *The Code of Hammurabi*, The Avalon Project <http://avalon.law.yale.edu/ancient/hamframe.asp> (accessed 15 Oct 2018)

Hannibal, M. and Mountford, L., *The Law of Criminal and Civil Evidence: Principles and Practice* (Harlow: Pearson Education, 2002)

Harcourt, B., *Against Prediction* (Chicago: University of Chicago Press, 2007)

Harrod, R. F., *The Life of John Maynard Keynes* (London: Macmillan and Co., 1951)

Hartley, L. P., *The Go-Between* (Oxford: Heinemann Educational, 1985)

Hastings, M., *Vietnam: An Epic Tragedy 1945–75* (London: HarperCollins, 2018)

Hausman, D. M., 'Philosophy and Economic Methodology', *PSA: Proceedings of the Biennial Meeting of the Philosophy of Science Association 1984*, No. 2 (1984), 231–49

HC Deb (4 June 1940), Vol. 361, cc. 787–98

Hendry, D. and Mizon, G., 'Why DSGEs Crash During Crises', *Vox CEPR* (2014) <https://voxeu.org/article/why-standard-macro-models-fail-crises> (accessed 9 Oct 2018)

Henrich, J., *The Secret of Our Success: How Culture is Driving Human Evolution, Domesticating Our Species, and Making Us Smarter* (Princeton: PUP, 2017)

Herbranson, W. T. and Schroeder, J., 'Are Birds Smarter than Mathematicians? Pigeons (Columba livia) Perform Optimally on a Version of the Monty Hall Dilemma', *Journal of Comparative Psychology*, Vol. 124, No. 1 (2010), 1–13

Hermanns, W. and Einstein, A., *Einstein and the Poet: In Search of the Cosmic Man* (Brookline Village: Branden Press, 1983)

Hiam, L., Harrison, D., McKee, M. et al., 'Why is Life Expectancy in England and Wales "Stalling"?', *Journal of Epidemiology & Community Health* (2018)

Hicks, J. R., 'Mr Keynes and the "Classics": A Suggested Interpretation', *Econometrica*, Vol. 5, No. 2 (1937), 147–59

Himmelreich, C., 'Germany's Phantom Serial Killer: A DNA Blunder', *Time* (27 Mar 2009)

HM Treasury, *TAG Data Book* (May 2018a)

HM Treasury, *The Green Book: Central Government Guidance on Appraisal and Evaluation* (2018b)

Hobbes, T., *The English Works of Thomas Hobbes of Malmesbury*, Vol. I (1843)

Hofstadter, D., 'The Shallowness of Google Translate', *The Atlantic* (30 Jan 2018)

Holmes Jr, O. W., *The Common Law* (1881)

House of Commons Treasury Committee, 'The Run on the Rock' (2008)

House of Commons Treasury Committee, 'Second Report: Fixing LIBOR: Some Preliminary Findings' (2012)

Howe, G., *Conflict of Loyalty* (London: Macmillan, 1994)

Hubbert, M. K., 'Nuclear Energy and the Fossil Fuels', *Shell Development Company: Exploration and Production Research Division* Publication No. 95 (1956) <https://web.archive.org/web/20080527233843/http://www.hubbertpeak.com/hubbert/1956/1956.pdf> (accessed 15 Jan 2019)

Hume, D. (ed. Beauchamp, T. L.), *An Enquiry Concerning Human Understanding: A Critical Edition* (Oxford: OUP, 2000)

Ignatieff, M., 'Defending Academic Freedom in a Populist Age', *Project Syndicate* (2 June 2017) <https://www.project-syndicate.org/onpoint/defending-academic-freedom-in-a-populist-age-by-michael-ignatieff-2017-06> (accessed 16 May 2018)

Ioannidis, J. P. A., 'Why Most Published Research Findings Are False', *PLoS Medicine*, Vol. 2, No. 8 (2005)

Ipsos MORI, 'Online Polls for Gapminder in 12 Countries' (Aug 2017) <gapm.io/gt17re>

Isaacson, W., *Steve Jobs* (New York: Simon and Schuster, 2011)

Ishiguro, K., *The Remains of the Day* (London: Faber and Faber, 1989)

Izhakian, Y., Yermack, D. and Zender, J. F., 'Ambiguity and the Tradeoff Theory of Capital Structure', *NBER Working Papers* (2017)

J. G. W., 'The Fourteenth International Congress of Actuaries', *Transactions of the Faculty of Actuaries*, Vol. 22 (1954), 441–5

Jallais, S. and Pradier, P-C., 'The Allais Paradox and its Immediate Consequences for Expected Utility Theory' in Fontaine, P. and Leonard, R. (eds), *The Experiment in the History of Economics* (London: Routledge, 2005), 25–49

Janis, I. L., *Victims of Groupthink: A Psychological Study of Foreign Policy Decisions and Fiascoes* (New York: Houghton Mifflin, 1972)

Jensen, K., Call, J. and Tomasello, M., 'Chimpanzees are Rational Maximizers in an Ultimatum Game', *Science*, Vol. 318, No. 5847 (2007), 107–9

Jevons, W. S., *The Coal Question: An Inquiry Concerning the Progress of the Nation, and the Probable Exhaustion of Our Coal-Mines* (1865)

Jevons, W. S., 'Commercial Crises and Sun-spots', *Nature*, Vol. 19 (1878), 33–7

Joint Committee of the European Supervisory Authorities, 'Questions and Answers (Q&A) on the PRIIPs KID' (4 July 2017) <https://esas-joint-committee.europa. eu/Publications/Consultations/Questions%20and%20 answers%20on%20the%20PRIIPs%20KID.pdf> (accessed 9 Oct 2018)

Kafka, F. (trans. Muir, E. and Muir, W.), *The Trial* (London: Pan Books, 1977)

Kahneman, D., 'Remarks from Daniel Kahneman', *NBER Economics of AI Conference* (2017) <youtu.be/gbj_NsgNe7A> (accessed 5 Oct 2018)

Kahneman, D., *Thinking, Fast and Slow* (London: Penguin, 2011)

Kahneman, D. and Tversky, A., 'On the Reality of Cognitive Illusions', *Psychological Review*, Vol. 103, No. 3 (1996), 582–91

Kahneman, D. and Tversky, A., 'Prospect Theory: An Analysis of Decision Under Risk', *Econometrica*, Vol. 47, No. 2 (1979), 263–92

Kaplan, I., 'The "Getty Kouros" was Removed from View at the Museum After it was Officially Deemed to be a Forgery' (16 Apr 2018) <https://www.artsy.net/news/artsy-editorial-getty-kouros-removed-view-museum-officially-deemed-forgery> (accessed 24 Apr 2019)

Kasparov, G., *Deep Thinking* (London: John Murray, 2018)

Katz, V. J., *A History of Mathematics* (New York: HarperCollins, 1993)

Kay, J. A., 'The Concept of the Corporation', *Business History, Special Issue: Leslie Hannah Festschrift* (2019)

Kay, J. A., 'Gambling is a Feature of Capitalism – Not a Bug', *Prospect* (14 March 2017)

Kay, J. A., *Obliquity* (London: Profile, 2011)

Kay, J. A., *Other People's Money* (London: Profile, 2015)

Kay, J. A. and King, M. A., 'USS Crisis: Can the Pension System be Reformed?', *Times Higher Education* (6 Sept 2018)

Keating, J., 'In his Heart, Rick Santorum Knows that Dutch People are Forcibly Euthanized', *Foreign Policy* (12 Mar 2012)

Kennedy, G., *The Art of Persuasion in Greece* (London: Routledge, 1963)

Kennedy, R. F., *Thirteen Days: A Memoir of the Cuban Missile Crisis* (New York: Norton, 1999)

Kennes, R. and Smets, P., 'The Transferable Belief Model', *Artificial Intelligence*, Vol. 66, No. 2 (1994), 191–234

Keren, G., 'A Tale of Two Systems: A Scientific Advance or a Theoretical Stone Soup? Commentary on Evans and Stanovich (2013)', *Perspectives on Psychological Science*, Vol. 8, No. 3 (2013), 257–62

Keren, G. and Schul, Y., 'Two Is Not Always Better than One: A Critical Evaluation of Two-System Theories', *Perspectives on Psychological Science*, Vol. 4, No. 6 (2009), 533–50

Keynes, G. and Keynes, J. M., *Essays in Biography* (London: Macmillan and Co., 1933)

Keynes, J. M., 'Economic Possibilities for Our Grandchildren' (1930) in Keynes, J. M., *Essays in Persuasion* (London: Macmillan and Co., 1931)

Keynes, J. M., 'The General Theory of Employment', *Quarterly Journal of Economics*, Vol. 51, No. 2 (1937), 209–23

Keynes, J. M., *The General Theory of Employment, Interest and Money* (London: Macmillan and Co., 1936)

Keynes, J. M., 'Professor Tinbergen's Method', *Economic Journal*, Vol. 49, No. 195 (1939), 558–77

Keynes, J. M., *A Treatise on Probability* (London: Macmillan and Co., 1921)

Keynes, J. M., 'William Stanley Jevons 1835–1882: A Centenary Allocation on his Life and Work as Economist and Statistician', *Journal of the Royal Statistical Society*, Vol. 99, No. 3 (1936), 516–55

Keynes, J. M., Johnson, E. and Moggridge, D. (eds), *The Collected Writings of John Maynard Keynes: Volume IX: Essays in Persuasion* (1978)

Khaw, M. W., Stevens, L. and Woodford, M., 'Discrete Adjustment to a Changing Environment: Experimental Evidence', *NBER Working Paper* (2016)

Kimes, M., 'The Sun Tzu at Sears', *Bloomberg Businessweek* (15 June 2013)

King, M. A., *The End of Alchemy* (London: Little Brown, 2016)

King, M. A. et al., 'Education and Employment – Minutes
of Evidence', House of Commons Education and
Employment Subcommittee (27 May 1999) <https://
publications.parliament.uk/pa/cm199899/cmselect/
cmeduemp/547/9052701.htm> (accessed 3 Oct 2018)

Klein, G. A., *Sources of Power: How People Make Decisions*
(Cambridge, Massachusetts: MIT Press, 1998)

Klemperer, P., 'What Really Matters in Auction Design', *Journal
of Economic Perspectives*, Vol. 16, No. 1 (2002), 169–89

Knight, F. H., *Risk, Uncertainty and Profit* (New York: Houghton
Mifflin, 1921)

Knight, F. H., 'What is Truth in Economics?', *Journal of Political
Economy*, Vol. 48, No. 1 (1940), 1–32

Knights, L. C., *How Many Children Had Lady Macbeth? An Essay
in the Theory and Practice of Shakespeare Criticism* (Cambridge:
Folcroft Library Editions, 1933)

Kolm, S-C. and Ythier, J. M., *Handbook of the Economics of
Giving, Altruism, and Reciprocity, Volume 1: Foundations*
(Amsterdam: North Holland, 2006)

Korzybski, A., *Science and Sanity* (New York: The International
Non-Aristotelian Publishing Co., 1933)

Kruglanski, A. W. and Gigerenzer, G., 'Intuitive and
Deliberative Judgments are Based on Common Principles',
Psychological Review, Vol. 118, No. 1 (2011), 97–109

Krugman, P., 'What Do We Actually Know About the
Economy?', *New York Times* (16 Sept 2018)

Kydland, F. E. and Prescott, E. C., 'Time to Build and Aggregate
Fluctuations', *Econometrica*, Vol. 50, No. 6 (1982), 1345–70

Lakoff, G. and Johnson, M., *Metaphors We Live By* (Chicago:
University of Chicago Press, 1980)

Lampert, E., 'Chairman's Letter', Sears Holdings (23 Feb 2010)
<https://blog.searsholdings.com/eddie-lampert/chairmans-
letter-february-23-2010/> (accessed 12 Oct 2018)

Lampert, E., 'Evolving the Sears Mastercard With Shop Your Way', Sears Holdings (27 Oct 2016) <https://blog. searsholdings.com/eddie-lampert/evolving-the-sears-mastercard-with-shop-your-way/> (accessed 12 Oct 2018)

Laplace, P. S. (trans. Truscott, F. W. and Emory, F. L.), *A Philosophical Essay on Probabilities* (New York: Dover, 1951)

Laplace, P. S., *Théorie Analytique des Probabilités* (1812)

Larsen, P. T., 'Goldman Pays the Price of Being Big', *Financial Times* (13 Aug 2007)

Laura and John Arnold Foundation, 'Public Safety Assessment: Risk Factors and Formula' (2016) <https://www. arnoldfoundation.org/wp-content/uploads/PSA-Risk-Factors-and-Formula.pdf> (accessed 24 Jan 2019)

Laville, S., 'Roulette Arrest Trio Keep £1.3m in Winnings', *Guardian* (6 Dec 2004)

Lawrence, C., 'Obama Ending Two-War Strategy', CNN (4 Jan 2012) <http://security.blogs.cnn.com/2012/01/04/panetta-ending-two-war-strategy/> (accessed 15 Oct 2018)

Leamer, E. E., 'Let's Take the Con Out of Econometrics', *American Economic Review*, Vol. 73, No. 1 (1983), 31–43

Leamer, E. E., *Specification Searches: Ad Hoc Inference with Nonexperimental Data* (New York: John Wiley and Sons, 1978)

Leamon, N., *The Test: A Novel* (London: Hachette, 2018)

Leeson, N. W., *Rogue Trader* (London: Little Brown, 1996)

Lenin, V. I. (trans. Dutt, C.), 'Letter to Rosa Luxemburg' (1909) in *Lenin Collected Works: Volume 34* (Moscow: Progress Publishers, 1975)

LeRoy, S. and Singell, L. D., 'Knight on Risk and Uncertainty', *Journal of Political Economy*, Vol. 95, No. 2 (1987), 394–406

Lewis, M., *The Undoing Project: A Friendship that Changed the World* (London: Penguin, 2017)

Libet, B. et al., 'Time of Conscious Intention to Act in Relation to Onset of Cerebral Activity (Readiness-Potential). The Unconscious Initiation of a Freely Voluntary Act', *Brain*, Vol. 106, No. 3 (1983), 623–42

Lipshaw, J. M., 'Dissecting the Two-Handed Lawyer: Thinking Versus Action in Business Lawyering', *Berkeley Business Law Journal*, Vol. 10, No. 2 (2013), 231–86

Lo, A., *Adaptive Markets: Financial Evolution at the Speed of Thought* (Princeton: PUP, 2017)

Lohr, S., 'Without Its Master of Design, Apple Will Face Many Challenges', *New York Times* (24 Aug 2011)

Lovallo, D. P. and Mendonca, L. T., 'Strategy's Strategist: An Interview with Richard Rumelt', *McKinsey Quarterly* No. 4 (2007), 56–67

Lowe, D. L., Hopkins, C. and Bristow, T., 'Survation was the Most Accurate Pollster this Election – How Did we Get it Right?', *Survation* (2017) <https://www.survation.com/survation-most-accurate-pollster/> (accessed 27 Nov 2018)

Lucas, R., 'Econometric Policy Evaluation: A Critique', *Carnegie-Rochester Conference Series on Public Policy*, Vol. 1, No. 1 (1976), 19–46

Lucas, R., 'What Economists Do', University of Chicago Commencement Address 1988, published in *Journal of Applied Economics*, Vol. 14, No. 1 (2011), 1–4

Lucas, R. E., *Lectures on Economic Growth* (Cambridge, Massachusetts: HUP, 2002)

Lucas, R. E., 'Macroeconomic Priorities', *American Economic Review*, Vol. 93, No. 1 (2003), 1–14

Lux, H., 'The Secret World of Jim Simons', *Institutional Investor* (1 Nov 2000)

MacIntyre, A., *After Virtue: A Study in Moral Theory* (London: Gerald Duckworth and Co., 2003)

Mackay, C., *Extraordinary Popular Delusions and the Madness of Crowds* (1841)

Mackin, J. H., 'Rational and Empirical Methods of Investigation in Geology' (1963) in Slaytnaker, O. (ed.), *Fluvial Geomorphology* (Abingdon, Oxon: Routledge, 2013), 271–98

Maddison Project Database, version 2018. Bolt, Jutta, Robert Inklaar, Herman de Jong and Jan Luiten van Zanden (2018), 'Rebasing "Maddison": New Income Comparisons and the Shape of Long-run Economic Development', *Maddison Working Paper 10*

Mandel, T., 'Happy Birthday to Science', *Chicago Sun-Times* (28 May 1990)

Mandelbrot, B., 'The Variation of Certain Speculative Prices', *Journal of Business*, Vol. 36, No. 4 (1963), 394–419

Mandeville, B., *The Fable of the Bees* (1732)

Marconi, D., *My Father, Marconi* (London: Guernica, 2001)

Markowitz, H. M., 'Foundations of Portfolio Theory', Nobel Prize lecture (1990)

Markowitz, H. M., 'Portfolio Selection', *Journal of Finance*, Vol. 7, No. 1 (1952), 77–91

Márquez, G. G. and Stone, P. H., 'Gabriel García Márquez, The Art of Fiction No. 69', *The Paris Review*, No. 82 (1981)

Marshall, A., *Principles of Economics* (1890)

Marshall, B. J., 'Helicobacter Connections', Nobel Prize lecture (8 Dec 2005)

Marshall, B. J. and Adams, P. C., 'Helicobacter Pylori: A Nobel Pursuit?', *Canadian Journal of Gastroenterology and Hepatology*, Vol. 22, No. 11 (2008), 895–6

Martin, V., *The Ghost of the Mary Celeste* (London: Hachette, 2014)

Marwell, G. and Ames, R. E., 'Economists Free Ride, Does Anyone Else? Experiments on the Provision of Public

Goods, IV', *Journal of Public Economics*, Vol. 15, No. 3 (1981), 295–310

Mauss, M. (trans. Halls, W. D.), *The Gift: The Form and Reason for Exchange in Archaic Societies* (London: Routledge, 1990)

May, R. M., 'Uses and Abuses of Mathematics in Biology', *Science*, Vol. 303, No. 5659 (2004), 790–3

Maynard Smith, J., 'Group Selection and Kin Selection', *Nature*, Vol. 201 (1964)

Mayzner, M. S. and Tresselt, M. E., 'Tables of Single-letter and Digram Frequency Counts for Various Word-length and Letter-position Combinations', *Psychonomic Monograph Supplements*, Vol. 1, No. 2 (1965), 13–32

McCoy, J., Prelec, D. and Seung, H. S., 'A Solution to the Single-Question Crowd Wisdom Problem', *Nature*, Vol. 541 (2017), 532–5

McGonagall, W., *McGonagall: A Library Omnibus* (London: Duckworth, 1980)

McNamara, R. S., *In Retrospect: The Tragedy and Lessons of Vietnam* (Collingdale, Pennsylvania: DIANE Publishing, 1995)

Meadow, R., 'Fatal Abuse and Smothering' in Meadow, R. (ed.), *ABC of Child Abuse* (London: BMJ Publishing, 1997)

Meadows, D. L. et al., *The Limits to Growth* (New York: Universe Books, 1972)

Mearsheimer, J. J., *The Tragedy of Great Power Politics* (New York: Norton, 2001)

Mees, C. E. K., 'Scientific Thought and Social Reconstruction', *Sigma Xi Quarterly*, Vol. 22, No. 1 (1934), 13–24

Menand, L., *The Metaphysical Club* (London: HarperCollins, 2011)

Mercier, H. and Sperber, D., *The Enigma of Reason: A New Theory of Human Understanding* (London: Allen Lane, 2017)

Merton, R. K., *Social Theory and Social Structure* (Glencoe, Illinois: Free Press, 1960)

Met Office, 'The Science of "Probability of Precipitation"' (8 Aug 2014) <http://www.altostratus.it/previsorideltempo/2014_Probabilita_Precipitazione_MetOffice.pdf> (accessed 23 Apr 2019)

Midanik, L., 'The Validity of Self-Reported Alcohol Consumption and Alcohol Problems: A Literature Review', *British Journal of Addiction*, Vol. 77 (1982), 357–82

Mill, J. S., *A System of Logic, Vol. II* (1843)

Mill, J. S. (ed. Ashley, W. J.), *Principles of Political Economy with Some of their Applications to Social Philosophy* (London: Longmans, Green, and Co., 1909)

Miller, A., *Death of a Salesman* (New York: Viking, 1949)

Mintzberg, H., Ahlstrand, B. and Lampel, J., *Strategy Safari: A Guided Tour Through the Wilds of Strategic Management* (New York: Simon and Schuster, 2005)

Mintzberg, H. and Mangelsdorf, M. E., 'Debunking Management Myths', *MIT Sloan Management Review* (1 Oct 2009)

Monahan, J., 'A Jurisprudence of Risk Assessment: Forecasting Harm Among Prisoners, Predators, and Patients', *Virginia Law Review*, Vol. 92, No. 3 (2006), 391–435

Monahan, J. and Skeem, J. L., 'Risk Assessment in Criminal Sentencing', *Annual Review of Criminal Psychology*, Vol. 12 (2016), 489–513

Mooney, A., '€2.5bn Cost of MiFID II Rattles Asset Managers', *Financial Times* (27 Jan 2017)

Moore, H. N., 'Congress Grilled Lehman Brothers' Dick Fuld: Highlights of the Hearing', *Wall Street Journal* (6 Oct 2008)

Morris, S., 'The Sting: Did Gang Really Use a Laser, Phone and a Computer to Take the Ritz for £1.3m?', *Guardian* (23 Mar 2004)

Moscati, I., 'How Economists Came to Accept Expected Utility

Theory: The Case of Samuelson and Savage', *Journal of Economic Perspectives*, Vol. 30, No. 2 (2016), 219–36

Nahl, P. C., 'Perham C. Nahl's Notes from Frank H. Knight's Course on Business Cycles' (1936) in Cristiano, C. and Fiorito, L., 'Two Minds That Never Met: Frank H. Knight on John M. Keynes Once Again – A Documentary Note', *Review of Keynesian Economics*, Vol. 4, No. 1 (2016), 67–98

NASA, *MESSENGER: Mercury Orbit Insertion* (2011)

Nelson, E., 'Karl Brunner and UK Monetary Debate', *SSRN* (2018), available at <https://ssrn.com/abstract=3256826>

Nelson, E. and Nikolov, K., 'Monetary Policy and Stagflation in the UK', Bank of England Working Paper No. 155 (2002)

Nelson, L. D., Simmons, J. P. and Simonsohn, U., 'False-Positive Psychology: Undisclosed Flexibility in Data Collection and Analysis Allows Presenting Anything as Significant', *Psychological Science*, Vol. 22, No. 11 (2011), 1359–66

NEST, 'Investment Approach' <https://www.nestpensions.org.uk/schemeweb/nest/aboutnest/investment-approach.html> (accessed 10 Jan 2019)

Newhouse, J., 'A reporter at large: A sporty game – I betting the company', *New Yorker* (14 June 1982)

Noble, S. U., *Algorithms of Oppression: How Search Engines Reinforce Racism* (New York: NYU Press, 2018)

Norman, J., *Adam Smith: What He Thought, and Why it Matters* (London: Penguin, 2018)

Nunn, G. A., 'The Incompatibility of Due Process and Naked Statistical Evidence', *Vanderbilt Law Review*, Vol. 68, No. 5 (2015), 1407–33

Nwauwa, N., 'Improving Care and Response in Nigeria', *Journal of Emergency Medical Services*, Vol. 42, No. 6 (2017)

Obama, B. H., 'Remarks by the President at a Campaign Event in Roanoke, Virginia', Office of the Press Secretary (13 July 2012) <https://obamawhitehouse. archives.gov/the-press-office/2012/07/13/remarks-president-campaign-event-roanoke-virginia> (accessed 17 Jan 2019)

Odurinde, T., 'UK Household Water Consumption 2015: Facts & Figures', *Hope Spring* (12 Oct 2015) <https://www. hopespring.org.uk/uk-household-water-consumption-2015-facts-figures/> (accessed 25 Oct 2018)

Office for National Statistics, 'Appendix Tables: Homicide in England and Wales' (2018)

Office for National Statistics, 'English Life Tables No. 17: 2010 to 2012' (2015a)

Office for National Statistics, 'Infant Mortality (Birth Cohort) Tables in England and Wales' (2015b)

Office for National Statistics, 'Population of the UK by Country of Birth and Nationality, June 2016 to June 2017' (2017)

Ohno, T., *Toyota Production System: Beyond Large-scale Production* (New York: Productivity Press, 1988)

Ohuchi, N. et al., 'Sensitivity and Specificity of Mammography and Adjunctive Ultrasonography to Screen for Breast Cancer in the Japan Strategic Anti-Cancer Randomized Trial (J-START): A Randomised Controlled Trial', *The Lancet*, Vol. 387, No. 10016 (2016), 341–8

O'Neil, C., *Weapons of Math Destruction: How Big Data Increases Inequality and Threatens Democracy* (London: Penguin, 2016)

Orange, V., *Tedder: Quietly in Command* (Abingdon: Frank Cass, 2012)

Ortiz-Ospina, E. and Roser, M., 'Trust' (2019) <https:// ourworldindata.org/trust> (accessed 25 Apr 2019)

Oxford Dictionary, 'Rationality' <https://en.oxforddictionaries.com/definition/rationality> (accessed 14 Jan 2019)

Oxford Dictionary, 'Risk' <https://en.oxforddictionaries.com/definition/risk> (accessed 16 Jan 2019)

Oxford Dictionary, 'Uncertainty' <https://www.lexico.com/en/definition/uncertain> (accessed 30 Aug 2019)

Pardo, M. S. and Allen, R. J., 'Juridical Proof and the Best Explanation', *Law and Philosophy*, Vol. 27, No. 3 (2008), 223–68

Pascal, B. (trans. Trotter, W. F.), *Pascal's Pensées* (New York: E. P. Dutton & Co, 1958)

Paul, M., *Frank Ramsey (1903–1930): A Sister's Memoir* (London: Smith-Gordon and Co., 2012)

Phillips, A. W., 'The Relation Between Unemployment and the Rate of Change of Money Wage Rates in the United Kingdom 1861–1957', *Economica*, Vol. 25, No. 100 (1958), 283–99

Pierce, A., 'The Queen Asks Why No One Saw the Credit Crunch Coming', *Daily Telegraph* (5 Nov 2008)

Pilkey, O. H. and Pilkey-Jarvis, L., *Useless Arithmetic: Why Environmental Scientists Can't Predict the Future* (New York: Columbia University Press, 2007)

Pinker, S., *The Blank Slate* (London: Penguin, 2003)

Planck, M. (trans. Gaynor, F.), *Scientific Autobiography and Other Papers* (Westport, Connecticut: Greenwood Press Publishers, 1968)

Plato (trans. Jowett, B.), *Phaedrus* (1892)

Plender, J. and Persaud, A., 'The Day Dr Evil Wounded a Financial Giant', *Financial Times* (22 Aug 2006)

Plomin, R., *Blueprint: How DNA Makes Us Who We Are* (London: Allen Lane, 2018)

Poisson, S-D., *Recherches sur la Probabilité des Jugements en Matière Criminelle et en Matière Civile* (1837)

Potter van Loon, R. J. D., van den Assem, M. J. and van Dolder, D., 'Beyond Chance? The Persistence of Performance in Online Poker', *PLoS One*, Vol. 10, No. 3 (2015)

Powell, J. H., 'Monetary Policy in a Changing Economy', *Changing Market Structure and Implications for Monetary Policy: A Symposium Sponsored by the Federal Reserve Bank of Kansas City, Jackson Hole, Wyoming* (24 Aug 2018) <https://www.federalreserve.gov/newsevents/speech/powell20180824a.htm> (accessed 10 Oct 2018)

Quetelet, A., *Sur l'homme et le Développement de ses Facultés, ou Essai de Physique Sociale* (1835)

Quine, W. V., 'Main Trends in Recent Philosophy: Two Dogmas of Empiricism', *Philosophical Review*, Vol. 60, No. 1 (1951), 20–43

R&A, 'Rules Modernisation: A Fundamental Revision to the Rules of Golf for 2019' (2019) <https://www.rules.golf/en> (accessed 11 Jan 2019)

Rajan, R. G., 'The Greenspan Era: Lessons for the Future', *Financial Markets, Financial Fragility, and Central Banking: A Symposium Sponsored by the Federal Reserve Bank of Kansas City at Jackson Hole* (26 Aug 2005) <https://www.imf.org/en/News/Articles/2015/09/28/04/53/sp082705> (accessed 16 May 2018)

Ramis, H. (director), *Groundhog Day*, Columbia Pictures (1993)

Ramsey, F. P., 'Truth and Probability' (1926) in Mellor, D. H. (ed.), *Philosophical Papers* (Cambridge: CUP, 1990), 52–109

'Reasonable Doubt: An Argument Against Definition', *Harvard Law Review*, Vol. 108, No. 8 (1995), 1955–72

Reed, C. (director), *The Third Man*, British Lion Film Corporation (1949)

Rhodes, R., *The Making of the Atomic Bomb* (New York: Simon and Schuster, 1988)

Ricardo, D., *On the Principles of Political Economy and Taxation* (1817)

Rittel, H. W. J. and Webber, M. M., 'Dilemmas in a General Theory of Planning', *Policy Sciences*, Vol. 4 (1973), 155–69

Roberts, P. and Aitken, C., '3. The Logic of Forensic Proof: Inferential Reasoning in Criminal Evidence and Forensic Science: Guidance for Judges, Lawyers, Forensic Scientists and Expert Witnesses', Royal Statistical Society (2014)

Robertson, D. H., 'The Snake and the Worm' (1936) in *Essays in Monetary Theory* (London: P. S. King and Son, 1940), 104–13

Romer, P. M., 'Mathiness in the Theory of Economic Growth', *American Economic Review*, Vol. 105, No. 5 (2015), 89–93

Romer, P. M., 'The Trouble With Macroeconomics' (14 Sept 2016a) <https://paulromer.net/wp-content/uploads/2016/09/WP-Trouble.pdf> (accessed 9 Oct 2018)

Romer, P. M., 'Trouble With Macroeconomics, Update' (21 Sept 2016b) <https://paulromer.net/trouble-with-macroeconomics-update/> (accessed 17 May 2018)

Rorty, R., 'Is Truth a Goal of Enquiry? Davidson vs. Wright', *Philosophical Quarterly*, Vol. 45, No. 180 (1995), 281–300

Rosling, H., Rosling, O. and Rönnlund, A. R. (eds), *Factfulness* (London: Sceptre, 2018)

Rothschild, M. and Stiglitz, J. E., 'Increasing Risk: I. A Definition', *Journal of Economic Theory*, Vol. 2, No. 3 (1970), 225–43

Royal Statistical Society, 'Royal Statistical Society Concerned by Issues Raised in Sally Clark Case' (2001)

Rumelt, R., *Good Strategy/Bad Strategy: The Difference and Why it Matters* (New York: Crown Business, 2011)

Samuelson, P. A., 'Alvin H. Hansen, 1889–1975', *Newsweek* (16 June 1975)

Samuelson, P. A., 'An Enjoyable Life Puzzling Over Modern Finance Theory', *Annual Review of Financial Economics*, Vol. 1 (2009), 19–35

Samuelson, P. A., 'Risk and Uncertainty: A Fallacy of Large Numbers', *Scientia*, Vol. 57 (1963)

Samuelson, P. A. and Murray, J. (eds), *The Collected Scientific Papers of Paul Samuelson: Volume 7* (Cambridge, Massachusetts: MIT Press, 2011)

Sargent, T. J., *Macroeconomic Theory* (New York: Academic Press, 1979)

Sargent, T. J., Evans, G. W. and Honkapohja, S., 'An Interview With Thomas J. Sargent', *Macroeconomic Dynamics*, Vol. 9 (2005), 561–83

Savage, L. J., *The Foundations of Statistics* (New York: John Wiley and Sons, 1954)

Schelling, T. C., *Arms and Influence* (New Haven: YUP, 2008)

Schoemaker, P. J. H., *Brilliant Mistakes: Finding Success on the Far Side of Failure* (Philadelphia: Wharton Digital Press, 2011)

Schulte, P. et al., 'The Chicxulub Asteroid Impact and Mass Extinction at the Cretaceous-Paleogene Boundary', *Science*, Vol. 327, No. 5970 (2010), 1214–8

Scott, J. C., *Seeing Like a State: How Certain Schemes to Improve the Human Condition Have Failed* (New Haven: YUP, 1998)

Scottish Widows, 'Our History' <https://www.scottishwidows.co.uk/about_us/who_we_are/our_history.html> (accessed 10 Oct 2018)

Self, R., *Neville Chamberlain: A Biography* (Aldershot: Ashgate, 2006)

Sellar, W. C. and Yeatman, R. J., *1066 and All That* (London: Methuen, 1930)

Selvin, S. et al., 'Letters to the Editor', *American Statistician*, Vol. 29, No. 1 (1975), 67–71

Serling, R. J., *Legend and Legacy: The Story of Boeing and its People* (New York: St Martin's Press, 1992)

Shackle, G. L. S., *Epistemics and Economics: A Critique of Economic Doctrines* (Cambridge: CUP, 1972)

Shackle, G. L. S., 'Probability and Uncertainty', *Metronomica*, Vol. 1, No. 3 (1949), 135–85

Shackle, G. L. S., *Uncertainty in Economics and Other Reflections* (Cambridge: CUP, 1968)

Shakespeare, W. (ed. Pooler, C. K.), *The Merchant of Venice* (London: Methuen and Co., 1912)

Shiller, R. J., 'Narrative Economics', *American Economic Review*, Vol. 107, No. 4 (2017), 967–1004

Shiller, R. J., *Narrative Economics: How Stories Go Viral and Drive Major Economic Events* (Princeton: PUP, 2019)

Shubber, K., 'Theranos Founder Charged with "Massive" Securities Fraud', *Financial Times* (14 Mar 2018)

Shulman, L. B. and Driskell, T. D., 'Dental Implants: A Historical Perspective' (1997) in Block, M., Kent, J. and Guerra, L., *Implants in Dentistry* (Philadelphia: Saunders, 1997)

Silver, N., *The Signal and the Noise: The Art and Science of Prediction* (London: Allen Lane, 2012)

Silver, N., 'When We Say 70 Percent, It Really Means 70 Percent', *FiveThirtyEight* (4 Apr 2019) <https://fivethirtyeight.com/features/when-we-say-70-percent-it-really-means-70-percent/> (accessed 23 Apr 2019)

Silver, N., 'Why FiveThirtyEight Gave Trump a Better Chance Than Almost Anyone Else', *FiveThirtyEight* (11 Nov 2016) <https://fivethirtyeight.com/features/why-fivethirtyeight-gave-trump-a-better-chance-than-almost-anyone-else/> (accessed 23 Apr 2019)

Simon, H., *Models of Man: Social and Rational* (New York: John Wiley and Sons, 1957)

Simon, R. J. and Mahan, L., 'Quantifying Burdens of Proof: A

View From the Bench, the Jury, and the Classroom', *Law and Society Review*, Vol. 5, No. 3 (1971), 319–30

Simons, D. J. and Chabris, C. F., 'Gorillas in Our Midst: Sustained Inattentional Blindness for Dynamic Events', *Perception*, Vol. 28, No. 9 (1999), 1059–74

Sinn, H-W., 'EU Enlargement, Migration, and Lessons from German Unification', *German Economic Review*, Vol. 1, No. 3 (2003)

Skousen, M., *The Making of Modern Economics: The Lives and Ideas of the Great Thinkers* (Armonk: M. E. Sharpe, 2001)

Slaughter, A-M., 'On Thinking Like a Lawyer' (2002) <https://www.princeton.edu/~slaughtr/Commentary/On%20Thinking%20Like%20a%20Lawyer.pdf> (accessed 8 Oct 2018)

Sloan, A. P. (ed. McDonald, J.), *My Years with General Motors* (New York: Doubleday, 1964)

Smith, A., *An Inquiry Into the Nature and Causes of the Wealth of Nations*, Volume I (1776a)

Smith, A., *An Inquiry Into the Nature and Causes of the Wealth of Nations*, Volume II (1776b)

Smith, E., *Luck: A Fresh Look at Fortune* (London: Bloomsbury, 2013)

Smolin, L., *The Trouble with Physics: The Rise of String Theory, the Fall of a Science, and What Comes Next* (London: Penguin, 2006)

Smyth, J., 'New Zealand Bans Foreigners From Buying Homes', *Financial Times* (15 Aug 2018)

Soros, G., 'Soros: General Theory of Reflexivity', *Financial Times* (26 Oct 2009)

Spence, M., 'Job Market Signalling', *Quarterly Journal of Economics*, Vol. 87, No. 3 (1973), 355–74

Sprat, T., *The History of the Royal Society of London*, Vol. I (1734)

Statistical Abstract of the United States: 2011, United States Census Bureau (2011)

Sterling, B., Grootveld, M. and van Mensvoort, K., 'Interview: Bruce Sterling on the Convergence of Humans and Machines' (22 Feb 2015) <https://www.nextnature.net/2015/02/interview-bruce-sterling/> (accessed 14 May 2018)

Stevenson, M. T., 'Assessing Risk Assessment in Action', *Minnesota Law Review*, Vol. 103, No. 1 (2019), 303–84

Stevenson, R. L., 'The Day After To-Morrow', *The Contemporary Review*, Vol. 51 (1887), 472–9

Surowiecki, J., *The Wisdom of Crowds* (Boston: Little Brown, 2004)

Swanson, I., 'Revealed: Final Cost of Edinburgh Tram Scheme Will be £1 Billion', *The Scotsman* (13 Dec 2017)

Taft, J. G., 'Why Knight Capital Was Saved and Lehman Brothers Failed', *Forbes* (20 Aug 2012) <https://www.forbes.com/sites/advisor/2012/08/20/why-knight-capital-was-saved-and-lehman-brothers-failed/> (accessed 14 Jan 2019)

Taleb, N. N., *Antifragile: Things that Gain from Disorder* (London: Penguin, 2013)

Taleb, N. N., *The Black Swan: The Impact of the Highly Improbable* (London: Penguin, 2008)

Taleb, N. N., *Fooled by Randomness: The Hidden Role of Chance in Life and in the Markets* (London: Penguin, 2007)

Taleb, N. N., *Skin in the Game: Hidden Asymmetries in Daily Life* (London: Allen Lane, 2018)

Tetlock, P. E., *Expert Political Judgement: How Good Is It? How Can We Know?* (Princeton: PUP, 2005)

Tetlock, P. E. and Gardner, D., *Superforecasting: The Art and Science of Prediction* (London: Random House, 2016)

Thaler, R. H., *Misbehaving: The Making of Behavioural Economics* (London: Penguin, 2016)

Thaler, R. H. and Benartzi, S., 'Save More Tomorrow™: Using Behavioural Economics to Increase Employee Saving', *Journal of Political Economy*, Vol. 112, S1 (2004), S164–S187

Thompson, W. S., 'Population', *American Journal of Sociology*, Vol. 34, No. 6 (1929), 959–75

Thomson, W., 'To Baden Powell' (1896) <https://zapatopi. net/kelvin/papers/letters.html#baden-powell> (accessed 15 May 2018)

Thorp, E. O., *A Man For All Markets: Beating the Odds, from Las Vegas to Wall Street* (New York: Random House, 2017)

Tolstoy, L. (trans. Edmonds, R.), *War and Peace* (London: Penguin, 1978)

Torricelli, R. and Carroll, A., *In Our Own Words: Extraordinary Speeches of the American Century* (New York: Washington Square Press, 2000)

Trenerry, C. F., *The Origin and Early History of Insurance, Including the Contract of Bottomry* (London: P. S. King and Son, 1911)

Treverton, G. F., 'Risks and Riddles', Smithsonian Institution <Smithsonian.com> (1 June 2007)

Tribe, L. H., 'Trial by Mathematics: Precision and Ritual in the Legal Process', *Harvard Law Review*, Vol. 84, No. 6 (1971), 1329–93

Trichet, J-C., 'Reflections on the Nature of Monetary Policy, Non-Standard Measures, and Finance Theory', opening address at the ECB Central Banking Conference (18 Nov 2010) <https://www.ecb.europa.eu/press/key/date/2010/ html/sp101118.en.html> (accessed 16 May 2018)

Truman, H. S., 'Longhand Note' (17 June 1945)

Tucker, A. W., 'The Mathematics of Tucker: A Sampler', *Two-Year College Mathematics Journal*, Vol. 14, No. 3 (1983), 228–32

Tuckett, D. and Nikolic, M., 'The Role of Conviction and

Narrative in Decision-Making Under Radical Uncertainty', *Theory and Psychology*, Vol. 27, No. 4 (2017), 501–23

Tversky, A. and Kahneman, D., 'Availability: A Heuristic for Judging Frequency and Probability', *Cognitive Psychology*, Vol. 5, No. 2 (1973), 207–32

UNAIDS, 'South Africa: People Living with HIV (All Ages) and South Africa: New HIV Infections (All Ages)', UNAIDS Estimates 2018 <http://www.unaids.org/en/regionscountries/countries/southafrica> (accessed 7 Jan 2019)

United Nations, *The Millennium Development Goals Report* (2015)

Universities Superannuation Scheme, 'Report & Accounts' (2017)

University of Chicago, *Annual Register* (1896)

Upton, J. and George, P., 'The Prevalence of Lactose Intolerance (Adult Hypolactasia) in a Randomly Selected New Zealand Population', *New Zealand Medical Journal*, Vol. 123, No. 1308 (2010), 117–8

US Department of Defense, *DoD News Briefing: Secretary Rumsfeld and Gen. Myers* (12 Feb 2002)

US Energy Information Administration, 'Short-Term Energy Outlook, January 2019' <https://www.eia.gov/outlooks/steo/images/Fig14.png> (accessed 15 Jan 2019)

Vaihinger, H. (trans. Ogden, C. G.), *The Philosophy of 'As If': A System of the Theoretical, Practical and Religious Fictions of Mankind* (London: Kegan Pual, Trench, Tubner & Co., Ltd, 1924)

Vandevelde, K. J., *Thinking Like a Lawyer: An Introduction to Legal Reasoning* (London: Hachette, 2010)

Ventola, C. L., 'The Antibiotic Resistance Crisis', *Pharmacy and Therapeutics*, Vol. 40, No. 4 (2015), 277–83

Vickrey, W., 'Counterspeculation, Auctions, and Competitive Sealed Tenders', *Journal of Finance*, Vol. 16, No. 1 (1961), 8–37

Viña, G. et al., 'Brexit Will Cost Households "£4,300 a Year"', *Financial Times* (18 Apr 2016)

von Hayek, F. A., 'The Pretence of Knowledge', Nobel Prize lecture (1974)

von Neumann, J. and Morgenstern, O., *The Theory of Games and Economic Behavior* (Princeton: PUP, 1972)

von Ranke, L. (trans. Iggers, W. A., ed. Iggers, G. G.), *The Theory and Practice of History* (Abingdon, Oxon: Routledge, 2010)

Waldfogel, J., *Scroogenomics: Why You Shouldn't Buy Presents for the Holidays* (Princeton: PUP, 2009)

Waldfogel, J. 'The Deadweight Loss of Christmas', *American Economic Review*, Vol. 83, No. 5 (1993) 1328–36

Walras, L., *Éléments d'économie Politique Pure* (1874)

Walton, S. and Huey, J., *Made in America: My Story* (New York: Bantam Books, 1993)

Wansell, G., 'Whatever the Coroner May Say, Sally Clark Died of a Broken Heart', *Independent* (18 Mar 2007)

Welles, O. (director), *Mr Arkadin*, Warner Bros. (1955)

Wells, J. D., 'Prof. von Jolly's 1878 Prediction of the End of Theoretical Physics as Reported by Max Planck' (6 Mar 2016) <http://www-personal.umich.edu/~jwells/manuscripts/jdw160306.pdf> (accessed 17 Jan 2019)

Whately, R., *Detached Thoughts and Apophthegms: Extracted From Some of the Writings of Archbishop Whately* (1854)

Wiessner, P. W., 'Embers of Society: Firelight Talk Among the Ju/'hoansi Bushmen', *Proceedings of the National Academy of Sciences*, Vol. 111, No. 39 (2014), 14027–35

Wilde, O., *The Picture of Dorian Gray* (1891)

Williamson, O. E., *Markets and Hierarchies: Analysis and Antitrust Implications* (New York: Free Press, 1975)

Wilson, E. O., *Consilience: The Unity of Knowledge* (London: Vintage, 1999)

Wolfe, T., *The Bonfire of the Vanities* (London: Cape, 1988)

Wood, D. (director), 'The Missing Page' in *Hancock's Half Hour: Volume I*, BBC (1960)

World Bank, 'How are the Income Group Thresholds Determined?' <https://datahelpdesk.worldbank.org/knowledgebase/articles/378833-how-are-the-income-group-thresholds-determined> (accessed 11 Jan 2019)

World Bank, 'Poverty Headcount Ratio at $1.90 a Day (2011 PPP) (% of Population)' (2019)

World Health Organization, *WHO Guidelines on Hand Hygiene in Health Care* (2009)

Wrangham, R., *The Goodness Paradox: The Strange Relationship Between Virtue and Violence in Human Evolution* (New York: Pantheon, 2019)

Zabell, S. L., 'The Rule of Succession', *Erkenntnis*, Vol. 31, No. 2–3 (1989), 283–321

Zipf, G. K., *Human Behaviour and the Principle of Least Effort* (Boston: Addison-Wesley, 1949)

Zipf, G. K., *The Psycho-Biology of Language* (New York: Houghton Mifflin, 1935)

Zweig, J., *Your Money and Your Brain* (New York: Simon and Schuster, 2007)

FURTHER READING

A century ago, Frank Knight and John Maynard Keynes wrote their critiques of the application of probabilistic reasoning to economic and social problems. As we describe in the text, they lost the intellectual battle and the social sciences have been increasingly dominated by probabilistic reasoning – though George Shackle was a rare exception.

As the importance of radical uncertainty came to shape our own thinking, two authors seemed to us to be on the right track. They came from very different backgrounds. One was a British academic, Ken Binmore, a mathematician and economist specialising in game theory, at London University, whose 2009 book *Rational Decisions* explained clearly the limitations of Bayesian reasoning and the foundations of statistical theory espoused by Jimmie Savage. The other was a Lebanese-American former trader turned writer, Nassim Nicholas Taleb. His 2001 book *Fooled by Randomness*, followed in 2007 by *The Black Swan*, provided a powerful demonstration of why the unthinking application of probabilistic reasoning to financial risks failed. His writings constitute a series entitled *Incerto* which, although following many detours, contains very important insights into how to cope with a world of radical uncertainty.

George Lakoff and Mark Johnson's *Metaphors We Live By* (1980) is a short, seminal account of the extent to which human reasoning is guided by narratives. This theme has been recently developed in the context of economics and finance by Jens Beckert and Richard Bronk in *Uncertain Futures* (2018) and Robert Shiller in *Narrative Economics* (2019). The relationship between narratives and models is a subject taken up by Nancy Cartwright and Mary Morgan; see, for example *Nature, the Artful Modeler* (2019) and *The World in the Model* (2012). Hugo Mercier and Dan Sperber provide important insights into communicative rationality – the links between reasoning and narrative – in *The Enigma of Reason* (2017).

As this book went to press, arguments similar to ours were presented in a popular manner by the writer and BBC journalist Michael Blastland in *The Hidden Half* (2019). Critical discussions of what is meant by rationality when information is imperfect – as it necessarily is in the face of radical uncertainty – are *A Call for Judgment* by Amar Bhidé (2010) and *Beyond Mechanical Markets* by Roman Frydman and Michael Goldberg (2011).

Nicholas Christakis's *Blueprint* (2019) is a masterful account of how evolution has shaped human reasoning. Nick Chater's *The Mind is Flat* (2018) is a provocative critique of any attempt to base an account of reasoning on computational science rather than neurophysiology and Joseph Henrich's *The Secret of our Success* (2017) demonstrates the extent to which economic development is the result of the growth of collective knowledge. We think these three recent books, along with Joel Mokyr's *A Culture of Growth* (2016), are indispensable for anyone who wishes to understand how economics fits into science (and social science) more broadly.

Peter Bernstein's *Risk* (1998) is a highly readable account of the ways humans have attempted to manage risk over the millennia. Lorraine Daston provides a comprehensive account of the development of probabilistic reasoning in *Classical Probability in the Enlightenment* (1995) and its application to insurance is described in Niall Ferguson's *The Ascent of Money* (2008). In 2019 the American Statistical Association devoted an entire issue to the misuse of probabilistic reasoning to make inferences about causation. The editorial concluded 'it is time to stop using the term "statistically significant" entirely'.* The study of power laws was pioneered by Benoit Mandelbrot, and Mark Buchanan's *Ubiquity* (2002) is a survey of many applications. Again as we went to press, we saw Ian Stewart's *Do Dice Play God?* (2019) which reviews several of the puzzles and paradoxes in the early chapters of this book.

---

* Ronald L. Wasserstein, Allen L. Schirm and Nicole A. Lazar, 'Editorial: Moving to a world beyond "$p<0.05$"', *American Statistician*, Vol. 73, No. 51 (2019), 1–19.

INDEX